PORTF

CIVILIAN WARRIORS

Erik Prince, a former Navy SEAL, founded Blackwater in 1997. He served as its CEO until 2009 and its chairman until 2010, when the company was sold. A native of Michigan, he now splits his time between homes in Virginia and Abu Dhabi, where he pursues a variety of business ventures.

CIVILIAN WARRIORS

The Inside Story of
BLACKWATER
and the Unsung Heroes
of the War on Terror

ERIK PRINCE
with Davin Coburn

Afterword by Max Boot

PORTFOLIO / PENGUIN

PORTFOLIO / PENGUIN
Published by the Penguin Group
Penguin Group (USA) LLC
375 Hudson Street
New York, New York 10014

USA | Canada | UK | Ireland | Australia | New Zealand | India | South Africa | China
penguin.com
A Penguin Random House Company

First published in the United States of America by Portfolio / Penguin,
a member of Penguin Group (USA) LLC, 2013
This paperback edition with a new preface published 2014

THE LIBRARY OF CONGRESS HAS CATALOGED THE HARDCOVER EDITION AS FOLLOWS:
Prince, Erik, 1969–
Civilian warriors: the inside story of Blackwater and the unsung heroes of the War on
Terror / Erik Prince ; with an afterword by Max Boot.
pages cm
Includes bibliographical references
ISBN 978-1-59184-721-2 (hc.)
ISBN 978-1-59184-745-8 (pbk.)
1. Blackwater USA—History.   2. War on Terrorism, 2001–2009.   3. United States—
Military policy—History—21st century.   4. Civil-military relations—United States—
History—21st century.   5. Prince, Erik, 1969–   I. Title.
UB149.P75 2013
355.3'5—dc23
2013033302

Printed in the United States of America

Set in Chronicle Text G1
Designed by Sabrina Bowers

To all the Blackwater team, especially the forty-one men who
gave their all and those who were wounded and still
inspire us today with their perseverance.
I'm extremely proud of what we accomplished together.

CONTENTS

PUBLISHER'S NOTE

PRIOR TO THE PUBLICATION OF *CIVILIAN WARRIORS*, ERIK PRINCE SUBMITTED the manuscript to the Central Intelligence Agency for review, honoring the confidentiality agreement he had signed when hired by the agency. The CIA review resulted in numerous redactions, and Mr. Prince accordingly deleted all material considered classified from the text, including his accounts of several widely publicized events.

While Mr. Prince's memoir stands alone despite the cuts, we have asked Max Boot, one of America's leading military historians, to write an outsider's account of the experiences Mr. Prince is unable to recount himself. This afterword is based on information drawn from public sources, and Mr. Prince has had no input or involvement in its writing.

PREFACE TO THE PAPERBACK EDITION

A LOT HAS HAPPENED SINCE I STEPPED AWAY FROM BLACKWATER. THE BIPOLAR world of the Cold War, already fragmented when I founded Blackwater, has given way to a panoply of rising conflicts over religious fanaticism, natural resources, poverty, corruption, theft, trade disputes, and tribalism. The Arab Spring has rapidly turned into a bitter winter. What started in some cases as a hue and cry for economic and political freedom was quickly hijacked by Islamist forces and the Muslim Brotherhood.

Western governments continue to struggle to find real solutions to these crises. They spent trillions of dollars during that Cold War preparing the mightiest of hammers, but when you have a magnificent hammer everything looks like a nail. NATO nations and the United States continue to deploy large and expensive conventional forces to tamp down minor conflicts that should be easily resolved. This "hammer" of traditional forces lacks the nimbleness and fiscal efficiency of either small active-duty units or contracted special forces. Even more troubling, traditional forces can inflame a situation instead of pacifying it.

Pundits may fuss over the validity of using the private sector to sort out conflicts, but one thing is clear: The government agencies currently responsible for security and peacekeeping are failing and are likely to keep failing. Having been involved in military and security operations for more than twenty years, I can assure you that the so-called interagency process is in shocking dysfunction. The CIA, Department of State, and Department of Defense are so cumbersome and unresponsive that their attempts to cooperate actually make matters worse.

Even the "successes" are failures since they are economically unsustainable. Witness the totally failed economic development of the Afghan economy after nearly thirteen years of U.S. forces on the ground. The aid community spent billions in dead-end boondoggles while ignoring the mineral and energy sectors that could make Afghanistan an independent nation instead of a welfare case.

Everyone talks about reform, but it's becoming clear that Congress and the executive branch are incapable of fixing their problems. The only solution that remains is to turn to what made America great in the first place: individual initiative and competition. We must allow the private sector to contribute by contracting to sort out peace-making, logistics, political warfare, and intelligence operations. But good luck to any private company that accepts those contracts—I recommend that they carefully consider the government's betrayal of Blackwater before signing on the dotted line.

These days I'm operating a small fund (FRG) that invests private dollars into the African energy, mining, and agriculture spaces. We pursue the development of the basic commodities that Africa needs to feed its emerging economies and that the rest of the world, Asia in particular, imports to sustain development. I'm also building a new business called Frontier Services Group. We will provide aviation, construction, and logistics services first throughout Africa and then throughout the rest of the world. We will assist large extractive energy and infrastructure companies and even some governments to accomplish their projects on time and on budget.

I'm learning that it's easier to start a business in your twenties than in your forties. Like my Blackwater work, my job today requires a lot of travel and long, hard days. The worst part is that it takes me away far too often from the ones I love the most. I hope they will understand someday.

After you read *Civilian Warriors* I hope you, too, will understand why I have unfinished business. Enjoy the true Blackwater story.

INTRODUCTION

December 6, 2003

AT ELEVEN P.M., EIGHTEEN CARS, WATCHED OVERHEAD BY U.S. ARMY APACHE
and Kiowa Warrior helicopters, as well as by a pair of Blackwater helicopters, known as Little Birds, stormed out of the Green Zone.
They turned onto a pockmarked roadway, drove past scorched traffic barriers and burned-out remains of vehicles once used for suicide
bombings, and sped toward Baghdad International Airport. A motorcade escorting a head of state and the U.S. secretary of defense
doesn't travel light. Especially not on the "Highway of Death."

That multilane stretch of asphalt connects Iraq's largest international airport with the coalition-occupied Green Zone. For years,
insurgents had effectively owned the five or so miles, ambushing
convoys, diplomats, and American troops roughly once a day. So
dangerous was the road that the State Department would ultimately
outlaw its personnel from using it at all. And even before that, no one
took that road without a plan.

But sometimes Paul Bremer wouldn't take no for an answer.

Shortly before eleven p.m., Bremer, the United States presidential envoy and administrator in Iraq, had finished a meeting with Secretary of Defense Donald Rumsfeld outside the Green Zone. To the surprise of his Blackwater security detail, Bremer insisted he would see the secretary off at the airport.

Frank Gallagher, the barrel-chested head of the detail charged with keeping Bremer alive, quickly recalibrated travel plans. "Needless to say, some of the radio traffic back to me expressed grave concern about doing the mission and questioned my sanity," Gallagher later remembered. "But I could see the look in [Bremer's] eyes that this was not open for debate."

The trip out was uneventful, but Gallagher sensed the worst was yet to come. The show of force had certainly tipped off the insurgents that something unusual was going on at the airport. And Bremer's Blackwater motorcade would have to travel back to the Green Zone without the Pentagon detail that had accompanied Rumsfeld.

Once Bremer had said his good-byes to the secretary, the Coalition Provisional Authority leader and his right-hand man, Brian McCormack, climbed into the back of an up-armored Chevy Suburban SUV. Gallagher gathered his Blackwater team. "I explained that getting back to the Green Zone was going to be an adventure, and made sure that everyone was aware of the dangers," he said. "We promised to have a cup of mead in Valhalla later that evening."

Contractor humor.

Around eleven twenty p.m., Bremer's pared-down convoy pulled away from the airport. The nimble Blackwater helicopters darted out front, providing top cover and scanning the roadway for threats. Gallagher, in the front passenger seat, wrapped his fingers around his matte black M4 carbine and stared out into the darkness that enveloped the roadway. Bremer and McCormack chatted about meeting schedules for the next day.

Suddenly, a call from a Blackwater bird above: "Be alert—a vehicle ahead is *backing* down an on-ramp onto the road." The driver of

Bremer's SUV pulled into the far left lane, closest to the highway median. The lead and follow armored cars maneuvered to flank Bremer on the right.

There was a jarring *crack* against the bulletproof window on Gallagher's door—what he later learned had been an AK-47 round that had marked him for death. And then, with a horrible flash of light, an improvised explosive device (IED) rocked the armored Humvee behind Bremer's SUV, destroying the Humvee's axle with a deafening blast.

Bremer's driver swerved and battled to keep all four tires of the SUV on the ground. From the darkness, insurgents opened fire with AK-47s, rattling machine-gun fire off the right side of the car. There was nowhere to hide; flames and headlights provided just enough light to grasp what was unfolding. "We'd been ambushed, a highly organized, skillfully executed assassination attempt," Bremer later wrote. "I swung around and looked back. The Suburban's armored-glass rear window had been blown out by the IED. And now AK rounds were whipping through the open rectangle."

"*Tuna! Tuna! Tuna!*" shouted the voice from the radio in Bremer's SUV. It was Blackwater's shift leader, limping along in the battered armored vehicle, calling out the code for the SUVs to drive through the ambush: *Leave the Humvees*, he was saying; *get Bremer out of there now.*

Contractors in the two helicopters above unloaded enough ammunition to repel the attack, while Blackwater's drivers ignored the burns on their feet from the heat of the blast and stomped on the gas through the fog of smoke on the roadway. One of the trailing Suburbans pulled immediately alongside Bremer's car, shielding it while speeding down the Highway of Death so close together that the cars' sideview mirrors touched. "I asked for a casualty report and learned that two of our four vehicles were damaged, but limping along," Gallagher said.

The stench of explosives lingered in the ambassador's vehicle as they made it to the Green Zone. And soon, the Humvees and helicopters made it back as well.

Miraculously, no one was injured.

Since I first enrolled in the Naval Academy after high school, my life's mission has been to serve God, serve my family, and serve the United States with honor and integrity. I did it first as a midshipman, then as a SEAL, then—when personal tragedy called me home from the service—as a contractor providing solutions for some of the thorniest problems on earth. The business of war has never been pretty, but I did my job legally, and I did it completely. Too well, perhaps, growing Blackwater until it became something resembling its own branch of the military and other government agencies.

During my dozen years as company CEO, we filled contracts for the State Department, the Department of Defense, the CIA, elite law enforcement agencies around the world, and many others. We did everything from protecting heads of state to delivering the mail. Blackwater expanded from a simple training center in the North Carolina swampland to encompass dozens of business divisions ranging from surveillance blimp development and construction to intelligence services to K9 operations. We became the ultimate tool in the war on terror, pushing a thousand contractors into Iraq and hundreds more into Afghanistan under the Republican Bush administration, then continuing a connection to Democratic president Barack Obama that was closer than he has ever wanted to admit. My company's history is a proud tale of performance excellence and driven entrepreneurialism.

The public relations battle at home, however, was very different from a firefight on the front lines. Those conflicts my men and I were trained for. Stateside, though, thanks to endless waves of frivolous lawsuits, congressional hearings, and inaccurate press reports, Blackwater was slagged as the face of military evil. Gun-toting bullies for hire. We were branded mercenaries and murderers, and were made the whipping boy for the public's fury over the Bush administration's policies in the Middle East. After failing in their multiyear effort to win hearts and minds in Iraq, the bureaucrats decided a company that had repeatedly answered this government's pleas for help was suddenly more valuable as a scapegoat. I was strung up so the politicians could feign indignation and pretend my men hadn't done exactly what they had paid us handsomely to do.

There is much the government doesn't want told about the work we did: the truth about our State Department–sanctioned operational tactics in Iraq, for instance, including our rules of engagement; or Blackwater's crucial involvement with President Obama's ever expanding terrorist-hunting tactics in Pakistan and beyond; or even the depth of government reliance on contractors today and the outsourcing of its war machine. Government agencies don't want that spotlight being shone on our work, nor to applaud the greatest advantage Blackwater offered them: increased capability. They want increased deniability.

For years my company's work was misconstrued and misrepresented. At the time, our government contracts explicitly barred Blackwater from responding to the public broadsides. We were never allowed to explain things such as how we secured the contracts we did, or what really happened during a bloody Baghdad shoot-out in September 2007, or the way shifting political tectonic plates crushed my company as an act of partisan theatrics. Or how the one job I loved more than any other was ripped away from me thanks to gross acts of professional negligence at the CIA.

So now I'm done keeping quiet. What's been said before is only half the story—and I won't sit idly by while the bureaucrats go after me so that everyone else can just go back to business as usual. The true history of Blackwater is exhilarating, rewarding, exasperating, and tragic. It's the story of men taking bullets to protect the men who take all the credit, a tale of patriots whose names became known only when lawyers and politicians needed to blame somebody for something.

Our critics have spoken. Now it's my turn.

CHAPTER 1
MY FATHER'S SON
1969–1996

THE SOUND OF A BOAT EXPLODING IS EXACTLY WHAT YOU'D THINK IT WOULD BE.

I was thirteen the first time I heard it, way up in Ontario's North Channel, where my family was vacationing aboard our forty-three-foot Viking powerboat. My dad had driven my mother, Elsa, one of my three older sisters, and a buddy and me up through Lake Michigan and past the Upper Peninsula. Towed behind us was an aging thirteen-foot Boston Whaler my dad had bought through a newspaper ad, and which I'd subsequently poured my heart into.

Just before six a.m. one morning during that vacation, my friend and I jumped from the Viking into that Whaler and motored out to a nearby fishing spot. We'd barely cast our first lines when suddenly an orange flash on the horizon jerked my head, followed by a baritone thunderclap that rattled across the water. White smoke billowed from the blown-open motor yacht; in the distance I saw debris raining down and the shards of a mast pinwheeling out of the sky.

I could hear screaming. There were no cell phones at the time, and no radio in my boat to call for help. We cranked the forty-horsepower outboard motor my father and I had recently mounted in the Whaler, crouched low inside that robin's egg blue hull, and zoomed toward the chaos.

With the water spray whipping against my face, I thought about one of the first boating lessons my father had taught me: *Always ventilate!* Gas engines on board require particular attention, he'd emphasized—it's different than with car engines. In automobiles, he'd said, the airflow under the vehicle blows away dangerous gas fumes. But there's little natural ventilation through a bilge compartment, and even during a routine refuel, heavy gas fumes can pool there. If you don't adequately ventilate those fumes, he said, you'll literally create a bomb just waiting for a spark. I remembered reading in *Popular Mechanics* a few years earlier that one cup of gasoline had the same explosive power as a dozen sticks of dynamite. And there in the North Channel I figured I was about to see what that actually looked like.

The Whaler cleared the half-mile distance to the accident in one minute flat. The damage to the motor yacht shocked me. The coach roof had been blown off, and there was a sickening hole by the bow. The deck was on fire.

Two people, a woman who appeared to be in her seventies and a middle-aged woman I assumed was her daughter, had been catapulted from the boat. Unbelievably, they were alive, though the burns they had suffered, and the sounds of their pain, were evident before we could even pull alongside them. They struggled to stay afloat.

Together, my friend and I hoisted each of them into the Whaler, laying the women across the wide wooden bench seats my father and I had spent so many hours sanding and revarnishing back in Michigan. To this day, I remember the smell of their burnt hair.

Luckily for the women, as I cranked the Whaler into a U-turn and gunned it for shore, locals back on land who'd also seen the explosion were calling for the emergency personnel. The paramedics arrived soon after we reached the shore, and we helped load the women into the ambulances on stretchers. I never did learn their names, or what became of them. In fact, the last thing I remember about that morning was puttering back out to the Viking, tying off the Whaler, and climbing back on board with my family. Hardly anyone else was even awake yet.

"Perseverance and determination," my father used to say. "Perseverance and determination." It's a mantra that defined his life. I hope it defines mine.

As a child, my father accompanied his father, Peter, on his daily delivery route for Tulip City Produce Company around the scenic town of Holland, Michigan. My grandmother, Edith, was a seamstress. There, in the quiet town along the eastern edge of Lake Michigan, my father was taught to be industrious and to chip in with home improvement projects as soon as he could swing a hammer. When Peter died suddenly of a heart attack in 1943, my grandmother sought no government handouts, no charity from the church, not even money from family. Edgar, who had two sisters, was the man of the house now. He would provide for them. He was twelve.

My father's first job, for a local painter, paid him a few cents an hour to scrape and sand houses. That summer, when the hot water heater at home broke, he measured all the piping connections for the new appliance, walked to the hardware store, and had galvanized pipe cut and threaded. Piece by piece he installed the new water heater, no plumber necessary. There was no money to afford one, anyway.

There were few stories of happy times from my father's childhood. He never spoke of vacations to the beach, or family celebrations. He played high school football for only one season. He was studious because he was expected to be, and hardworking because he needed to be. At age thirteen, Dad took a job at the local Chrysler-Plymouth dealership that paid him forty cents an hour. He devoured everything there was to know about cars—how to take them apart, how to diagnose problems, how to sell them. Three years later, he was running the dealership whenever the owner was away.

Dad supported his family, and saved enough money to put himself through college. An engineering major at Michigan Technological University, he earned a Reserve Officers' Training Corps (ROTC) scholarship and soon served two years as an Air Force photoreconnaissance officer at bases in South Carolina and Colorado. He returned to Holland after his service and took a job as a die caster at the local Buss Machine Works, working his way up to chief engineer. He married a lovely young schoolteacher named Elsa Zweip, whom he'd met while waterskiing on summer break two years earlier. Soon my oldest sister, Elisabeth, was born. Then came Eileen and Emily. I was born in the summer of 1969.

In 1965, Buss was sold. During that transition, Dad gathered two coworkers, remortgaged the house, and borrowed $10,000 from his mother. He was convinced that nearby manufacturers would soon need to perform their own in-house die casting. He had clever ideas about how to answer that call—for which he can thank my mother, and the opera. Dad found their date nights at Opera Grand Rapids so interminably boring, he spent the whole time pondering novel designs for die-casting machines. Amid a forest of competitors, with his finances overextended thanks to a growing family at home and his aging mother's nest egg at risk, he struck out to create Prince Manufacturing.

A staff of six labored around the clock to construct the six-hundred-ton die-casting machines. A few months after its founding, Prince filled its first order for Honeywell International, which needed a pair of the machines to manufacture military ordnance. Soon, Honeywell returned for three more. Then fifteen. Then General Motors started buying them, manufacturing each of its new engine blocks with Prince machines. Everyone at the company saw the hard work paying off. "If my employees are part of the game, if they desire to know what the game plan is, they will be part of its success," my father said. "People win games because they have the group working together."

The size of the machines grew as the orders did: In January 1969 GM demanded a sixteen-hundred-ton die caster to manufacture aluminum transmission cases. Sixteen-hour workdays became eighteen-hour workdays. For my father, filling even the most outlandish order was about more than business. It was about even more than *losing* the business. It was pride. "If you have high expectations for your own life, you have to put those same expectations into your work," he said. And seven months later, Prince Manufacturing had the die caster in place and operational at GM's factory.

Soon he was diversifying, and Prince Manufacturing was growing into Prince Corporation. Dad's company was no longer just manufacturing machines to make machines, but creating products of its own. In 1972, he invented a lighted mirror sun visor for Cadillac—an accent so ubiquitous today, it's hard to imagine a time when cars didn't have them. Prince then began designing interior consoles for cars—then dashboard cup holders, movable armrests, a digital compass/thermometer, programmable garage door openers. My father could envision whole new industries to create. David Swietlik, then Chrysler's procurement manager for large cars, once told *Forbes* magazine, "Prince comes in saying, 'You don't know you want this yet.'"

The Big Three automakers loved that my father backed his research and development with his own funds; if prototypes failed, he took on all the losses. The approach made him relentless and tactical; every mistake the company made was documented and chronicled in a notebook he stored in his office desk. He called those mistakes "humbling gifts." It worked: Seven years after its founding, Prince Corporation was Holland's largest employer.

Not that success came without a price. In 1972, a heart attack almost killed my father. He was forty-two. For three weeks, he lay in bed at Holland Hospital reflecting upon how hard he'd been driving himself—and everyone around him. He thought about his own father dying at the age of thirty-six. He thought about how his temper had been getting the better of him. I remember when my mom and I found him at home before rushing him to the hospital. It was the first time I'd ever seen him lying down in the middle of the day. "It was then, while he lay in a hospital bed reflecting on what all his labor had won for him, that he committed himself anew to his faith in Jesus Christ," family friend Gary L. Bauer would later say. "Ed turned his future and the future of his business over to God." As a result, Dad soon focused less on work and became a much larger part of my life.

It was important for my father to show me my grandparents' European heritage. The old country. The Dutch-German roots were not subtle: I grew up in a town named Holland, settled in 1847 by Dutch immigrants fleeing religious persecution in their homeland. We were surrounded by tulip festivals and traditional architecture from the Netherlands—even an imported ancient windmill from the old country. There were wooden shoes everywhere. The Dutch Christian Reformed Church was a cornerstone of our town, and my mother a devoted member.

I was fascinated by my family's history, and world history in general—particularly its association with the military. The first group of soldiers I ever assembled was made of solid lead—two inches high, standing in neat rows on my bedroom windowsill. There were hundreds of them, painted to match their real-life British, French, and Continental Army counterparts. I created them from molds I got on trips abroad and forty pounds of lead Dad and I melted down in a cast-iron plumber's pot. I was only seven, but I'd heard amazing stories about the military from my father, and his uncles, who'd also served.

A sense of duty to family was also important. Mom was strict but gentle, especially with me. Dad was six feet tall, with an average build and giant hands that had grown thick through endless hours at the milling machine. He traveled often for business, and I saw myself becoming the man of the house, as my father had been. Family was intertwined with business, and I got a feel for the business when Dad designated my mom, my sisters, and me as major shareholders of the ever expanding Prince Corporation. He led family meetings so everyone could be involved with company decisions. On Saturdays, he'd walk me through the various plants and offices at the company, teaching me about manufacturing and pointing out inefficiencies in production. The whole place smelled like hydraulic fluid. He never let me miss shaking even one person's hand, from machinist to executive, to acknowledge their contributions. Even when I was just seven.

In the years following the heart attack, Dad truly changed. Family and health became more important. In addition to the road trips across foreign continents, we saw places like Dachau and Normandy. He became obsessed with his physical fitness—there were no more doughnuts around the house—and that obsession caused him to worry about the health of his fifteen hundred employees.

Three afternoons a week, Prince Corporation executives met at the nearby Holland Tennis Club, which Dad had purchased when it threatened to go bankrupt. In the era of three-martini lunches elsewhere, the Prince top brass came together over double faults and backhand winners. Then, in 1987, Prince Corporation opened a massive new company complex complete with basketball and volleyball courts. Dad also offered his employees regular screenings for life-threatening illnesses.

To him, business wasn't just about making money. It was about relationships. My father's employees were loyal to him, and so, he felt, he was responsible for their welfare. He delighted in seeing them prosper with the company's success, from the hardworking machinist who could send his kids to college to the engineer who could afford the best care for a child with special needs. He sent planes from the company fleet to pick up salespeople at distant meetings so they'd be home in time for family dinners. The office stayed closed on Sundays.

His success made giving back important. Outside of work, Dad gave away at least 10 percent of his income every year. The fourth point on the Prince Corporation's mission statement said, "Make maximum charitable contributions," and my parents did so with devotion. In the 1980s their aid helped revitalize downtown Holland— including a donation of more than a million dollars to build one of the first dedicated senior centers in the country, Evergreen Commons. (Then vice president George H. W. Bush toured the center in December 1985.) Their contributions also enabled the restoration of the grand sandstone Tower Clock, which had stood downtown since 1892 and had become a beloved local landmark. The appreciation was mutual. Today a series of bronze footsteps in the sidewalk in downtown Alpenrose Park leads to statues of musicians and children singing; a plaque there memorializes my father. "We will always hear your footsteps," it reads. "The people of Downtown Holland honor your extraordinary vision and generosity."

Dad gave millions to the local Hope College, and Calvin College, my mother's alma mater, in nearby Grand Rapids. Both were schools built around the Christian Reformed faith, which my father had deeply embraced since his first brush with mortality. In 1988, his support helped Gary Bauer and James Dobson launch the Family Research Council, an influential public policy group that promoted conservative values. "We're blessed," Dad told us time and again. "We have a responsibility to be a force for good in the world."

Dad didn't let me hold a job during high school; unlike his hardscrabble youth, he wanted me to enjoy those years. I was on the basketball, soccer, track, and wrestling teams at Holland Christian High School; my senior year we won the Class B state soccer championship. I remember Dad flying in from anywhere in the world to sit on those metal bleachers with my mom during that rainy autumn.

I was never the most popular kid in high school. I didn't drink and I didn't smoke. Being an athlete gave me a social network, yet I didn't have many close friends growing up. My family background was a gift, but also had its disadvantages. I was never sure whether people saw me as my own person, or simply as the son of Holland's largest employer. I spent endless hours discussing politics with Dad, and thinking about my future. I got involved with the church. I learned to fly, earning my private pilot's license at nearby Tulip City Airport at the age of seventeen.

I loved studying history—particularly military history. I argued with teachers and classmates who hadn't seen what I'd seen on those family vacations. Those trips and stark contrasts between communist and free Europe had made an impression. *How can they not demand we oppose communism? Don't they know the Iron Curtain turns nations into prison camps?* Once in class I challenged a teacher who called then president Ronald Reagan's Cold War military buildup a waste of taxpayer dollars. I countered by rattling off every Strategic Defense Initiative weapons system we needed to counter various Soviet threats. I'd analyzed Reagan's "Star Wars" the way my classmates picked apart the University of Michigan's football roster. I wanted to battle the Soviets myself.

Because I'd been such an early and avid sailor, Dad encouraged my interest in the Navy. His time in the ROTC had helped him develop leadership qualities, he said, and a military academy could do the same for me. After the heart attack, my father was generous with his time—but never with handouts. He didn't want me relying on the family business. He made clear that I'd been given every advantage in life, and that I had no excuse for not making something of myself. Independently. I would not be working for Prince Corporation after college, he said, and I would receive no trust fund. I had to make it on my own.

On July 1, 1987, I reported to the United States Naval Academy in Annapolis, Maryland. I loved the newfound sense of purpose, and the connection to history. I loved spending a month aboard the World War II–era oiler USS *Caloosahatchee*—even if I did come down with chicken pox and suffer through three weeks of quarantine. But it wasn't long before I realized the academy wasn't the right fit: It was just after *Top Gun* had come out and the environment was an uncomfortable mix of Tailhook-era frat boys on one hand and a nonsensical policing of political correctness on the other. I felt as if I was expected to learn from graduate student instructors who knew little more than the fact that they'd been there longer than I had. I quickly began to wonder whether the academy created great leaders—or if great leaders just enrolled there, endured it, and made it out the other side.

I left the antics of Annapolis after three semesters and looked to get back to a serious academic path. I chose Hillsdale College, a liberal arts school of fourteen hundred students in southern Michigan, about twenty-five miles north of the Ohio border.

The thing that truly appealed to me about Hillsdale was its focus on libertarian, free-market economics. The courses were anchored in the ideologies of the Austrian School of economics, which lionizes long-term laissez-faire policies without government intervention. President Reagan gave a speech at Hillsdale in 1977 titled "What Ever Happened to Free Enterprise?" I wish I had been there to see it. I was an economics major and a political science minor, and began to see that I might one day have an impact as a businessman, much like my father.

A staunchly religious institution, Hillsdale was also notable for its approach to federal and state grants: There would be none. The college administration was determined to protect its academic freedom through fierce independence, without need or want of the bureaucratic oversight attached to those grants. And I remember that when the college offered me a full institutional scholarship, we turned it down. "Leave it for someone who needs the money," Dad said.

Back in 1986, I'd seen one of my favorite actors, Clint Eastwood, in the film *Heartbreak Ridge*. In it, Eastwood's Marine gunnery sergeant character mutters, "You can rob me, you can starve me, and you can beat me and you can kill me. Just don't bore me." To this day I love that line—I've never been one to sit still for long. I had long had a childhood dream of becoming a fireman, for instance, so I soon became the first student ever to sign up for Hillsdale's city fire department.

Now, most Hillsdale students came from money. The butchers, painters, and slaughterhouse workers who volunteered or worked at the firehouse initially figured me for a snot-nosed college kid. But I showed up at the firehouse early to change the blades on the K12 rescue saws, and I stayed late to clean the pumps. I handled the heavy canvas hoses and carried the ladders. After a call, when the other volunteers sat back and cracked open a drink, I rolled the hoses. Gradually I earned their respect—and seven dollars an hour—and I began branching out.

Having gotten scuba certified in Annapolis, I took up rescue diving with the sheriff's department, helping recover drowning victims and their vehicles that had plunged into the nearby lakes. I remember using a chain saw in the winters to cut holes in the ice that formed there, then dumping a few repurposed orange juice bottles full of hot water into my wet suit before striding in, all in an attempt to not freeze down there.

I had never before felt the focus or the adrenaline rush that came from descending into black water with no sound at all but my breath through the regulator, or clinging to a fire truck with its sirens raging. And I loved it. Everything had to be done fast. Lives depended upon our being prepared and executing our mission. That was more important than any class I was taking. I wore my fire department radio during exams. I was ready to move at the sound of the alarm.

Meanwhile, there was a girl: Joan. I first laid eyes on her in a picture on a fellow midshipman's wall back in Bancroft Hall, in Annapolis. She had long blond hair and blue eyes that shone across the room. I thought it must be Jimmy Keating's girlfriend—and then I thought about stealing Jimmy's girlfriend. It was worse: Joan Nicole Keating was his sister. "I won't let any midshipmen near her," he warned. Then he smiled. "They can't handle the heartbreak."

I finally met Joan in January 1989, when an old friend at the

academy called with extra tickets to the youth inaugural ball for incoming president George H. W. Bush. It was one of eight inaugural
balls Bush would hold, this one at a Marriott. My friend's daughter
wanted to go with Jimmy—so I promptly refused him a ticket until
he agreed to bring his sister. I flew in from Michigan to meet her.

Joan completely captivated me that night. She was from upstate
New York, near Saratoga, and was studying at Penn State University.
She could speak at length about anything and sound good doing it.
Joan knew nothing about my family or my background—virtually no
one at the Navy did—I was simply an ex-midshipman two years her
junior. She wore a ruffled navy blue taffeta dress that she'd bought
for the occasion—even though the occasion didn't seem to impress
her all that much. The floor-length dress brought out the color in her
eyes, but did nothing to complement her figure. Truth be told, that's
probably why I never really cared for it. But I'll never forget the first
moment I saw Joan wearing it. I'd have been happy spending the entire night just standing there with her in the security line.

In 1990, after my junior year at Hillsdale, I applied to be an intern in
George H. W. Bush's White House. Hillsdale had strong relationships
with the Reagan and Bush administrations, and they were campaigns
I believed in. A few months earlier, I'd made the first political
donation of my life: $15,000 to the National Republican Congres-
sional Committee, which came from investment income from stocks
my parents had long ago bought for me.

At the same time, Joan had graduated from Penn State and was
also working in Washington D.C., at a nonprofit foundation and a law
office. We spent all our free time together, and as quickly as I fell in
love with her, I fell out of love with national politics. I went to the nation's capital expecting a bastion of selfless service to one's country.
Where I came from, the Reagan administration had been hailed as
a triumph of vision and dedication. It was evidence that government could be a force for good in the world—through policies that

supported innovation and entrepreneurship at home, and ones that would tear down communist walls abroad. But in Washington I found career politicians and bureaucrat straphangers who existed purely to serve their own best interests—including those politicians at the highest levels of government.

I worked at the Office of Public Liaison in what was then called the Old Executive Office Building, an ornate Second Empire palace that houses most of the White House staff. The office served as the primary avenue through which the general public offered feedback to the White House—and I had some opinions about the administration myself. Before long, I came to feel that President Bush was bargaining with people who wanted to weaken the sanctity of marriage, raise taxes with budget compromises, and push environmental policies that meant undue expenses for major national employers. I know I could be a bit headstrong, and that outspokenness earned me my one visit to the West Wing. Deputy Chief of Staff Andrew Card had heard about my frustration with the administration. He wanted to chew me out.

That sole encounter with a top administration official lasted about five minutes, and my White House internship quickly wrapped up after just five months. But as luck would have it, one night while bowling with friends I ran into Congressman Dana Rohrabacher.

Today, Rohrabacher is serving his thirteenth term as representative from Southern California, currently its 48th District. Prior to his first election in 1988, Rohrabacher served as special assistant to President Reagan and for seven years was one of his senior speechwriters. At the White House, Rohrabacher played a key role in formulating the president's "Economic Bill of Rights," which championed free markets with little government interference. He also helped create the Reagan Doctrine, an aggressive military policy that publicly supported anticommunist insurgencies. "Freedom is not the sole prerogative of a chosen few," Reagan said during his 1985 State of the Union address; "it is the universal right of all God's children." Those words had inspired me. When Rohrabacher offered me an internship,

I jumped at the chance to learn from him. And it would be another Rohrabacher staffer, Paul Behrends, who led me to my next adventures.

Behrends, then a Marine reserve major—he would retire as a lieutenant colonel in 2005—conducted fact-finding missions for the House International Relations Committee. He was big into foreign policy and national security, and we had no trouble finding things to talk about. Also, I noticed that he ducked out of the office every day at lunchtime and never discussed where he was going. Only later did I learn he was going to mass. Behrends ultimately became influential in my exploration of becoming a Catholic.

In March 1991 I visited Zagreb with him to meet with Croatian leaders as they discussed plans to break away from Serb-dominated communist Yugoslavia. I remember visiting a major hospital in the city and seeing the rows and rows of wounded Croats.

The next month I accompanied Behrends to Nicaragua to investigate reports of mass graves in the countryside. The Nicaraguan Association for Human Rights believed that Daniel Ortega, a Marxist who'd come to power when his militant group, Frente Sandinista de Liberación Nacional, overthrew the Nicaraguan government in 1979, had been murdering civilian dissenters. In Managua, we had to shake a surveillance tail from a Sandinista in a Soviet-made Lada. Ninety minutes north of town, farmers led us to a secluded rolling hillside—and grim evidence of the atrocities. We found the remains of dozens of peasants who'd been bound at the wrist, shot in the head, and thrown into pits. I remember the shattered bones, the piles of broken skulls that stared up at me from the earth.

Eight days after I returned from Nicaragua, Joan and I stood at the altar of St. Mary's Catholic Church in Alexandria, Virginia. I was twenty-one; she was twenty-three. All of our friends and family were there. And as frustrated as she might have been about my conveniently being out of the country during the peak of our wedding planning, we were thrilled to be married on April 27, 1991.

When my congressional internship ended soon after, Joan and I took our honeymoon. We started with what we called our "Baltic liberation tour"—through Poland, Lithuania, Latvia, and Estonia. From there, we added stops in Belgrade, Sarajevo, and Mostar, in Bosnia and Herzegovina. We marveled at the medieval stone fortresses of Split and Dubrovnik. We even looped across North Africa before returning to Michigan, where I finished my senior year at Hillsdale. I remained a volunteer fireman—and still loved diving, and flying, and hunting—but I needed to fulfill a deeper mission.

I was also determined to keep my word. I'd first learned about the Navy's Sea, Air, and Land teams—better known as the SEALs— during my short time at the Naval Academy. During my exit interview in Annapolis, I told the registrar I'd one day become a SEAL—without the academy's help. He scoffed. I just nodded. So I applied to Officer Candidate School (OCS), the necessary first step for my reentry into the Navy, before graduating from Hillsdale. "We'll only do the Navy thing for a few years, okay?" Joan said.

There were eight operational SEAL teams in the United States, each comprising six platoons. Within the platoons there were sixteen SEALs—two officers, one chief, and thirteen enlisted men. Once accepted to OCS, I threw myself into training: swimming hours a day, ramping up the pull-ups and the dips. In the SEALs, it's not about how much you can lift, but how well you can move your weight on land and over water. Every SEAL has to be an expert at combat swimming, high-altitude parachuting, navigation, demolitions, and a host of other skills.

I packed up our house as soon as I handed in my last college exam— I didn't even attend graduation—and reported immediately to OCS in Newport, Rhode Island. Sixteen weeks later, Joan and I relocated again to Coronado, California, for my BUD/S—or Basic Underwater Demolition/SEAL—training at the Naval Special Warfare Center.

In total, BUD/S lasts six months, but it's the initial "Basic Conditioning" phase that's the stuff of legend: timed two-mile swims; four-, six-, or fourteen-mile runs in soft sand; and far worse. It's the most awful workout of your life, every day for seven weeks. As the Navy describes it: "Because of its particularly challenging requirements, many candidates begin questioning their decision to come to BUD/S." Once, a teammate and I were punished for goofing around—while freezing in the surf, he decided to start a class-wide conga line as a show of solidarity—and the instructors made us go "beached whale." We had to lie facedown in the sand as the waves crashed over our heads, then spit out the water before the next wave crashed. Breathing became a question of timing. Sand ended up in the unholiest of places. It was pure misery.

Our sixth week of training was called "Hell Week": 132 straight hours of mud, cold, and pain. We candidates ran more than two hundred miles and suffered through physical training for twenty-two hours a day. We got some four hours of sleep total in five and a half days. Consuming seven thousand calories a day didn't stave off weight loss; by the end of it, "running" wasn't really running so much as a furious stumble on pulled muscles and buckling knees.

And our class had it even worse than many. Traditionally, Hell Week is held on and around Naval Amphibious Base Coronado. But six weeks of above-average rain before our early February test meant that San Diego Bay and the surrounding ocean were full of sewage runoff, medical waste, and whatever in God's name washed up from Tijuana, ten miles south. Instead, instructors took us to Naval Auxiliary Landing Field San Clemente Island—a chilly little Channel Island sixty miles west of San Diego that could most charitably be called "rustic." Mostly I remember it because on San Clemente the low crawls went through a cactus patch. I might have preferred the sewage back at Coronado.

For days, trainers taunted the candidates to fold, to end the misery by ringing an ever present brass bell that hung in the camp. In our class, nearly 100 of the 120 candidates did. Many of those sailors went on to do great things in the Navy—but they would never be SEALs. The ones who somehow fought through will never quit anything in their lives.

When I got home from Hell Week, my parents sent me an extraordinary gift: a bronze statue of a cowboy. The artist had inscribed, "In the unwritten laws of the range, the work ethic still exists. When you sign for an outfit, you ride for their brand. True commitment takes no easy way out." It was an ethos I was proud to embrace: the months away from home, if need be, at the mercy of the elements, constantly under threats seen and unseen. The cowboy survived thanks to his courage and his wits. He protected those in his charge. Having survived that week, I knew my brand would be the Navy SEALs. It would be one of the greatest honors of my life.

We stayed in Coronado for only a few more weeks after my training. Joan wrapped up her time teaching at a local elementary school. Because I was a married officer, we'd been living off base; our place in town had become known to the other trainees as "Hotel Tango." During those last weeks, Joan followed her mother's Italian tradition and cooked staggering amounts of lasagna for the SEALs in my class. She was the extrovert in the household—she could, and did, make friends with anyone. She brought nuns and officers and fellow teachers over for dinner, and carried on late into the night about everything from fashion to philosophy. Exhausted as I was after days in the mud, I loved shining my boots at home, watching her captivate the room until I could no longer keep my eyes open.

My daughter Sophia was born on December 22, 1994, in Virginia Beach, Virginia, the first of seven beautiful children I've been blessed with. Joan and I had moved to town when I joined SEAL Team 8 the year before. At Sophia's baptism, the priest invited her grandparents to trace the sign of the cross on her forehead. I remember my father, a handsome man of sixty-three, tracing a giant finger along my baby's face. He had made the trip in from

Michigan and looked as vigorous as ever. But for some reason, when I saw him off, I kept going back to say good-bye. I kissed him. "Dad, I love you," I said. "I miss you and I can't wait to see you again."

Four days later, on March 2, 1995, Edgar Prince left the executive dining room at his company's headquarters, stepped into the elevator, and suffered a massive heart attack. Employees found him fifteen minutes later; by then, attempts to resuscitate him would prove unsuccessful. My hero was gone.

In the following days, flags in Holland flew at half-staff. At the time, Prince employed some forty-five hundred people. A young female engineer at the company told the local newspaper, "You felt in a way like you were part of his family. When I heard he died, I cried, and I didn't even know him." More than a thousand people arrived at the Christ Memorial Reformed Church to attend his funeral. "Ed Prince was not an empire builder," Gary Bauer later wrote to members of the Family Research Council. "He was a Kingdom builder."

At my father's funeral, I reflected on seeing him at Sophia's baptism, and how Joan had asked him how he was feeling. "You know," my father said, "I just don't feel very well." I realized that might have been only the second time I heard the eternal optimist say that.

Shortly after the service, Mom called a family meeting to discuss the substantial legacy Dad had left us. I had just finished a few weeks of combat search and rescue training in Fallon, Nevada; I asked my commanding officer for leave time, and two fellow sailors drove me to the airport. It wasn't a typical drop-off, however. Mom had sent a plane to get me: one of Dad's planes, a midsize executive jet that landed at Fallon and taxied toward the three of us standing in the small terminal. No one in the SEALs had known about my family background. I liked it that way; I had earned their trust and respect the same as everyone else. I was horrified when my father's vanity N-number on the tail of that plane came into full view, ending with a giant "EP." The pilots brought the jet to a stop and stepped out from the cockpit.

"Hey, Erik!" they called.

My buddies were speechless. Finally, one blurted out, "If you weren't in the Navy, could you just retire?"

I met back up with the SEALs in Virginia a few days later. The two sailors from Fallon had kept my family's secret. Or maybe they told everyone and no one believed them. Regardless, with SEAL Team 8, I deployed to Haiti in 1994 as part of the package President Bill Clinton sent to oust General Raoul Cédras from power. We were responsible for mapping landing beaches and performing special reconnaissance, though by the time we landed there it had become largely a peacekeeping mission. I remember the ride home to Norfolk almost as well as our time in Haiti: We hit a major nor'easter, my first on a ship, and they had to chain down the tables in the mess decks to keep them from becoming projectiles. We all ate peanut butter and jelly that night because there was no way anyone was going to try cooking.

Then, in late 1995, as Yugoslavia broke apart into warring states, SEAL Team 8 deployed to Bosnia-Herzegovina. The shattered buildings and war-torn streets were a far cry from the peaceful communities I'd once seen there with my wife. We SEALs were performing combat search and rescue for downed pilots, or taking direct action against radar sites.

My time abroad was hard for both me and Joan, especially with a newborn daughter at home. Then, in May 1996, while pregnant with our second child, Christian, my wife found a lump in her breast. She was twenty-nine. I finished out the year with the SEALs, but as much as I'd looked forward to the missions that might lie ahead, I knew I would soon have two young children at home with their mother facing a cancer battle. My being gone was suddenly impossible. I requested my discharge from the Navy.

Meanwhile, there were endless family debates about the future of Dad's business. Just over a year after my father's death, my mother, sisters, and I sold the Prince Automotive unit to Milwaukee-based Johnson Controls Inc. for $1.35 billion, which was split between a number of Dad's business partners, employee stockholders, and my mother, sisters, and me. We retained Prince Machine, as well as

Lumir Corp., Dad's real estate operation, and Wingspan Leasing, which leased airplanes. Johnson Controls renamed the 750,000-square-foot complex Dad had built in Holland the Edgar D. Prince Technical Campus.

My father had created an amazing enterprise. I was blessed to inherit a fortune. Now I had to use it wisely.

CHAPTER 2

THE GREAT DISMAL SWAMP

1996–1998

THE CONCEPT OF BLACKWATER ORIGINATED IN THE READY ROOM OF A 1960s-
era aircraft carrier sailing across the Mediterranean Sea. It was the
summer of 1995; SEAL Team 8 had just wrapped a training operation in the Adriatic in preparation for supporting the NATO mission
to beat back Serbian forces that had advanced on Srebrenica in
Bosnia-Herzegovina. Largely, training was what we did: a few weeks
in Nevada here, a few weeks in Puerto Rico there, then in Missis-
sippi, Indiana, West Virginia, North Carolina. . . . Special operations
personnel are never *not* training, wherever they can find space. When
your life depends on the ability to make snap judgments and execute
in an instant, training isn't something taken lightly.

The Bosnia exercise taught me well about that endless, inefficient
predeployment travel schedule—an issue that was growing all too
common across the armed forces thanks to dramatic defense spending cuts after the fall of the Berlin Wall in 1989 and the collapse of
the Soviet Union in 1991. Our SEAL deployments may have lasted six

months, but I'd been on the road for ten of the prior twelve months just for training.

Those spending cuts are a recurring part of American history, harkening all the way back to the Revolutionary War. Our military complex ramps up for conflict, then "skeletonizes" after. It's the "guns or butter" question of priorities—that somewhat simplistic theory suggesting a government can spend money bolstering its defense or it can invest money in civilian goods, but it cannot do both. In October 1993, President Bill Clinton picked up that baton and left no doubt about where the military was headed. That year, the introduction of the Department of Defense's "Bottom-Up Review," submitted to Congress, began: "The Cold War is behind us. The Soviet Union is no longer the threat that drove our defense decision-making for four and a half decades—that determined our strategy and tactics, our doctrine, the size and shape of our forces, the design of our weapons, and the size of our defense budgets."

That view wasn't wrong, and I believe strongly that it is important to rein in unnecessary defense spending. But the focus was on the wrong things, because amid that drawdown traditional conflict was quickly giving way to unconventional attacks. Aboard the USS *America*, we talked about the peacekeeping failure in Bosnia that had brought us there: Ratko Mladic, the top commander for the Bosnian Serb army, and wartime political leader Radovan Karadzic had been accused of orchestrating the massacre of eight thousand Bosniak (Bosnian Muslim) men and boys after the fall of Srebrenica in July 1995. Both men were accused by the UN International Court of Justice in The Hague, Netherlands, of genocide, along with "unlawful confinement, murder, rape, sexual assault, torture, beating, robbery and inhumane treatment of civilians; the targeting of political leaders, intellectuals and professionals; the unlawful deportation and transfer of civilians; the unlawful shelling of civilians; the unlawful appropriation and plunder of real and personal property; the destruction of homes and businesses; and the destruction of places of worship." Their trials were ongoing when this book was completed.

The assault on Srebrenica was revenge for the deaths of Serb civilians at the hands of Muslim guerrilla warriors. United Nations peacekeepers had prevented Mladic from overrunning the UN-declared "safe haven" once before, but in July the roughly six-hundred-strong Dutch UN Protection Force did little to stop the Serbs, resulting in the worst European atrocity since World War II. In 1999, UN secretary-general Kofi Annan admitted, "There was neither the will to use decisive air power against Serb attacks on the safe areas, nor the means on the ground to repulse them." The whole thing could have been avoided, the rest of the SEALs and I thought, with a modest peacekeeping force of U.S. special ops personnel.

The question was where they'd all train. We SEALs could barely find space. From 1989 to 1997, the Defense Department's spending cuts had reduced total active-duty U.S. military personnel by 32 percent, and personnel employed in "infrastructure" activities like training programs by 28 percent. More than a hundred military bases had been closed. Shooting ranges had been cut so drastically that personnel from different services basically stacked themselves on top of one another. Once, in 1995, at the thousand-yard sharp-shooting range at the North Carolina National Guard's Camp Butner, we SEALs practiced from the two-hundred-yard line on the range's right side while Army Special Forces marksmen shot from the thousand-yard line on the left. That would have failed any range safety policy anywhere—but there simply wasn't anyplace else to go.

Meanwhile, we grumbled, the SEALs got dumped in places like Camp Butner only because we didn't have a dedicated training area of our own. We had no outdoor ranges, indoor shoot houses, or ship simulators. We flew to the Army's Fort Pickett in Virginia for land warfare training, then to naval facilities in Puerto Rico for diving and submarine operations, then to an Army National Guard camp in Indiana for sniper training, and then to wherever we could go for airborne training. And once we arrived at those places, we could still lose our training slot if a range safety officer didn't show up, or an ambulance wasn't available to have on hand, or if base support couldn't tell us what radio frequencies to use. And then some endangered species of bird would fly through, and everything would come to a standstill. There were times Army officers didn't show up to training activities because it was *raining*. "I didn't figure you boys wanted to get wet," they'd say.

All the travel was a waste of taxpayer dollars—and it was miserable for a young family like mine. On those training stints I constantly thought about Joan and little Sophia, and about that second child on the way, and about our future. My time with the SEALs had changed my life, but by late 1996 I was considering what might come next. I'd been poring over *Entrepreneurs Are Made Not Born*, Lloyd Shefsky's book of business advice from pioneers such as Bill Gates and the guys behind Ben & Jerry's ice cream. It glorified risk taking and defying conventional wisdom. There on the USS *America*, I told my teammates I wanted to build a world-class training facility once I left the service, a one-stop shop near our base in Norfolk where special operations personnel could get the best of everything they needed.

Largely I was tailoring my sales pitch, because I knew the real challenge would be convincing my wife. I often wrote Joan letters from the road, and she had excellent common sense. "In reading that book, my confidence in starting a business was bolstered," I wrote to her in November 1995. "The book encourages readers to make a dream sheet of all the businesses they might want to start someday. But the only one that keeps coming to my mind is a training facility."

A center just west of Williamsburg, Virginia, I said, could draw SEALs, Virginia State Police, Marine snipers from Quantico, as well as CIA officers and SWAT teams. I could find a retired officer to run the place, so I wouldn't have to be there nine to five. The military drawdown meant the government was practically begging to outsource those training functions to the private sector—especially exotic niches like special operations, in which the entire premise is to equip the man as the weapon, instead of treating the man as the technician who operates the weapons, as conventional units do. The SEALs had long been too targeted for most strategic planners to worry about, and too low budget to interest politicians who wanted to funnel money toward megawarships and billion-dollar airplanes. But it only made sense that in an era of dramatic defense spending cuts, those niche groups might see greater action, and that their training would become an even higher priority.

I'm the first to admit, it wasn't exactly reinventing the wheel: If you want to run a marathon, there are clubs that will train you. Want to become a pilot? You go to flight school. If you want all manner of elite military training, it's only logical to have a place for that. Some people told me the idea was so straightforward, the only reason they hadn't already done it was because they didn't have the capital.

I was fortunate. As part of my parents' emphasis on stewardship and hard work, Dad's original will had stipulated that I wouldn't have access to any hypothetical inheritance until I turned thirty. He changed that once I became a SEAL, though—from then on, he said, there wouldn't ever be a reason to question my work ethic. So even at the age of twenty-six, the finances weren't a problem for me. "I think the whole thing could get done for less than a million," I told Joan. "If we rented the place for forty weeks a year, we might gross $200,000 annually."

She agreed that it sounded reasonable, though I'm also not convinced she fully understood the concept. Joan didn't care about firearms and hadn't ever been to a facility like the ones I described. But she knew I had the passion, the skills, and a clear vision for what I wanted to accomplish.

Turned out, I didn't have a clue what I was getting into, either.

As my father had done with Prince Manufacturing, I knew that launching my own business would require a tight team of skilled personnel—people who not only were subject matter experts, but also understood determination and persistence in a way that most people don't. I recalled my SEAL training and the way Team 8 had spent hour after hour at shooting ranges—squeezing off rounds until our fingers blistered and bled in the pursuit of excellence. I was prepared for building a business to be the same way, and my team had to understand that. The first people I brought on were Al, Jim, and Ken.

Al Clark was a senior weapons SEAL instructor in Virginia Beach in the early 1990s—one of the best I've ever known—and shared my vision for what the facility could become. He had long wanted to create his own firearms training center, but lacked the financial resources to launch it. Al was a great person to spearhead our training programs.

We then convinced Jim Dehart, a man who'd spent fifteen years designing shooting ranges for the military, to create shoot houses for us. He understood drafting and schematics, electrical engineering, even plumbing. I joked that when the zombie apocalypse came, he'd be the first guy I'd grab to keep the lights on and the fences up. Jim had phenomenal ideas and, just as important, could figure out how to make them into reality for twenty cents on the dollar.

Ken Viera, a former SEAL who'd led numerous missions worldwide and had been my training officer with Team 8, agreed to be the general manager. I got along well with the lanky long-distance runner because of his discipline and focus, and his intensity. He's not a relaxed kind of guy. Neither am I. But he was a terrific businessman and also a terrific competitor for the lunchtime physical training sessions that we would organize at Blackwater. He was regularly out there with us dragging tires, or pushing cars, or bombing through the swamp on mountain bikes, building camaraderie with any employee who wanted to show up, much as my father had done in Holland.

Our founding team selected, we chose the location of our facility with a map and a compass, marking off circles with a radius of four hours' driving distance from key surrounding military bases. The first was Naval Amphibious Base Little Creek, in Virginia Beach, home to Navy SEAL Teams 2, 4, 8, and 10.

Other foci were a pair of North Carolina bases. The Marines'

Camp Lejeune, south of Jacksonville, is home to the II Marine Expeditionary Force, 2nd Marine Division, 2nd Marine Logistics Group, and other combat-ready units. Meanwhile, the Army's Fort Bragg, outside Fayetteville, houses its Special Operations Command and the 82nd Airborne Division.

It was important that we have easy access to Virginia and the CIA's clandestine services training center there, often referred to as "the Farm." And finally, there was Washington D.C., the nerve center of the federal military and law enforcement agencies.

Connecting all those dots would put Blackwater in the midst of the largest military-industrial complex in the world. The circles overlapped just across the North Carolina border outside a ten-thousand-person town called Moyock, on the eastern edge of the Great Dismal Swamp.

Our team's vision for the facility was a cross between a shooting range and a country club for special forces personnel. Clients would be able to schedule all manner of training courses in advance, and the gear and support personnel would be waiting when they arrived. There'd be seven shooting ranges with high gravel berms to cut down noise and absorb bullets, and we'd carve a grass airstrip, and have a special driving track to practice high-speed chases and real "defensive driving"—the stuff that happens when your convoy is ambushed. There would be a bunkhouse to sleep seventy. And nearby, the main headquarters would have the feel of a hunting lodge, with timber framing and high stone walls, with a large central fireplace where people could gather after a day on the ranges. This was the community I enjoyed; we never intended to send anyone oversees. This chunk of the Tar Heel State was my "Field of Dreams."

I bought thirty-one hundred acres—roughly five square miles of land, plenty of territory to catch even the most wayward bullets—for $900,000. We broke ground in June 1997, and immediately began learning about do-it-yourself entrepreneurship. That land was ugly: Logging the previous year had left a moonscape of tree stumps and tangled roots lorded over by mosquitoes and poisonous creatures. I killed a snake the first twelve times I went to the property. The heat was miserable.

While a local construction company carved the shooting ranges and the lake, our small team installed the culverts and forged new roads and planted the Southern pine utility poles to support the electrical wiring. The basic site work was done in about ninety days— and then we had to figure out what to call the place. The leading contender, "Hampton Roads Tactical Shooting Center," was professional, but pretty uptight. "Tidewater Institute for Tactical Shooting" had legs, but the acronym wouldn't have helped us much. But then, as we slogged across the property and excavated ditches, an incessant charcoal mud covered our boots and machinery, and we watched as each new hole was swallowed by that relentless peat-stained black water.

Blackwater, we agreed, was a name.

Meanwhile, within days of being installed, the Southern pine poles had been slashed by massive black bears marking their territory, as the animals had done there since long before the Europeans settled the New World. We were part of this land now, and from that heritage we took our original logo: a bear paw surrounded by the stylized crosshairs of a rifle scope.

The final piece of the puzzle was Gary Jackson. Had two sailors not gotten their ears bitten off in a fight with a SEAL, I might never have met him. In 1993 I was an ensign with the Navy, an O1, at the bottom of the officers' pay scale. Like most junior SEAL officers, I was assigned "collateral duties"—that's the Navy's term for what is largely administrative grunt work. Many of my collateral duties were helping out with Judge Advocate General investigations, and when I met Jackson I'd been tasked with looking into a fight at the Naval Air Station in Brunswick, Maine. A group of sailors had been there for Survival, Evasion, Resistance, and Escape school, which teaches personnel what to do when they're lost behind enemy lines or being interrogated as prisoners of war. It clearly didn't teach those two not to pick a fight with a SEAL outside the enlisted men's club, however—and now all three were subject to disciplinary action. Jackson was the chief warrant officer overseeing the facility where the SEAL was now assigned.

A British-born naturalized American ten years my senior, Jackson had spent two decades as a SEAL. I remember him telling me once that he actually hadn't joined the Navy in the early 1970s by choice, but rather because he'd gotten into some mischief as a high schooler back in Tennessee. When his civil infraction case came before the judge, he said, the judge told him, "I can't put you in jail for a full year—but I can certainly put you there for eleven months and twenty-nine days. Or you can go talk to that recruiter in the blue uniform in the back of the room. Your call."

I also knew that Jackson was good with computers, which was still a novel skill in the 1990s. I don't know how much of an impression I made during our meeting in Brunswick, but Jackson remembered my name more than a decade later when Viera suggested he come check out the joint being built in Moyock. After twenty-three years with the Navy, Jackson was nearing retirement. And intrigued by our business plan, he hammered out a rudimentary Blackwater Web site on his trunk-size laptop. It arrived in the mail on a 3.5-inch floppy disk. By today's standards, that first site would be a Model T in an F150 world—the sort of thing we look back on and laugh about. But we were impressed by the effort, and in 1998, as soon as he submitted his retirement papers, Jackson came to work for us.

As we cleared that swampland, our ambitions grew—and by the time the Blackwater Lodge and Training Center officially opened on May 15, 1998, it was the largest shooting facility in the United States. We had the only twelve-hundred-yard shooting range on the East Coast. We had created an entirely new kind of shoot house, a heavy steel building with movable interior doors and walls where we could constantly change layouts and scenarios, complete with an observation deck above to instruct and grade trainees. We even dug a twenty-acre lake to practice maritime special operations, allowing personnel to practice boarding ships from portside, by helicopter, and from underwater. The property had practically doubled in size, to six thousand acres—nearly half the size of Manhattan. I'd invested more than $6 million of my own money into all of it . . . and then, early on, no one came, for days at a time.

There was one small contract right at the start: training SEAL Team 1, ironically from California, in a deal worth $25,000. The Navy paid with a credit card—and thank God, because that 1.5 percent credit card fee was well worth it for the cash flow. We couldn't afford to wait thirty days—or sometimes ninety days—for the government to cut us a check, because we were already sending hourly workers home early. Jackson would try to drum up business at gun shows—and then get booted because we couldn't afford a proper booth. His wife chipped in at the headquarters, helping us manage the books.

Understand, Blackwater didn't have some unlimited cash spigot to drink from. I was able to make a significant investment to launch the company, but part of my initial deal with Joan was that, no matter what happened with it, I wouldn't gamble our children's college funds. Managers in Moyock had budgets to stick to, and they understood that I expected them to accomplish three things for the cost of two. Jackson, thankfully, knew how to squeeze the buffalo dime until it squealed.

We offered firearms safety courses to local hunters, just to bring in *something*. Blackwater saw about $400,000 in revenue that first year, mostly through training nearby law enforcement and FBI SWAT teams.

Meanwhile, life at home offered different struggles. Soon after I left the Navy in 1996, Joan began her long battle with cancer—and won, for a time. In 1997, we moved our growing family back to Michigan to be closer to our relatives. There, I took over as chairman at Prince Machine, and regularly flew my single-engine bush plane back to North Carolina to oversee Blackwater's development. But that same year, as Joan was expecting our third child, doctors gave us an ominous prognosis. They talked about the elevated estrogen levels women have during pregnancy, and how that heightened the risk for more serious tumors to come. They recommended the extreme solution.

"Joan," one doctor told her, "we have to interrupt your pregnancy."

"When will it be resumed?" she shot back. Joan wouldn't abort our child under any circumstances—and our second daughter, Isabella, was born in September 1997.

Five months later, the breast cancer returned. Joan suffered through cancer surgery, then chemotherapy and radiation. We were told her long blond hair—which I had come to know in photos, even before I'd actually met her—wouldn't make it through the treatments. Joan and I visited a salon in Beverly Hills, where it was cut short. She cried. The stylist cried.

By the morning of May 10, 1998, the predictions were coming true. Joan's hair was falling out in handfuls. I'd flown back from Blackwater to spend the weekend in Michigan with her and the kids, and that Sunday morning, she asked me to shave off the rest of it. I can't forget that date: It was Mother's Day. That was the day I cried.

CHAPTER 3

COLUMBINE, THE *COLE*, AND CANCER

1999–2001

WHEN HE CAME ON BOARD, GARY JACKSON CALCULATED THAT, AT MAXIMUM capacity, Blackwater could bring in as much as $1.7 million a year in revenues. That was multiple times my original estimate; we really had no idea of what the numbers could become. But early on, we were all too aware of what the numbers actually were. Our small team clawed through eighteen-hour workdays, seven days a week, just as my father had done, trying to build the business. I found an odd comfort in following in my father's footsteps and in the distraction from Joan's illness—though Blackwater at the time was an environment rife for what we'll call "philosophical differences."

The staff we'd put in place was long on special operations know-how, but much shorter on business background. With all the skills they have, elite military personnel don't necessarily have any experience at all with increasing business productivity, or managing costs down, or grinding out supply chain inefficiencies. We saw that same problem eat away at other major contracting companies that employed scores of generals and colonels just for their name recognition. But at a startup like Blackwater, I knew that the question of whether we could quickly transition from operators to businessmen was going to decide the fate of the company.

Viera and Jackson, for example, were able to make that jump, and I tip my hat to them. Some others, such as Clark, had less success finding a comfortable role and a set of responsibilities on the team, and ultimately left during those challenging times.

Those who stayed understood one thing very clearly: We had to figure out how to start making money. Dehart started with shooting range targets.

The courses he designed for Blackwater tested shooters' reflexes, with moving targets that could represent an enemy combatant or an innocent civilian. Trainees had to determine which one to put, or not put, a bullet through in less than a heartbeat. It helped them master precision in high-adrenaline situations and sharpened their judgment—and absolutely shredded the equipment. Chains, tracks, hinges, and pivots—all made of heavy steel—controlled the moving targets. We pushed clients so hard, even the highest-end, $12,000 commercial Action Targets were reduced to bullet-riddled junk within months. And manufacturers don't exactly offer warranties against assault by special forces. "Train hard or don't train at all" was our motto, but it was also becoming a legitimate budgetary problem.

Thankfully, Dehart had a solution. He machined a new kind of target system, named the BEAR, from Hardox 500 steel, the same alloy used in things like excavator buckets and armored personnel carriers. The BEAR featured a dozen spinning targets that were controlled either by specially designed computer software or by remote control.

Then he created a modified dueling tree, featuring six steel targets that swung from one side of a central column to the other when shot. A pair of trainees would fire simultaneously at the targets; the first person to knock all the targets to the other side won. It was like Blackwater tetherball.

Dehart's targets drew such rave reviews, trainees in Moyock all wanted to take them home with them. So soon enough, a metal building sprung up on our grounds beside the bunkhouse, full of men cutting and welding Blackwater-branded systems—everything from self-contained ranges inside shipping containers to pneumatic pop-up targets. That equipment brought in 50 percent of our revenue in the early days. Dehart's designs—not the training we'd originally intended to provide—kept Blackwater out of the red.

And gradually, with the targets keeping us afloat, Jackson's salesmanship began to pay off. At the end of his naval career, Jackson had headed a counterdrug platoon in the Caribbean, and the connections he'd made down there came in handy in 1999. People he'd known at the Coast Guard asked if Blackwater could train marksmen for its new Helicopter Interdiction Tactical Squadron. HITRON, as it's known, is based out of Jacksonville, Florida, and was the country's first law enforcement unit authorized to employ airborne use of force. At the time, the Coast Guard estimated it was stopping less than 10 percent of the drugs being smuggled into the country over the water, and in Stingray helicopters that could cruise at 140 knots, the agency found a solution. But disabling those arrow-shaped go-fast boats—which would allow cops to seize shipments and apprehend smugglers—is far more nuanced than simply blowing them out of the water. The Coast Guard wanted us to adapt SEAL techniques to train their shooters to destroy outboard engines with massive .50-caliber rifles.

It was, at the time, our first classified contract—and a real step forward for a small company searching for some traction. Very quickly, we found that the one thing we could do better than anyone else was to learn from current events and find creative solutions for real-world problems. And unfortunately, in 1999 and 2000, two events shone spotlights on problems that needed to be solved.

Just after eleven a.m. on Tuesday, April 20, 1999, Eric Harris and Dylan Klebold carried an arsenal of shotguns, semiautomatic weapons, and homemade pipe bombs into Columbine High School, just south of Denver. In one of the worst school shootings in U.S. history, the teenagers spent forty-nine minutes patrolling the building, murdering thirteen people before ultimately turning the guns on themselves. Following the massacre, the public fixated on potential causes—antidepressant use in teens, goth culture, or listening to shock rock, for instance—many of which have since been proven to be unfounded speculation. The Blackwater team, however, saw something very different.

We noticed that more than seventy-five police officers had surrounded the school by the time the shooters committed suicide, yet it would be three hours before anyone entered the building and found the two of them. We heard that a reported one thousand personnel from forty-seven different agencies had arrived at the scene throughout the day, and most were never given an assignment from commanders there. We lamented the passing of teacher Dave Sanders, the final of the fifteen casualties that day, who'd been shot at 11:26 a.m. yet who bled to death in a classroom before paramedics reached him nearly four hours later. It was clear that SWAT teams needed better training for a situation like this. Established policies that had patrol officers securing a perimeter and waiting for the cavalry—instead of charging inside to get the shooter—clearly didn't work when the gunmen weren't taking hostages.

Blackwater already had a fifteen-thousand-square-foot range on its property that looked like a small town, complete with paved streets and buildings outfitted with video cameras, allowing trainees to simulate urban environments. We conferred with the National Tactical Officers Association (NTOA), a nonprofit founded back in 1983 to oversees training programs for police patrol officers and special operations units around the country. Within six weeks of the Columbine shootings, Blackwater was home to a sixteen-room steel building that allowed for live gunfire inside, and even explosions outside for practice with "dynamic entry." There was a sound track of alarms, and people screaming. We called the massive structure "R U Ready High School."

The NTOA committed $50,000 to start the construction—but never delivered the funds. So we forged ahead and funded the project ourselves, hoping that if we built it, tactical teams would come to update their training. It was another leap of faith.

In September 1999, the NTOA sent a class of four hundred SWAT team members to Moyock. We had actors playing students, covered in blood and pleading for help. Backpacks contained mock bombs; "shooters" hid among the "students" to lie in wait for police. It was a grisly scene, intentionally so—the sort of thing critics point to when they call us callous for using tragedy to grow the company. They don't get it. As a reporter once described our work: "Somebody has to be in the business of worst-case scenarios."

Those mock injuries—the "moulage," as it's known in medical and military circles—were a key part of instilling in the officers a profound sense of the morality and necessity of their mission. Tying in that psychological component created something we called "full competency." It was sometimes horrifying training that most of the participants—police officers at local and state levels—had never encountered before. Larry Glick, the NTOA's executive director, later described his team's first visit to Blackwater: "There was no back-slapping or celebration at the end of the simulation," he said. "Several officers told us they never believed in their worst nightmares that such an event could take place, let alone that they would have to train for it." It was the sort of thing they needed to see to be able to respond to a real-life event of that magnitude.

Soon, the NTOA was sending officers from all fifty states, plus Canada, Haiti, Belgium, and England, to our facility. One year after the Columbine shooting, we'd trained a thousand of its men. Other police officers were so eager to take the course, they paid for the program out of their own pockets if their departments wouldn't cover the expense. Trainees were battering and blowing open so many doors that we had a standing monthly order at the local Home Depot for truckloads of new ones.

That pair of teenagers outside Denver had rocked the nation's law enforcement community, and in the process had given Blackwater a chance to grow. Just over a year later, two men half a world away, in Aden, Yemen, would shake the entire U.S. Navy—and alter the course of our company.

The USS *Cole* is a billion-dollar warship—a 505-foot-long Arleigh Burke–class guided-missile destroyer armed with torpedoes, machine guns, Tomahawk missiles, and a vast array of advanced radar equipment. In August 2000, the destroyer sailed from Naval Station Norfolk en route to a deployment with the U.S. 5th Fleet in the Arabian Gulf. Two months later, as the ship refueled in Aden harbor under security posture Threatcon Bravo—the third of the five alert levels the military uses to label impending terrorist threats—two al-Qaeda operatives steered a small fiberglass fishing boat full of C4 plastic explosive to the *Cole*'s port side. Witnesses watched the men stand at attention. Then the duo set off a blast equivalent to the detonation of seven hundred pounds of TNT, shaking buildings along the waterfront and opening a forty-foot-by-forty-foot gash in the destroyer's reinforced steel hull. Seventeen sailors were killed instantly or mortally wounded; thirty-nine more were injured. At the time, it was the worst terrorist attack on an American target since the 1998 bombings of U.S. embassies in Nairobi, Kenya, and Dar es Salaam, Tanzania.

Yet even more shocking than the attack itself was what the Navy subsequently discovered about its own outdated policies and training procedures. Crew members reported that the sentries' rules of engagement, set by the ship's captain following Navy guidelines, would have prevented them from defending the ship, even if they'd detected a threat: They weren't permitted to fire on an enemy without being fired upon first. Petty Officer John Washak told the *Washington Post* that he was manning a gun at the rear of the *Cole* when a second boat approached, but that he was ordered to turn his weapon away unless he was actively shot at. "In the military, it's like we're trained to hesitate now," Washak said. "If somebody had seen something wrong and shot, he probably would have been court-martialed."

The Navy's own Judge Advocate General (JAG) investigation into the bombing carried additional and unsettling weight. The report concluded that the *Cole*'s commanding officer had failed to implement roughly half the force protection measures required during the refueling stop. Far more important, a full implementation of those measures still wouldn't have stopped the carnage. In his statement to the JAG report, Vice Admiral Charles W. Moore Jr., commander in chief of United States Naval Forces Central Command and the Navy's 5th Fleet, noted that "had the *Cole* implemented the Threatcon Bravo measures perfectly, there is total unity among the flag officers who have reviewed this investigation that the ship would not have prevented or deterred this attack."

One can imagine the reaction at the Pentagon when the commander of the 5th Fleet—which patrols five million square miles, including the Red Sea, the Arabian Gulf, the Arabian Sea, and parts of the Indian Ocean—suggests men aboard his destroyers couldn't stop bad guys in fishing boats. It led to an "urgent and compelling" training contract—a short-term emergency stopgap measure used when the government doesn't have months to engage in the traditional, cumbersome open bidding process. Not long after the bombing, we got a phone call from the Navy asking if Blackwater's personnel could instruct twenty thousand sailors in force protection over the next six months, at facilities in four separate locations.

That call was part of a standard market survey conducted by the DoD to figure out how many providers might be able to satisfy the demands of an upcoming contract. "With those surveys," explained Fred Roitz, Blackwater's former vice president of contracts and compliance, "the Navy is basically saying, 'We have to train X number of sailors at X types of ranges, within X miles of Hampton Roads. How many companies can even accomplish that?'" It turned out, travel time was a sticking point. "The Navy wasn't going to be putting sailors on planes to go train," Roitz said—which is exactly what Blackwater's founders had anticipated when we drew those compass circles that led us to Moyock.

We were the only company that checked every box on the Navy's list. Still, we had to think carefully about whether we would accept that challenge. Blackwater was, at the time, a company with thirty full-time employees. We hadn't trained three thousand people *total* since opening our doors three years earlier; now the Navy was asking if we could train twenty thousand sailors in six months. We weren't entirely sure how we would do it, but our company culture was always aggressively proactive, and management never shied away from a challenge. Jackson's commitment to action was so intense that he had even gone so far as to start keeping a database of business resources with a "T" or a "D" marked next to names: The letters stood for "Talker" and "Doer."

Committed to being "doers" ourselves, we said yes. The Navy gave us thirty days to be up and running, and they made it simple: The contract was worth almost $7 million—and everything we needed to execute it came out of our own pocket. It was like my father footing the bill for all his R&D—we bought our own equipment, firearms, and ammunition. With Dehart's guidance, we built a "ship in a box"—a floating superstructure made of forty-foot steel tractor trailer cargo containers, painted battleship gray and fitted with watertight doors and railings. Think of an elaborate ship's bridge on a movie set, only one designed to withstand real-life firefights. No one slept much that month, but the structure was ready for the Navy on Day 30, and inspected by the Occupational Safety and Health Administration the day after.

For the next six months we trained nearly a thousand sailors a week to identify threats, engage enemies, and defeat attacks under way on ships in port and at sea. Almost immediately, one of the

Navy's problems was clear: It had been years since some of those guys had held a gun. Our instructors were stunned to find that sailor after sailor had never used a firearm, except in boot camp.

Filling that contract created a funny juxtaposition between our fledgling operation and the type of business we did. Blackwater Lodge and Training Center was still a small business, but hundreds of sailors flooded Moyock every week. We were bringing in tens of thousands of dollars. And yet, every Friday, some Blackwater employee had to stand in our simple pro shop, swiping the Navy's credit card through the countertop reader next to a little magazine rack and a stack of old PowerBars. (And swipe it multiple times. When the card's individual charges were capped at $5,000, ringing up $60,000 on a Friday afternoon meant he was going to be there a while.)

But we impressed the right people. In May 2001, Admiral Vern Clark, then the chief of naval operations, was able to report to the Senate Armed Services Committee, "The attack on the USS *Cole* was a terrible tragedy and dramatic example of the type of threat our military forces face worldwide on a day-to-day basis, emphasizing the importance of force protection both today and in the future. The Navy has taken action at home and abroad to meet this challenge, undergoing a sea change in the way we plan and execute self-defense. We have enhanced the manning, training, and equipping of naval forces to better realize a war fighter's approach to physical security, with ATFP [Anti-Terrorism Force Protection] serving as a primary focus of every mission, activity, and event. Additionally, we are dedicated to ensuring this mindset is instilled in every one of our sailors."

Our work was so successful that two years later, once the "urgent" part wore off, the Navy put up for bid a five-year contract to conduct two-week training sessions for its personnel on sentry duty, weapons use aboard a ship, and how to board, seize, and search other vessels. We would win that deal, ultimately worth more than $40 million, and by 2008 Blackwater would train roughly seventy thousand sailors at our facility, busing them in from Norfolk daily to train on that ship in a box. We felt like a scrappy little dog that finally caught the school bus he'd been chasing.

After scoring that first major government contract, plus growing business from local police officers and SWAT team members, plus a $400,000 September order from the FBI for BEAR target systems, we felt flush. I could envision my future here—helping train our military and police forces, eventually breaking even, having old friends visit to test their skills at Blackwater. It could be a nice life. A simple one.

We expanded again—up to seven thousand acres, more than twelve square miles. We set aside conservation areas to preserve wetlands and restore wildlife habitat, and reseeded hundreds of acres with native swamp oak and cypress. And we made one other addition to the Moyock facility: a massive black bear that had been shot on the Blackwater grounds. He stood now on his hind legs in the lobby of our main lodge, a 598-pound symbol of Blackwater's tenacity—jaws frozen open, right paw raised high, ready to strike.

Things were equally busy back in Michigan. Earnings at Prince Machine had quadrupled, increasing the company's value, and we sold that division to an Italian competitor, IDRA Presse, in 2000 at the peak of the market. The 225 employees owned 20 percent of the company and they did well with the sale, too—the newly formed IdraPrince became the world's largest supplier of die-casting equipment, carrying on my father's legacy. And now I was freed up to make Blackwater my top business priority.

By then, Joan and I also had a fourth beautiful child at home, Erik Xavier, born in July 1999. We called him "X." Joan was overjoyed; after having beaten cancer into remission a second time, doctors had predicted that the extensive treatments would prevent her from getting pregnant again. We were a proud Roman Catholic family, and proud to prove the doctors wrong about having another child. That faith—one she introduced me to—gave her strength, and she in turn was my greatest source of strength.

I got from Joan a sense of loyalty and trust that I'd never felt before. She never cared about the money I'd inherited, or the money we might make—something, unfortunately, I can't say about an awful lot of people I've met over the years. I learned years later that during one trip home while we were dating, my father slipped a thousand dollars in her pocket as he hugged her good-bye. He hoped she would buy herself something special. Instead, she found it when she got home, then divvied it up among her siblings.

There's no doubt that Blackwater never would have existed without her support and encouragement. In 2000, Joan agreed that we should move back to Virginia, near friends and closer to Moyock. A Navy wife, she loved the SEALs and shared our passion for what we were creating there. She could charm anyone she met at my various Beltway functions—she always said the key to the endless small talk was just knowing when to say, "That is so interesting!"

We chose McLean, Virginia. I knew I could rent an office there for Prince Group, the parent company I'd created to oversee Blackwater and various smaller business ventures. Joan was excited about living fifteen minutes from the Catholic Diocese of Arlington. I looked forward to spending more time at home with my family. Besides, Joan said, there were excellent medical facilities in the region in case we needed them.

That observation proved to be awful foreshadowing. As Joan packed boxes for that move, she felt a nagging twinge in her lower back, as if she'd pulled a muscle. X-rays, an MRI, and a bone scan confirmed her cancer had metastasized, and had spread throughout her spine and pelvis. There was nothing upbeat about the doctors' demeanors this time. It was January 2001, and my wife was thirty-three. They gave Joan two and a half years to live.

CHAPTER 4

THE RISE OF BLACKWATER

2001-2002

TUESDAY, SEPTEMBER 11, 2001, WAS A BEAUTIFUL LATE SUMMER DAY IN northern Virginia. A little after eight a.m. I dropped the kids off at school. I cranked up the radio in the car and headed off to a haircut; Joan was resting at home, steeling herself for another awful chemo treatment scheduled the next morning at St. Vincent's Hospital in lower Manhattan. Needless to say, that appointment was canceled.

In the car, I heard that American Airlines Flight 11 had just struck the World Trade Center. My barber, Ali, and I watched United Flight 175 slam into the South Tower as I sat in his chair. Then came news of American Flight 77 hitting the Pentagon, and United Flight 93 crashing in Shanksville, Pennsylvania.

My company's staff showed up in Moyock as always that Tuesday. Everyone sat transfixed by the TV. Gary Jackson was in Dallas; with commercial flights grounded, he rented a car and began the twenty-eight-hour drive to the facility. We were horrified by the news—but, unfortunately, we weren't shocked. We had seen a

low-cost, low-technology strike slip through our nation's basic security procedures a year earlier in Aden harbor.

Military insiders and intelligence officials had been monitoring,
if some of them discounting, swelling anti-American extremism for
years. It seemed clear to me that these sorts of attacks were bound to
become more common. I remembered seeing that two senior colonels in China's People's Liberation Army had gone so far as to pub-
lish an entire book in 1999 called *Unrestricted Warfare*. The book
advocated "a multitude of means, both military and particularly
non-military, to strike at the United States during times of conflict,"
according to the CIA's Foreign Broadcast Information Service,
which translated the text. "Hacking into websites, targeting financial institutions, terrorism, using the media, and conducting urban
warfare are among the methods proposed." Watching the Twin
Towers collapse on TV, I could see the American public had suddenly
come face-to-face with unrestricted warfare at home. The question
was what our politicians would do about it.

At the time, those of us on the Blackwater staff didn't care much
for policy debates. We were soldiers and sailors and cops and Marines. We thought pragmatically, with an eye toward the future.
Soon after 9/11, while some talking heads debated whether we should
strike back at all against those who murdered American civilians,
conversation in Moyock centered on what the inevitable strike
would look like—and what role Blackwater could play. Certainly, we
could train the special operations guys who would hunt down the
al-Qaeda leadership, but we wanted to do more and needed to find
someone who would let us help.

As focused as I'd been on building the company and tending to my
family, I hadn't worried about keeping up with my few political contacts in Washington. I hadn't set foot in the White House complex
since leaving as an intern years before—and President George W.
Bush's national security team was dominated at that point by career
professionals and President Bill Clinton's political holdovers. The
closest I ever got to any of them was when Joan and I bought tickets

to the president's inaugural ball eight months earlier—which is to say, we had no relationship at all.

I rifled through my desk in Moyock for the one business card I had for somebody at the CIA. His name was "Buzzy"—Alvin Bernard "Buzzy" Krongard, the agency's executive director, whom I'd known since Krongard's son, a Navy SEAL, had trained at Blackwater.

Krongard agreed to meet right away. Why the urgency? Besides wanting to provide training, we knew we had intelligence that could help in the fight. We brought contact information for a warlord.

Amid Afghanistan's ever shifting historical political winds, Abdul Rashid Dostum transformed himself more often, and more successfully, than most anybody else. In the era of Soviet control, the ethnic Uzbek worked for a time as a communist union boss at a gas field, then joined the Afghan military in 1978 to battle the insurgent mujahideen, who sought to oust the Russians. In just a few short years, Dostum rose to the rank of army general, commanding a twenty-thousand-strong militia in the northern provinces of Afghanistan. By 1997, thanks in large part to his willingness to switch sides whenever it became politically expedient (including aligning himself with the new mujahideen government when it successfully took control in 1992, before defecting again to ultimately join the Northern Alliance), the forty-three-year-old Dostum lorded it over a sort of multiethnic six-province miniature state in Afghanistan's northern steppe. Its main city was Mazar-i-Sharif, a thriving home to two million—including the cantankerous leader who reportedly once put a thief to death by running over him with a tank. Dostum was not what anyone in the U.S. intelligence community considered predictable.

In 1998, Dostum was ousted by the ultraconservative Taliban, which, since taking over Afghanistan's capital of Kabul in 1996, had been dismembering the Northern Alliance to expand its power base. Dostum was forced into exile in Turkey, but by early 2001 had reunited with loyal followers in the inaccessible Hindu Kush mountains of eastern Afghanistan. The return was possible thanks to an alliance forged with legendary mujahideen commander Ahmad Shah Massoud—a man Dostum had once fought against, but who was also the final Northern Alliance leader left to stave off the Taliban. Massoud, known as the "Lion of Panjshir" in homage to his hometown, had played a leading role in driving the Soviets from Afghanistan in 1989, had served for a time as the country's minister of defense, and had been receiving aid for his military efforts, on and off, from the CIA since 1984.

On September 9, 2001, in a preemptive strike by al-Qaeda and the Taliban to destabilize the alliance and remove a key CIA asset before 9/11, Massoud was killed by a pair of Arab suicide bombers posing as journalists. Dostum was suddenly thrust to the head of the Northern Alliance. He needed the sort of friends Massoud had.

Through my prior congressional contacts, we at Blackwater had gotten word that Dostum didn't have much more faith in the Americans than they had in him. There was only one U.S. contact the general trusted, we were told: Charlie Santos, an American representative for Saudi Arabia–based Delta Oil, who had previously worked with United Nations mediators in Afghanistan. In the late nineties, Delta had sent Santos to negotiate the building of an oil pipeline across the country, which would have handed the Taliban a massive free revenue stream. When those talks broke down, the Taliban effectively declared Santos persona non grata—which was all the recommendation Dostum needed to trust the guy.

It also happened to be the case that Paul Behrends had worked with Santos on Delta's pipeline project, and the two were in regular contact. I was still in regular contact with Paul—and that made Charlie our friend.

A few days after 9/11, I got a call from Behrends. He had news: "Dostum's been calling Charlie, saying, 'What do you want me to do? Nobody's calling me. I want to help,'" Behrends reported. Apparently Santos and Dostum had been chatting daily.

In the days following the attack, the CIA was scraping for information from contacts in Islamabad, Pakistan, and wondering how much they could trust the intelligence sent by Pakistan's notoriously untrustworthy Inter-Services Intelligence agency. They had no relationship with the general; a few years prior, the CIA under director John Deutch had purged its rolls of "dirty" assets—those with shady backgrounds, or worse. From May 1995 to December 1996, the agency cast aside roughly a thousand paid informants under those so-called "Deutch Rules"—especially in places like Afghanistan, where political alignments seemed to change by the hour. The policy protected the CIA from a PR standpoint, but it also kept them from working with men like Dostum, a leader and a fighter who at the very least bought into the idea that the enemy of his enemy was his friend. He was certainly no Boy Scout—but Boy Scouts don't command rebel armies. And after 9/11, his influence and authority made him just the sort of contact the agency needed.

As plans were drawn up for America's military response to the attacks, a number of higher-ups at the CIA had been urging something less conventional. They knew the Pentagon's U.S. Central Command, or CENTCOM, was considering a raft of options for destroying al-Qaeda and removing the Taliban from power in Afghanistan—including grotesquely conventional approaches that would have led with Special Forces personnel, then seen thousands of soldiers and Marines battling the remaining Taliban fighters. But the CIA and DoD are often at loggerheads, and those in Langley understood that President George W. Bush had publicly insisted the military campaign was not an assault upon Islam or the Afghan people. To that end, military strategists needed to remember two things: First, a large coalition ground force might inflame the Afghan population; and second, time was of the essence. The faster the coalition could accomplish its mission and hand political power back to the anti-Taliban Afghans, the better off we'd all be.

These factors swayed CIA planners toward a new form of warfare—and a sudden reliance on the fifteen-thousand-strong

Northern Alliance. The hope in Langley was that small teams of CIA operatives and Army Special Forces personnel could spread out across Afghanistan with Northern Alliance commanders, liberating villages and calling in air strikes on Taliban strongholds. That would minimize the American contingent of ground forces for the campaigns, planners understood, and put a local face on the mission as well. But that meant coordination with contacts the CIA didn't have.

Working through the contacts Behrends and Santos helped us establish, Blackwater provided the agency with a list of in-country assets. Beyond Dostum, we delivered Haji Mohammed Mohaqiq, who commanded anti-Taliban forces in central Afghanistan, and Ishmael Khan, a former officer in the Afghan National Army, who was jailed by the Taliban in 1997 but escaped three years later hungry for payback. That list also included Payenda Mohammad Khan, a former commander under Dostum, who served as an interlocutor, translator, and idea man. These were men with nasty reputations but an appreciation for getting things done. None of Afghanistan's officials were clean. Even Massoud had financed his rebel alliance partly by smuggling opium and heroin into Europe. Handcuffed by politics, the CIA had not been able to cultivate relationships with the key but messy leaders. Fortunately, though, Blackwater had no such political restrictions. We were careful to maintain the highest ethics while dealing with these contacts, and we were able to set the CIA up with some of the most useful men in the region.

With that assistance, the CIA's seven-man Northern Afghanistan Liaison Team, code-named "Jawbreaker," arrived in the Panjshir valley, about sixty miles north of Kabul, just fifteen days after 9/11. They began coordination on the ground for the Green Berets to come, and the team's mission was unmistakable. Before leaving, CIA counterterrorism chief Cofer Black gave the team leader a mandate straight from a Hollywood script. "I don't want bin Laden and his thugs captured, I want them dead," Black said. "I want bin

Laden's head shipped back in a box filled with dry ice. I want to be able to show bin Laden's head to the president."

Then on October 7, 2001, Operation Enduring Freedom began with a volley of fifty Tomahawk cruise missiles fired from land-based bombers, two dozen strike aircraft, and U.S. and British ships and submarines. They destroyed much of Afghanistan's spartan air defenses in advance of the American bombers to come.

The Army's first twelve-man Special Forces Operational Detachment Alpha (ODA)—literally, an A-team—reached the Panjshir valley and the Jawbreaker contingent on October 17, 2001. As one prong of Task Force Dagger, which aimed to gain control of Afghanistan's northern cities, those Green Berets would focus on Kabul. Two days later, a second A-team, ODA 595, was choppered in the dead of night to a landing zone roughly seventy miles south of Mazar-i-Sharif, where they linked up with General Dostum and his fifty men on horseback. From CENTCOM headquarters in Tampa, Florida, Santos coordinated with Dostum via satellite phone, telling him when his men should light the landing zone.

What came next was "the Flintstones meets the Jetsons," according to the men of ODA 595, and one of the most remarkable military campaigns in American history. For weeks, the Green Berets suffered on horseback, Dostum leading them north in wooden saddles, across parched plains and along two-foot-wide cliffside trails. It had been the better part of a century since the cavalry galloped into battle, and in 2001 the Army didn't exactly train Green Berets in horsemanship. But with their artillery a phone call away, and Dostum's cunning, the Special Forces and Northern Alliance liberated dozens of towns. They called in such ferocious air strikes on enemy encampments that the laser target designators ODA 595 used to guide the bombs became known to Afghans as "death rays."

In the early morning darkness of November 9, 2001, Dostum's cavalry, six hundred strong, flowed from the mountains down into Mazar-i-Sharif and soon reclaimed the city. Four days later, Task

Force Dagger retook control of Kabul. Nearly two-thirds of the country changed hands in a few weeks, and the Taliban regime was completely toppled in Afghanistan a grand total of 102 days after 9/11—led by only a relative handful of U.S. personnel. "I asked for a few Americans," Dostum would later say of the Special Forces. "They brought with them the courage of a whole army." And the international connections provided by an ever expanding training center in the North Carolina swamp.

Blackwater's contribution to Operation Enduring Freedom wasn't ever conceived as a business decision. We certainly received no money for it. The team in Moyock wanted to help the United States strike back at the men who'd attacked it, and opening our Rolodex and acting as facilitators was one way we could do so. I had another idea as well: I applied to work in the Special Activities Division of the CIA's National Clandestine Service, the agency's most elite and secretive paramilitary wing. I went through the extensive vetting process, including a polygraph, standard tests of my loyalty, and a battery of psychological exams. To this day I chuckle about one of the ultimate ironies in my career: The CIA shot me down. They said I didn't have enough field experience. Nonetheless, more people at Langley were learning my name—and seeing how a private business like Blackwater could serve as a vital asset for the government's military and intelligence services. They knew we wanted to help.

Soon the agency offered us a way to do that: by standing guard. With the Taliban leveled, CIA bases sprang up in Kabul and elsewhere across the country. When Krongard visited the Afghan capital shortly after it changed hands, he found the locals ill-equipped to handle the crucial security details there—particularly when some of their allegiances remained uncertain. He knew the agency didn't directly have the manpower to staff those roles. He also knew just the man to call.

In fact, Krongard's trip overseas dovetailed perfectly with

conversations already happening in Moyock. Guarding officials or military installations had initially felt pretty far afield for our shop, but thanks to the client list from Blackwater's training programs, we knew we had a network of retired special forces personnel who might be interested. In the 1990s, many special ops missions had revolved around security for high-value individuals. Elite personnel from those missions already understood threat assessments, radio protocols, and convoy procedures, and we realized they could slip into similar Blackwater roles with a minimal learning curve. As we watched Operation Enduring Freedom unfold, the idea of joining in suddenly made sense.

We incorporated the offshoot Blackwater Security Consulting early in 2002. In April of that year, Blackwater received the CIA's urgent and compelling contract to provide security guards—and to have them on a plane in a matter of days—for the agency's headquarters in Kabul. The first six months of work there was a sole-source deal, and beyond that my company competed and won the contract to keep going.

Critics contend that Blackwater must have landed that first international deal by greasing wheels someplace. Over the years, all of us associated with the company have heard that claim often. The reality is that during the life of the company, 95 percent of our contracts were won through open and competitive bidding. And to the CIA in 2002, it was clear that our performance record and our "Say yes first, iron out the details later" mind-set justified the deal. "Blackwater got a contract because they were the first people that could get people on the ground. We were under the gun, we did whatever it took when I came back from Kabul," Krongard said in 2006. "The only concern we had was getting the best security for our people. If we thought Martians could provide it, I guess we would have gone after them."

I was part of the first rotation of our guards. It wasn't exciting work—and we certainly weren't frontline vigilantes kicking down doors and shooting our way through Taliban strongholds, or whatever the public perception of Blackwater's men seemed to become. Security meant being the defense—standing outside the front gate to investigate the vehicles that drove up, and ensuring there were none of the rebel attacks that would plague other diplomatic missions in the future. We brought a steely focus to our jobs—I was there to personally guarantee Blackwater's men checked cars and stood guard better, and more cost-effectively, than anybody else—and quickly learned the rhythms of our new location. One of my most enduring memories from that inaugural trip to Afghanistan was lurching bolt upright in bed at four thirty a.m. my first night there. I'd never before heard a call to prayer—and the massive loudspeakers right outside the hooch ensured that no one anywhere nearby would miss it.

Blackwater's dedication to efficiency formed the cornerstone of our entire corporate culture. It was perhaps the ultimate benefit of our streamlined hierarchy: The company had one owner—me—so no stockholders to answer to. There was no board of directors to argue with, and no interminable bureaucracy of a government organization. I could delegate much of my authority, or choose to stand a post overseas. We were nimble and aggressive. And as I learned a few short months later, that approach to our work made quite an impression.

CHAPTER 5
INHERENTLY TRADITIONAL

CRISTOFORO COLOMBO IS MY FAVORITE GOVERNMENT CONTRACTOR.

Sure, most people remember Christopher Columbus as the mariner from the Republic of Genoa, the man who received backing from Spain's Queen Isabella and King Ferdinand to launch the voyage that discovered the New World. But I love that Columbus was far more entrepreneur than seafarer, crazy enough to brave the open ocean in tiny trade ships—especially when his speculation on the distance to reach the East was off by a factor of three. He was a doer, trying to persuade royalty to back his vision even after being rebuffed multiple times. Finally, at the start of 1492, his timing was right: The Castilian crown had wrestled control of Granada away from the Moorish forces, and a more efficient Western route to the East Indies would again expand Spain's global footprint in the name of Christendom. With the Capitulations of Santa Fe, Columbus was promised wealth and prestige if he could discover those shipping lanes. With the stroke of Isabella's pen, Columbus effectively became a private military contractor, or PMC.

The mariner's demands were grand, but given the huge stakes—Columbus's son later admitted those monarchs never actually believed he would make it back alive—they were not unreasonable. The forty-year-old wanted the military rank of admiral, a hereditary post to be handed to his son and descendants, not unusual for the time in Europe. In addition, he sought to govern any lands he would discover or acquire on behalf of his royal clients. Columbus demanded one-tenth of the net wealth from those lands as payment. He also wanted options on future business ventures in the lands he would claim as payment for his enterprise and his risk.

Shortly thereafter, Isabella and Ferdinand appointed their new PMC to the royal offices he sought. The Italian explorer was now a Spanish admiral. The *Niña*, *Pinta*, and *Santa María* arrived in the New World on October 12, 1492, as armed, privately owned merchant vessels requisitioned by the Crown. And for more than five centuries to follow, the fate of our nation would be inextricably tied to military contractors.

Today in Washington D.C.—a district named after Columbus—there is a seven-acre public park just north of the White House called Lafayette Square. It's a lovely place full of regional trees and open spaces, and wide brick paths that lead to a central statue of Andrew Jackson on horseback. I often visit the park when I'm in the city—at its four corners are additional statues, honoring General Thaddeus Kosciuszko, Major General Baron Friedrich Wilhelm von Steuben, General Marquis Gilbert de Lafayette, and Major General Comte Jean de Rochambeau. None of them are Americans, yet they were all instrumental in the United States winning its independence. They're instrumental in how I look back on what we built at Blackwater.

It might seem incongruous that America owes its greatest military triumph largely to the help of contractors—foreign ones at that—but only to those people who don't know the history of the business model. In 1607, for instance, Captain John Smith, whose relationship with Pocahontas would become the stuff of legend (and Disney films), arrived in Virginia clapped in shackles and leg irons. The twenty-seven-year-old English soldier and war hero was sent to the New World by the joint-stock business Virginia Company of London and was tasked with overseeing security operations in the dangerous North American wilds. The company intended to mine for gold in what is today the Chesapeake Bay area and explore the countryside for other lucrative natural resources in hopes of establishing a more permanent English settlement there. They needed a military contractor to safeguard their business interests.

Historical accounts suggest Smith was as aggressive as a wolverine, and only half as likable—it seems he arrived in leg irons because he so irritated expedition leaders during the voyage, they charged him with mutiny. But he quickly proved himself indispensable in the New World. He explored the bay area, creating detailed maps that stood as the definitive charts of the region for nearly a century. Smith helped establish the colony's settlement, Jamestown, which he named after England's King James I, and supervised construction of the colony's fort. His organization of a security force, which he trained with English weapons, ultimately led to his becoming president of Jamestown. The pale-faced PMC with the fiery red beard also reached out to the area's indigenous populations—with varying degrees of Disneyfied success—and, more than anyone else, shepherded the English colony through potentially crushing setbacks during his two years in the region. His tenacity was an inspiration to me as I built Blackwater and we began to grow our own security operations.

In 1614, Smith mapped the northern American coastline, naming it "New England," which enabled another English firm, and another PMC, to shape our nation's history. In 1620, the Council for New England, previously known as the joint-stock Plymouth Company, was granted a royal charter by King James to explore the new region Smith had mapped. They just needed colonists. Puritans and Separatists, meanwhile, needed a new homeland away from religious persecution in England. So the company leased a veteran freighter built for the wine trade, called the *Mayflower*, and sent the pilgrims on their way. One key passenger on that fateful voyage? Thirty-five-year-old Captain Myles Standish, who may have sympathized with the Separatists but who had no religious reason for joining their expedition. Standish was, in fact, an English soldier who had fought in the Netherlands before joining the private sector. He was a military contractor hired by the pilgrims to lead the defense of the colony to come.

Prior to landing, Standish was one of the forty-one signers of the Mayflower Compact. And ultimately, the fortifications and training he oversaw in Plymouth Colony proved so successful, he became the first PMC immortalized on an official government emblem. Approved by Governor John Hancock in 1780, the Great Seal of the Commonwealth of Massachusetts features the state's coat of arms, first sketched out five years prior. That coat of arms shows an Algonquian Native American holding a bow and arrow; above the shield is a uniformed right arm brandishing a golden sword. That arm and sword are believed to represent Standish, whom the National Guard proudly remembers as "a professional soldier hired to train the colonists to defend themselves in the New World. He instructed them on the proper handling of muskets and other arms, helping to make them a more effective defensive force."

By the time our fledgling nation revolted against the British Crown, the use of private citizens to carry out what are today thought of as traditionally government military functions was practically habit. On the brink of war in 1775, one prominent Southern plantation owner volunteered to personally fund a military force to battle the British if the Continental Congress failed to create a standing army. The forty-two-year-old, who'd been an officer in the Virginia militia, trusted the private sector's ability to provide solutions when the government could—or would—not. Luckily for the fate of the nation, the Continental Congress consolidated the colonial militias into a national army, and George Washington didn't actually have to fund the force himself.

But that ragtag Continental Army did face huge gaps in capability, training, experience, and organization—which is where those statues in Lafayette Park come in. The Continental Congress had to fill the gaps by turning to foreign professionals to staff, train, and even command Washington's soldiers. It was a blueprint for outsourcing that I admire to this day. In Paris, Benjamin Franklin, the U.S. envoy to France, personally recruited Tadeusz—or Thaddeus—Kosciuszko, a skilled Polish freedom fighter with an expertise in artillery and engineering. The fortifications he built at Philadelphia, Saratoga, and West Point were so successful, Kosciuszko is today considered the father of American artillery.

Prussian officer Baron Friedrich Wilhelm von Steuben was similarly recruited to help oversee the training and staffing of the Continental Army, and effectively became the first inspector general of the U.S. military. Meanwhile, the French aristocrat the Marquis de Lafayette was only nineteen when he first met Washington in the colonial capital of Philadelphia in 1777, but he impressed the general enough to quickly become one of his closest aides. That "pushy French teenager," as the Smithsonian Institution would later describe him, rose to the rank of major general in the Army, and today there are some two dozen towns or cities in the United States named Fayetteville, Lafayette, or some variation of La Grange, in honor of Lafayette's estate in France.

Finally, in 1780 Comte Jean de Rochambeau was sent by French king Louis XVI to command the fifty-five hundred or so French troops who fought alongside the colonialists and ultimately overpowered the British at the Siege of Yorktown, in Virginia. Because the upstart Americans had French support, Rochambeau's assistance helped lay the groundwork for modern military aid. As Washington wrote to Congress just days before British lieutenant general Lord Cornwallis surrendered there and effectively ended the war, "I cannot but acknowledge the infinite obligations I am under to His Excellency, the Count de Rochambeau."

While all of that happened on land, privately owned warships played an equally key role in safeguarding our harbors. So powerful was the Royal Navy in the 1770s, with some 150 ships, that any challenge seemed futile. The Continental Navy, such as there was one, consisted of sixty-four ships. Without disrupting British supply lanes or port blockades, however, the American cause was doomed. So in late 1775 John Adams, then a Massachusetts delegate for the First and Second Continental Congresses, proposed a turnkey solution: private warships that could wage naval insurgency on the high seas. Privateering—essentially government-sanctioned piracy—wasn't an original idea, but when the Massachusetts legislature passed "An Act for encouraging the fixing out of Armed Vessels to defend the Sea-Coast of America" in November of that year, New England's merchants and fishermen were given the green light to convert their fishing vessels into nimble little warships. Suddenly the twelve hundred guns of America's tiny Continental Navy were backed by nearly fifteen thousand guns from seventeen hundred privateer vessels.

Soon after, the Second Continental Congress, under its president, John Hancock, authorized privateer and Navy attacks on "all vessels" flying the British flag. The Navy pledged to split the plundered bounty with the privateers, keeping its part to fund the war effort. Congress printed blank commissions for "private ships of war" and authorized "letters of marque and reprisal" for the entrepreneur-soldiers, giving privateers the legal authority to attack. The men in our nation's history who drafted the very bedrock declarations and articles upon which this nation was built clearly grasped the value of private companies in larger governmental operations. That Congress issued legislative guidelines on how private warships could carry out their work, marking some of this nation's first government regulations for private business.

Encouraging entrepreneurs to build and run their own warships had a profound effect: By the end of the war, privateers had captured

2,283 British ships, compared to fewer than two hundred by the standing Continental Navy.

Over the ensuing 240 years, the use of private military contractors in American conflicts has only increased. Privateers again took to the high seas to help defeat the British during the War of 1812.

Then, a half century later, Abraham Lincoln relied upon the Pinkerton National Detective Agency—the original "private eye" sleuthing firm, founded by Allan Pinkerton in 1850—to build his domestic intelligence network. In 1861, Pinkerton uncovered an assassination plot against President-elect Lincoln, and Union general George McClellan soon hired the Scottish immigrant to create a "secret service" to gather military information in the South during the Civil War. The CIA credits him with "developing a different view of espionage, pursuing what today would be called actionable intelligence."

A year before the United States entered World War I, American aviators determined to battle Kaiser Wilhelm II volunteered for the French Air Service. The colloquially known "Escadrille Américaine" was created in 1916; soon after, the squadron of thirty-eight pilots was officially renamed in honor of the Marquis de Lafayette, becoming the Lafayette Escadrille. Two years later, with the United States involved in the war, they were merged into the 103rd Pursuit Squadron of the U.S. Army Air Service.

Perhaps the most famous contract aviators arose from World War II, however. I remember sitting in bed at night as a boy in Michigan, reading about the American Volunteer Group, better known as the Flying Tigers. I read about how in early 1941, months before the attack on Pearl Harbor, the Japanese had invaded the Republic of China. To support Nationalist Party leader Chiang Kai-shek, President Franklin D. Roosevelt sent retired U.S. Army Air Corps captain Claire Lee Chennault to create an air force in China that would help repel the imperial forces—but not directly involve the U.S. military. The three squadrons commanded by Chennault—consisting of about twenty aircraft each and flown by pilots recruited from the Army, Navy, and Marines—are officially credited with destroying 297 Japanese aircraft. The Flying Tigers were heroes to me when I was younger—they seemed larger than life. I couldn't believe how cool those Curtiss P40s looked with the shark faces painted on them. Even thirty years after those men had completed their missions, they were the ones who first made me dream of becoming a pilot someday.

After World War II, the government began leaning more and more heavily on PMCs. That intermarriage was a trend noted by no less than President Dwight D. Eisenhower, who'd previously been supreme commander of the Allied forces in Europe during World War II. Twenty years after receiving that command, the then president gave his farewell address from the White House in 1961. In it, he warned: "In the councils of government, we must guard against the acquisition of unwarranted influence, whether sought or unsought, by the military-industrial complex. The potential for the disastrous rise of misplaced power exists, and will persist."

Yet reliance on contractors continued unabated. During the politically explosive Vietnam War, the Pentagon paid private firms to build and operate bases, as well as supply water and ground transport from the beginning of the American involvement in 1954. "The airfields, roads, and bridges [built in Vietnam] that now bear military traffic can serve as lifelines for the distribution of goods and services throughout the nation," Ellsworth Bunker, the American ambassador to South Vietnam, said in 1972. "At a time when all too many forces are bent on destruction, RMK-BRJ's ten years of accomplishment have been in my opinion one of the finest episodes in our nation's history."

PMCs were again used in the first Gulf War, in early 1991, which I saw from inside the bubble in Washington, as the conflict coincided with my brief internship in the George H. W. Bush White House. And following the war, the Pentagon turned to contractors to bolster UN peacekeeping missions throughout the rest of the decade.

I'm proud that when our first Blackwater team stepped foot in Afghanistan in 2002, we became part of a deeply rooted American tradition: private business supplying logistical, intelligence, and military support services that the government can't provide on its own. (To be clear, it's hardly a tradition unique to the United States. Globally, PMCs operate in more than fifty countries as part of a $100 billion annual industry.) Perhaps the Army said it best. In describing its nearly thirty-year-old LOGCAP—or Logistics Civil Augmentation Program—contract, the service's official logistical bulletin wrote, "LOGCAP provides contingency support to augment the Army force structure. With large global commitments, the Army must use contractors to provide logistics support in theaters of operations so that military units can be released for other missions. In essence, contractors provide the Army with additional means to adequately support its forces. This is not a new concept for the Army, which has used contractors to provide supplies and services since the Revolutionary War."

One big shift, however, came in the 1990s. During the first Gulf War, PMCs made up about 2 percent of U.S. manpower. But their usage grew exponentially throughout the decade—not only because of contractors' demonstrated versatility, but also because they allowed Pentagon planners to fudge the numbers. During the NATO-led peacekeeping mission in Bosnia in 1995, for instance, Congress imposed a twenty-thousand-strong cap on American troop involvement. But the DoD wanted a larger presence, so it quietly augmented that number with two thousand contractors who did not constitute "troops" and who could fulfill various logistical duties behind the scenes. The end run worked so well that in the coming years DoD contracts with PMCs grew from $85.1 billion in 1996 to more than $150 billion in 2006.

That, of course, included Iraq and Afghanistan. Those conflicts have been described as the first contractor wars, and rightly so: PMCs—more than two hundred thousand of them—ultimately made up 54 percent of the Defense Department's workforce in those countries (and that figure doesn't include approximately three thousand contractors, including Blackwater's men, working directly for the State Department). The vast majority of the DoD's PMCs provided transportation and engineering services, or worked laundry details, or staffed dining halls at forward operating bases—the necessary support functions that enable the military to project combat power. The "tail-to-tooth ratio," as some analysts describe it. And those PMCs quickly became such indispensable parts of the U.S. war machine that the Pentagon's 2006 Quadrennial Defense Review included contractors—along with active-duty military, reserves, and civilian employees—as one of the four key components of the DoD's "Total Force."

Those sorts of statistics underscore an uncomfortable reality for some analysts: Waging war requires sheer numbers of personnel this country's military no longer possesses. During the first Gulf War, the Army had 780,000 troops; a decade later that number had fallen 40 percent, to about 480,000. Not since the last men were conscripted in December 1972 has the United States faced a draft—yet without one, the manpower necessary for the United States to effectively wage war simply doesn't exist today.

At the height of the Iraq conflict, in 2007, even with contractors providing more than half the workforce, the Army could still meet recruiting benchmarks only by lowering standards, raising the maximum enlistment age, accepting more troops with "moral waivers," and offering $20,000 bonuses for recruits who agreed to report to basic training in thirty days or less. (Only 71 percent of Army recruits that year had graduated high school, the lowest rate in twenty-five years.) "We cannot operate without private security firms in Iraq," Patrick F. Kennedy, the undersecretary of state for management, said in 2008. "If the contractors were removed, we would have to leave Iraq." Former Marine colonel Jack Holly put it slightly differently: "We're never going to war without the private security industry again in a nondraft environment."

The reliance on contractors crosses administrations and political affiliations. The 1995 Bosnia peacekeeping contracting came during the Clinton administration, the ramp-up in Iraq and Afghanistan under President Bush. And today under President Obama, left-wing critics seem somehow surprised that little has changed. In fact, in Obama's first year in office, the DoD increased the use of PMCs in Afghanistan by 29 percent and in Iraq by 23 percent. The 2010 Quadrennial Defense Review, released well after the term "private military companies" had become venomous in public debate, describes ongoing efforts by the DoD to "reduce the number of support service contractors, thereby helping to establish a balanced workforce that appropriately aligns functions to the public and private sector."

Yet it also clearly states: "The [Defense] Department is facing mission requirements of increasing scope, variety, and complexity. To ensure the availability of needed talent to meet future demands, we are conducting a deliberate assessment of current and future workforce requirements. This effort will ensure that the Department has the right workforce size and mix (military/civilian/contractor) with the right competencies.... The services provided by contractors will continue to be valued as part of a balanced approach."

And that's the crux of the issue here. PMCs that provide laundry service or drive trucks or empty toilets—the crucial "life support" tasks that support our troops—are as old as America itself. But of the thousands of contractors who worked in Iraq and Afghanistan, a small fraction—only about 10 percent—were employed in a relatively new subset of the industry. It's the one the State Department needed then, and still needs at locations around the world now: security. The active protection of a *noun*—a person, facility, or property—"for which," the National Defense Authorization Act reads, "contractors are required to be armed."

For many critics, that final clause makes all the difference: Blackwater's men carried guns. And the subjective moralizing is fascinating.

At home, armed private security guards help protect airports and banks and office buildings. They staff checkpoints at military bases across the country and they're stationed at government offices in Washington D.C. Meanwhile, the private sector supplies the U.S. military with bullets and bulletproof vests, rifles and communications gear, tanks and ships and jets. The general public—much less Congress—never really questions whether or not those duties should be outsourced. Yet Blackwater became famous—some might say infamous—for combining the two. We were a private company providing armed guards to a war zone. For that, critics branded us "war profiteers." No one ever says that about the contractors delivering the mail to the soldiers every day.

I understand security work can be dramatic. Blackwater's men— elite special forces personnel, far better trained than the average enlisted man on the ground—protected the most important figures in the region and performed what might have been the most dangerous work there. By 2009, more contractors were dying in Iraq than military personnel; that same bloody rubric flipped in Afghanistan in 2011. "Privatizing the ultimate sacrifice," as one George Washington University law scholar described it. Unlike the guy cleaning the mess hall, doing security work well meant that it was possible someone would have to die.

I realize, too, that my conservative politics made us a target for critics on the left who saw our work as a threatening usurpation of what they considered "inherently governmental functions."

Still, I never understood the singular spotlight that seemed to be trained on my company. We were not the largest military contractor in Iraq or Afghanistan, nor were we making the most money. Odds are, though, the average citizen can't name even a handful of the other providers. It seems nearly impossible to talk about military contractors today without reflexively mentioning Blackwater—and in the past few years, there's been a lot of talk. The brand still comes up in one-sided magazine articles and newspaper editorials—and, unfortunately, in hearings by various committees on Capitol Hill.

But those mentions just underscore what those editorial writers and politicians—in every chamber and across every aisle—would rather the public overlook: Contractors were here long before my company was, and the job will still need to be done long after I'm gone. Debates about pay rates or operational tactics or contractor immunity—all of which I'll clarify in the coming pages—simply obscure this momentous realization: "The United States no longer can project power of any significance over any protracted period of time without reliance on the private sector," read a 2010 assessment by the Lexington Institute, a public policy research center named for the spot where more than two centuries ago Americans defied the military might of the most powerful empire on earth. "Civilians are now the equivalent of a new service."

As part of this service, it seemed only fitting that our next key step forward came from protecting the most important civilian in Iraq.

CHAPTER 6

BREMER AND THE BUSINESS MODEL

2003

I FIRST MET L. PAUL BREMER III WHEN WE MEASURED HIM FOR BODY ARMOR.

That was early in May 2003, nearly two months after President George W. Bush had stood behind a blue podium in Cross Hall at the White House and looked directly into a TV camera. "For more than a decade, the United States and other nations have pursued patient and honorable efforts to disarm the Iraqi regime without war," President Bush said. "Peaceful efforts to disarm the Iraqi regime have failed again and again because we are not dealing with peaceful men." He issued this ultimatum: "All the decades of deceit and cruelty have now reached an end. Saddam Hussein and his sons must leave Iraq within forty-eight hours. Their refusal to do so will result in military conflict, commenced at a time of our choosing."

They refused.

Two days later, March 20 dawned in Baghdad with air raid sirens. Blackwater executives all watched the footage on TV as U.S. warships in the Red Sea pummeled targets across Iraq with Tomahawk cruise missiles. Operation Iraqi Freedom had begun; by April 9, U.S.

troops would secure Saddam's presidential palace in the capital city and, surrounded by celebrating Iraqis, Marines would topple the despot's statue in central Firdos Square. Less than a week later, as Iraqi troops laid down their weapons before advancing coalition forces, the United States captured Tikrit, the final major bastion of the Hussein regime. On May 1, 2003, Bush stood on the flight deck of the USS *Abraham Lincoln* and delivered his infamous "Mission Accomplished" speech to the nation. Forty-five days after his initial threat to Saddam, the president declared, "Major combat operations in Iraq have ended. In the battle of Iraq, the United States and our allies have prevailed." It was what came next that was the problem.

As far back as December 2001, the Iraq War plan delivered to President Bush had four basic stages: Phase I, building an international coalition and support for the war; Phase II, gathering intelligence and drawing up decisive battle plans; Phase III, successful combat operations; and Phase IV, rebuilding a shattered nation. Much like the war plans for Operation Enduring Freedom in Afghanistan, Phase IV in Iraq called for minimal continued military presence thanks to the rapid handover of power to a provisional local government. That same December, the Afghan Interim Authority had appointed Hamid Karzai chairman of its temporary administration and cemented plans to soon establish the Afghanistan Transitional Authority. Eschewing long-term U.S. nation building in favor of striking quickly and moving on had seemed to work in that country. It made sense to many DoD planners that it would work in Iraq, too.

Besides, military leaders thought, Phase IV was the job of civilians, particularly the State Department. As CENTCOM's former commander General Tommy Franks wrote in his memoirs, "While we at CENTCOM were executing the war plan, Washington should focus on policy-level issues.... I knew the president and Don Rumsfeld would back me up, so I felt free to pass the message along to the bureaucracy beneath them: *You pay attention to the day* after *and I'll pay attention to the day* of." (Emphasis in Franks's original.) The general retired just weeks after the president's speech announcing his mission was accomplished, saying that it was now the responsibility of civil organizations to ensure safety and stability. "As I had said throughout our planning sessions, civic action and security were linked—*inextricably* linked," Franks wrote. "There was a commonly held belief that civil action would not be possible in Iraq without security. I would continue to argue that there could be no security without civic action."

From the start of the war planning, however, those civilians had warned that the transition in Iraq might not be so easy. State Department officials believed that the country's exiled leaders wouldn't be hailed as returning heroes, the way Karzai had been in Afghanistan. Further, as outlined in a December 2002 memo titled "A Perfect Storm" by Deputy Assistant Secretary of State for Near Eastern Affairs Ryan Crocker and Special Assistant to the Secretary of State William Burns, the fall of Hussein's Ba'ath regime had the potential to unleash violent competition among Iraq's ethnic and sectarian groups. Neighboring nations such as Iran, Syria, and Saudi Arabia might try to exert their influence. In part because of that memo, it is believed, the State Department's head civilian, Secretary of State Colin Powell, issued his well-known warning to President Bush: "When you hit this thing, it's like a crystal glass. It's going to shatter," Powell told the president. "There will be no government. There will be civil disorder. You'll have twenty-five million Iraqis standing around looking at each other."

The predictions proved frighteningly accurate. Looting and killing in Baghdad began almost the moment Hussein's statue was toppled. According to a 2009 report by the Special Inspector General for Iraq Reconstruction, the military's rush through the country—and toward central Iraq, where it was believed Hussein was hiding weapons of mass destruction—meant that only about twenty-five thousand soldiers remained to occupy Baghdad, with its population of six million. In comparison, a city that size would easily be the second largest in the United States; with so few American troops scattered across it, organized crime in the war-torn capital was unstoppable.

Soon, violence spread across the country. Millions in cash was stolen or destroyed at the Rasheed and Rafidain bank branches and at the Central Bank of Iraq. "In a military compound under nominal guard by U.S. soldiers," according to the inspector general's report, "one of these gangs smashed through a rear wall and used a crane to remove valuable precision milling equipment used to manufacture Scud missiles." In Mosul, the report added, a prison guard sold all the prison beds for scrap metal. In the capital, the Ministry of Health was set on fire multiple times because there was insufficient U.S. force to stop it. Iraqis were not, in fact, greeting U.S. forces as liberators, as Vice President Dick Cheney had predicted. Mere days after the downfall of a tyrant, the vengeful lawlessness of Iraq's citizenry threatened to plunge the country into even greater darkness.

Into that chaos stepped Bremer, a State Department veteran and former chairman of the National Commission on Terrorism. Appointed by Bush to head the Coalition Provisional Authority (CPA) and take charge of the rebuilding, the then sixty-two-year-old Bremer was given a clear and sweeping directive by Secretary of Defense Donald Rumsfeld: "You shall be responsible for the temporary governance of Iraq, and shall oversee, direct and coordinate all executive, legislative, and judicial functions necessary to carry out this responsibility, including humanitarian relief and reconstruction and assisting in the formation of an Iraqi interim authority."

With the stroke of a pen, the career diplomat had been made the most powerful man in Iraq. The invasion was about to become a bloody occupation that would last for nearly a decade, and as the head of the CPA, Bremer would become the insurgents' primary target. For a free Iraq to take shape, someone had to keep him alive. For Blackwater Security Consulting, it was our introduction to Iraq.

The safety of the ambassador in Baghdad was overseen by a small component of the Army known as the Criminal Investigation Command, within which its even smaller Protective Services

Battalion provides security for executive-level Defense Department personnel during wartime. If that sounds niche, that's because it is: The Army's main function is to project force, not protect targets. Protective Services is one of the few divisions in all the military forces trained in this sort of thing—and so there's little manpower to go around. So to bolster Bremer's security detail, the Defense Department added a pair of Blackwater's ex–Navy SEALs to the team. I joined them for their first meeting with Bremer at the Pentagon.

As with every "principal," or the figure being guarded, we discussed his goals and mission and what we would be doing to protect him. I couldn't go with them to Iraq, but I wanted Bremer to know I would still be personally involved—and that I understood the dangers he faced: When the new head of the CPA landed in Baghdad, on May 12, 2003, the city was on fire. The ambassador was taking control of a country in political and economic chaos, as the inspector general's report later described it, "with no government, no electricity, and no functioning security forces." Prior to the invasion, one of Hussein's final acts of power had been to throw open his prisons and release roughly a hundred thousand convicts into the streets—many of them violent criminals. There wasn't enough personnel to protect humanitarian convoys and staging areas, much less government installations—a problem made all the more acute by one of Bremer's first acts in Iraq: He disbanded Iraq's entire military.

The CPA's "Order 2"—a directive second only to removing loyalists of Hussein's Ba'ath Party from positions of authority in Iraqi society—left half a million members of Iraq's army, navy, air force, Republican Guard, Special Republican Guard, and intelligence system out of work. And the CPA wasn't big on severance packages. Major General David Petraeus, who would be named to head Iraq's Multi-National Security Transition Command, would later say the decree fueled the growing insurgency, finally offering disparate rebels something they could unite around: hatred of the CPA. Order 2, Petraeus said, created "tens of thousands, if not hundreds of thousands, of additional enemies of the Coalition."

For three harrowing months, Blackwater's men helped protect the ambassador from ambush attempts on the roads, rocket attacks in the Green Zone, and increasingly hostile Iraqis in general. "When I got here," Bremer would later say, "I slept with earplugs, the noise [from all the gunfights outside] was so loud." He was never harmed. But by August 2003, lousy conditions on the ground were rapidly getting worse.

Early that month, a car bomb had destroyed the Jordanian embassy in Baghdad, killing nineteen. Less than two weeks later, during a single twelve-hour stretch, insurgents blew up the pipeline that supplied much of Baghdad's water, killed or wounded sixty-five Iraqis by firing mortar rounds into Abu Ghraib prison, and set fire to a major pipeline carrying Iraqi oil into Turkey. On August 19, a cement truck carrying a five-hundred-pound bomb from Hussein's prewar arsenal exploded outside the Canal Hotel in Baghdad, home of the United Nations' offices. Among many other casualties, Sergio Vieira de Mello, the UN's top envoy in Iraq, lay trapped amid the rubble for hours before dying of his injuries. Then, at the end of August, a car bomb exploded outside the Imam Ali mosque in Najaf during morning prayers, killing more than eighty—including Ayatollah Mohammed Baqir al-Hakim, leader of the largest Shia movement in postwar Iraq. Those terrorist attacks "clearly suggested a new order of magnitude of violence," Bremer would later say. "I mean, we had certainly been losing soldiers and we'd been having some problems, but nothing on that scale."

In response, the ambassador's security detail was immediately contracted out in full. The Pentagon's protective services had been stretched increasingly thin, and in the three months since major combat operations had ended, DoD planners had seen some hundred fifty members of the U.S. military killed in Iraq, and more than six hundred wounded. They were happy to let someone else take the heat for a while. And this detail was guaranteed to get fiery: "At Rumsfeld's request," Bremer would later write in his memoirs, "the U.S. Secret Service had done a survey of my security and had

concluded that I was the most threatened American official anywhere in the world."

The turnover in security teams was so rapid, the DoD didn't initially have time to choose among competing bids. In late August
2003, the Pentagon awarded my company a $21.3 million no-bid
contract to protect the ambassador until the Iraqi Interim Government could take power eleven months later. For us, it was another
chance to chase the school bus. Keeping the ambassador safe would
prove we could keep anyone safe, anywhere. Screwing it up, on the
other hand, could cripple Blackwater. We couldn't pitch security
services to prospective clients by saying, "Everything with Bremer
went well—you know, until he got killed." The DoD's entire contract
was twenty-two pages long—laughably short, we would later learn,
for this sort of work. The Pentagon basically said, "Do whatever you
have to. Just keep him alive."

The "Bremer detail," as it became known, was a sole-sourced,
fixed-price deal. "That contract process was based on urgency," Fred
Roitz, Blackwater's former vice president of contracts and compliance, remembers now. "They needed men around him really fast.
Someone in the Army's contracting department recommended
Blackwater, the company was thoroughly vetted, and they determined Blackwater could get the job done." We made it easy for them
to say that, because that agreed-upon fee was all the money we'd
get—meaning we accepted all the financial risk if costs began to spi-
ral. It was how I preferred to operate—I'd seen it work in Holland,
Michigan, and it ought to work in Baghdad, too. But the potential for
runaway costs became immediately apparent.

Blackwater initially provided a thirty-six-man team headed by
Frank Gallagher, a former special warfare operator with the Marines and onetime director of security for Secretary of State Henry
Kissinger. Bremer had first met Gallagher during the CPA leader's
time working as managing director of Kissinger Associates in the
1990s. They got along well, and we knew Bremer would listen when
Gallagher advised him on safety issues.

We paid each member of Bremer's security detail $600 per day. The security plan also included a special addition from our special operations days: helicopters. Three of them, in fact, to grant us air cover for ground convoys, high-speed reconnaissance capabilities, and, if necessary, medevac options.

In April 2003, just as Blackwater first expanded into Iraq, we'd purchased Melbourne, Florida–based Aviation Worldwide Services, which added aircraft to the training and logistical assistance we could offer clients. For the Bremer detail, Blackwater bought three McDonnell Douglas 530s, whippy little black and silver helicopters developed during the Vietnam War for Army scouting operations, which were later adapted for special operations forces. Their size and maneuverability meant they could land on rooftops and in city streets that larger military choppers couldn't access. Decades ago, special ops personnel nicknamed the teardrop-shaped four-man aircraft "Little Birds."

In addition to the millions of dollars we poured into hardware, having a helicopter fleet meant that we were providing not only bodyguards and professionally trained defensive drivers, but suddenly helicopter pilots, door gunners, and mechanics. That raised Blackwater's investment considerably. And the Pentagon contract gave us a scant thirty days to buy the Little Birds, outfit them with the necessary gear, assemble and train their crews, and deliver it all to Charleston, South Carolina, to have it all shipped over to Iraq. Doing so over our internal financial estimates would cost us money, but delivering late meant Blackwater could be debarred, the giant governmental black mark that rescinds a company's eligibility for contracts for a period of time.

Richard Pere, our newly appointed aviation chief, understood the pressure, and even managed to deliver the helicopters early. Not just to Charleston, mind you—he packed the Little Birds into the cargo hold of a military C5A aircraft, then flew with me on the plane from Charleston to Dover Air Force Base in Delaware, then to Spain for a stopover before delivering them personally at Baghdad International

Airport at three a.m. on Day 28. This was our first big chance to serve in Iraq, and we weren't about to start by being late.

There really was no prior design for the sort of protection Bremer required. When the ambassador walked out of a building, he was often surrounded by ten of my men in khakis and polo shirts, wearing beige vests packed with extra ammunition, their M4 carbines at the ready. When Bremer traveled through the city, there might be three dozen men, helicopter support, surveillance, and counterassault teams involved.

His motorcade had grown to include two armored Humvees at the front of the pack, three lead-armored Chevy Suburbans—the middle one carrying Bremer, the other two carrying Blackwater "shooters"—in the center of the line, and then another pair of Humvees at the rear. The Little Birds above provided extra shooters and emergency evacuation capabilities, but, just as important, they provided navigational guidance for uncertain traffic conditions, cutting valuable minutes off Bremer's trips across town.

American civilians watching Baghdad on their televisions might have thought the precautions were excessive, but threats appeared in even the most secure of places. Contingency plans had to be drawn up in case Bremer's villa was struck by one of the mortar rounds routinely fired indiscriminately into the coalition's fortified Green Zone while he slept. Meanwhile, he had been moved into that villa—as opposed to living in Hussein's converted Republican Palace with other CPA officials—only because intelligence reports kept reaffirming that he was at the top of insurgents' hit lists. "And, among the hundreds of Iraqis working in the palace in jobs ranging from janitor to high-level liaisons with our ministry teams, there was lots of room for an assassin," Bremer wrote in his memoirs. "One report Blackwater took seriously suggested that one of the Iraqi barbers in the palace had been hired to kill me when I got a haircut." On the fly, Gallagher and his Blackwater team adapted to these threats—including that

December 2003 ambush attempt on the Highway of Death—and created the protection schemes the U.S. government would later adopt for protecting its highest-risk personnel.

The ambassador's security detail proved so impenetrable that, by mid-2004, Osama bin Laden himself was seemingly growing impatient. "We in the al-Qaeda organization will guarantee, God willing, ten thousand grams of gold to whoever kills the occupier Bremer," an audiotape from the terrorist leader declared. At the time, those twenty-two pounds of gold would have been worth more than $130,000. Even those close to Bremer found bounties on their heads, as insurgents reportedly offered $30,000 for the body of a Blackwater guard. Yet Gallagher's planning and the skill of Blackwater's men not only kept Bremer safe; no one on his security detail was injured over the eleven-month assignment, either.

On the morning of June 28, 2004, after a brief ceremony during which Bremer handed power over to Iraq's new prime minister, Ayad Allawi, the ambassador's Blackwater team escorted him to a West Virginia Air National Guard C130 on the tarmac at Baghdad International Airport. They stayed with Bremer as he posed for farewell photographs, then boarded the plane with him. The stairs were drawn up and the cabin door was secured for takeoff. And then they just sat there in the 120-degree heat and didn't go anywhere.

In the days before the handover, terrorists had been blowing planes out of the sky with surface-to-air missiles, and they knew Bremer always flew in a C130. Rather than risk an attack on the outgoing head of the CPA, Blackwater's team waited until the crowds had cleared, helped him climb over cargo and out the rear of the aircraft, and then escorted him across the airport to a second, smaller jet for the flight to Jordan. It was one final precaution to make sure the job was done right. And with that sort of track record, Blackwater was soon guarding everyone.

We were tasked with protecting British prime minister Tony Blair when he visited Baghdad, and Secretary of State Powell when he met with top Iraqi officials there. Blackwater teams protected the

Iraq Survey Group, the CIA contingent combing the country for proof of weapons of mass destruction. Over U.S. objections, the UN had largely pulled out of Iraq after the truck bombing of its headquarters the summer before, dropping its humanitarian presence from some five hundred personnel to a few dozen international aid workers scattered across the northern part of the country. But those remaining workers received protection from our men. Meanwhile, any CPA official, regardless of age or rank, made a viable terrorist target—and the State Department was funneling hundreds of them into Iraq to aid the reconstruction efforts. We guarded them, too.

By mid-2004, Blackwater was filling security and training contracts for the DoD, the State Department, and the CIA, in multiple countries. And as well known as we were becoming within the halls of power in Washington D.C., we were gaining similar cachet on the streets of Baghdad. Suddenly our bear paw logo was everywhere—on T-shirts and baseball caps worn by everyday security guards, Iraqi civilians, and ironically everyone *but* my employees, who hardly ever dressed in branded gear. Even more important, we were earning the respect of the other men and women putting their lives on the line to rebuild Iraq. Owen Powell, a former soldier in Iraq who was originally published under the pen name "Sgt. Roy Batty," offered this great description in a piece for U.S. Cavalry's *ON Point* blog, titled "Rock Stars of Baghdad":

There is a low buzz on the horizon, somewhere behind the buildings surrounding the tiny [forward operating base], insectile at first, barely audible, but quickly rising on the morning breeze.... The sound fades again for a second—they must be behind another building—and then increases expectantly, louder now, and I feel the anticipation in the noise, like the sound of a huge audience applauding before a show, and WROOOOOOOMMMM!!!, the tiny helicopters burst upon the stage above us, a roar and a black flash of motion fifty feet above our heads, and they're past, instantly, the sound quickly fading with the sudden Doppler effect of something very loud, moving very fast.

More important than the security they provide for [a] convoy, the Little Birds bring a precious sense of élan, of esprit de corps, of being something elite, to our usual morning grind. You can't help but feel like you are in a really good action movie every time you see these guys, and how could you lose when you have guys and toys as cool as these on your team? The soldiers around me always say the same thing whenever Blackwater is overhead—"Man, I would do anything to have that job!" Me, too.

It was a time of extraordinary triumph for Blackwater—and one of personal tragedy at home. Joan wasn't responding well to her cancer treatments, and each round of chemotherapy seemed more brutal than the last. She was on Cytoxan, a medication literally derived from the chemical weapon mustard gas, and Adriamycin, which some people refer to as the "red devil" because of its color and ability to burn your skin. Joan called it "the cranberry juice from hell."

I can only hope that twenty years from now the way we treat cancer today—by cutting it out, burning it out, or poisoning it out—will be looked back on as something as barbaric as bloodletting. But those are the best options anyone currently has. As encouragement during her third cycle of treatment, I suggested Joan start planning what we endearingly came to know as the "chemo cruise": "While you're sitting there suffering, just think about anywhere in the world you want to go," I said. "Think about who'll be there with you and all the amazing things you'll eat. Just get through this, and we'll do it. Anywhere."

I remember the nights spent lying awake in a sleeping bag on the floor of her Hackensack, New Jersey, hospital room thinking over and over, *My wife is dying—and there isn't a damn thing I can do about it.* For the first time in my life, I felt helpless. I had been raised to believe that with enough resources and creativity—and I had both— any problem had a solution. But money and determination didn't matter here. I couldn't stop her cancer.

And Lord, we tried. Joan and I had traveled the world to find the most innovative doctors with the most aggressive cures. We relied on the advice of brilliant physicians like William Grace, then the chief of medical oncology at St. Vincent's. When radiation and chemotherapy failed, we turned to stem cell treatments. When those failed, Joan and I funded a clinic in Prague with a $500,000 grant to develop experimental treatments that might not get approved in the States. Nothing in my character, or my SEAL training, gave me the courage my wife had. And through it all, she seemed more concerned about my loss, my impending grief, than her own death. "Remember, Erik, you can live without me," she would say. "But you can't live without God."

We searched for humor where we could find it. No matter how many beautiful wigs Joan had, my wife couldn't ever seem to find one when the doorbell randomly rang in the middle of the day. "Quick, kids, find Mommy's hair!" she'd yell. "Winner gets Fruit Roll-Ups for dinner!"

As a goof, I began affectionately calling her *Frau*, German for "Mrs.," which always made her chuckle, because in our travels Joan had never found Germans particularly warm or fuzzy. "OK, Frau," I'd say, "I need your thoughts on something."

And when she made it through that third round of chemotherapy, almost four dozen of her friends and family came together for a weeklong tour of the Caribbean aboard the Cunard yacht *Sea Goddess*, bouncing from St. Thomas and St. Croix in the Virgin Islands, east to St. Barths, then south to St. John, Guadeloupe, and Barbados. I'd never been a huge fan of cruises—I figured I'd had enough of them aboard massive gray ships with five thousand of my closest friends. Yet I'm so glad we went. That "chemo cruise" created lifelong memories.

As her health deteriorated, Joan's enormous and devoted family descended on McLean, Virginia. I rented them a town house a mile from our home so they could be with her all day, then have a place of their own to return to in the evening. Joan began keeping a personal voice recorder by the bed, which had but a single message she and her friends put on it: "Note to self: Wake up tomorrow."

I remember sitting by my wife's bedside and scooping up her delicate body in my arms when Etta James's "At Last" came on the radio, and the way we used to dance there in the room together in the middle of the night. And even on the worst of days, suffering with an oxygen mask, she put on a strong show. I didn't know until I was told about it later, but my wife would apparently pinch her cheeks and pull herself up on the pillows when she heard me come home, just to look cheerful for me.

Not that I deserved it. With the pressures of so many things around us, Joan and I had been become isolated from each other. As Blackwater began to take off, I had been pushing myself at work harder than ever. We had four beautiful little kids at home, but even with help around the house, caring for them was exhausting. Then, with Joan's family around all the time, I began to feel like a stranger in my own home. By early 2003, my wife and I didn't have much time alone together to begin with, and those stresses—as well as the effects of cancer and surgery and chemotherapy—eliminated most of the romance or intimacy when we did.

I felt as if it was all I could do to keep things from spinning completely out of control, and I found comfort in the arms of a woman named Joanna Houck, who had worked as our nanny in Michigan. In mid-2002, when we all moved back to Virginia, she was hired to perform administrative functions at our Moyock facilities. She became pregnant before Joan died.

In March 2003, on a ski trip in Vail, Colorado, Joan wrote me a long letter. She left it on the dresser in our vacation home there. My wife understood it would likely be her last time visiting a place we both loved, and that I would find the letter when I returned at Christmastime, nine months later. Without her. It was the most caring, most awful thing I've ever read.

She knew about everything with Joanna. I had devastated her, yet in her final months Joan had found the strength to forgive me. There are no excuses for what happened—there's not a day that goes by that I don't regret the way I hurt her.

After years of pain and treatments, on June 14, 2003, my beautiful wife surrendered her body to her Creator and passed from this life. She was thirty-six years old. I cut a small lock of her hair to keep, and I asked the doctor for the chemotherapy port that had been implanted in her upper chest.

"Really?" the doctor said. "That thing was the bane of her existence."

"That was the closest thing to her heart," I said. I've got it to this day.

Soon after, surrounded by family and friends, we laid Joan to rest in that same ruffled navy blue taffeta dress she wore the night I met her. Our children were eight, seven, five, and three years old.

With her passing, and my shame, the screaming jet noise of life overwhelmed me. I dug ever deeper into my work. Days at a time morphed into a single blur, and I know that for a while I lost focus on those around me, and even those at home—our four beautiful kids, who'd just lost their mother. Not knowing what else to do, I turned my all-consuming sense of loss into an all-consuming drive to forge Blackwater into everything Joan and I had dreamed it could be. *Whatever it takes,* I told myself, *I'm going to make that happen.*

CHAPTER 7

THE EXPANSION PLAN
2004

ONE AFTERNOON IN EARLY 2004, RICHARD PERE SAT IN BLACKWATER'S staging area on the ramp at Bagram Airfield in Kabul, Afghanistan. He was there with a pair of pilots from Presidential Airways, a loadmaster, and a crew chief. Behind them sat one of the company's boxy, Spanish-built EADS CASA C212 airplanes. A Blackwater plane.

Presidential Airways was the operating subsidiary of Aviation Worldwide Services, the company I'd bought the year before. The purchase had been part of my deep focus on expanding Blackwater's capabilities while I was facing struggles at home. But regardless of the impetus, few business decisions I've made have had a bigger impact on the company.

Partly I bought Presidential for those two twin-engine Spanish workhorses it owned. But also I bought it for the airmen. Pere, Presidential's cofounder and president, was a veteran of the Army's 160th Special Operations Aviation Regiment, known as the "Night Stalkers" because of their pilots' strike capabilities in complete darkness.

His experience stretched all the way back to flying a nighttime helicopter mission to start the liberation of Grenada in 1983.

Then there was John Hight, vice president of Presidential and the man who became director of our aviation operations in Afghanistan. He was a fellow veteran of Army's 160th who had served this country with distinction since Vietnam. He was also there with Pere at Bagram that day. They were there for standard Blackwater cargo and passenger movements.

Suddenly, a frantic phone call came in from a junior Army officer. The 82nd Airborne had been on long patrol when they encountered insurgents in the mountains near Pakistan, Pere was told. The firefight had now gone on for days. The soldiers were almost out of ammunition. The Air Force wouldn't resupply them because the drop zone hadn't been "surveyed," or officially approved. Could we help?

Everyone at Blackwater knew it was only a matter of time before something like this unfolded. As the military mission in Afghanistan shifted from toppling the Taliban to rousting insurgents in the mountains along the Pakistan border, the Army's Special Forces had to venture deep into some of the most isolated and inhospitable areas on earth. Rebel camps thrived in the snowcapped Hindu Kush range, with peaks twice as high as many of those in the Rockies or the Alps. In the barren Safed Koh mountains south of Kabul, the thirty-three-mile-long Khyber Pass winding between Peshawar, Pakistan, and the Afghan border was littered with the roadside remnants of NATO supply vehicles blown apart by militants hiding in the hillsides. And thirty miles west of the pass was Tora Bora—or "Black Dust" in the native Pashto—Osama bin Laden's notorious cave and tunnel stronghold, which at the time was manned by a few hundred of his loyal followers. "The tyranny of distance and terrain, a long history of conflict and occupation, an extraordinarily complex tribal mosaic, an adaptive and committed enemy, and primitive and often corrupt governance all posed extraordinary challenges for soldiers and diplomats alike," read a National Defense University assessment of the region.

Without any significant civil infrastructure in the region, America's elite counterinsurgency troops were stuck creating forward operating bases (FOBs) that were little more than heavily armed campsites in the wilderness, often no larger than a city block. And to do their jobs, they constantly needed supplies: food, water, fuel, ammunition.

Delivering cargo by road just invited an ambush—and that's when there were any roads at all. (With only about thirty miles of paved road in the entire country, it was hardly a given.) Helicopters could get to the FOBs, but the noise would only advertise troop locations and leave the choppers vulnerable to antiaircraft fire. The Air Force has a rock-and-roll collection of strategic bombers and high-speed ground attack planes—classic vestiges of big wars no longer being fought—but few landing zones in the Afghan highlands can handle a 150,000-pound supply plane. By the time Pere got that call, the Pentagon had been making do by airdropping six-hundred-pound pallets of gear. But it's hard to hit a postage stamp–sized base from the altitudes the Air Force drops from in order to protect those multimillion-dollar warplanes. Too many loads were drifting away, then forcing our troops into dangerous recovery missions to prevent the matériel from falling into enemy hands.

Presidential's boxy little turboprops, meanwhile, were decidedly blue collar, but also cheap to fly and easy to maintain. They could haul just over two tons of personnel and cargo. A rear cargo ramp made them perfect for parachute drops. In the right hands, a C212 could pull off exactly the harrowing sort of low-cost, low-altitude (LCLA) resupply missions the soldiers on the ground desperately needed. The "low cost" refers to the less expensive parachute system employed for smaller package sizes. And the "low altitude"? That's ripping through the mountainside at 160 knots less than fifty feet above ground level—close enough to study a stunned goatherd's face as we soared above him. Close enough to be sure not to miss the drop zone. Close enough that mistakes become fatalities.

Pere's crew agreed on the spot to help out—no haggling, or

contracts, or attorneys. Just a simple yes to a request from an officer in need, and then Blackwater's plane, packed with shrink-wrapped ammunition, headed into the mountains to find the troops. A soldier there placed the drop zone's big orange RAM, or raised angle marker, on the hood of his Hummer; less than an hour later, our men flew in low and tight enough to knock the RAM off the Hummer with a pallet. I gladly paid the costs of that mission myself; soon, after a few more of those emergency runs, the Pentagon asked us to make it official. Air Force solicitation of competitively bid contract FA4428-04-D-0036 began in July 2004; in September of that year we completed negotiations with Air Mobility Command out of Scott Air Force Base in Illinois, which oversaw the contract. The deal was to provide fixed-wing short takeoff and landing aircraft to move the troops and supplies of Combined Joint Task Force 76 in and around Afghanistan, Uzbekistan, and Pakistan. In no time at all, Presidential was dropping 5.5 million pounds of cargo a year in a deal worth $34.8 million—more than the combined total of our federal contracts to that point.

Which meant, of course, that we suddenly needed to put a fleet of C212s on the ground in Afghanistan. Our team found secondhand CASAs in Texas, Latin America, and Australia, but the little planes had an average range just shy of nine hundred miles. They were designed for coastal patrols, not oceanic crossings. John Hight sat down and calculated how much fuel each C212 would need to make the flight, then filled the planes with fifty-five-gallon fuel drums and a pump system he engineered himself. Every thirty-seven minutes on those transatlantic flights, a crewman shifted the pump from one barrel to the next as the engines wolfed down the gas. For forty hours straight.

There's no autopilot on these clattering little planes, mind you, no cabin pressure—and there certainly aren't bathrooms. But over and over, Presidential found dedicated pilots and other crew members who wanted to be part of a mission again and contribute to a team doing something larger than themselves. We had no problem recruiting crews to pump their way across the Atlantic.

Soon I, too, was joining on those LCLA flights in Afghanistan, harnessed at the rear of the plane, standing alongside six supply bundles and a jumpmaster team. With the cargo ramp raised, the khaki countryside disappeared behind us in a furious blur. The countdowns came from the loadmaster and pilots at one minute, thirty seconds, ten seconds—then "*Go, go, go!*" When that tinny "go" bell rang, one team member slashed the tether and the rest of us shoved pallets through the tail chute. The payloads smacked down on the ground in mere seconds, just as the CASA pilots pulled spine-bending banks away from the drop zones that left even the most battle-tested veterans airsick. It was some of the most dangerous, exhilarating fixed-wing flying I've ever been a part of.

For some members of my team, Blackwater was strictly a business. Others saw it as a larger mission, like a sixth branch of the military. Contractors were, after all, viewed by the Pentagon as part of its "Total Force," and some of our jobs came from urgent and compelling contracts for which the government needed somebody to solve a problem right away. I saw my growing company as a perfect combination of the two: a way to benefit the armed forces in all sorts of ways, without all the bureaucracy. "The DoD has a lot of great people trapped in it," I often told people.

Some of the most dedicated, most passionate people I've ever met have been part of the United States armed forces. But I also know that where the Pentagon needs a hundred men to get a job done, a private company can do it with ten. Blackwater, I figured, could be the FedEx to the DoD's postal service: We didn't want to replace the military; we just wanted to make it more efficient and help patch the inevitable logistical gaps that cropped up in Pentagon planning. The approach benefited the Pentagon—and it benefited our bottom line.

In 2001, Blackwater earned some $735,000 in federal contracts. In 2002, that increased to $3.4 million. Then, in the space of eighteen months from 2003 through 2004, our business grew 600 percent. By the time we signed the Presidential Airways supply contract, money was coming from every direction—not just from Iraq and Afghanistan. The small staff in Moyock could hardly manufacture Dehart's target systems, costing as much as $15,000 apiece, fast enough. Corner office corporate warriors decided $1,500 pistol courses were more fun than golf vacations, and they shared space at the training facility with the international collection of police, military personnel, federal agents, forest rangers, and security guards who streamed through. Soon, the uniform patches those units left as souvenirs filled a pair of wall-size bulletin boards in our mess hall—a far cry from the days when we were sending employees home early. So many bullets were being fired on our Moyock ranges—some 1.5 million rounds per month—we invited local Boy Scout troops to come sweep up the brass shell casings, then recycle them and keep the cash.

Just past the fifteen-acre lake on the North Carolina campus, we upgraded the headquarters to a 65,000-square-foot command center, making it the largest building in Camden County. We even added imitation .50-caliber machine-gun barrels as handles on the front double doors. To accommodate all the foot traffic, the original modest sleeping quarters were rebuilt into a 206-bed hotel.

Overseas, we were filling contracts from the State Department, the CIA, and the DoD, including facility and personnel protection in multiple countries. We trained Afghan border agents and narcotics officers for the U.S. Drug Enforcement Agency. State even asked us to train security personnel to combat unusual threats at the Athens Olympic Games. Then there was a collection of classified contracts I'm not at liberty to discuss, even today. It made up only about 15 percent of our business—but as Gary Jackson liked to say, there were times we couldn't tell one government agency what we were doing for another.

We opened offices in Baghdad and Amman, Jordan, and Blackwater USA became Blackwater Worldwide. During our rapid rise, the company created numerous affiliates, branching far beyond Blackwater Lodge and Training Center, Blackwater Armor and Targets, and Blackwater Security Consulting. One early addition was Blackwater K9, which trained law enforcement dog units in Moyock and deployed nearly one hundred teams around the world with bomb-sniffing German shepherds and malamutes.

For water-based practice and antipiracy protection in the Gulf of Aden, we created Blackwater Maritime Security Solutions, the centerpiece of which was the *McArthur*, a 183-foot-long former National Oceanic and Atmospheric Administration research vessel that we retrofitted to carry two Little Bird helicopters, three rigid-hull inflatable boats, and a few dozen Blackwater personnel. Soon we were working with Azerbaijan's navy, at the approval of the U.S. government, to provide facility upgrades and maritime interdiction training. Those on Capitol Hill supported efforts by the tiny former Soviet republic to send its Caspian Sea oil out to the international market without having to go through neighboring Russia or Iran. But protecting its oil and gas infrastructure required top-notch tactical teams Azerbaijan didn't yet have. I'm proud that over the course of roughly ten months Blackwater's trainers took those Azerbaijan naval commandos from the most basic training to the most advanced techniques in hostile ship boarding.

Meanwhile, in Moyock, another team focused on vehicles. Having seen our convoys attacked in Iraq, we began designing and manufacturing our own heavily armored personnel carrier, called the Grizzly. The fifteen-ton beasts could carry ten men, cruise at sixty-five miles per hour, and stop rounds as large as .50 caliber—a vast improvement over the Humvees that had been taking bullets in Iraq. We figured Blackwater Armored Vehicle might sell three hundred of the trucks a year.

Then we built a blimp. No joke. The airships have been used for defense since World War II, when Goodyear convinced the Navy they could be cost-effective submarine scouts. From 2000 to 2005, defense spending on unmanned aerial vehicles (UAVs) had increased nearly tenfold, according to the Congressional Research Service. So Blackwater Airships prototyped a 170-foot-long remote-controlled blimp that could hover for days, for half the price of a fixed-wing UAV. "We can sit it over the top of Baghdad at 18,000 feet and watch all that goes on," Jackson told a reporter at the time. "The problem is if it really does work, it will be hard to produce them fast enough. I believe airships will be a multi-billion-dollar business."

Then, incorporating all these growing capabilities, we pitched to the State Department a privately trained, seventeen-hundred-man peacekeeping package with its own air force, helicopters, cargo ships, aerial surveillance, medical supply chain, and combat group. We called the offshoot company Greystone and registered it in Barbados as an international affiliate that could better ship out to war-torn regions like Darfur, Sudan, in place of the ineffectual UN peacekeepers, who are slow to deploy and hampered by red tape.

It's true that not all those ideas panned out. The Army ultimately decided against buying the Grizzly. There were no Blackwater blimps in the skies over Baghdad. And the idea of "relief with teeth," as I called the humanitarian team, didn't sit well with some Washington insiders. But such is the price of continually innovating: Whatever the government needed—whatever the government might suddenly realize it needed—my team was determined to offer it.

All told, I probably spent $100 million on various Blackwater projects that never went anywhere. But I knew that if we threw enough darts at the board, we were bound to hit the bull's-eye—more than once. I'd learned that early on, watching my father design a propeller-driven snowmobile that never caught on. Then he built a ham-deboning machine—which sold all right, apparently, in Bulgaria—and a light for a sock drawer. They were misfires, all of them, but he was never at a loss for ideas. And then one day he decided to stick that light in a car visor. GM ordered five thousand of those before Prince Manufacturing had even manufactured the first one. And by the end of

2006, Blackwater had hit the bull's-eye enough to bring in a total of one billion dollars in federal contracts.

Growing up in Michigan, I knew the "Big Three" as Ford, GM, and Chrysler. With Blackwater, they became the State Department, the CIA, and the Department of Defense. Large clients are an obvious blessing, but when there are only a few of them, they're guaranteed to set prices as low as possible. It's logical business from their standpoint—you squeeze the producer to get a better deal. In my father's line of work, auto parts manufacturers competed with one another by accepting slim profit margins. I was forced to do the same with Blackwater. And you know what? I was all for it.

From 2000 to 2005, the span when my company really gained traction, government procurement spending rose by 86 percent, to $377.5 billion annually, according to a special investigation by the House Committee on Oversight and Government Reform. By 2005, the federal government spent a record forty cents of every discretionary dollar on contracts with private companies. Considering world events, it's no surprise the department with the largest contract dollar growth during that time was the DoD: "In 2000, the Defense Department spent $133.5 billion on federal contracts. By 2005, this spending had leaped by $136.5 billion to $270 billion, an increase of 102 percent," according to the report. "In 2005, the Defense Department consumed over 70 percent of the total federal procurement budget."

Meanwhile, the department with the largest contract *percentage* growth over that span? State. In 2000 it spent $1.2 billion on federal contracts. Five years later, the department's contract spending had increased by $4.1 billion, to $5.3 billion—a jump of more than 330 percent.

My company was working for both of them. But the huge difference between the customers I sold to and the ones my father did was that the government is buying contractor services with your money. And my money. It's taxpayer dollars that fund wars, and fund private military contracts. The government *should* be fighting for the best deal it can get. And to do that, it should procure those goods and services at fixed costs. Make the provider assume the risk of losing money if he's sloppy. In exchange for that risk, assuming he does his job, the supplier can anticipate a reasonable profit. That fixed-cost approach is how Blackwater did business every time we could. You might not think it's so revolutionary, but with government contracting it is.

Traditionally, suppliers angle for a cost-based model, wherein the contractor is reimbursed for his total costs to get the job done, whatever they end up being. Or even worse, they use a "cost-plus" model that then tacks on an extra percentage of those total costs as pure profit. Not only does that system disincentivize a contractor from being careful with taxpayer dollars, but it achieves exactly the opposite. "The incentive for businesses in a regular free market is to drive down costs to maximize profit margins," says Peter W. Singer, the Brookings Institution scholar. "In the cost-plus mechanism, an incentive exists to raise costs, because your profit is based on the costs and goes up the more there are. It's a wicked reversal of the free market. [The cost-plus model] completely turned Adam Smith on his head."

Put another way: It's an absurd way to do business. And equally absurd is that it isn't just cavalier contractors who seem to prefer it. We found many preprogrammed federal contracting officers were just as fond of the lazy accounting of simply paying a set percent on top of the total costs. In fact, between 2000 and 2005 the government's use of cost-plus contracts increased by 75 percent, to $110 billion, according to that congressional investigation. Worse, according to the report, "nearly half was spent on cost-plus-award-fee contracts, a type of cost-plus contract in which it is possible for the contractor to receive millions in profits even if the contract goes over budget." No wonder some contractors get such a reputation for greed—and that the issue came up in the very first presidential debate between Senators John McCain and Barack Obama in 2008. "Particularly in defense spending, which is the largest part of our appropriations," McCain insisted, "we have to do away with cost-plus contracts."

By 2005, less than two years after the invasion of Iraq, the Defense Department was responsible for roughly 70 percent of the federal government's expenditures on cost-plus contracts—and it oversaw seven of the eleven individual contracts worth over a billion dollars apiece. (NASA and the Department of Energy each had a pair of projects on that list.) Combined, those seven DoD contracts were worth nearly $18 billion in 2005 alone. At the top of the cost-plus list, Halliburton-Kellogg Brown & Root took home more than $5 billion in 2005 for its LOGCAP contract with the Army to provide food, shelter, and other support services to troops in Iraq, Afghanistan, and beyond.

That's important for two reasons: First, Blackwater wasn't on those lists. My background, and my company's name recognition, always led to some cartoonish public perception of how much revenue we must be generating. And it's true we didn't argue when people suggested we were successful. But compared to a DoD provider making $5 billion on one contract in one year, our cumulative total of $1 billion in contracts by 2006 meant we were always punching way above our weight class. The second reason: There was plenty of money flying around without having to rig the system with shadowy cost-plus contracts. Looking back on it, I'm almost embarrassed I didn't make *more* money with Blackwater. But here's one example of why I didn't:

On November 22, 2003, not long after our Little Birds made it to Baghdad, terrorists shot down a DHL Airbus cargo plane with a surface-to-air missile. The heroic landing by the three members of the flight crew—who wrestled the severely damaged A300 to the ground from eight thousand feet up without the use of any functional flight control surfaces while the plane was leaking fuel and on fire—has become famous in aviation circles. It also led to a prompt reevaluation of risks by DHL's insurance company, which happened to be our insurance company, too. They immediately yanked our aircraft coverage, then offered to sell it back to us at twice the rate for half the protection. So after a little back-of-the-envelope math, we decided to self-insure our helicopters—meaning that if any were shot down, Blackwater would simply eat the material loss. And those losses would come.

Under a cost-plus contract, a firm could simply bundle those insurance fees in with their overhead, slide it past a contracting agent, and let the taxpayers foot the bill. Yet my company could still be aggressive, I knew, still be profitable, and that didn't require padding the paperwork. Our tack was more honest, more straightforward, and saved the taxpayers money by keeping us focused on delivering a great product at a competitive price.

No surprise: That approach appealed to a number of high-ranking personnel trapped in the federal bureaucracy. And soon they brought us another opportunity for Blackwater to expand.

Joseph Cofer Black once told me he thought about leaving government work when he found himself climbing out a car window.

The man who would one day become vice chairman of Blackwater began his CIA career in 1974. Nearly twenty years later, he became the agency's station chief in Khartoum, Sudan. His appointment coincided with the State Department labeling the country a state sponsor of terrorism, thanks in part to its harboring the leadership of what was then a fledgling militant group known as al-Qaeda. At the time, thirty-five-year-old rebel leader Osama bin Laden was largely unknown to anyone outside the Muslim world or intelligence circles. And people within those circles had a far larger target in Khartoum, anyway: Ilich Ramírez Sánchez, a Venezuelan-born killer aligned with the Popular Front for the Liberation of Palestine, whose nearly two-decade-long bombing spree had earned him the nickname "Carlos the Jackal." He was perhaps the most famous terrorist of his time—and a figure Cofer Black was hell-bent on hunting down.

For months under Black's watch, CIA personnel in Khartoum collected intelligence about the Jackal, eventually collaborating with French secret service agents who would apprehend the terrorist. After a minor surgical procedure on August 13, 1994, Sánchez was reportedly moved from Ibn Khaldoun hospital to a private villa by Sudanese police, who claimed they'd uncovered a plot to kill him. In reality, the police were cooperating with Black's team—and the villa's "security guards" tranquilized the terrorist in the middle of the night, bound his hands and feet, and tossed him onto a private jet bound for France.

It was a career-making success, leading to Black's appointment as CIA task force chief for the Near East and South Asia Division in 1995, followed by a prominent role with the agency's Latin America Division in 1998. By then, however, bin Laden had proven himself an international menace. The CIA knew that the terrorist, now living in Afghanistan, was responsible for the 1993 deaths of eighteen Army personnel working in Somalia as part of Operation Restore Hope, which delivered food to starving children. Bin Laden was also behind the murder of five more Americans in a November 1995 truck bombing at a U.S.-operated Saudi Arabian National Guard training center in Riyadh, along with the hundreds dead from the embassy bombings in Nairobi and Tanzania in 1998.

Al-Qaeda's ambition, and destructive power, were growing. In December 1998, CIA director George Tenet circulated a memo among the intelligence community declaring "we are at war" with the terrorist organization. Soon after, Black was named the head of the CIA's Counterterrorism Center, or CTC, and tasked with overseeing Alec Station—a special unit focused on stopping bin Laden.

The twenty-five-year intelligence veteran was a logical choice for the job. For one, Black held the distinction of being one of the few people bin Laden had ever personally marked for death yet failed to kill. Back in Khartoum in 1995 bin Laden had discovered Black was CIA—and put the crosshairs on him. Black's travel through town was soon watched by insurgents; intelligence personnel countersurveilling the terrorists even saw them stage a mock ambush on a city back-street as practice for murdering the station chief. (Ultimately, the U.S. ambassador to Sudan complained about the threat to the local government, shutting down the plot.) Tenet knew Black would have a personal stake in bin Laden's downfall.

Black was also a colorful character. This was, after all, the man who would one day demand the Jawbreaker team in Afghanistan bring back bin Laden's head in a box. (Little wonder why.) The veteran's confidence has been misrepresented by some as loose-cannon cockiness, but make no mistake: That swagger is just what the intelligence realm needed at the time. Even Richard Clarke, the White House counterterrorism czar with whom Black would later publicly butt heads about pre-9/11 intelligence failures, saw Black as a key member of the team. "He had a reputation as a bit of a cowboy," Clarke said. "So when I was urging Tenet to get someone to run CTC who had balls, he came back to me and said, 'Well, all right. I found this guy, and I don't know him personally, but by all reports he's got big *cojones*.' And when [Black] showed up, it was really a breath of fresh air."

In the days following 9/11, Black spearheaded the agency's push to crush al-Qaeda and the Taliban in Afghanistan. It would be a de-cade, of course, before bin Laden was finally killed; in that time, the CTC chief's role with the government, and his interest in working for it, would shift.

In late 2002 President Bush appointed Black the State Depart-ment's coordinator for counterterrorism, making him the man re-sponsible for coordinating America's counterterrorism cooperation with foreign governments. Black was granted the rank of ambassa-dor at large.

His transition away from the CIA came at a time the intelligence community was undergoing its own transition. By the early 2000s, the CIA and National Security Agency were outsourcing intelli-gence work almost as feverishly as the Defense Department farmed out security. At the start of the decade, government agencies were spending roughly $20 billion per year on intelligence contracts. By 2003, a snowballing dependence on contractors had pushed that number to more than $40 billion.

Beyond budgets going haywire, the politics within the intelligence community had become more volatile than usual after 9/11, and the overnight escalation of sheer manpower was dizzying. Black saw that firsthand as a new ambassador at State, driving back to Langley one afternoon for a friend's retirement party. He reportedly pulled into the CIA's parking lot, only to find it completely packed. Even the VIP lot was full, but for a tiny spot way too narrow for his car. Black wedged into the space, shut off the ignition—and with no other option, climbed out the driver's-side window.

He lasted about two more years in the bureaucracy of the State Department before following the lead of its top two officials— Secretary of State Colin Powell and Deputy Secretary of State Richard Armitage—and resigning before the start of President Bush's second term. On February 4, 2005, Black came to work for Blackwater, bringing with him his intelligence expertise.

Soon after, we incorporated the Black Group, helmed by the eponymous CEO with three decades of government experience, which focused on security for *Fortune* 500 companies. "We seek to anticipate and defeat the next terrorist tactic—disruptions of supply chains, coordinated attacks on key assets or customers, or even assassinations of top executives," said a statement on the company Web site. "Corporations are the most vulnerable targets. It's our job to keep them safe."

The idea of working in the intelligence field never occurred to me while sketching out plans for a shooting range and training center, but the market was undeniably there. We'd seen over the years how larger corporations assessed risk and planned for security, often poorly. Those were skills we knew well. Black, meanwhile, brought his own impressive background, and together we saw the chance to assemble an intelligence team in Virginia every bit as formidable as the former military men on the ground in Moyock.

That same year, another heavy hitter joined our ranks: Robert Richer resigned his position as associate deputy director of operations at the CIA to become Blackwater's vice president of intelligence. After twenty-two years with the agency, the former Marine saw in our company a level of efficiency that simply doesn't exist within the federal bureaucracy—and the potential to expand business intelligence on a global scale. "Cofer can open doors," Richer said then. "I can open doors. We can generally get in to see who we need to see. We don't help pay bribes. We do everything within the law, but we can deal with the right minister or person." Under their guidance, we soon combined the Black Group with a pair of independent companies, the Terrorism Research Center and Technical Defense, to create Total Intelligence Solutions (TIS): a sixty-five-man, twenty-four-hour operation based in Arlington that provided threat analysis, political briefings, and security training services to companies around the world.

Before long, oil companies, cruise lines, banks, and biotech firms—even the Walt Disney Company (which needed threat assessments for filming locations overseas)—were spending hundreds of thousands of dollars on TIS's services. Black quickly became so impressed by the private sector, he publicly suggested that every mid-level government official should spend a two-year sabbatical there to learn about efficiency and effectiveness.

Hiring the ambassador was certainly a coup for Blackwater. Our critics like to contend there was something devious about his transition to corporate America. In reality, it's far simpler than that: Business intelligence companies have been around for ages; if we were going to expand in that direction, we wanted the most experienced personnel to offer the highest-quality services. It's the same thing every company strives for. Back in 2002, for instance, retired Army lieutenant general Harry E. Soyster, then an executive at giant contractor Military Professional Resources Inc., made waves by bragging, "We've got more generals per square foot here than in the Pentagon." However, in my mind, bringing in retired DoD brass was

the *last* thing a PMC should brag about. I wanted executives who accomplished things, not senior leaders who'd been paralyzed by years
in the bureaucracy.

As for why Black wanted to work with us: He'd seen what our
manpower could accomplish at home and overseas. He'd seen how
streamlined our corporate hierarchy was. And he'd seen that this
team would never shy away from doing whatever it took to support
American troops. That message hit close to home: At the time, Black's
son was a lieutenant in the Army, stationed at Forward Operating
Base (FOB) Tillman—a base named for the professional football
player who joined the Army, only to be killed by friendly fire. FOB
Tillman sat along Afghanistan's rugged southeast border, separated
from Pakistan by harrowing peaks that American troops nicknamed
"Big Ugly" and "Big Nasty." Blackwater regularly carried in supplies
for the troops there; I personally flew on one of those missions that
dropped on Tillman. As a father and an American, our service appealed to Black. "The reason I came to Blackwater was its mission to
support the United States government," Black would later say. "I'm
proud of the fact that Blackwater provided air resupply to my son."

CHAPTER 8

FALLUJAH

2004

BY MID-2004, THE INITIAL GROUND WAR IN IRAQ HAD GIVEN WAY TO OPERATION Iraqi Freedom II (OIF 2), military shorthand for the new American mission to stabilize the shattered nation. At that point, the Pentagon rotated in and out of Iraq more than 200,000 pieces of equipment and 235,000 personnel to relieve those reaching the ends of their one-year deployments. It was the largest troop rotation since World War II—one described by Air Force general Richard Myers, then chairman of the military's Joint Chiefs of Staff, as "a logistics feat that will rival any in history." He told reporters, "There's going to be a lot of turbulence in the system, as you would expect." That turbulence, Defense Secretary Donald Rumsfeld added with significant understatement, "is always undesirable."

A year after Saddam Hussein was ousted from the country, attacks across Iraq numbered in the dozens per day. More than two hundred American troops had been killed there since the end of major combat operations, and casualties continued to mount among civilians and the sloppy patchwork of Iraq's security forces, both of which were increasingly targeted by an equal-opportunity insurgency. During the OIF 2 rotation, the massive influx of U.S. troops without established situational awareness and an understanding of the rapidly evolving Iraqi enemy provided nearly free rein for terrorist strikes—nowhere more so than in what's known as the Sunni Triangle, a few hundred square miles of central Iraq bounded roughly by Baghdad to the east, Tikrit to the north, and Ramadi to the west. At the time, some 80 percent of all guerrilla attacks in Iraq came within that triangle, where well-armed Hussein loyalists preyed on coalition forces with a combination of IEDs—improvised explosive devices, or roadside bombs—and artillery scavenged from the collapse of the former regime's internal security apparatus.

Those Hussein forces, abruptly disbanded by CPA Order 2, had employed well over one hundred thousand Sunni men—and now they were eager for bloodshed. "The coalition and Iraqi Security Forces face a composite insurgency whose elements act on diverse motives. These include former regime members and Iraqi Islamists, foreign jihadists, angry or aggrieved Iraqis, tribal groups, and criminals, who draw considerable strength from political and religious ideologies, tribal notions of honor and revenge, and shared solidarities deeply ingrained in the Sunni Triangle," read a 2005 analysis by the Washington Institute for Near East Policy, a nonprofit think tank that promotes peace and security in the Middle East. "Fundamentally the insurgency is about power: who had it, who has it now, and who will have it in the future."

Though attacks in Baghdad still dominated headlines, perhaps no part of the Sunni Triangle was more volatile in early 2004 than a city seated on the banks of the Euphrates River, forty miles west of the capital: Fallujah. Home to roughly three hundred thousand people, the city had been largely left to police itself thanks to DoD planning that stretched the Army's 82nd Airborne Division precariously thin in an effort to have it patrol the entire triangle.

Tensions in Fallujah were permanently high, and bloody battles common: At an April 2003 rally there to celebrate Hussein's sixty-sixth birthday—the ousted leader had not yet been captured by the coalition—the Army's troops insisted they were fired upon by demonstrators. The 82nd Airborne shot back, killing more than a dozen Iraqis and injuring seventy-five. Not long after, insurgents retaliated by shooting down an American transport helicopter just outside town, killing sixteen soldiers. Townspeople danced on the wreckage. By March 2004, roughly a hundred days before U.S. authorities handed over power to the fledgling Iraqi government, the archconservative Sunni stronghold had become the flashpoint of anticoalition hostility.

That month, the 1st Marine Division relieved the 82nd Airborne in the triangle as part of the OIF 2 troop rotation. That meant turnover in logistical support teams as well: When American forces move, the contractors who feed them move, too—in this case, ESS Support Services Worldwide. ESS was the subcontractor to Halliburton subsidiary KBR, the lead contractor being paid through that massive Army LOGCAP. ESS needed to transfer truckloads of pots and pans and kitchen equipment out of Camp Ridgeway, just west of Fallujah. With the Marines moving in, the Army's contractors were clearing out—which meant someone had to protect ESS's convoys on their trips through the desert. It was the sort of thing Blackwater was good at.

We staked a partnership with Kuwaiti firm Regency Hotel & Hospitality Company to become the subcontracted security provider for ESS, making Blackwater the subcontractor to the subcontractor of the contractor for the Army. We signed that deal on March 8, 2004. And then there was even an additional layer of paperwork added: Blackwater's security missions were so carefully planned, we soon feared that wrangling with a business partner might force us into logistical compromises we weren't comfortable with. So four days later we signed a restructured deal with Regency making us subcontractors under *them*, putting Blackwater fourth on the contracting chain but giving us control over the actual security procedures in place. We agreed to provide a squad of thirty-four men to protect ESS's personnel and convoys. Regency was to pay my company

$11,082,326 for a year of work—just shy of a million dollars per month—with an option to renew for a second year.

Blackwater took over the lucrative assignment from ESS's previous security team, Control Risks Group (CRG), a move some have since contended must have involved shady backroom dealings. The reality is far simpler: CRG refused to do it. That British firm had twice been asked by ESS to guard its convoys in the Sunni Triangle. "This was refused both times due to the obvious risk of transporting slow-moving loads through such a volatile area," CRG's operations manager would later write in a report. So ESS found someone who would take the job.

During security handovers among private firms, there's often a thirty-day transition during which the incoming teams ride along on missions and monitor the established provider's movements from the local command center. It also provides sufficient time for the new contractor to acquire the appropriate vehicles and weaponry to do its job. The Blackwater-Regency team signed our initial deal with ESS on March 8, meaning that thirty-day window would have put my men on duty April 8—but upon losing the contract, CRG promptly announced its personnel would continue to support ESS only for another three weeks, through March 29.

ESS, meanwhile, had its own contracts to fill and wanted its manpower and matériel on the move before April 8. Starting our work before the contractual date meant that tactical SUVs and heavy machine guns to be provided to us by Regency might not have yet arrived. My men wouldn't have had a full month to fully explore the area. Yet ESS was a major global supplier—a company well worth making a good impression upon. Blackwater's men always said yes first. We would figure out the details as we went.

On March 30, the four men of Blackwater Team November 1 arrived at the Army's Camp Taji, located a dozen miles north of Baghdad. The men—forty-eight-year-old Wes Batalona, thirty-two-year-old

Jerry Zovko, and thirty-eight-year-old Mike Teague, all former Army Rangers, as well as thirty-eight-year-old former Navy SEAL Scott Helvenston—had been on a mission transporting an ESS employee north from the capital. They delivered the principal without an issue.

There, however, the plan changed: With Blackwater's team now at Camp Taji, ESS management called our site manager in Baghdad, Tom Powell, and requested that November 1 make an additional run. The food service provider still needed to collect its sixteen truckloads' worth of kitchen equipment from Camp Ridgeway, on the other side of Fallujah. Could the four-man Blackwater team leave right away from Taji with a caravan of empty flatbeds to pick up the matériel?

November 1 was made up of talented men, for sure. Batalona, a native of Hawaii's Big Island, had served as an Army Ranger for two decades. As a retired sergeant first class, the veteran was exactly the kind of guy to lead a small unit in a tight situation. The silver-haired forty-eight-year-old, whose penchant for flip-flops and Hawaiian shirts would follow him even to Baghdad, had joined the Army at the end of the Vietnam War. Batalona was part of the first invasion force in Panama in 1989, and the liberation of Kuwait the following year; then, in 1993, he served in the Somalia operation. He retired the year after, moved back to Hawaii and to his wife, June, whom he'd been with since high school. He eventually took a job as a security guard at the Hilton Waikoloa Village, but the night shift wasn't exactly thrilling for a man with his background. So in late 2003 Batalona found himself on contract with the firm MPRI to train Iraq's new army. On that job, he became fast friends with another former Ranger sixteen years his junior, Jerry Zovko.

Zovko, a Cleveland native, had spent a year at Ohio State before enlisting in the Army at age nineteen. He served six years, starting out as a military policeman with the 82nd Airborne but spending most of his career as a Ranger. The Croatian-American saw action in Bosnia in 1995 before retiring from the Army two years later. He was six foot three and built to bench-press the world. He spoke Croatian,

Spanish, Russian, Japanese, Thai—and Arabic, which made him particularly valuable in the contracting realm. He caught on first with the PMC DynCorp to provide security at the U.S. embassy in Qatar, then reported to Iraq in the summer of 2003 on that MPRI deal. In February 2004, he and Batalona signed contracts with Blackwater to work security in Iraq: $600 a day for missions, $150 for standby days.

The third Ranger on November 1 was Teague. The giant Tennessean was a former Night Stalker with the Army's 160th Special Operations Aviation Regiment, based out of Fort Campbell, Kentucky. Teague had served in the invasions of Grenada and Panama, and had earned the Bronze Star in Afghanistan. He had retired from the military as a staff sergeant in January, and on that day had been with Blackwater for only two weeks. He'd signed up just after his seventh wedding anniversary with his wife, Rhonda. "He was aware of the conditions," friend Johnny Ratliffe later said. "He volunteered his services to try to help more people." That was in keeping with his character: At home, the thirty-eight-year-old donated his time to help out his son's high school wrestling team and was active in the local Cumberland Drive Baptist Church. "Mike, from the men of Task Force DAGGER," a fellow Night Stalker would later write on a military message board, "drop your rucksack, and stand at ease as you enter the gates of Heaven, 'cause your time in Hell has already been served."

Even on a team of remarkable veterans, the final member stood out: Stephen "Scott" Helvenston had dropped out of high school before finding his true calling in the Navy. After earning his GED, he enlisted and went directly to SEAL training. Helvenston was only seventeen years old when he completed BUD/S training; not yet old enough to vote, and needing special parental consent to be there, he became the youngest SEAL in naval history. The Florida native was deployed by the SEALs four times before transitioning to become an instructor for BUD/S training and accelerated-freefall parachute jumps in his home state. That lasted until 1994, when his canopy malfunctioned during a jump: He broke both legs—then stood up and tried to walk it off.

Like many members of the special forces, Helvenston struggled to find a niche for his extraordinary skills in civilian work. While in the Navy, he'd won two gold medals in the world championship of the Military Pentathlon—once described as "perhaps the closest thing to being named the best military athlete on the planet"—so he started a fitness company, Amphibian Athletics, in Southern California. He became an occasional stuntman for Hollywood films, and trained actress Demi Moore for her SEAL role in *G.I. Jane*. But times were tight, and with Blackwater he saw a chance to again serve a war effort he believed in, and to save a little money for his two young children, whom he adored. When he arrived in the Middle East in early 2004, Helvenston became instantly recognizable to our staff as the guy constantly saying, "I'm just damn glad to be here!" He was unflinchingly optimistic; a fellow SEAL and friend would later remember, "His feeling was, 'If your time is up, there's going to be a bullet out there with your name on it.'"

At Camp Taji, Powell conferred with Batalona, November 1's team leader. They all knew Fallujah was nasty. And there, prior to the official contract start date with ESS, November 1 didn't have the heavy-duty squad automatic weapons that were still en route from Regency. Worse, the men knew they'd be driving a pair of ESS's old Mitsubishi Pajeros that were being used only until Regency could deliver us vehicles with protection kits—armor plating that reinforces an SUV better than anything you'd drive off your local sales lot, but not as well as full armor. ESS's Pajeros were just regulation SUVs with armor plates mounted behind the back seats. The men knew that if they were attacked from behind, that level of protection wouldn't mean much.

Lastly, there was the question of manpower. The contract that Blackwater and Regency had initially signed with ESS specifically acknowledged the threats our men could face in Fallujah, and the number of men necessary to do our job. "Further to Blackwater's analysis of ESS requirements and the current threat in the Iraqi the-ater of operations as evidenced by the recent incidents against civil-ian entities in Fallujah, Ar Ramadi, Al Taji and Al Hillah," the contract read, "there are areas in Iraq that will require a minimum of three Security Personnel per vehicle." That allowed for one driver, a navigator riding shotgun—which isn't just a colorful phrase in this line of work—and a third team member in the backseat watching their six.

We stipulated that in the contract because, as always, Blackwa-ter's executives had been following the news. Earlier in 2004, nine men had been killed when a U.S. Black Hawk helicopter was shot down outside Fallujah—even though Iraqi witnesses said the chopper had been clearly marked with a red cross. The next month, insur-gents fired rocket-propelled grenades (RPGs) at a convoy carrying General John P. Abizaid, who had succeeded Tommy Franks as head of U.S. Central Command. And in the three weeks before we signed on with ESS, more than ten foreign civilian contractors had been killed across Iraq. November 1 hadn't needed six men—that is, three in each of the SUVs—to simply drive someone from Baghdad up to Camp Taji, but Fallujah, where merely looking American had become a potential death sentence, was something else entirely.

A mission to Camp Ridgeway and back would mean Batalona and deputy team leader Zovko would have to ride in the lead Pajero, while the other SUV, driven by Helvenston and Teague, book-ended the fleet of ESS trucks, which would be driven by Iraqis. And because it was an urgent request from ESS, Blackwater's men had to make a go-no-go decision on the spot—unusual, because our security teams normally had twenty-four hours to perform risk assessments before missions.

Batalona determined that even without the fully armored vehi-cles and standard manpower the team he had could accomplish the task—but for three of those flatbeds, not sixteen. The men weren't forced into the mission or somehow ordered to do it—a private com-pany doesn't have that sort of military authority. Risk assessments like those were the sorts of judgment calls Blackwater contractors on the ground routinely made to ensure operational safety. No one questioned Batalona's decision to accept the mission, especially since his insistence on shrinking the convoy showed he was aware of the risks.

At three p.m. on the same afternoon they'd arrived at Camp Taji, Team November 1 and three red ESS flatbeds set off from Taji on their new mission. The caravan made it as far as the Marine base Camp Fallujah, five miles east of the insurgent hotbed, before stopping for the night.

At approximately nine in the morning on March 31, Blackwater's four men and the three ESS trucks left the base along Highway 10, heading west for Camp Ridgeway. Batalona called back to our operations center in Baghdad to report that November 1's exact route was still to be determined; a straight run through Fallujah would be far more direct, though far more dangerous. Dozens of minarets stood across the City of Mosques, reaching as high as 150 feet, but otherwise the city's finished buildings were wedged in next to one another, low and flat, the color of the desert upon which they sat. They offered endless rooftops and alleyways where shooters could hide. Then there were the strings of half-finished homes, with junked automobiles dumped in the streets outside next to piles of loose garbage. One never knew how traffic might flow through Fallujah on a given day— or if some new barricade was part of a plot by insurgents. There was a reason that by the end of its rotation three weeks earlier the Army had rarely entered town with fewer than a caravan of vehicles stacked with troops.

To avoid the city, another route could take the Blackwater convoy north and then west around Fallujah—a road known to the military as Route Mobile—but that was three hours longer each way. It would not only add time, but also increase the exposure and risk to the convoy. Besides, the Marines in charge now were also regularly blocking roads in the area, and Batalona wouldn't know for sure which arteries were even open until his team reached an Iraqi Civil Defense

Corps (ICDC) checkpoint fifteen minutes closer to Fallujah. As civilian contractors, Blackwater's men didn't have formal access to military intelligence, and the same was true in reverse. The Marines had no idea November 1 was approaching the city that morning.

At that checkpoint, manned by as many as twenty members of the ICDC, the Blackwater team was simply waved through without so much as a word. What happened next remains the subject of intense debate. U.S. intelligence reports have determined that Batalona intended to link up with other ICDC personnel on the gritty eastern edge of the city; there, ICDC would lead November 1 on a route through Fallujah that bypassed the morning traffic jams. That plan would have required coordination with ICDC the night before, from Camp Fallujah, and Batalona never told Blackwater's operations center he'd done so. But there's no doubt he could have pulled that off. And as the cloverleaf exit for Route Mobile disappeared into their rearview mirrors that morning, the Blackwater team did indeed connect with a pair of run-down pickup trucks full of tan-uniformed ICDC personnel all too eager to guide my men through the city.

Within a mile, November 1's convoy was led to an intersection with broken traffic lights. An Iraqi policeman standing there directed traffic; Blackwater's men asked him how to get to Camp Ridgeway—perhaps confirmation that they trusted their ICDC escorts only so far.

We knew corruption was rife within Iraqi police forces; the security environment at Iraq's Ministry of Interior, which oversees the forces, had become so perilous that Western officials sometimes wore body armor to meetings at the ministry offices. Just weeks prior, General Abizaid had testified before the Senate Armed Services Committee that "there's no doubt that terrorists and insurgents will attempt to infiltrate the security forces. We know it's happening, and we know it has happened." The House Armed Services Subcommittee on Oversight and Investigations would later report, "The Ministry of Interior, concerned about a pattern of unprofessional and even criminal behavior on the part of many National Police units, started pulling National Police brigades out of counterinsurgency operations for retraining." And the officers simply waving Batalona's convoy through the checkpoint a few minutes earlier wouldn't have exactly inspired confidence in Blackwater's men—especially when just through the intersection Fallujah's morning traffic, penned in by barricades throughout the city, snarled around their convoy. So much for that shortcut.

Crawling west through town, the men of November 1 scanned the sidewalks and kebab shops and storefronts for threats. Zovko, who spoke Arabic, would have demanded the ESS truck drivers behind him stay close, stay in line. Helvenston and Teague surely monitored the convoy from the rear as the ICDC trucks came to a stop up ahead. The caravan was at a standstill.

At about nine thirty a.m., a group of boys approached the vehicles. It's a familiar scene wherever U.S. military personnel appear around the world, as curious children want to chat, or maybe ask for candy. One boy put his hands on the passenger-side door of Batalona's Pajero. Blackwater's men rolled down the window and made friendly conversation.

Upon leaving the SUV, two of the boys hurried back to a crowd that was now gathering on the sidewalk. They spoke to two men in their thirties, both clad in white dishdashas with matching black-and-white scarves over their shoulders. Yes, the boys said, the men in the first and last vehicles were Americans. They sat down on the ground and faced the lead SUV.

Within moments, at least five gunmen charged from the surrounding shops, their AK-47s erupting with thunder cracks that echoed through the crowded streets. Round after round ripped into the rear SUV; 7.62-mm cartridges tore through the back of the vehicle, then the armor plate, then poured in through the side windows. Helvenston and Teague never even had a chance to lift their weapons.

Hearing the assault behind him, Batalona stomped the gas in the lead SUV. Ahead, the road was blocked. Insurgents swept forward alongside the flatbed trucks. The supposed ICDC escort trucks sped away; one terrified ESS driver would later report seeing a heavily armed blue-and-white pickup truck—a police vehicle, he believed—escape the scene down a side street. Batalona wrenched the steering wheel to the left, barreling over the median and destroying one of the Mitsubishi's rear tires in a desperate U-turn. Now facing east-bound, the two men met a new blockade of stopped cars, and a hail of machine-gun fire from the oncoming attackers. The black Pajero slammed into a stopped car, then came to rest, Batalona's body slumped over into the passenger seat, Zovko's head rolled back. As one investigation would later ominously report, "There was no evidence of return fire by the Blackwater personnel."

The entire assault was over in seconds. Four men had been be-trayed and ambushed; had there been six in the vehicles that morn-ing, the other two surely would have died as well. Larger guns would have made no difference without time to fire. Facing this sort of cal-culated, close-quarter execution, even protection kits on the SUVs wouldn't have saved the men inside. The three ESS truck drivers were allowed to leave—because they, of course, were not Americans.

Only then did the worst part begin. Insurgents burned and muti-lated the four bodies, dragged one of them through the streets, then strung up two others from the city's steel trestle bridge spanning the Euphrates. Crowds of crazed men—and children—beat the bodies and chanted, "Fallujah is the graveyard of Americans." No police of-ficers or firefighters stepped in to halt the brutal desecration, which lasted for hours. Later, nurses from the nearby hospital reportedly tried to remove the bodies from the bridge; gunmen threatened to kill them, too. Marines, who learned of the assault only when foot-age showed up on Fox News, couldn't save lives already lost—and they couldn't quell the riot without more bloodshed. So they did nothing.

Two of the attackers, meanwhile, had carried their AK-47s in one hand and video cameras in the other. They'd recorded the entire savagery. Soon, just as the insurgents had hoped, TV newscasters were broadcasting it around the world.

My phone in Virginia rang around three thirty a.m. By then—eleven thirty a.m. Baghdad time—our operations center there had learned of a brutal attack in Fallujah. Details were sketchy, but they were awful. It sounded like our men. If so, they would mark not only Blackwater's first casualties, but—in my entire military career—the first for anyone under my responsibility.

Everyone at Blackwater understood that in our line of work losing men was likely inevitable at some point. But that phone call shook me far more than I would have ever expected. I stood there thinking back over my time as a SEAL. I couldn't help but imagine my family's grief if they'd been told I wasn't coming home—and the grief that would soon come to the parents and spouses and siblings of those men who'd been killed. I thought of my children in their bedrooms down the hall, tucked under their covers. I threw on whatever clothes were within arm's reach; in a haze, I drove through the darkness to my office in McLean.

On the television, Al Jazeera had the footage first—the burning, the cheering, the shattered bodies hanging from that green bridge. Soon it was splashed across American networks, edited somewhat, as if a little pixilation could ease the sight of the dead being torn apart by a mob. It immediately brought to mind Somalia and the famous Black Hawk Down mission to Mogadishu in 1993. There, videotaped desecration of Army Rangers so turned public opinion at home, President Clinton ultimately withdrew American forces from the country entirely. We were watching a modern spin on a psychological weapon as old as war itself: The more horrific—and widely seen—the attack, the smaller the actual death toll had to be to generate maximum disgust. The insurgents in Fallujah "knew how to stage that [attack]," John Pike, director of the terrorism research group GlobalSecurity.org, said at the time. "They want to frighten us out of Iraq. It was premeditated, planned, skillfully staged terrorism. They know the degree of dread it will inflict in American family members."

Whether they were Blackwater's men on the TV or not, my first thought was to send in a young man with whom I'd spoken outside Fallujah three weeks earlier, during a site visit to our security operations there. I'd been impressed by the former Ranger's knowledge of the region, its languages, and its people. If anyone could track down the insurgents who'd done this to Americans, I thought, it'd be Jerry Zovko.

By midmorning on the East Coast, however, we got confirmation that the slain men were Blackwater's, and I learned to my sorrow that Zovko had already gone in. The first thing I wished I could do, more than anything else, was talk to my dad. I'd thought that often as I built a company of my own, but right then, at that moment, my father would have known the right thing to say to the staff, to those families, even to me.

I have always remembered a book he pointed me to when I first joined the Navy: *On War,* a nineteenth-century philosophical exploration of combat by the Prussian general Carl von Clausewitz. "War is the province of danger, and therefore courage above all things is the first quality of a warrior," Clausewitz wrote. "Courage is of two kinds: first, physical courage, or courage in presence of danger to the person; and next, moral courage, or courage before responsibility, whether it be before the judgment-seat of external authority, or of the inner power, the conscience."

I wished I could talk to my father about that idea of moral courage—about the right way to be a leader, right then. But he was gone. Joan, the only other person whose opinion ever meant as much to me, was gone. As the leader of Blackwater, I needed to swallow my own grief, comfort the bereaved families, and investigate the disaster—all without the support of the two who had been there to help with my most difficult decisions. I felt deeply alone, but I knew we would get through. We had to.

In Moyock, Gary Jackson took the news with similarly grim acceptance. There, Ana Bundy, who was then in charge of our logistics department, instituted a casualty assistance program she'd mapped out for this eventuality. Jackson, who'd seen Teague at our training center just a few weeks prior, headed to Clarksville, Tennessee, to locate the veteran's widow. Chris Taylor, another Blackwater VP, left for Oceanside, California, to meet Helvenston's ex-wife. Mike Rush, our head of security consulting, left for Hawaii to speak with June Batalona. Years later, we would learn that Bundy's notification protocols were so comprehensive, the State Department would adopt them for all its private security contractors. I didn't know that at the time, of course. I just knew that I was getting on a plane to Cleveland, to go see Zovko's mother, Donna. I had no idea what I would say.

It was a dreary, ugly night in Willoughby, Ohio. Jerry had listed his brother as next of kin on company paperwork; around seven thirty p.m., a local U.S. marshal and I knocked on the door of Tom Zovko's home. Jerry's sister-in-law answered the door. She called Donna and Jerry's father, Joe, who soon arrived at the house as well. The names of those killed had been leaking out through the day, and they'd all seen the news footage. Nothing in the world could ease a family's pain over that. But seated at the dining room table, I told Donna and Joe that I'd met their son. That I thought if anyone could have survived this war, it was Jerry. I listened to their stories about him as a boy; I told them of my own sons. We talked about family, and loss, and Joan's battle with cancer. We prayed together. They were gracious, even in their profound grief.

As I left that night, I gave the Zovkos money for funeral expenses—it only seemed right. Blackwater matched the insurance funeral expense payout for each of those who were killed. Once the military released custody of the men's remains, a Blackwater representative met each of the families at Dover Air Force Base in Delaware, where DNA, dental, and medical records were evaluated and death certificates issued. We escorted the bodies from Dover to the designated funeral homes; that included sending one of our CASA C212s to Dover to fly Mike Teague's body home to Tennessee.

In the days following the attack, reporters contacted everyone. And soon, we heard, the grief-stricken homes were flooded with unrelenting phone calls. A member of the Helvenston family in Florida emailed us with a cell phone number "that we are giving out to family and friends in case anyone has to get through. We are attempting to prepare statements to give out in hopes [of getting] the press taken care of all at once." No luck. Two days after the killings, Helvenston's mother, Katy Helvenston-Wettengel, emailed us: "OK, we give up. Please have the police shoo the press away." So we did—Blackwater called the local cops and asked them to keep the reporters at bay.

We would have done that for anyone at Blackwater. The hours and stresses and life events each of us had endured the past six years had created an indelible bond among our team—and that extended to Wes and Jerry and Mike and Scott, and everyone who worked for us. They were part of the "family at Blackwater," as June Batalona described it in an email soon after her husband's death. "First of all, how do I start to thank you—all of you at Blackwater—for everything you have done to help me, and most of all [our daughter]?" she wrote. "My family is [in] awe just talking about Blackwater; they are so proud of each and every one of you, and believe me, we will never forget all of you. Please pass along our thanks to everyone, and I am so proud to be part of your family at Blackwater."

Everyone on our team enjoyed getting to know these families, even amid tragic circumstances. Patricia Irby, Scott Helvenston's ex-wife, emailed us about summer plans with their kids, and settling into a new house—even ideas for a pig roast. Six months later, when Irby wrote that she couldn't cash Scott's last paycheck of $9,000 because the family hadn't gotten an executor to the estate, but their children needed the money, we immediately issued a new check in her name. "If the estate comes after us for the $$, then so be it," reads one of our internal staff emails from the time. "It sounds like the kids need the money."

We remembered birthdays and anniversaries—and I fondly remember now the calls and thank-you notes in reply. Mike Teague's widow, Rhonda, sent Ana Bundy a short note after the observance of his birthday following his death. "I felt so touched that you guys remembered his birthday and us," she wrote. "I know he is not forgotten. Thank you for that." Blackwater's team even arranged for a condolence letter to be sent from Croatian prime minister Ivo Sanader to Jerry Zovko's parents. I felt that was important.

Ten days after the attack, I joined roughly eight hundred other people at the Cathedral of St. John the Evangelist in Cleveland to celebrate the former Ranger's life. The entrance procession, "Nearer My God," was sung in the family's native language by the St. Paul Croatian Church choir. They chose a reading from the second book of Maccabees, about a noble warrior who made peace with Arab nomads. Jerry's brother, Tom Zovko, told mourners, "He wanted to help the Iraqis, and he wanted to do it on their terms." The congregation then drove thirty-five miles to Ohio Western Reserve National Cemetery, where Jerry Zovko's remains were buried with full military honors. The service there included a seven-gun salute, two Army buglers, and a police bagpiper. The words "Proud," "Patriotic," "Strong," and "Brave" were carved into his granite headstone.

Six months later, with the families of the fallen by our sides, we dedicated a memorial garden at the Blackwater training center for Wes, Scott, Mike, and Jerry—and the others who would give their lives while working for us. It's a quiet place near the original Moyock lodge, where a pebbled footpath encircles a small pond. Large stones along the walk bear the names of the Blackwater dead. Benches and shade trees offer solitude. The entrance is marked by a life-size bronze sculpture of a boy clutching a folded American flag.

While Blackwater and the families of the fallen men dealt with grief and the practical details of funerals and estates, press coverage of the killing began to escalate. Initially, news reports simply described the slain men as civilians. Which was accurate: The four security contractors were hired by a private company and reported to corporate bosses. They certainly weren't riding in military vehicles. Furthermore, Blackwater's men weren't operating under the Pentagon's command structure; there had been no coordination with the Marines before heading into Fallujah, and there had been no help from the military after. But to the general public, "civilian" suggested something like Red Cross or UN personnel, or perhaps a contractor delivering the mail. Maybe crazy tourists. So the disconnect with the news footage was immediate: The Blackwater men were wearing body armor and carrying machine guns into insurgent strongholds, just like soldiers. They had elite military backgrounds and were working on behalf of the Defense Department's mission in Iraq. Tracked all the way back up the chain of subcontracts, the money ultimately flowed to them from the Pentagon. Article 3 of the Geneva Conventions clearly defines noncombatants in war zones as "persons taking no active part in the hostilities," which historically keeps those contractors on mail runs from being considered combatants. Yet had they had a moment to react that morning in Fallujah, the four Blackwater men would have become a very active part of the fight.

So they weren't combatants—but they weren't noncombatants. Batalona, Zovko, Helvenston, and Teague were civilians, but they were armed, ultimately at the behest of the DoD, pursuing dangerous missions. The four fell into a glaring gray area of international law that experts in Geneva and beyond have continued to debate for years.

At the same time, the relentless rolling of the awful footage seared my company's name into the public consciousness. As Joseph Neff, a reporter who would extensively cover the attack, later described it: "I first met the private security company Blackwater at the breakfast table on April 1, 2004. The *News & Observer*, the newspaper where I work in Raleigh, North Carolina, displayed a photo of a burning truck and an exultant mob on the front page; inside, there was an even grislier photo of a crowd, including children, cheering at the sight of two burnt corpses hanging from a bridge. I quietly pulled aside the front section, making sure my kids, six and nine at the time, stuck with the sports and comics."

People who previously hadn't known a thing about PMCs now had but one horrible scene—and one name—to associate with the industry. I have always been leery of the mainstream media—another thing that came from my father, who gave one newspaper interview about his company around 1980, felt he was misquoted, and basically said, "Never again." Suddenly, it seemed, the feeling was mutual. Rabid-left pundits and politicians who either didn't grasp the history of Blackwater's business or simply weren't interested in learning called my men "mercenaries." It was the start of my being labeled a war profiteer. It began a growing howl of inflammatory rhetoric that would, in the years that followed, drown out any sense of reasoned discussion.

The attack also had major political and military implications: Ambassador Bremer's CPA clearly hadn't managed to bring stability to entire cities in Iraq—yet the American public was to believe this was a country that would somehow be ready for handover three months later? Moreover, these were the chanting barbarians American troops had been sent to liberate? At home, President Bush was deep in his reelection battle with Senator John Kerry in March 2004—and that "Mission Accomplished" speech given nearly a year earlier looked more off base than ever. In Moyock, we wondered how the Pentagon might respond to the killing of our men; it was a question that was suddenly one part military planning, one part moral imperative, and one part reelection campaign gambit.

We had all watched, for the better part of a year, coalition forces trying to win the "hearts and minds" of Fallujans in hopes of promoting peace and security. U.S. troops had helped with infrastructure repairs, provided cash, and tried to build relationships with town officials. It never worked. Insurgents in the city had fought the coalition from the outset—with everything from violent attacks to petty insults. In one memorably odd incident, soldiers spent days building a new community soccer field in the city center, only to see insurgents rip down the goal nets, scrape the dirt off the field, and cover the site with garbage as soon as they left. "What kind of people loot dirt?" one soldier asked. Then, when the Marines relieved the 82nd Airborne in the Sunni Triangle, insurgents began spreading leaflets around town nicknaming the new troops "awat," a delicate cake that crumbles on contact.

The day before the attack on Blackwater's men, General James Conway, then commander of the 1st Marine Expeditionary Force, which was conducting counterinsurgency operations throughout the Sunni Triangle, had conceded, "Fallujah is probably our center of gravity. We know that there are more bad guys around Fallujah than anywhere else in our whole area of operations." After the atrocity on March 31, it was clear that some within the DoD would want to reduce the city to rubble.

On the other hand, we knew that Marines on the ground, who shared their superiors' disgust with the news footage, were hesitant about an all-out invasion. Conquering a ten-square-mile city is a massive undertaking, even for a force as well equipped as the American military. Additionally, available manpower would be limited to just two Marine infantry battalions and the two most combat-ready nearby ICDC battalions—far less than an overwhelming force for the deadly house-to-house slog of urban warfare. Further, a major military response would set a complicated precedent: Blackwater's "civilians" weren't staffing a hospital, after all—our men were carrying guns in a war zone. Would the Pentagon lay siege to a city of three hundred thousand to retaliate for the deaths of four armed contractors? Would it now exact vengeance upon anyone who harmed security contractors? The Marines, Conway would later explain, "felt . . . that we ought to probably let the situation settle before we appeared to be attacking out of revenge."

I didn't begrudge the Marines that. It's not the military's job to protect security contractors. Men and women in uniform have important jobs to do; my men were in Iraq supporting them. The truth is, I didn't expect the Pentagon to respond. But did everyone at Blackwater appreciate the consideration and camaraderie? Absolutely.

Among the most influential decision makers, the response to the killing of civilians was clear: President Bush was reportedly highly upset and emotional. Hours after the murder of Blackwater's men, Brigadier General Mark Kimmitt, the chief U.S. military spokesman in Iraq and a man not particularly given to sentimentality, told a roomful of reporters, "Somewhere out in this world there are going to be families who are getting knocks on the door from people telling them what happened to their loved ones. It is not pleasant to be on either side of that door, I can tell you." With Defense Secretary Donald Rumsfeld advocating harsh action in closed-door meetings, Kimmitt soon added that the military response would be "deliberate, it will be precise, and it will be overwhelming."

Less than twenty-four hours after the attack on Blackwater's men, the Phase IV rebuilding effort in Fallujah was no more. Assault plans were drawn up for the Marines and ICDC battalions to surround the city, then strike simultaneously from the southeast and northwest. They would be supported by tanks, helicopters, fighter jets, and massive AC130 Spectre gunships, the heavily weaponized cousins of C130 cargo haulers. Army lieutenant general Ricardo Sanchez, the overall commander of U.S. forces in Iraq, briefed the Marines on the decision to attack Fallujah. "The president knows this is going to be bloody," he said. "He accepts that."

As coalition forces took their positions on the outskirts of town, rebels from elsewhere in the Sunni Triangle and beyond took theirs, streaming into the city to help fortify the insurgency. On April 4, the Pentagon issued an ultimatum, demanding Fallujah's town elders turn over those responsible for murdering Blackwater's men. They refused.

Soon, half a world away, a condolence letter from Ambassador Bremer's office arrived in a mailbox outside Cleveland, at the home of Joe and Donna Zovko. "Rest assured that our authorities are actively investigating Jerry's murder and that we will not rest until those responsible are punished for this despicable crime," it read. "Your family will remain in our thoughts and prayers as you confront this terrible tragedy in the difficult days ahead. I will do my part to ensure Jerry's contribution to this county will be forever remembered by the Iraqi people."

On April 5, 2004, five days after the murder of Blackwater's men, the Pentagon unleashed hell upon Fallujah.

Operation Vigilant Resolve commenced with approximately two thousand total men, plus M1A1 tanks with seventeen-foot-long cannons that could hit targets from four thousand yards out; a lineup of tracked assault vehicles that carried eighteen Marines apiece; and a battery of M198 howitzers, the Marines' eight-ton cannons that can fire a variety of lethal munitions up to fourteen miles. The 1st Battalion, 5th Marine Regiment attacked from the southeast of the city, quickly capturing the industrial district. The 2nd Battalion, 1st Marine Regiment stormed into the residential Jolan district of northwest Fallujah, where they launched into thirty-six hours of sustained fighting against pockets of insurgents who fired at them from inside mosques and school buildings and defended their fortifications with rocket-propelled grenades and machine guns.

Lithe little Bell AH1W Cobra and heavier UH1N Huey helicopters fired Hellfire missiles at rebel strongholds. Fighter jets flew more than a hundred sorties, dropping dozens of laser-guided bombs on entrenched positions and destroying as many as seventy-five buildings. Marines in tanks on the ground called in nighttime strikes from the AC130 gunships, known to the men as "slayers," then thundered into downtown Fallujah as insurgents scattered. But hemmed in by the city's walled streets, Marine infantry squads advancing through town on foot faced hit-and-run attacks by Fallujah's two thousand insurgents, among them two hundred foreign fighters, mainly from Syria and Yemen, as well as former members of the Iraqi Special Republican Guard. The rebels hid among civilians and darted into neighborhood households.

Those homes, originally built to shield their residents from the scorching Iraqi summers, were generally made of concrete walls, and concrete roofs three feet thick, often with three more feet of dirt on top. Their front doors were either metal or wood doors protected by a locked metal gate. They were basically bunkers—and they all had to be cleared, room by room, in a bloody procession that led to the deaths of more than a dozen Marines and wounded almost a hundred others. It was the start of what would become, to that point, the deadliest month for U.S. forces in Iraq.

Some seven hundred insurgents were killed in the April 2004 offensive. Unfortunately, in the accelerated ramp-up to the attack, little planning was in place to prevent civilian casualties. After just days of fighting, the media—Arab outlets fed information by insurgents, while Western reporters faced kidnappings or beheadings in Fallujah—estimated total civilian deaths there as high as 700. The Iraqi minister of health estimated a far smaller number: 220. Neither is confirmable. Both are tragic. What is clear is that, as grisly imagery from the war zone spread across the country, Sunni members of the Iraqi Governing Council—the collection of political, religious, and tribal leaders advising Bremer's CPA—threatened to resign unless the ambassador initiated a cease-fire. Two months before the handover of power, democracy in Iraq stood at a perilous crossroads—and the message from the Governing Council was clear. So five days after the Marines began their siege of Fallujah, they were ordered to stop advancing. They pulled out of the city entirely three weeks later.

In the coming months, anti-American sentiment only deepened in the devastated City of Mosques. Fueled by news reports from the first assault, Fallujah grew into a staging ground for insurgent attacks across Iraq, which exploded from approximately two hundred per week at the start of 2004 to more than five hundred per week over that summer. By fall, it was clear to all of us in Moyock and beyond that if the Bush administration intended to ensure a secure first democratic election for the Iraqi people in January 2005, U.S. forces would have to return to the city.

On November 7, 2004, seven months after slinking out of Fallujah the first time—after Bush had been safely reelected at home and power in Iraq transferred from the CPA to the transitional government—as many as fifteen thousand U.S. troops launched their largest urban battle since Hue in Vietnam in 1968. They intended to finish what they started.

Operation Phantom Fury soon became one of the bloodiest single engagements of the Iraq War, as two armored Army battalions rolled heavy into the streets of Fallujah, rustling out insurgents for the four Marine infantry battalions that swept in behind. U.S. forces carried out hundreds of additional air strikes; between the two assaults on Fallujah, they unloaded enough munitions to damage or destroy roughly half the city's thirty-nine thousand buildings. After two days of intense battle, military officials announced that U.S. forces controlled 70 percent of the city. The rest was secured just over a week later. More than ninety soldiers died and more than five hundred were wounded. In their wake, U.S. forces left a bombed-out wasteland of approximately 1,350 dead insurgents—and, if studies are correct, a level of unrelenting toxicity in the flattened city that appears to have led to a staggering rise in birth defects there today.

On Sunday, November 14, 2004, Marines with 3rd Battalion, 5th Marine Regiment rolled away the bundles of concertina wire that had been spread along on the shore of the Euphrates. They became the first Americans to walk across Fallujah's infamous bridge since two of my men had been strung up on it nearly eight months before. Back in the States, it was an emotional time for our staff. We printed eight hundred Blackwater shirts with "3/5" embroidered on the sleeve as a thank-you to the Marines. "It's symbolic because the insurgents closed the bridge, and we reopened it," Major Todd Desgrosseilliers, the battalion's executive officer, told reporters.

In black marker, one of the Marines left a message on one of the bridge's green trestles: "This is for the Americans of Blackwater that were murdered here in 2004. Semper Fidelis 3/5."

"PS," it concluded. "Fuck you."

CHAPTER 9
BLACKWATER VERSUS THE MAHDI ARMY

2004

IN THE WEEKS LEADING UP TO BLACKWATER'S CONVOY THROUGH FALLUJAH,
Paul Bremer's attention had been increasingly drawn to a small
town far south of the Sunni hotbed called Najaf. Located just outside
the ancient Mesopotamian city of Babylon and its fabled hanging
gardens, Najaf was chosen as the final resting place of Ali ibn Abi
Talib, the cousin and son-in-law of the prophet Muhammad. In the
years following Muhammad's death in 632, Talib's rise through the
caliphate—the political and religious government of the early Muslim world—led to the major schism between the Sunni and Shia
branches of Islam. Today, Imam Talib remains Shia Islam's most re-
vered figure, and the massive, golden-domed mosque that houses his
tomb in Najaf is one of the world's holiest sites for the sect's hundreds of millions of followers.

When coalition forces invaded Iraq in 2003, Shias made up
roughly 60 percent of the country's population, dominating its
southern regions. Yet from nearly the moment modern-day Iraq was
created from the disintegrating Ottoman Empire at the end of World

War I, the country's Sunni contingent—about only 20 percent of its population—had dominated Iraqi politics, sometimes brutally suppressing sectarian dissension. Amid the turmoil of the occupation, Shia leaders in Najaf, home to more than a half million people, saw a chance to rebel—violently—against not only coalition forces but also decades of religious and political oppression. And by mid-2004, as the CPA faced its impending government handover, Bremer was largely focused on one particular Shia: Muqtada al-Sadr, the frumpy thirty-year-old commander of the nascent "Mahdi Army," a militia named for a messiah yet backed by Iranians who were anything but holy saviors.

Almost entirely unknown prior to the fall of Saddam Hussein's regime, al-Sadr is the son of Ayatollah Muhammad Sadiq al-Sadr, an outspoken critic of Hussein and one of the most powerful Shia clerics in Iraq during the late 1990s. The third of four sons, Muqtada al-Sadr has no grand educational background to speak of; he was once derided as "Ayatollah Atari" because of his love of video games. But he was smart enough to ride his famous father's coattails, and reportedly oversaw his family's security during the time of Muhammad Sadiq al-Sadr's heaviest criticisms of the Iraqi government. If that's true, however, he failed: On February 19, 1999, gunmen working for the Iraqi secret police killed the sixty-year-old and two of his sons, Mustafa and Muammal, as they left a mosque in the holy city of Kufa, right outside Najaf. Suddenly the twenty-five-year-old Muqtada al-Sadr was thrust into the lead of his father's swelling movement.

The amazing part? He pulled it off. While initially dismissed by fellow religious leaders as a *za'tut*, or ignorant child, al-Sadr had the famous ancestry that appealed to some educated Shias. At the same time, restless young men oppressed under Hussein's regime could relate to those dismissals, and they rallied behind al-Sadr's underdog scrappiness. The man wasn't known for nuance: Al-Sadr found his voice in lashing out against the U.S. presence—and anyone who disagreed with him, allegedly going so far as to orchestrate the murder of a rival Shia cleric, Abdul Majid al-Khoei, who had supported

the American overthrow of Hussein. Al-Sadr's was a social movement more than a religious one, and against much conventional wisdom, it was taking hold. "The most puzzling aspect of Muqtada's
ascent is that he possesses none of the more obvious criteria of political success and little that can account for the existence and resil-
ience of his social base," according to a report by the International
Crisis Group (ICG). "Although coming from a prominent family, he
is neither particularly charismatic nor a particularly adept speaker.
He does not enjoy the backing of a party apparatus. He has few religious credentials. By most accounts, even his material assets are
scanty."

While it was tempting to try to dismiss al-Sadr at first as a petty
rabble-rouser—that ICG report noted, "His critics, and even a few of
his allies, have accused [al-Sadr] of mental deficiency"—the cleric's
influence quickly became as unmistakable as it was unexpected. In
a show of force in the summer of 2003, al-Sadr cobbled together a
black-clad militia guided by the theology of his father, who'd declared that an army of believers would be led by the Shia messianic
figure Imam Mahdi. Supplied with guns, roadside bombs, and training by forces in the predominantly Shia Iran—which had great interest in helping shape the unfolding political climate in neighboring
Iraq—al-Sadr's Mahdi Army attacked Americans, they attacked
Sunnis, they even attacked rival Shia parties in the Iraqi government. "In the Najaf-Kufa area, al-Sadr's militia demonstrated better
structure and organization than the local government," according
to a 2004 Marine Corps battle study. "The militiamen roamed the
streets, set up roadblocks, and intimidated whomever they pleased.
On one occasion, al-Sadr's men kidnapped an Iraqi policeman and
tortured him while broadcasting the atrocity over a government
radio frequency."

Al-Sadr's terrorist group grew over the course of the U.S. occupation to include as many as sixty thousand disenfranchised fighters—
replacing al-Qaeda as the country's "most dangerous accelerant
of potentially self-sustaining sectarian violence," according to the

Pentagon. Amid the power vacuum in Iraq after the American invasion, this small-time cleric was beginning to cast quite a shadow over politics in his homeland, and by the spring of 2004 al-Sadr's influence was cause for alarm both in Baghdad and in Washington D.C.

In addition to following his firebrand speeches, Blackwater's security teams used to monitor the eight-page weekly newspaper, *al-Hawza*, that al-Sadr published for fifteen thousand readers. It was full of the expected propaganda and false reports—including a list of those al-Sadr labeled the "124 traitors," who'd cooperated with the coalition, leading to the immediate killing of two of them. One February 2004 article headlined "Bremer Follows in the Footsteps of Saddam" accused the CPA leader of deliberately starving Iraqi children. And when, a few weeks later, *al-Hawza* transcribed a fiery sermon from al-Sadr describing the September 11 attacks as "a miracle from God," the ambassador had heard enough. "We've got to shut that damned paper down," Bremer snapped. "I'm not going to tolerate this."

The CPA head ordered al-Sadr's paper closed for sixty days. On March 28, U.S. soldiers escorted the newspaper staff into the streets of Baghdad and padlocked chains on the doors.

The strategy backfired. I remember reading reports of hundreds of protestors rallying outside the newspaper offices for days. They held portraits of al-Sadr and chanted, "Just say the word, Muqtada—we'll resume the 1920 revolution!" The chants escalated from there: "Today is peaceful," they warned; "tomorrow will be military!"

Three days after the closing of the newspaper, the four Blackwater men were slaughtered by Sunni insurgents a hundred miles away in Fallujah. Taken together, the events ushered in confrontations on two fronts, and the most serious crisis the CPA would face in Iraq. "For the first time," Ali Allawi, Iraq's first postwar civilian minister of defense, wrote in his book *The Occupation of Iraq*, "important constituencies in both the Shia and Sunni communities simultaneously rose up in arms in two widely separate locations." Bremer later stated in a PBS inverview, "The Iraqi political system was on the brink of flying apart. The Sunni members of the Governing Council were outraged by the nightly broadcasts on Al Jazeera television, which were especially provocative about the civilian deaths in Fallujah [during Operation Vigilant Resolve]. The Shia were concerned about what was happening with Moqtada al-Sadr, because he was a Shia."

Believing an additional show of force—if of a different severity than was about to be meted out in Fallujah—was the only way to restore order in Baghdad, Bremer cracked down even harder on al-Sadr. On Saturday, April 3, coalition forces arrested the cleric's senior deputy, Mustafa al-Yaqubi, for his alleged connection to the killing a year earlier of rival cleric Abdul Majid al-Khoei. Now even further incensed, al-Sadr responded by loosing his protestors and army throughout southern Iraqi cities and towns, catching coalition forces off guard. Or at least certain members of the coalition: "The fledgling Iraqi police had no intention of stopping [al-Sadr's men]," reports Patrick Cockburn in his book *Muqtada*. "The security in important cities in southern Iraq was in the hands of Italian, Polish, Ukrainian, Salvadoran and Spanish troops sent there at the high tide of U.S. success in 2003 and whose governments had never expected them to fight."

The crux of al-Sadr's plan was to overrun Najaf, the Iraqi Shias' symbolic capital. From there, he would demand al-Yaqubi's freedom.

No U.S. combat unit served in Najaf at the time; the few uniformed Americans in the city were communications technicians. Security there was the responsibility of the Spanish army, which in turn commanded small contingents of troops from El Salvador, Honduras, and the Dominican Republic. But the safety of the CPA headquarters there—and the State Department's Philip Kosnett, the top coalition official in Najaf—was the responsibility of eight men from Blackwater, who in early April 2004 were about to rewrite the rules of the contractor-combatant relationship.

As the sun rose over Najaf on April 4, busloads of Shia protestors flooded the city and overwhelmed Spanish forces, who didn't exactly try to stop them. Spain's thirteen hundred soldiers in and around Najaf were officially on a civil support mission, helping farmers irrigate their land and helping local justices set up court systems. They had their own atrocity on their minds: Three weeks earlier, al-Qaeda had murdered 191 people in the Madrid train bombings, the worst Islamic terrorist attack in European history. More attacks were threatened unless the Spanish troops were pulled from Iraq. And three days after the bombing, in a surprise upset in Spain's national elections, Socialist José Luis Rodríguez Zapatero defeated conservative People's Party candidate Mariano Rajoy to become prime minister.

Zapatero's first move after taking office was to make good on his campaign promise to withdraw Spain's troops from Iraq. And quite clearly, none of the Spaniards in Najaf that April morning wanted to risk getting shot a few weeks before leaving the war zone. They were "security" in name only.

Similarly, the local Iraqi police remained indifferent to the throng sweeping through the city. And in no time at all, nearly one thousand of al-Sadr's protestors flowed through to the northeast corner of Najaf and up to the main gates of the regional CPA headquarters. Inside, Kosnett and his Blackwater detail began considering their options.

The aerial photos of the compound Blackwater used to plan our security procedures showed government offices occupying a small building at one end of the city's as yet unfinished Kufa University complex. That complex sat midway between the built-up, relatively metropolitan infrastructure of Kufa and Najaf. The whole area surrounding Kosnett's walled compound was flat and beige, with patches of scrubby grass and a few stubborn trees. At the time, almost no structure in or around the complex was taller than two stories; the whole spread was mostly a rat's nest of exposed rebar that jutted out from the half-built shells of concrete school buildings to come. The tallest structure in the area, the university's eight-story teaching hospital, sat a third of a mile across the street from the front gate, gazing down upon the rooftops and courtyards of the compound.

Officials in the CPA offices could hear the chanting from the growing crowd at the gate. The anger was palpable; it was only a matter of time before a spark ignited the crowd. As the team responsible for Kosnett's security, Blackwater's guards advised the regional CPA head of the obvious: Now might be a good time to leave. Our men were not contracted, authorized, staffed, nor armed and equipped to engage in any sort of offensive operations. Quelling rebellions was the military's job. As a defensive security unit, Blackwater's duty was to protect the principal—and from that standpoint, the safest option is not be there when an attack begins. "Get off the X," we drilled into our contractors: The first plan should always be to avoid the spot the militants plan to assault. Holding one's ground in a shoot-out is almost always the last.

Kosnett, on the other hand, was a career diplomat who'd volunteered to be there. "I had joined the [State Department's] Foreign Service to serve my country when called," he later recounted. "Iraq was center stage; I wanted to contribute." In Iraq for only three months at that point, Kosnett had already survived one attack outside Najaf, when nearly two dozen insurgents ambushed the diplomat's convoy on a ride in from Baghdad, only to be fought off by his El Salvadoran escorts. Choppering out of the city at that point would effectively hand al-Sadr the CPA offices—and the city—and Kosnett refused to be run off his post by a mob. "Our union is fond of saying that more American ambassadors have died in action than American generals since the end of World War II," Kosnett said. "There's more to being a modern American diplomat than conference tables and cocktail parties."

Just after eleven a.m., Blackwater's team, led by a middle-aged former Navy SEAL named Chris White, caught an early lunch with CPA staff, a few Salvadoran soldiers, and two members from Bravo Company of the Alabama National Guard's 711th Signal Battalion. One of those National Guardsmen, Specialist Michael Acquaviva, was installing communications networks at the base. Meanwhile, behind the CPA building a small team of Marines had just finished wiring a base station radio in the Spanish force's headquarters. Corporal Lonnie Young, a burly twenty-five-year-old Defense Messaging System administrator from Dry Ridge, Kentucky, reckoned he had a few minutes before chow time, so the Marine climbed into the backseat of his truck for a quick nap.

Outside the front gates, al-Sadr's crowd continued to demand freedom for al-Yaqubi. Then, around eleven twenty-five a.m., a very different sound rang out from the road: Bursts of AK-47 fire echoed though the complex as bullets rattled off the concrete buildings. The protest was no longer peaceful—and instantly everyone was on the move.

Blackwater's team rushed the CPA personnel out of the cafeteria and into their fortified section of the complex. The guards grabbed their body armor, whatever ammunition they could carry, and their government-issued weapons. Mostly that meant M4 carbines, a descendant of the famous M16 assault rifle with a short barrel that makes it easy to handle on security details. But it's not something you'd choose to defend a compound with: Beyond about a thousand feet, accuracy becomes a problem for the M4, especially with moving targets—and a thousand feet doesn't feel like nearly enough space between you and an angry militia. A few of the carbines had attached M203s, single-shot 40-mm grenade launchers that would scatter the crowd—but they weren't especially practical at longer ranges, either.

As they gathered their gear, my men noticed Acquaviva had brought with him an M249 squad automatic weapon (SAW)—a belt-fed, bipod-mounted light machine gun that can rip off eight hundred rounds per minute. The Guardsmen heard reports of potential unrest in the area, Acquaviva said; just in case, he'd packed a weapon perfect for long-range suppressive fire. It was strongly recommended the Guardsmen come along, and the growing security team raced around the corner in a Humvee to the two-story CPA building, picking up a few Salvadoran soldiers along the way. They headed for the roof; soon Young, who'd been jarred awake by sounds of gunfire, was roaring up the steps behind them, his own SAW in hand.

Eight Blackwater men and the handful of coalition troops spread out around the satellite dishes and ventilation systems on the CPA roof until they had a 360-degree view of the city. That roof was actually made up of two adjoining rooftops that met at a central, reinforced tower that encased the stairwell. A short sand-colored wall ran along the perimeter, offering a protected vantage point to monitor the gathering crowd. But there was no cover from above. The men remained vulnerable to surveillance from the hospital tower beyond, and as the Mahdi Army overtook government installations in its march across the city that morning, Blackwater's men would soon learn they had also overrun the health care facility, turning a 450-bed hospital into a sniper's nest.

Suddenly, more unrest in the street—and the sickening sound of an explosion. Four Salvadoran soldiers rushing back into the compound were mobbed outside the front gate. The men were ripped from their truck, beaten by the crowd—and then members of al-Sadr's army reportedly forced a grenade into the mouth of one of the young Salvadoran soldiers and pulled the pin. Less than fifteen hundred feet from the coalition position, the protest had deteriorated into frenzy.

Through his gun aperture, Young watched men spill out from a Mahdi truck, then run to shooting locations on the street below. They were clad in white robes, customary Iraqi burial dress. They had come to fight to the death. "One of the Iraqis quickly dropped down into a prone position and fired several rounds at us," Young would later recount in a local newspaper interview. "I started yelling that I had [a target] in my sights and asking if I could engage. '*With your permission, sir, I have acquired a target!*'" He yelled again, "*With your permission, sir, I have acquired a target!*"

But there was no commanding officer to answer his call.

The twenty-five-year-old communications specialist would later say that as the only American in uniform on his part of the rooftop, his first inclination upon bursting from the stairwell was to call out orders to the contractors around him. "But I realized real quick that these guys knew what they were doing," he said. "I was up there within thirty seconds of the first incoming [shots], and Blackwater was already there—binoculars out, weapons locked on, picking out targets. So instead of telling them what to do, I started working with them."

It was a smart decision: Half the Blackwater men atop the CPA building that day were former Navy SEALs. The rest were veterans of other military and police special operations units. They formed by far the most highly trained team—civilian or military, of any nationality—in Najaf. It also marked the first time in memory that private contractors commanded active U.S. military personnel—in the midst of a firefight, no less.

Blackwater's men gave Young permission to commence firing. The Marine leveled his sights on the shooter in white, who was now sprinting for cover. He fired a short burst of 5.56-mm rounds, then watched the man fall to the pavement. "I stopped for a second," Young remembered, "and raised my head from my gun to watch the man lay in the street motionless."

Acquaviva took a position along the wall next to the Marine; on the National Guardsman's other side was an Army captain, Matthew Eddy. Blackwater's men instructed Acquaviva to cover an arc from eleven to three on the clock dial, corresponding with the road ahead, over to the southwest corner of the hospital building. Below him, Iraqi rebels were trying to crash through the wall of the CPA compound. Rocket-propelled grenades hissed over the rooftop; Blackwater's contractors were beginning to pick off targets within range. The forty-three-year-old Acquaviva had never been in a firefight before— back at home, just north of Birmingham, the specialist had been a heavy machinery operator on construction sites for the Cullman County Road Department. *This is too surreal*, he thought, as if he'd just stepped into some big-budget war movie.

He spied buses in the distance unloading more Iraqis. Acquaviva could see they were all armed. He focused his machine gun at the reinforcements 650 feet away—and for the first time in his career, was ordered to fire. "When I first had to pull that trigger, it took a moment," Acquaviva later told a reporter. "You look at these people and you know you're about to take the life of one or several of them. So I hesitated for what seemed like an eternity but was just a split second. But once a bullet whizzed by and I heard it ricochet off the roof, I just fell back on my training and did what I had to do." The communications technician single-handedly destroyed the busload of Mahdi Army soldiers. *Eliminate the threat*, Acquaviva kept telling himself. *Eliminate the threat.*

He and Young unloaded belt after belt of ammunition at the militia convoys in the distance. As insurgents rushed closer to the gate, they were met by Blackwater's grenade launchers. Soon, however, the threat also came from above, as a sniper on the fifth floor of the hospital found his range with a Russian-made Dragunov rifle—nearly four feet in length, the slender weapon is deadly from three-quarters of a mile away. With a short scream, Eddy, the Army captain, suddenly collapsed on the rooftop between Young and Acquaviva. The sniper had hit Eddy sideways through his left arm, chest, and back, a 7.62-mm round knifing in behind his Interceptor body armor. Acquaviva lunged for him—just as another sniper round cracked into a tin air duct where his head had been an instant before.

At the captain's side, Acquaviva and Young unhooked the buttons and heavy Velcro on the front of Eddy's vest, then cut a long diagonal hunk off his brown T-shirt underneath. The captain was alive, but blood poured from his arm and back, pooling beneath them on the gray cement tiles. Young grabbed gauze pads from the medical kit on his own vest; Acquaviva forced them down onto the wounds to stanch the bleeding.

One of Blackwater's gunners, Donald Roby, a former Navy SEAL medic who went by the call sign "Doc," screamed from the edge of the stairwell: Young and Acquaviva had to get the captain off the rooftop. "We came up with a plan," Young remembered. "[Eddy] said that he could run, so I put his right arm around my neck and called for covering fire. I heard everybody firing their weapons rapidly as we made our run for the door." The burly Marine hauled the captain down a flight of stairs to the makeshift medical room that had been established on the first floor. From there, Young dashed across the base to Blackwater's ammunition supply room, strapped on 150 pounds of ammunition, and raced back to the action on the rooftop.

Young dropped the supplies for the contractors, but no sooner had he found his familiar position on the wall than the Dragunov in the hospital coughed again and a sharp *crack* buckled Blackwater's Arabic linguist right beside him. Blood shot out from the contractor's face. Again, Young leaped to a fallen man's side, but this time, applying pressure to the quarter-size hole in the linguist's jaw did no good. Blood spilled out between Young's fingers. "I thought to myself that his carotid artery had to be cut," Young said. "Using my index finger, I reached inside the hole and began to feel around. It took a few seconds to find it, but finally I felt something like a large vein. I wrapped my finger around it and pinched as hard as I could."

With his free hand, Young grabbed hold of the contractor's body armor and began dragging him toward the stairwell. Bullets ricocheted off the rooftop around them—and then another *crack* floored the Marine. A round, probably from the gunman in the hospital, had hit him on his left shoulder just outside his armored vest, drilled into his back behind his heart, and stopped an inch from his spine.

Battling pain like he'd never felt before and a left eye suddenly swollen shut by shrapnel, Young forced himself off the ground and looked around. "I knew that I heard the unmistakable *smack*, but no one appeared to be shot," he said. With adrenaline surging, the Marine grabbed the wounded contractor and finished dragging him to safety behind a concrete air duct. Blackwater's "Doc" came sliding in from the other side, pouring coagulant powder on the translator's gaping jaw wound. Then, once more, Young hauled the wounded man downstairs to the medical area; again he lugged ammunition back to the rooftop, where round after round was fired by the contractors in a deafening haze.

The team needed to take out the sniper. One of Blackwater's men, Eric Saxon, a former Navy SEAL who went by the call sign "Pyro," pointed at the hospital and yelled for a Salvadoran soldier to fire a grenade. But the shooter above was ready, and as the Salvadoran took aim, a round from the sniper's Dragunov caught him in the face. One of Blackwater's men swept in and pulled the wounded soldier to safety; Pyro picked up the gun and finished the job: With a hollow *thoonk* from the grenade launcher, followed moments later by an orange flash and a debris cloud from the hospital's fifth floor, the sniper fell silent.

For that moment, everyone exhaled. Looking at the blood smeared across the rooftop and the innumerable shell casings collecting at the defense's feet, Acquaviva couldn't help but do the math: "Here [we] just got three people shot in two minutes," he remembered thinking. "And if three people got shot in two minutes, then in less than fifteen minutes all of us could be gone."

Those SAWs were chewing through so much ammunition, Acquaviva and Young had to take breaks every few minutes to make sure they didn't melt their gun barrels. Yet for every Iraqi who fell outside the gate, nearly a dozen more seemed to climb over the bodies. Another sniper would be perched in the hospital soon enough. The men atop the CPA took count of their remaining ammunition and looked at each other: one magazine each.

As the National Guardsman turned his SAW back toward the militia below, the question began to pound in his mind: *Are you going home?*

It was lunchtime in Baghdad's Green Zone when word of the demonstrations across southern Iraq reached Bremer and our Blackwater managers. The ambassador had been reading a report about the apprehension of al-Yaqubi, al-Sadr's lieutenant, when an urgent call came in from Ricardo Sanchez, the top U.S. commander in Iraq. "All hell is breaking loose with Muqtada," Sanchez told Bremer. "We're getting reports from a lot of different sectors.... Demonstrators flooding the streets. A lot of them carrying AKs and RPGs." Soon, a second call from Sanchez: "Muqtada's people are really swarming around our bases, especially in Sadr City and down in Najaf. They seem to think they can get the Spanish to cave in."

The Mahdi Army had reason to believe it: The Spanish in Najaf hadn't agreed with the coalition move to arrest al-Yaqubi—and, apparently under political direction from Madrid, the Spaniards tried to distance themselves from the confrontation. As Bremer later wrote in his daily journal, "This morning, the Spanish put out an idiotic statement about the Yaqubi arrest, saying that the Spanish did not conduct the operation, that it was done by 'the Coalition from Baghdad,' and that it was for Yaqubi's part in the killing of an American soldier. I've instructed [CPA spokesman] Dan Senor to have the Ministry of Interior put out a statement that Yaqubi was arrested on an Iraqi arrest warrant for the murder of Ayatollah Khoei. The Spanish statement should be disavowed root and branch."

By twelve forty-five p.m., the word reaching Baghdad was far more threatening than mere demonstrations. Hundreds of militants were attacking the CPA compound in Najaf, Bremer was told, and CPA region chief Kosnett needed Army gunships and reinforcements on the ground. The ambassador became livid that the Spanish army was, as he put it, "refusing to fight." He wrote in his memoirs, "I got Sanchez's deputy Maj. Gen. Joe Weber down here and asked what they are doing to reinforce the CPA in Najaf. I said I thought CJTF [Combined Joint Task Force] should relieve the Spanish commander forthwith. I called the Spanish ambassador and gave him unshirted hell."

At that same time, Blackwater's men were issuing their own urgent call to Baghdad—to the head of Bremer's security, Frank Gallagher. The CPA compound in Najaf was in danger of being overrun, they told Gallagher. They needed more ammunition and more men—probably extraction capabilities for CPA officials, and evacuation capabilities for wounded soldiers. The word from the Army was that they'd have to hold tight for a few more *hours* until help arrived. That wasn't possible.

Gallagher told them he understood—and immediately called Steven "Hacksaw" Chilton.

Blackwater's top helicopter pilot in Iraq, Chilton was another esteemed veteran of the Night Stalkers—and now a proud "Ass Monkey." That radio call sign came from Bremer's Blackwater security team on the ground, who gave their hotshot pilot brethren a good-natured hard time because of all the time those pilots spent sitting around their hangars waiting to scramble. Mounted outside the Ass Monkeys' trailer at LZ Washington, the landing zone inside Baghdad's Green Zone that the pilots called home, Chilton had responded with a sign displaying the Ass Monkeys' unofficial motto: "Fuck you—we already have enough friends." And Chilton was about to leave no doubt why you didn't want them as enemies.

Hacksaw coordinated the planning of a route to the stricken city, putting all Blackwater helicopters on standby for the mission. This was a highly unusual development; every bit of paperwork with the State Department stipulated that those Little Birds were in Baghdad for Bremer's protection detail. Nothing in our contracts said anything about military rescue or resupply operations—though, technically, our men reasoned, nothing explicitly forbade it, either. The horrors of Fallujah were fresh in everyone's minds—so much so that when Gallagher put out the word that Americans were in trouble in Najaf, more Blackwater personnel volunteered to go than our four-man helicopters could carry. Bremer also didn't need persuasion to free up the Little Birds. "Gentlemen, I've got nothing until eight o'clock tomorrow morning," he said. "Do what you need to do."

There was one more person who had to sign off. Since the aircraft weren't U.S. government property, Bremer's security detail had to ask permission from their owner. Gallagher called the local air boss, who called Richard Pere, our aviation chief, in Moyock, who called me in Virginia just shy of five a.m. "Our guys in Najaf are in a bad way," Pere said. "Can we send the Little Birds in to help them?"

"Of course," I said. "Send everything you've got."

"They're not insured," Pere replied.

"Doesn't matter," I said. "Send 'em in."

On the CPA rooftop in Najaf, the firefight was well into its second hour when Young felt a tug at his back. It was one of Blackwater's men, getting Young's attention to ask about the blood pooling at the young man's feet. Together, they unfastened Young's body armor, then slashed off half his stained green T-shirt with a Ka-Bar combat knife, exposing the garish wound on his left shoulder. By the time Young made it downstairs to the makeshift infirmary, his head was spinning and his body temperature had spiked. Doctors knew he needed to be evacuated as soon as possible. Luckily, the Little Birds were already inbound, loaded down with food, water, medical supplies, two dozen additional weapons, and thousands of rounds of ammunition. "And this is before we put all the personal weapons and gear in," Travis Haley, a Blackwater door gunner who'd previously spent fifteen years in the Marines' Special Operations Regiment, later recalled. "The pilots were worried we would have trouble getting off the ground."

By two p.m., General Sanchez alerted Bremer that Army AH64 Apache attack helicopters and Air Force fighter jets had been sent to Najaf to provide air support for the men on the rooftop. For Blackwater's pilots, that meant flying into a combat zone where massive military airpower was engaging the enemy—which would be particularly harrowing if our civilian airmen couldn't communicate with those pilots. Our team of Little Birds stopped en route to Najaf at the coalition's Camp Babylon, situated at the historic archaeological site, to top off their fuel tanks and learn the possible radio frequencies being used by the Apaches. Then, five miles outside of Najaf, Hacksaw made contact with "Attack 6," an Army gunship that paused its blasting of militia targets long enough to offer cover for Blackwater's arrival.

Hacksaw set his helicopter down in a dusty parking area behind the CPA facility; the other two Little Birds circled the rooftops—so close their skids nearly scraped the perimeter wall—and dropped their bundles of gear. Then they, too, set down next to Hacksaw's Little Bird, at which point Haley deplaned with his sniper rifle and sprinted up to the rooftop.

At the makeshift infirmary, Blackwater's men from Baghdad tried to coordinate an Army evacuation for Young. But the military contended the fighting was too fierce to send in one of its medevac teams—unfortunately, the wounded men, the Army said, were on their own. So Hacksaw took charge, in a surreal scene for everyone involved. As the former Night Stalker fired up his Little Bird, the woozy Marine was helped out of the infirmary, surely wondering what was going on. He found no heavily armored military chopper waiting for him; rather, he saw Blackwater's trio of unarmored, open-doored navy-and-silver helicopters. Hacksaw ordered him into the passenger seat. "I felt very nervous as we took off from the ground," Young later remembered. "I didn't have any body armor at all, nor did I have a weapon. I looked all around the base and saw that everybody was firing their weapons. I felt almost helpless sitting there."

From the CPA rooftop, Acquaviva laid down yet another blanket of suppressive fire as Hacksaw lifted away from the compound. The restocked defensive team on the roof followed suit—and in the process, Haley, the Blackwater marksman, found himself the star of a video that would soon spread across the Internet and make him famous on military fan sites and message boards.

In the footage, Haley crouches in a corner, shaded on his right by the roof's central tower. His orange earplugs stand out amid the beige of the building, his beige T-shirt, and his beige backward baseball cap. Extra ammunition sits on the wall within arm's reach. He's peering through the scope mounted atop his rifle, which is steadied on the sunbaked perimeter wall. "Guy on the wall runnin'?" Haley asks his spotter.

"Yup."

Haley's gloved trigger finger twitches. *Boom! Boom! Boom!*
Silence.

Haley ejects the empty magazine and grabs a fresh one off the wall. Back to the scope. "We got a big group comin'," he says. "On the wall, squeezin' off." *Boom! Boom!* He shifts his aim slightly. *Boom!*

"Wow," the spotter says. "You got a whole group of 'em."

More shots. A calm exhale from the Blackwater sniper. It almost sounds like a casual whistle.

When the attack began, insurgents "were just coming straight on at first, and as they got suppressed they would get smart and stay out of range," Haley later recalled. "Then I hopped on the [special purpose rifle] and took that advantage away from them." In the video, the spotter can be heard coordinating with the other Blackwater men in the area as Haley clears militia hiding spots half a mile away: "We've got a bunch of bad guys at twelve o'clock, eight hundred meters from Building Two," the spotter says into his radio. "We've got about fifteen of 'em on the run up here."

Quickly, insurgents abandoned their earlier positions and attempted flanking maneuvers around the camp's perimeter. Shooters in flowing robes darted out from behind trees and walls, fired wildly for a moment, then sprinted off again. "You could sit there and watch them run out and spray-and-pray," Haley said. Which isn't to say they couldn't get lucky: "We did have mortar fire on the CPA, [and] one of the rounds hit right behind us [about fifteen feet away]—but was a dud," Blackwater's sniper said. "You should have seen the looks on our faces after that one."

Soon the men on the rooftop identified reinforcements in the distance. In the video, Haley can be heard asking, "The guy with the green flag?" There's a surge of adrenaline across the rooftop. "That's Mahdi Army! Green flag is Mahdi Army!" says the spotter. "They're to be engaged at any opportunity."

Boom! Boom! Boom! Boom! Boom!

To Haley's left, a volley of shots erupts from Blackwater M4s, flinging empty shell casings through the air. "They're taking cover," says the spotter. "OK, there's one—looks like he's got an RPG. You see him?"

"Yeah, I got him," Haley says.

Boom! Then a crackle in the distance.

"That's return fire coming back at us," the spotter points out.

"Yeah," Haley says, "they're shootin' back." He barely seems to have a care in the world.

By four p.m., the worst of it was over.

Hacksaw returned to Najaf after his medevac run, his Little Bird again heavy with extra ammunition. Thankfully, enough had already been spent. By midafternoon, al-Sadr had instructed his supporters to cease demonstrations throughout southern Iraq, calling them futile—and instead issuing a new order: "Terrorize your enemy," he said. "Allah will reward you well for what pleases him." As the message reached Najaf, the crowd dispersed and Blackwater's men began cautiously leaving the rooftop. At least one sniper remained in the hospital tower, but he was soon ferreted out by El Salvadoran soldiers. The U.S. Special Forces were en route to supplement the defensive power at the compound and ward off any return by the Mahdi Army.

Soon Lieutenant General Sanchez himself arrived aboard a Blackhawk, along with Brigadier General Mark Kimmitt, to survey the scene. Sanchez was escorted to the roof, where empty intravenous bottles and a pool of blood greeted him as he stepped through the doorway.

The general would later recount that he saw an unnamed private and a sergeant—perhaps the National Guardsmen—huddled behind the roof's perimeter wall, shielded from the sniper in the hospital. In his 2008 memoir, *Wiser in Battle: A Soldier's Story*, Sanchez says he raced across the rooftop and dropped down next to the sergeant, who appeared rather stunned that a three-star general had suddenly plopped down beside him. The sergeant told the general that they had been unsuccessful in getting the sniper, but that another unit was inside the medical building to outflank him. The mob that had been outside, the sergeant added, was now gone. Sanchez directed the soldiers to cover him by firing at the hospital tower, and he disappeared down the stairs. "During the time General Sanchez was departing the building, he noticed me as I was headed for the roof and thanked us for quickly responding and supporting his troops," Hacksaw recorded in his after-action report. "His comment, while shaking his head, was, 'Blackwater, I should have known. Good job.'"

But that wasn't the version that would be told to the world. Less than twenty-four hours later, Kimmitt detailed for reporters in Baghdad some of the events that had unfolded in Najaf. The *Washington Post* reported, "Without commenting at a news conference yesterday on the role of the Blackwater guards, Kimmitt described what he saw after the fighting ended. 'I know on a rooftop yesterday in Najaf, with a small group of American soldiers and coalition soldiers . . . who had just been through about three and a half hours of combat, I looked in their eyes, there was no crisis. They knew what they were here for. They'd lost three wounded. We were sitting there among the bullet shells—the bullet casings—and, frankly, the blood of their comrades, and they were absolutely confident.'" No credit for or mention of Blackwater.

Accompanying the article, above the fold on page one, the *Post* ran a dramatic photo of our men on the rooftop, alongside the young Marine. In the photo, Chris White, Blackwater's team leader in Najaf, was wearing a polo shirt and sunglasses—but no body armor. I phoned him immediately: "Chris, I just saw your picture in the paper," I said. "Where the hell was your body armor?"

"Boss, we were eating when the shooting started," he said. "I threw my armor on Kosnett and told him to get downstairs and wait till it was over." Blackwater's team leader had gone through a four-hour battle unprotected.

In the years since the Najaf firefight, swipes from Pentagon brass against the men who saved their own soldiers would continue.

Lieutenant General Sanchez, in particular, has begun telling a confounding version of the events since his retirement from the Army. In his book, the general writes that he initially sent air support to Najaf in response to frantic radio reports from a Marine major who said that he and his men were under heavy attack and had been abandoned by Spanish forces. But Sanchez claims that when that air support flew over the area, they saw no enemies at all. The general writes that he radioed the major back for confirmation, and again was told, "Fighting everywhere. This may be the last radio call we can make before we get overrun. Send help." That inconsistency, Sanchez says, is what prompted him to visit in person.

The general then writes that while on the ground in Najaf, the Spanish commander dismissed the Marine's version of events. "Those Blackwater and CPA guys wanted us to put all of our troops back and surround their building," Sanchez says he was told. "But we didn't need to do that, because there was never any threat of being overrun." Sanchez writes that he then assured the Marine major in person that the compound had not, in fact, been under attack by a violent mob, that the Spanish had not folded in the face of conflict, and that they were never in any real danger. "Those [Blackwater] civilians were not providing you with accurate information," Sanchez told him. Upon returning to Baghdad's Green Zone, the general says, he briefed Bremer. "Although the Ambassador didn't want to believe it," Sanchez writes, "what had really happened was that the CPA personnel had panicked [at the sound of gunfire] and the Blackwater civilians were aggravating the situation by having the young major relay bogus information."

It's a baffling story that flies in the face of the evidence, and one I still don't understand. Perhaps Sanchez is angry that our actions that day made him look ineffective, or as if he'd lost control of the situation in Iraq. The general was ultimately in charge of security and stability there, after all, and a crucial outpost would have been overrun had it not been for a handful of Blackwater's men and our Little Birds. The first sentence of that front-page *Washington Post* article said it quite plainly: "An attack by hundreds of Iraqi militia members on the U.S. government's headquarters in Najaf on Sunday was repulsed not by the U.S. military, but by eight commandos from a private security firm, according to sources familiar with the incident."

Not only that, but Sanchez hadn't been able to get Army resources to the area for hours after the first shots were fired. He couldn't evacuate wounded military. And maybe the general is resentful of the fact that Blackwater's men on that rooftop proved that they didn't exactly need his help. As Phil Carter, a former military policeman and civil affairs officer with the Army, described it on his *Intel Dump* blog: "So these [Blackwater] guys work for the U.S. government, but not for the CPA and CJTF [Combined Joint Task Force] chain of command? ... What are these contractors doing that they have this much firepower, and a friggin' helicopter of their own? And what kind of command system does CPA and CJTF have that they had zero visibility of this incident until presumably the *Washington Post* reported on it?" Blackwater's vice president at the time, Patrick Toohey, drove the point home soon after in an interview with the *New York Times*. "This is a whole new issue in military affairs," he said. "Think about it: You're actually contracting civilians to do military-like duties."

Maybe Sanchez remains bitter at contractors in general, for the events in Najaf, or the military and political fallout in Fallujah, or because the general's three-decade military career came crashing down in June 2004 thanks to the infamous Abu Ghraib scandal, in which Iraqi detainees at the prison outside Baghdad suffered torture and sexual abuse at the hands of U.S. soldiers and contract interrogators from CACI International and Titan Corp. (A July 2004 report by the Army's inspector general found, "Of the contract interrogators in Operation Iraqi Freedom (OIF), 35% (11 of 31) had not received formal training in military interrogation techniques, policy, and doctrine," much less background in international law.) Several military personnel were ultimately convicted of the abuses, while lawsuits against the contractors still continue to wind their way through the court system nine years later. Sanchez was replaced as commander almost immediately after photos of the abuse shocked the American public. He has since said that Abu Ghraib was "the key reason, the sole reason, that I was forced to retire."

Had I known what the general would ultimately say about Blackwater, I would have gotten to the bottom of it myself when I met him at a U.S. Army dinner in Virginia shortly before his book was published. I wasn't impressed. Regardless, the general's account is directly refuted not only by Blackwater's men on the ground, but by the very military branches he once oversaw.

The Marines recognized Corporal Lonnie Young with a Purple Heart and a Bronze Star with Valor, which is awarded for heroism in combat. The Army also awarded Specialist Michael Acquaviva a Bronze Star with Valor. Blackwater's contractors in Najaf weren't up for any medals; they simply kept their heads down and prepared for the next mission.

Meanwhile, back at LZ Washington in Baghdad, the Ass Monkeys still weren't looking for new friends—though that part was getting harder. The morning after his makeshift medevac of Young, Hacksaw had a visitor at his hangar. It was a youthful Marine who had come to say thanks for helping out a fellow leatherneck. Knowing that Blackwater's team would always come for a man in trouble meant a lot, he said. He just wanted to shake Chilton's hand. As Hacksaw obliged, he could see over the Marine's shoulder that a crowd of tan uniforms and green T-shirts was flowing toward the Blackwater staging area. Chilton shook nearly a thousand hands that day.

CHAPTER 10
THE RULES OF THE ROAD
2004-2005

THREE MONTHS AFTER THE BATTLE IN NAJAF, THE COALITION PROVISIONAL Authority disbanded with the handover of power, and the United States established diplomatic relations with a newly sovereign Iraq. Under United Nations Resolution 1546, federal power in the powder keg of a country passed to temporary prime minister Ayad Allawi and his Interim Iraqi Government. Their main job was to ensure that a democratic national election—in which Iraqis would vote for a National Assembly, which would then select a president, prime minister, and cabinet—was held no later than January 2005.

With the transition, the key American figure in Baghdad was no longer Paul Bremer, but sixty-four-year-old John D. Negroponte, the newly appointed U.S. ambassador to Iraq. The veteran diplomat was responsible for overseeing a new U.S. embassy, established in Saddam Hussein's former presidential palace in the Green Zone. The embassy was to be staffed by approximately one thousand Americans reporting to nearly a dozen government agencies, including the Departments of State, Defense, Agriculture, Commerce, and Homeland

Security, as well as USAID and others. It was the largest U.S. embassy anywhere in the world. "It has been thirteen years since the American flag was last lowered at the United States Embassy in Baghdad, on a day as dark as today is bright," Negroponte said at the embassy's opening on June 30, 2004. "This afternoon we have the honor to once again see Old Glory back where she belongs."

The crucial question was how to keep the American personnel safe. The core of the Green Zone, including the presidential palace, was surrounded by blastproof concrete barricades, razor wire, and a raft of guarded checkpoints. But the State Department's job can't be conducted by "a thousand people hunkered behind sandbags," as former U.S. ambassador to Iraq Edward L. Peck put it. Indeed, at the time the United States transitioned to a bilateral relationship with the Iraqi government, Americans had overseen the creation, training, and advisement of 18 governorate councils, 90 district councils, 194 city councils, 445 neighborhood councils, and more than a dozen national ministries across the country, according to then deputy secretary of state Richard Armitage. There was much coordination to be done outside the protection of the "Emerald City," as some called the Green Zone—and no one at the embassy needed to be reminded how dangerous a place Iraq was at that point.

The overall size of active enemy forces in the country at the time, according to U.S. Central Command, was approximately twenty thousand men: roughly ten thousand former regime members, about three thousand members of al-Sadr's Shia militia, some one thousand in the Sunni terrorist network overseen by Abu Musab al-Zarqawi, and about five thousand criminals, religious extremists, and other rogue elements. Only six weeks prior to the opening of the U.S. embassy, Izzedin Salim, the president of the Iraqi Governing Council, was killed when a suicide bomber pulled his car up next to Salim's convoy, then detonated a bomb so powerful it melted the roadway. The attack—engineered to magnify its shock value—unfolded at a checkpoint to enter the Green Zone.

Moreover, another crucial transition was taking place inside the

Green Zone. Under DoD policy in Iraq, the military would provide security only to those contractors and government civilians deploying with the combat force or otherwise directly supporting the military's mission. Barring any special arrangements, other U.S. government agencies—including the State Department—had to provide their own security. And as much as cobbling together a diplomatic outpost on short notice is pretty standard for the department, ensuring safety for the sheer number of diplomats and associated personnel who would soon be funneled into Baghdad was a different logistical challenge.

To accomplish that task, State has long had an official Bureau of Diplomatic Security, known as DS or DipSec. That bureau "develops and implements effective security programs to safeguard all personnel who work in every U.S. diplomatic mission around the world," according to its stated mission. It's an extraordinary responsibility, vital to our country's development and humanitarian work abroad and for establishing the stability in war-torn regions that allows American troops to come home.

But there were only about a thousand special agents in DipSec in 2005, and nearly three hundred State Department missions worldwide. Those numbers just don't line up in any sort of practical way—something State has long recognized. "Starting in 1983 after the U.S. embassy bombing in Beirut, Lebanon, the State Department resorted to using contractors to provide perimeter security to U.S. diplomatic and consular posts around the world," read a Congressional Research Service report to Congress about private security contractors (PSCs). "The State Department's Bureau of Diplomatic Security first used PSCs in 1994 when MVM, Incorporated was hired to help protect Haitian President Jean-Bertrand Aristide as he returned to Haiti. This was followed with the use of PSCs in Bosnia, Israel, Afghanistan, and most recently, Iraq."

I saw it firsthand while serving in both Haiti and Bosnia as a SEAL. With contractors, State didn't need to spend some three years recruiting, vetting, and training a DipSec agent—and they didn't have to add those men to long-term payroll or offer them pensions. The contractors were disposable security, single-use guards hired for a particular mission, and then let go just as quickly when the work was done. As a defense employee of the government, I had welcomed the development, and I was thrilled to contribute to State's security now.

In 2000, the State Department had formalized an exclusive deal with contractor DynCorp to protect its diplomats in parts of the former Yugoslavia, the Palestinian territories, and Afghanistan. That contract was known as Worldwide Personal Protective Services, or the WPPS. In mid-2004, State added additional responsibilities under the WPPS to cover security for Ambassador Negroponte and other personnel at the massive new Embassy Baghdad, but DynCorp was unable to meet the expansive new task order. Suddenly, State was faced with the untenable prospect of sending waves of diplomats into Baghdad without the means to keep them safe.

Those of us at Blackwater, meanwhile, had just wrapped up the successful Bremer detail. We had the personnel, vehicles, and protection strategies necessary for a larger operation—already sitting right there in the Green Zone. We had become known for getting results, and for delivering without cost overruns or excuses. So once again the U.S. government found itself with an urgent and compelling problem that my company was uniquely positioned to solve. We were eager to help.

In June 2004 the State Department issued Blackwater a one-year sole-source security contract under the WPPS, which provided Embassy Baghdad and its personnel with the immediate security they needed. It also allowed State a window of time to create a competitive contract for the Baghdad work, which would be bid upon by various contractors in the summer of 2005. That "indefinite delivery, indefinite quantity" deal we signed was to provide for the "protection of U.S. and/or certain foreign government high-level officials whenever the need arises." That Baghdad task order, ultimately worth $488 million, launched Blackwater's lucrative, tumultuous, successful, and ultimately devastating relationship with the State Department.

Over the next five years, new iterations of the WPPS would pay my company the better part of one billion dollars and put nearly a thousand of our contractors—effectively a private regiment—on the ground in Iraq at any one time. But that hardly means things always went smoothly, and thanks to dramatic misunderstandings among the general public about the scope of that deal and the regulations governing contractor actions in Iraq, Blackwater quickly became the lightning rod for critics of the war effort. Our work fulfilling the WPPS brought my company unprecedented importance and visibility—and then, ultimately, destroyed it.

For the State Department, image was everything. The agency was a force for good in Iraq, its higher-ups said, and they wanted to be seen that way. The WPPS contract outlined a number of requirements based on how things would literally look to the Iraqi people, right down to the wardrobe demanded of Blackwater's men. "The Government requires a favorable image," the contract read, "and considers it to be a major asset of a protective force."

State insisted that American diplomats would not be cowed into slipping under rebels' radars in dented local cars that camouflaged their movements. They would not travel in the dead of night. When in Baghdad, I usually tried to blend in by traveling in standard dinged-up civilian cars, but State wanted its diplomats charging through Baghdad in gunned-up convoys of waxed SUVs bristling with antenna arrays. At the outset, we explained that the approach would practically taunt insurgents to strike when diplomats are most vulnerable—on the open road, getting from one meeting to the next—yet State insisted the show of authority was important.

By the terms of the contract, the department dictated the missions— where its personnel had to go, and when—as well as the vehicles to be used. It would provide Blackwater with the weapons my men would carry. Our job, in turn, was to create for them a "high-visibility deterrent" to attackers and keep State's personnel safe no matter what. It didn't matter if it was probably the worst approach for the department actually achieving its diplomatic objectives in Iraq.

For the former military men like me at Blackwater, those discussions were the start of a culture clash that lasted until the very end of our time in Iraq. No longer were our contracts twenty pages long. State's WPPS deal weighed in at a thousand—the contract's iterations ultimately filled five four-inch binders at Blackwater's headquarters—detailing everything from the Oakley wraparound sunglasses contractors would wear to the appropriate use of a nightstick to how long it should take a guard to run a mile and a half.

And unlike the Department of Defense, the State Department had a further requirement: absolutely no casualties. It might seem silly to underscore the fact that State didn't want its personnel to get killed, but by June 2004, when Blackwater took on our WPPS duties, more than five hundred U.S. servicemen had been killed by "hostile action" in Iraq since major combat operations had ended the year before. It's even crazier to expect to pump hundreds of high-value diplomats, aid workers, intelligence officers, and visiting VIPs into the middle of that kind of conflict and suffer zero loss of life—especially when your transportation demands made those workers conspicuous targets.

So how could Blackwater's men move those personnel through lawless pockets of Baghdad, in ostentatious convoys, at the times of State's choosing, and still safeguard their lives 100 percent of the time? My company's critics are quick to point out the answer: We drove aggressively, sometimes offensively—just as the contract demanded under its Tactical Standard Operating Procedure, which was more than 180 pages of instructions on everything from the planning of a security mission to postmission recovery efforts.

Everyone, including State, understood from Fallujah what could happen at a single clogged intersection with a broken traffic light. In Baghdad, a group of Iraqis huddled around a vehicle at the side of the road might be fixing a breakdown, or they might be insurgents lying in wait with heavy machine guns and rocket-propelled grenades. Any approaching car on the highway could be a vehicle-borne improvised explosive device, or VBIED. More than four hundred of those blew up in 2004, more than eight hundred in 2005. Contractors, businesspeople, journalists, and missionaries were getting maimed and abducted left and right—and none of them were as princely a target as an American diplomat. Meanwhile, some fifty-six hundred roadside bombs detonated in Iraq in 2004 (that number grew to almost eleven thousand in 2005), and Blackwater's holdovers from the Bremer detail had experience with the damage they caused.

So, yes, our motorcades sped through town, sometimes on the wrong side of the road. And absolutely, when hand signals or flashed lights didn't get the attention of local drivers who pulled too close to our motorcades, Blackwater's men threw water bottles at them. There were times we had to follow that up by putting a few bullets into the intruding car's hood, a tactic to stop the vehicle known as "shooting to disable." State demanded the appearance of American invincibility, but actually providing it meant getting their principals off the road as soon as possible. And almost immediately, some of my men sacrificed their lives to do it.

On June 2, 2004, Richard "Kato" Bruce, a forty-nine-year-old former SEAL and father of one from Menifee, North Carolina, became the fifth Blackwater casualty, and our first under the WPPS. He was killed when his speeding motorcade vehicle slammed into a ditch and flipped. Three days later, four more Blackwater men were killed during an ambush along Route Irish, the military name for the Highway of Death connecting Baghdad International Airport to the Green Zone, when insurgents roared up behind their convoy and sprayed the SUVs with small-arms fire and RPGs. Three of our wounded contractors in the motorcade's heavily armored Suburban fought off the assailants and scrambled back to the Green Zone. But the four men in the "soft skin," or unarmored, SUV perished.

I was even more infuriated at that loss of life because Blackwater's men were stuck with some of those unarmored Suburbans while we waited months for State to deliver us Wisconsin-built SUVs with appropriate armoring. In a classic case of unhinged bureaucracy, State could have simply sent over a few of the hundred or so armored Land Rovers and Toyotas it already owned, but thanks to the Depression-era Buy American Act—a federal regulation once derided in the DoD's *Acquisition Review Quarterly* as "one of the most visible and egregious remnants of U.S. protectionism"—the department could provide us with only American-made vehicles for the WPPS work.

That didn't mean I couldn't buy better armored cars myself, however. And regardless of the fixed-price contract, I wasn't about to watch more of my men get blown up because the government dragged its feet. If the agency wanted a show of force, I would give it one.

Within days of that attack, I was standing in an Army surplus yard outside London, buying retired armored personnel carriers (APCs) for roughly $10,000 apiece. I purchased two ten-ton Saxons— giant, boxy vehicles used by the British army—and four Mambas— distinctive South African APCs whose oblique-angled hulls help deflect bullets, rockets, and bomb blasts. Some of the fortified transporters had seen action in Northern Ireland, others in Kosovo, but all needed overhauls for a 130-degree desert environment. I had them shipped to Kuwait, where Blackwater's engineers installed air conditioners and modified them to carry civilians and their luggage for runs to the airport. From there, we drove them north across the border into Iraq. Mere days after I'd purchased the vehicles, Blackwater had an armored motorcade in Baghdad that trailed only the U.S. Army and Marines.

Those APCs arrived not a moment too soon. By late summer, Route Irish had deteriorated into a shooting gallery. There were numerous suicide VBIED attacks on the highway each week, all of which seemed to claim a handful of lives, and the Army's 1st Cavalry

Division, which guarded the highway with about a thousand soldiers, could do little to stanch the bloodshed. Yet thanks to the armored vehicles and our aggressive driving strategies, Blackwater's teams transported roughly a dozen people from the Green Zone to the Baghdad airport every day for months in those high-visibility motorcades, and returned with twice as many new arrivals. The APCs became such a key to our protection details, I eventually bought twenty of them, and State leased about half after incorporating them into its motor pool of contracted options for safe travel.

By early December 2004, enough carnage had befallen other motorcades that the U.S. embassy declared State's personnel were permitted to travel between the airport and the Green Zone only in helicopters. The rest of Baghdad was faring little better; the entire stretch of city surrounding the Green Zone had morphed into a barbarous hellscape that came to be known as the "Red Zone." Whereas State's motorcade policy initially relied upon ten-man protective details using as few vehicles as possible, convoys heading most anyplace outside the Green Zone soon required a number of additional guards plowing through town in a parade of massive vehicles. When we took the job, State had insisted they wanted their motorcades to be seen. There was no way any of us would be missed now.

When we signed the WPPS, Blackwater had roughly a hundred people working in Baghdad. By the end of 2004, that number had swelled to about 375. We had twenty teams in the Iraqi capital operating seven days a week. Approximately fifteen had permanently assigned VIPs to protect; the others were used in rotation for State's various transportation requirements each day. And much as my men had done with Bremer's detail, we had to rethink the fundamentals of a protective detail.

Three months after signing on for the WPPS, for instance, we developed a quick reaction force (QRF) of Humvees and armored SUVs that could race to an engagement and ferry back the wounded. The

QRF conducted mission planning and rehearsals, and coordinated with the State Department—and was always waiting in the wings should any of our motorcades find themselves in a tight spot. Similarly, we got those Little Birds—previously dedicated only to Bremer's security detail—redesignated as common-use support assets, to provide cover for all our State Department convoys. And we created an advance team to evaluate security at State's meeting locations and perform route reconnaissance ahead of the missions. That crew used those K9 explosives detection dogs we'd been raising on my farm in Virginia to sweep meeting areas prior to a visit.

Then we worked with State to create a TOC, or tactical operations center, inside one of Saddam Hussein's former palaces. There, we coordinated the security requirements dictated to us by the State Department's regional security officer, or RSO. By the explicit terms of our contract, Blackwater's personnel answered only to the RSO and to the U.S. ambassador in Baghdad—we were not to be under the military's chain of command. We worked for State.

On any given evening, a department officer would give us a list of their officials' itineraries for the next day. By the next morning, our protective details presented them with the equivalent of a preflight plan, including satellite imagery with the primary and backup routes; safe areas and other protective physical features where officials could seek shelter in case of an ambush; the locations of military forward operating bases adjacent to the security teams' paths of movement; and preidentified landing zones for medevac extractions. Each leg of the security teams' travel to and from was segmented in the plan, and the completion of those legs would be monitored as an individual event in real time.

Each Blackwater vehicle and aircraft had a specific designation number, every team was attached in our database to that particular piece of equipment, and every individual was assigned to a specific team. That enabled us to track the exact locations of every on-duty Blackwater security professional anywhere in the world, virtually in real time, using GPS signals from the vehicles superimposed over

Google Earth. As each milestone, or "event," was achieved throughout the mission, the team's progress appeared on status boards and
banks of flat-screen monitors that allowed Blackwater supervisors,
the RSO, and Ambassador Negroponte to monitor our teams. (It was
also the way we could definitively refute assertions from the military or the media that insurgents had taken Blackwater personnel
hostage. "All of our men are accounted for," we'd say. "But the hostage is wearing a Blackwater hat!" they'd say.)

On one eventful run in early 2005, insurgents along Route Irish
attacked one of our twenty-five-year-old Mambas with a powerful
roadside bomb known as an explosively formed penetrator, or EFP.
The weapon is a simple device about the size of a coffee can, often
built from a short section of well-casing pipe packed with high explosives. A copper liner is attached to the pipe's open end. When the
bomb explodes, that liner deforms into a shaped charge of molten
metal that screams toward its target at 4,500 miles per hour, or something approaching Mach 6. On that run to the airport, the Iranian-
made hypersonic projectile punctured the Mamba's armor, costing
one of our men his right arm at the elbow and spraying another Blackwater contractor with metal fragments that destroyed one of his eyes.
They were awful injuries—but that EFP could have cut an armored
Suburban in half, killing everyone inside.

The attack was significant for another reason. The shock wave
from the blast ruptured an eardrum of one of the principals in the
Mamba. Thanks to our equipment, preparation, strategies, and driving techniques, it was the only real injury ever suffered by someone
under Blackwater's protection.

The State Department got its 100 percent survival rate. And yet
somehow by doing exactly what the department demanded—
regardless of how miscalculated its strategy was—Blackwater got
the PR nightmare. Anonymous "U.S. military officials" told reporters
things like: "[Blackwater's men] tend to overreact to a lot of things.
They maneuver around town very aggressively, they've got weapons
pointed at people, they cut people off, of course their speeds—I mean

a whole bunch of things they do fairly consistently." As recently as the start 0f 2013, nearly a decade after my company was awarded that WPPS contract, Congresswoman Jan Schakowsky, a Democrat from Illinois, naively listed this screed on her Web site, among her positions "on the issues": "I am one of the few members of Congress who has focused particularly on the over 27,000 armed private security contractors in Iraq and Afghanistan who work for companies like the infamous Blackwater. Time and again, the cowboy-like behavior of these private contractors—or mercenaries—has endangered the men and women of our armed forces, damaged our relationships with foreign governments, and threatened our mission."

Critics contend we should have somehow toned down our vigilance on those convoys. I contend most of them have never been in a truck hit by a roadside bomb. Even more important, no other contractor filling the WPPS would have been able to act any differently. Retired Marine colonel Thomas X. Hammes, who served in Iraq in early 2004 and ultimately spoke out against PMC use in general, at least described the situation accurately. "Blackwater's an extraordinarily professional organization, and they were doing exactly what they were tasked to do: protect the principal," he told PBS's *Frontline*. "The problem is in protecting the principal they had to be very aggressive, and each time they went out they had to offend locals, forcing them to the side of the road, being overpowering and intimidating, at times running vehicles off the road.... [I]t puts Blackwater in an impossible position. They will be as aggressive and as muscular as they need to be to fulfill what we contracted them to do. They did a superb job doing exactly what we told them to do. The problem is what we told them to do hurt the counterinsurgency effort."

Even beyond our tactical approach, there is a grander fundamental misunderstanding about Blackwater's work for the State Department—one tied directly to the perception of "cowboy-like behavior" that my company's critics have feverishly latched onto:

the complete fallacy that contractors were somehow above the law while in Iraq.

As the public learned more about our contractually mandated aggressiveness in Baghdad, relentless headlines blared that Blackwater was getting "A Free Pass in Iraq," or suggested we operated in an area "Where Military Rules Don't Apply." Those stories inevitably got spun by bloggers to declare, "There is no law that restricts [Blackwater] from committing crimes."

Much of the focus fell on one of Paul Bremer's final acts as head of the CPA: issuing Order 17 to clarify legal guidelines for contractors in Iraq. Critics such as Tom Engelhardt at the *Nation* further fanned the flames of misinformation: "Order 17 gave new meaning to the term 'Free World,'" he claimed. "It was, in essence, a get-out-of-jail-free card in perpetuity.... These private soldiers, largely in the employ of the Pentagon or the U.S. State Department—and so operating on American taxpayer dollars—were granted the right to act as they pleased with utter impunity anywhere in the country." The implications of those assessments would be staggering—if they were true. But that sort of dogma is profoundly, dangerously wrong, showing at best a hasty mishandling of the facts and more likely, I suspect, a willful misrepresentation of reality.

In June 2003, Bremer's CPA issued a public notice establishing the initial legal framework for coalition forces and contractors operating in Iraq. The relevant part of that notice read: "In accordance with international law, the CPA, coalition forces and the military and civilian personnel accompanying them, are not subject to local law or the jurisdiction of local courts. With regard to criminal, civil, administrative or other legal process, they will remain subject to the exclusive jurisdiction of the State contributing them to the Coalition." That meant Blackwater (and the military, and CPA officials) faced no legal oversight from *Iraqi* authorities—who could hardly have provided a fair or thorough judicial system at a time when much of the country didn't even have running water—but were still subject to oversight from U.S. authorities. The CPA's public notice concluded (with emphasis in the original):

> The immunities provided will *not* prevent legal proceedings against Coalition personnel for unlawful acts they may commit. It simply ensures that such proceedings will be undertaken in accordance with the laws of the State that contributed the personnel to the Coalition. Furthermore, the immunity will only apply to acts or omissions during the authority of the CPA within Iraq.

So from virtually the moment Blackwater's men arrived in Iraq, they were subject to the American rule of law.

The question of contractors' legal oversight in the post-CPA landscape was even more clearly spelled out one year later, when Bremer signed Order 17 immediately prior to the handover of power. The order states in relevant part (emphasis mine):

> Contractors shall be immune from Iraqi legal process with respect to acts performed by them *pursuant to the terms and conditions of a Contract or any sub-contract thereto*. Nothing in this provision shall prohibit (Multi-National Force) Personnel from preventing acts of serious misconduct by Contractors, or otherwise temporarily detaining any Contractors who pose a risk of injury to themselves or others, pending expeditious turnover to the appropriate authorities of the Sending State.

That order laid out the crucial fact that contractors were immune from Iraqi civil or criminal liability only when their actions were a necessary part of fulfilling their U.S. government contracts. Order 17 "said any action that is required to fulfill an authorized and legal contract cannot be considered a crime under Iraqi law," former Blackwater vice president for strategic initiatives Chris Taylor told the *National Review* in 2007. "Rape, murder, smuggling, sex abuse, child molestation—those are never actions that are required to fulfill a contract. Therefore they could be tried under Iraqi law, under a Military Territorial Jurisdiction Act, under the War Crimes Act, under the Victims of Trafficking and Violence Protection Act—I can go on." He concluded: "Everybody says that Ambassador Bremer signed a piece of paper that makes contractors immune: 'They can't be charged with crimes in Iraq!' Horse doo-doo. That's not what Order 17 said."

Understand, as well: Unlike the State Department's thousand-page contracts detailing the behavior expected of Blackwater's men, CPA Order 17 was a total of sixteen pages long. Section 4—the component specifically relating to contractors—is one single page. It would almost seem difficult for my company's critics to so blisteringly misunderstand the information outlined in seven numbered paragraphs, especially when the legal accountability for American contractors in Iraq was so similar to their traditional accountability in other countries. For instance, NATO's official parties' agreement regarding the Status of Forces, signed in 1949, establishes: "The military authorities of the sending State shall have the primary right to exercise jurisdiction over a member of a force or of a civilian component in relation to . . . offences arising out of any act or omission done in the performance of official duty." It continues: "In the case of any other offence the authorities of the receiving State shall have the primary right to exercise jurisdiction."

Not only were Blackwater's men not immune from Iraqi law—much less U.S. federal regulations—Order 17 simply followed the general international framework in place for contractors for more than a half century.

Additionally, in January 2007 contractor accountability became even stricter. That year, the National Defense Authorization Act added a new provision to the long-standing Uniform Code of Military Justice (UCMJ), which had previously governed all military personnel and—"in time of war"—the government's contractors. That "time of war," however, meant that contractors acting in what were not officially war zones were not subject to the UCMJ. And while there have been innumerable instances in which the U.S. military was sent abroad for various reasons, the United States has fought only five officially declared wars: the War of 1812 against Great Britain, the Mexican-American War in 1846–1848, the Spanish-American War in 1898, World War I, and World War II. A case in 1970 exposed the limitations of the UCMJ, when the Court of Military Appeals reversed the conviction of a contractor in Saigon because Vietnam didn't officially constitute a war zone.

So in 2006, Republican senator Lindsey Graham of South Carolina, a reserve Judge Advocate General officer, added the key words "or a contingency operation" to the code. "The provision clarifies the [UCMJ] to place civilian contractors accompanying the Armed Forces in the field under the court-martial jurisdiction during contingency operations as well as in times of declared war," he said. That, too, covered Blackwater's men in Iraq.

The faulty reporting and mistaken assumptions about our motorcade policies and our accountability are things all of us in Moyock dearly wanted to correct. But there was another wrinkle: The WPPS strictly forbade contractors from talking to the media without express permission from the State Department. Section H.7 H-020 of the contract concerns the "Safeguarding of Information" (emphasis mine):

> The Contractor and its employees shall exercise the utmost discretion in regard to all matters relating to their duties and functions. They shall not communicate to any person any information known to them by reason of their performance of services under this contract which has not been made public, except in the necessary performance of their duties or upon written authorization of the Contracting Officer. All documents and records (including photographs) generated during the performance of work under this contract shall be for the sole use of and become the exclusive property of the U.S. Government. *Furthermore, no article, book, pamphlet, recording, broadcast,*

speech, television appearance, film or photograph concerning any as-
pect of work performed under this contract shall be published or dissem-
inated through any media without the prior written authorization of the
Contracting Officer.

As it happened, the public affairs officer in Washington involved
in managing Blackwater's contractual nondisclosure policy was a
career bureaucrat named Grace Moe. She had a fear of bad press that
was extraordinary. Rather than allowing us to defend ourselves
under proper official parameters, as we requested numerous times,
State threatened to terminate the contract if we did anything to halt
the repeated slams by ill-informed talking heads. Not only would we
have to take the bullets for their men in Baghdad, we were effectively
told, we had to take the heat at home, too. And when we deviated
from that role, the response was unequivocal.

One email from Moe to Blackwater higher-ups—regarding that
2007 interview Taylor gave to the *National Review*, which she hadn't
preapproved—highlighted the tensions. "I've had it with the egos,
the macho attitude and the total disregard of just how much trouble
[interviews like] this will cause," she wrote. Soon, to strike back at
us, State canceled Blackwater's contracts for WPPS work we'd also
won in Haiti and Israel.

That message was delivered loud and clear. And suddenly, "A Blackwater spokesman declined to comment" soon became an incessant
refrain in news stories. Each time it appeared, my team back in
Moyock wanted to whip a computer against the wall.

Regardless of what was said in the press at home, our effectiveness
on the ground in Baghdad spoke for itself. Amid a seemingly
overnight postinvasion boom in the contracting industry, which led
to all sorts of fly-by-night "two-guys-and-a-laptop competitors," as I
often described them, the Blackwater brand of professionalism
stood out. "They were there to assist, to do the right thing," Hammes,

the retired Marine colonel, said of my men. "I never had the feeling that Blackwater was about money. Obviously it is about money, because they've got to stay in business. But these guys were people who dedicated their life to America. They've served in our best special forces. They're very, very concerned and dedicated Americans. And they'll do anything, including put their life on the line, to do right."

While U.S. military personnel saw our commitment in Iraq, the State Department respected the results. So much so that in June 2005, once our yearlong contract had expired and State put the WPPS work up for bid, Blackwater came out of the open competition with the lion's share of the work.

Under the five-year contract generally referred to as the "WPPS II," personal security in Iraq was split among three firms: DynCorp would be responsible for State personnel in the relatively placid northern region, including the major cities of Erbil and Kirkuk; Triple Canopy was assigned the south, including the port city of Basra; and Blackwater undertook protection for Embassy Baghdad personnel and provincial reconstruction teams across volatile central Iraq, accounting for the bulk of the people in Iraq being protected under the WPPS II. "The contract was awarded on a best value basis, meaning its award was based on what was most advantageous to the federal government," a 2008 Congressional Research Service concluded. "The WPPS II considered technical merit more important than cost."

That cost was significant: a ceiling of $1.2 billion per contractor over the five years, which included a guaranteed first year plus four more optional years. The total price of each contract wasn't fixed, but the daily rate for each labor category was. It was expected that as requirements for various task orders evolved and increased over the years—and with it, the man-hours required—so, too, would the State Department payout. And soon, as Blackwater's role grew to safeguard the ever rising number of State personnel in Iraq, my company brought in some $340 million a year in revenue through the WPPS II. We oversaw the main centers of reconstruction while the other contracting companies safeguarded something akin to satellite offices.

It's not surprising that Blackwater's take dwarfed the payouts to DynCorp ($47 million) and Triple Canopy ($15.5 million). Of the more than $400 million annually State spent for that total contract's Iraq components, Blackwater came away with almost 85 percent of it. And our manpower—which soon rose to nearly one thousand men—made up more than 70 percent of the trained personnel filling the contract.

It was another dramatic success for our company. It also offered a watershed reflection upon nation building in the twenty-first century.

The Defense Department had blown apart Iraq under the promise of a brighter, more democratic future for its people. Amid the chaos of insurgency, the DoD handed over the restoration job to an undermanned State Department—and without contractors like us, U.S. embassy personnel simply couldn't accomplish that mission. "Security is key to establishing diplomatic relations," according to a 2005 Congressional Research Service report. "If the effort to achieve security [for State Department personnel] is unsuccessful, U.S. diplomacy will likely be ineffective." Then, with the WPPS II, State hired nearly three-quarters of its contractors, for its most crucial work, from one single company. From the *only* company that could get the job done in Baghdad.

The moment we signed that contract, any discussion of Blackwater in Iraq was actually about something far larger than security contracting: If our motorcades didn't run, the State Department didn't run. Without my company, *U.S. diplomacy in Iraq didn't run.* It was a terrifying realization for many on Capitol Hill—but one that also provided them with a perfect whipping boy.

By June 2005, comparisons between the conflict in Iraq and the morass of Vietnam were everywhere. A *Washington Post*/ABC poll found that nearly 60 percent of Americans believed that the war in Iraq should never have been fought in the first place, and 52 percent believed military action there wasn't contributing to the long-term safety of the United States. "It was the first time a majority of Americans disagreed with the central notion [President] Bush has offered to build support for war: that the fight there will make Americans safer from terrorists at home," the *Post* reported. Democrats looked to appease constituents by distancing themselves from the war effort—yet it proved more difficult than they anticipated.

Even as President Bush headed toward historical lows in approval ratings that summer, Democratic minorities in both the House and the Senate meant that members of Congress could marshal little more than impotent theatrical broadsides against the administration's policies. "With the presidency and control of Congress, we have an easier time setting the agenda," House Speaker J. Dennis Hastert, a Republican from Illinois, said in late 2005. "We can act when the other side can only talk and complain." Soon, columnists referred to Nancy Pelosi, Harry Reid, and Howard Dean—the House minority leader, Senate minority leader, and chairman of the Democratic National Committee, respectively—as the "Three Stooges," and their party's floundering led to newspaper headlines such as "For Democrats, Many Verses, but No Chorus" and "Democrats Struggle to Seize Opportunity." (The *Onion* was even more on point with its satirical current events roundup, "Democrats Vow Not to Give Up Hopelessness.")

Publicly sniping at our servicemen and -women was also risky. Four decades ago, veterans returning from Vietnam were smeared as "baby killers" and worse in what seemed to be an accepted tactic of the antiwar movement. In the Internet era, however, those boundaries have shifted. *Los Angeles Times* columnist Joel Stein, for instance, was nationally excoriated in 2006 for a piece that began, "I don't support our troops." He wrote, "I'm not for the war. And being against the war and saying you support the troops is one of the wussiest positions the pacifists have ever taken—and they're wussy by definition.... [W]hen you volunteer for the U.S. military, you pretty much know you're not going to be fending off invasions from Mexico and Canada. So you're willingly signing up to be a fighting tool of American imperialism, for better or worse. Sometimes you get lucky and get to fight ethnic genocide in Kosovo, but other times it's

Vietnam." The backlash Stein suffered was predictable—and no politician wanted that sort of heat.

Dead-set against any conflict—yet without the strength to rattle the administration that had launched it, and knowing the people who actually fought it were off limits—Democrats were in need of a new villain. They needed *somebody* to publicly push around. So they took aim at the "mercenaries."

CHAPTER 11
CHARACTER COUNTS

WHAT SORT OF PERSON WOULD WANT TO WORK FOR BLACKWATER? IT'S A question I've heard often—and the standard smear goes something like this: "Once I did a little reading, I was horrified at the secret, virtually unregulated army [President] Bush has at his beck and call. This mercenary army is arguably composed of conscienceless assassins who are among the best of the best, or worst of the worst, depending on your point of view, about being highly skilled at 'stability solutions' utilizing assault rifles."

That tired bit of rhetoric came from the blog *Capitol Hill Blue*, but the practice of equating Blackwater's men with "mercenaries" happens to this day everywhere from blog posts to book titles to the halls of Congress. It's an intentionally inflammatory term—evoking "vigorous condemnation of immoral killers and profiteers of misery and war," as the *International Review of the Red Cross* describes it—which affects not only the lawmakers who authorize funding for PSC operations abroad, but also—possibly fatally—the contractors whose potential treatment if captured by the enemy is legally tied to it. Yet no matter how many times the "mercenary" refrain is repeated, it doesn't make the description of Blackwater's contractors more accurate. And it's a distinction I take seriously.

At its essence, mercenarism is outlined by a pair of international conventions set in place to specifically criminalize and eliminate the practice: 1977's Additional Protocol I of the Geneva Conventions, and the UN's 1989 International Convention Against the Recruitment, Use, Financing and Training of Mercenaries. Under Additional Protocol I, there are six conditions to be satisfied for one to qualify as a mercenary. The term applies if that person:

(a) is specially recruited locally or abroad in order to fight in an armed conflict;

(b) does, in fact, take a direct part in the hostilities;

(c) is motivated to take part in the hostilities essentially by the desire for private gain and, in fact, is promised, by or on behalf of a Party to the conflict, material compensation substantially in excess of that promised or paid to combatants of similar ranks and functions in the armed forces of that Party;

(d) is neither a national of a Party to the conflict nor a resident of territory controlled by a Party to the conflict;

(e) is not a member of the armed forces of a Party to the conflict; and

(f) has not been sent by a State which is not a Party to the conflict on official duty as a member of its armed forces.

The result under the Geneva Conventions is that a mercenary, if captured, does not benefit from prisoner of war status, which otherwise guarantees detainees cannot be prosecuted for taking part in hostilities, demands their release and repatriation after the end of hostilities, protects them against violence and intimidation at the hands of their captors, and defines minimum conditions of detention regarding accommodation, food, clothing, hygiene, and medical care. The UN convention defines the term similarly, but adds as punishment that signatories of the document can also try mercenaries for the fundamental crime of mercenarism. Either way, if captured by the enemy, "mercenaries" are simply on their own—and probably gone for good. It's not a designation to be taken lightly.

Yet considered in the terms of the Geneva Convention qualifications, Blackwater's men were hired to protect civilians and buildings from insurgent attack, not overtly fight in an armed conflict; their engagements with enemies were purely defensive, as opposed to offensive action as a direct part of the hostilities; their motivations for being in Iraq were generally as patriotic as they were material; and perhaps most important, the men on our WPPS details were American citizens, working for U.S. agencies that were a lawful party to the conflict. (We periodically hired a small percentage of foreign nationals to fill nonsecurity roles with Blackwater, but they never worked protective details.)

Legal scholars can go on—and have—at further length about the myriad ways the term has been misapplied, but suffice it to say, it simply doesn't fit for Blackwater's men. "In truth, whenever I hear someone call a PSC a mercenary I just roll my eyes," David Isenberg, author of *Shadow Force: Private Security Contractors in Iraq* and an evenhanded critic of the industry, wrote at the *Huffington Post*. "It is a sign of mental laziness."

Moreover, as those standard smears go, it is a certainty that nothing in Blackwater's contracts with the government gave me the resources or constitutional authority to create a standing army. The security wing of Blackwater was basically a robust temp agency. We hired people from across the country for short-term contracts—and far from a militia, we simply had a database full of tens of thousands of subscribers to our *Blackwater Tactical Weekly* newsletter.

Gary Jackson launched that newsletter in the company's early days to keep the special operations and law enforcement communities apprised of the latest developments in Moyock. What began as a pre-Facebook attempt at social media, however, became an invaluable recruiting tool. By the time we took over the WPPS duties, filling our rapidly growing list of contracts in Iraq and Afghanistan meant we had to find guards, medics, intelligence analysts, armored vehicle mechanics, helicopter pilots, door gunners, and more. So we put job postings in the newsletter—and three days later, we'd have a few hundred applicants.

They were specialized skill sets we were looking for, to be sure. But we were able to find not only elite-level military and law enforcement professionals for the armed security work, but also our own collection of linguists, agricultural and sanitation experts, electrical power grid engineers, civil engineers, accountants, attorneys, psychologists, architects, managers, logisticians, machinists, and PhDs in everything from aerodynamics to communication. Even a chaplain—D. R. Staton, a retired officer and instructor from the Virginia Beach Police Department. Far from being suitable for reckless cowboys, those positions required sophistication and maturity, morality and discernment.

For people who wanted to work for Blackwater, character counted—I can't stress that enough. We needed thinking men behind the trigger, who had passion for the job in front of them. Because one never knew when those characteristics might be tested.

Muntazer al-Zaidi surely didn't realize that his life rested in the hands of a security contractor. To this day, few people do. But in December 2008, the thirty-year-old journalist with the Al Baghdadiya TV channel made global headlines when he interrupted a Baghdad press conference by yelling that President Bush was "a dog"—then chucking his shoes at him, one after the other. In video footage that immediately spread around the world, one fellow journalist, at the prime minister's palace to cover the joint appearance by Bush and Iraqi prime minister Nouri al-Maliki, can be seen trying to halt the shoe thrower from the front, while another claws at him from behind.

Then al-Zaidi is tackled—and, eventually, swarmed by U.S. Secret Service agents in their telltale suits and ties and earpieces.

Almost entirely unseen by the phalanx of cameras at the rear of the room was a bearded young man in khakis and wearing a short-sleeve black shirt over a long-sleeve gray one—the man who actually tackled and apprehended al-Zaidi. The reason he didn't look like Secret Service is that he wasn't. He was one of Blackwater's men, there in the room because high-ranking State Department personnel also attended the press conference. And within an instant of the commotion, he had his department-approved pistol drawn, with a front sight picture of the assailant's head, before the second shoe was thrown. Yet, grasping the lack of a more significant threat—and the magnitude of shooting a man in a crowded room in front of two heads of state and an international press corps—Blackwater's man reholstered his weapon, darted around the reporters, and brought the assailant to the ground.

The Secret Service closed in on the pile of bodies after the fact, and was left to endure public scrutiny over how a reporter had been able to hurl two objects—effectively committing assault and battery against the president of the United States—before they could stop him. "In a perfect world, [the Secret Service] would have been on the guy before he threw the first shoe," Joseph J. Funk, a former service agent told the *Los Angeles Times*. "But after looking at the tapes, [the throws] were pretty quick and they were one right after the other. I doubt any security force or any law enforcement could have reacted in time to stop the second shoe." Blackwater's man did. And then he held off. That's no accident.

The contractors who formed the ground teams we sent to Afghanistan and Iraq were mainly former noncommissioned military officers and former members of the special operations services and elite light infantry. They averaged thirty-seven years old, with ten years of experience in the armed forces and three years of professional security experience afterward. Roughly two-thirds were former

U. S. Army, about one-quarter were Marines, and the rest former Navy SEALs, police SWAT team officers, and former federal agents from the FBI, Secret Service, and other agencies. More than half were combat veterans. All knew how to make calm decisions in even the most stressful of situations. "You have to be disciplined to do this job," one of our WPPS contractors in Baghdad told the *Washington Post* in 2005. "If any one of them is a cowboy, he will ... get everyone killed." On the aviation side, the average age of our contractors was forty-eight, and many of the pilots came to us with more than seven thousand hours of flight time.

Some men and women came to Blackwater after injuries had curtailed their military careers and yet they still had the training, talent, and perspective to be tremendous assets in a war zone. "I like being someplace where stupidity can be fatal, because here you work with people who think about their actions," the *Washington Post* quoted another of our men saying. Route Irish, the contractor said, was a far cry from a pampered American society back home that "puts warnings on coffee cups."

The people who worked for my company were proudly patriotic. I could relate to the many contractors we hired for whom a military lifestyle no longer meshed with family obligations. Still others were retired from their previous DoD positions, but after the attacks of 9/11 felt compelled to rejoin the fight. Those contractors had all built successful first careers, during which the Defense Department received its return on investment for their training—and then, much like the aviation mechanics or submarine reactor technicians they served with in the military, the special ops guys found the chance to translate their skills to the private sector. The government should have been publicly thankful to have them back out there assisting its mission abroad, regardless of the company name on the ID card.

Our employees may have been retired from the military, but Blackwater didn't hire your typical "retiree." After the eight-week Moyock training programs that turned those veterans into diplomatic security professionals, our final physical fitness test standards required men to run one and a half miles in less than ten minutes, forty-five seconds; execute twelve pull-ups in a row, seventy-five push-ups done in two one-minute sets, and seventy-five sit-ups in two one-minute sets; and drag a 175-pound dummy eighty feet in under one minute. Those aren't far off Navy SEAL fitness standards—and they're ones that State Department personnel often supervised at the Blackwater facility to ensure quality and compliance with their needs.

Our trainers subjected those elite, dedicated applicants to the exacting screening procedures outlined in the WPPS—more than five hundred pages of which were devoted to specifications for each training element, going so far as to itemize how many pieces of furniture were required to be in the rooms of a building used in live-fire simulation exercises.

Then we scrutinized applicants' professional backgrounds and their psychological profiles. They all had to pass medical examinations and criminal background checks. Each recruit's biographical data was submitted to DipSec's High Threat Protection office, where State Department staff independently verified the recruits' qualifications. Once cleared by DipSec, each Blackwater WPPS contractor then underwent an additional State Department investigation in order to qualify for a national security clearance at least at the "secret" level.

Only U.S. citizens can be granted those security clearances, so all Blackwater personnel who accompanied American officials were Americans. We did, however, sometimes hire locals from the countries in which we worked, and also third-country nationals where the laws permitted, for periodic static security functions such as manning checkpoints and gates, or acting as housekeepers and cooks. In fact, during our time executing the WPPS II contract, nearly a quarter of the Blackwater contractors in Baghdad were Iraqis or third-country nationals.

Some have suggested this must have been a cost-cutting measure to lowball foreign workers, but that overlooks the obvious: Locals, with native fluency and an innate understanding of the culture, are invaluable to any security operation. They're able to detect inconsistencies and threats the way foreigners might not—and build personal networks with police and community leaders that no outsider can. Critics also miss the fact that, under our contract with State, we hired non-Americans only when so instructed: "In certain circumstances, *and when directed,*" the WPPS reads (emphasis mine), "contractors may be required to recruit, evaluate, and train, local foreign government or third-country foreign nationals in established personal protective security procedures, to conduct protective security operations overseas with them, and to provide trained protective security personnel for short or long-term special domestic security situations."

Any non-American Blackwater employees brought on underwent similar vetting procedures, and they were required to receive from the State Department a favorable Moderate Risk Public Trust determination—a designation that allowed them to work on sensitive assignments that didn't involve access to national security information but did involve situations in which the "public trust" might be at moderate risk because of potential disruptions to government programs or facilities. All told, Blackwater's men in Baghdad, American or not, received far tougher screenings than most U. S. soldiers and law enforcement personnel undergo at home—as exhibited by a U.S. Capitol Police fiasco in 2008, when it was revealed that fifteen of the force's new hires had actually failed criminal background checks and psychological examinations or had submitted false information on their applications.

Further, most if not all of the personnel Blackwater protected had been required at some point to take the traditional oath of office: "I, _____, do solemnly swear (or affirm) that I will support and defend the Constitution of the United States against all enemies, foreign and domestic; that I will bear true faith and allegiance to the same; that I take this obligation freely, without any mental reservation or purpose of evasion; and that I will well and faithfully discharge the duties of the office upon which I am about to enter. So help me God." With that in mind, I made it policy across the entire Prince Group that all officers, employees, and independent contractors of Blackwater who were required to have security clearances took the same oath when coming on board.

That's not to say we never got it wrong. It's true that with a workforce growing exponentially almost overnight to fill those contracts abroad, even the most careful scrutiny by Blackwater hiring managers and State Department clearance personnel didn't catch a handful of bad actors. It's a problem all companies face. (One survey I read recently showed that nearly 70 percent of American employers are affected by bad hires each year, and that more than 40 percent of them point to needing to fill a job quickly as the main culprit. I can relate.)

I believed strongly in standing by our employees and contractors when they made honest mistakes, allowing us all to learn from them. But if we hired fast, I fired faster when confronted with people who were wrongly motivated, or knowingly broke the law, or ignored the standards of professionalism I demanded. "You hire people, they don't work out, you move on"—that became a mantra of mine. No one ever accused me of coddling the people under me.

Those fireable offenses didn't even have to result in headline-grabbing situations. Of the thousands who contracted with us in Iraq over the years, we fired more than 120 of them for various things—such as possessing unauthorized weapons (that is, one whose serial number doesn't match the weapon assigned to that person, or his carrying a make or model weapon not authorized by the contract); or drug and alcohol violations; or sometimes just because someone had a bad attitude. One early situation that drew significant attention provided a perfect example of that hiring and firing cycle—and also of the major misunderstandings about the capabilities of a private company like mine.

On December 24, 2006, Blackwater contractor Andrew Moonen, who had served in the Army's 82nd Airborne Division from 2002 to 2005, left a holiday party in the Green Zone. By almost all accounts, he'd been drinking heavily. Soon after leaving the party alone, Moonen—an armorer who repaired weapons for us, not a protective security professional—encountered Raheem Khalif Sa'adoon, a thirty-two-year-old guard assigned to protect the compound of Iraqi vice president Adil Abdul-Mahdi.

Whatever exchange ensued is impossible to re-create with any certainty—though I've always found it interesting that some six months later, a number of Mahdi's security guards were arrested after robbing a Baghdad bank and making off with the equivalent of nearly five million dollars. The men on that protective detail were never known for their agreeableness.

Still, there on Christmas Eve, Sa'adoon was shot three times. He died early the next day at an American military hospital. Moonen was the only suspect in the killing, and the relatively rare shooting inside the Green Zone provided perfect fodder for those looking to accuse Blackwater's men of recklessness.

Our corporate response was every bit as tough as it—legally—could have been: Within hours, we fired Moonen for a "blatant and egregious" violation of Blackwater's policy prohibiting the possession of a firearm while under the influence of alcohol. Whatever else had transpired that night, the booze infraction alone got him canned. Then Moonen forfeited his $3,000 Christmas bonus and, at the State Department's direction, was immediately loaded on a plane back to the United States—at his own expense—while various American authorities investigated the shooting. Employees who didn't maintain our standards were always left with just one decision to make: window or aisle? (In fact, examining the full dollar amounts involved, Moonen also sacrificed the $3,000 Fourth of July bonus he would have earned a few months later on that contract, and a $7,000 completion bonus for finishing his time with us in good standing. Adding in the sudden $1,600 airfare home, that alcohol infraction cost the armorer nearly $15,000.)

Critics were dismayed at our response, apparently figuring that amid dramatic uncertainty about whether or not a crime was even committed, we were obligated to detain a civilian against his will. Even had the night's events been clearer, a private company like Blackwater is not empowered to enforce U.S. law; holding him could well have constituted false imprisonment. We fired Moonen for breaking company rules. We fined him. But, as I later said publicly, we couldn't flog him. We couldn't incarcerate him. We could only follow State Department demands for sending him back to the United States, and assist in the investigations however we could. We always welcomed that oversight, along with the prosecution of any of my men found to have broken the law. "We have supported the investigation, and if a grand jury sends it to trial, Blackwater will support that as well," Gary Jackson told reporters at the time. "As we have said all along, we strongly support holding responsible anyone who engages in misconduct."

Over the next four years, federal prosecutors and FBI agents traveled to Baghdad multiple times to interview witnesses and collect evidence on the case. Ultimately, in October 2010, the Justice Department decided not to bring murder charges against Moonen, citing the difficulty of preserving evidence in war zones, questions of legal jurisdictions, and immunity implied to him by the initial State Department investigators under what's known as a Garrity warning—the threat that Moonen would lose his job for not answering questions truthfully, but a simultaneous grant that anything he said could not be used to later prosecute him. Blackwater cooperated fully, every step of the way—and quickly replaced Moonen. Whenever a bad hire washed out, there was a line of applicants looking to take his place.

But it wasn't just for the money. Despite conventional wisdom, the reality is that my company didn't offer the massive financial windfall generally assumed. "[Blackwater's] armed commandos earn an average of about $1,000 a day," one early *Washington Post* report contended. "Many of these contractors make up to $1,000 a day, far more than active-duty soldiers," parroted an op-ed in the *Los Angeles Times*. The figure was repeated over and over. Yet no matter how often people said it, the thousand-dollars-a-day figure simply wasn't accurate.

Blackwater pay rates ranged from $450 to $650 per day in the hot zone, and averaged about $500 per day across the entire contractor force. Workdays often stretched twelve hours; company-wide, it wasn't unusual for contractors to average a little over $40 an hour in the most hazardous work environments imaginable. Which is not to say that couldn't add up: $500 a day in Baghdad over the course of a six-month contract could mean roughly $90,000. An average Navy SEAL makes about $54,000 a year before factoring in special skills bonuses that can bump his salary significantly higher. So of course Blackwater's base pay was a draw, and one I felt was only reasonable to attract men and women with the elite skills that we needed. But simply comparing those two numbers, as so many have been wont to do, offers a constrained and dramatically incomplete view of compensation. And you don't have to take my word for it.

"It's more than just salary," the Army's recruiting literature proudly declares. "The Congressional Budget Office (CBO) recently estimated that the average active-duty service member received a compensation package worth $99,000. Non-cash compensation represents almost 60 percent of this package. Non-cash compensation includes health care, retirement pay, childcare and free or subsidized food, housing and education. Coupled with regular cash compensation, this adds up to attractive compensation for Soldiers." That pitch is part of the Army's recent heavy push to try to draw top talent: For high school or home school graduates pledging three or more years of service, the enlistment bonus can be up to $40,000. Soldiers are offered as much as $73,836 to help pay for college, and the College Loan Repayment Program offers up to $65,000 for first-time enlistees who sign up for various military occupational specialties. Soldiers on active duty receive thirty days' paid vacation a year, with sick days as needed. The list of incentives goes on: a $16,000 housing allowance, a $3,900 food allowance, a $2,700 tax allowance—and those sorts of packages have become available throughout the armed forces.

At Blackwater, none of that applied, starting with the obvious. We hired contractors and let them go as needed—the concept of job security never really applied. We offered no regular salary or overtime to the contractors, and we didn't cover their Medicare, Social Security, or federal income taxes. There wasn't a retirement plan, health insurance, life insurance, or paid sick leave available, much less paid vacation. And Blackwater wasn't paying for anyone's college education. My company's base pay was solid in order to attract the best candidates, but in this line of work, that really is worth only so much. "Once you get here, the money isn't really an issue," Richard Hicks, Blackwater's operations manager in Baghdad told the *Washington Post* in 2005, "because you could be dead the next day."

An extensive nonpartisan Congressional Budget Office report from June 2007, "Evaluating Military Compensation," further explored the financial issue. The *Military Times* summarized the forty-four-page study this way:

> Neither service members nor the lawmakers and policymakers who decide pay levels understand the true value of cash compensation and non-cash military benefits, according to [the report].... The problem, the [study's] authors argue, is that service members fixate on basic pay and housing allowances, but fail to factor in the value of benefits like family health care, discounted shopping and subsidized child care. Add to that deferred compensation, like retirement and veterans benefits, they say, and the value of members' compensation is effectively doubled. So when all that is taken into account, the authors say, the so-called pay gap between military and civilian wages disappears.

Further, the incorrect and incomplete compensation figures thrown around led to suggestions that companies like Blackwater somehow poached from, or undermined, the military. A July 2005 analysis by the nonpartisan Government Accountability Office (GAO), however, cut the legs out from under that argument: "While both Special Forces and military police officials *believe*"—emphasis mine—"that attrition is increasing in their military specialties, partially because of increased employment opportunities with private security providers, our review of DoD data shows that the attrition levels in fiscal year 2004 increased compared to fiscal years 2002 and 2003, but are similar to the levels seen in fiscal years 2000 and 2001, prior to the establishment of stop loss." The GAO's investigators found that the stop loss, which "prevents servicemembers from leaving the service even though they may have reached the end of their enlistment or service obligation," artificially deflated attrition rates from 2002 to 2003. "This similarity indicates that former military members in the Special Forces and military police communities are leaving in the same proportions as before the attacks of September 11, 2001."

I can only speculate that the mistaken figure of a thousand dollars a day might have originated from confusion about Blackwater's charges to the State Department. That bit of accounting made numerous headlines in 2007, when an oft-cited congressional memo about my company announced: "Using Blackwater instead of U.S. troops to protect embassy officials is expensive. Blackwater charges the government $1,222 per day for the services of a private military contractor. This is equivalent to $445,000 per year, over six times more than the cost of an equivalent U.S. soldier."

The problem was that that treatment, prepared for members of the House Committee on Oversight and Government Reform, failed to grasp that the $1,221.62 Blackwater charged per protective security specialist per day—only for days he was in the hot zone, not the 365 days that congressional math presupposes—included all our overhead.

It covered the contractor's daily rate, the gear my company provided for him, his training, and aviation support. Every institution has overhead, whether in Moyock or West Point, as I later explained to Congress: "I don't believe it's as simple as saying, 'Well, this sergeant costs us this much,' because that sergeant doesn't show up [in Iraq] naked and untrained." On top of the overhead, our billing rate included a 10.4 percent profit margin—well below the allowable 15 percent on cost-plus deals, and one that was low enough to let us win competitively bid contracts.

The worst part of those accusations about runaway charges and pay rates is the insinuation that Blackwater somehow defrauded the government and, by extension, American taxpayers. "This war has produced some of the most lavish, most fiscally excessive, and most exorbitantly profitable contracts in the history of the world," Representative John Duncan, a Republican from Tennessee, said in 2007. "It seems to me that fiscal conservatives should feel no obligation to defend [Blackwater's] type of contracting. In fact, it seems to me that fiscal conservatives should be the ones most horrified by this!" It made for a great sound bite—yet not only was Blackwater not defrauding anybody, those pay rates that launched a thousand headlines were actually *saving the government money*.

For years, those of us at Blackwater beseeched lawmakers to analyze the true costs of the government providing its own security services, and how those numbers compared to the rates we charged. My company's entire business model was predicated upon hyperefficiency and excellent results; we would gladly have sponsored an activity-based study to determine the cost of our Diplomatic Security work being performed by the military, or brought in-house at the State Department. Ultimately, we didn't have to: An August 2008 Congressional Budget Office report, "Contractors' Support of U.S. Operations in Iraq," finally offered the first thorough, nonpartisan examination of the issue. It took immediate aim at those frequently quoted congressional memorandum figures, and concluded this:

Those figures...are not appropriate for comparing the cost-effectiveness of contracting the security function or performing it using military personnel.... A better comparison would involve estimating a soldier's "billing rate"—the total cost to the government of having a soldier fill a deployed security position for one year....

CBO performed such an analysis, comparing the costs of a private security contractor with those of a military alternative. That analysis indicates that the costs of the private contractor did not differ greatly from the costs of having a comparable military unit performing similar functions. During peacetime, however, the military unit would remain in the force structure and continue to accrue costs at a peacetime rate, whereas the private security contract would not have to be renewed.

That report firmly established Blackwater as a more cost-effective security option in Baghdad for the short term than the Defense Department. Then, in 2010, a GAO analysis of the WPPS II, "Warfighter Support: A Cost Comparison of Using State Department Employees versus Contractors for Security Services in Iraq," turned the microscope on the State Department.

"Because of the broad level of interest by Congress in issues dealing with Iraq," the report began, "the Comptroller General performed this review under his authority to conduct evaluations on his own initiative." The GAO's conclusion? "For the Baghdad Embassy Security Force contract for static security, State Department's estimated annual cost would be over $785 million more than [Blackwater's] cost if the decision was made to have the State Department provide these services rather than using a contractor."

The report noted that by using federal employees, State might be able to perform Blackwater's motorcade security services for less annually—$240 million vs. our approximately $380 million—but also that "because the State Department does not currently have a sufficient number of trained personnel to provide security in Iraq, the department would need to recruit, hire, and train additional employees at an additional cost of $162 million." Furthermore, "[The State Department] said it could easily take them three years or longer to hire, train, and fully staff all positions necessary to accomplish the [various security missions]." Those statistics echoed a 2007 refrain from Ryan Crocker, then the U.S. ambassador to Iraq, when he told the Senate Armed Services Committee, "[T]here is simply no way at all the State Department's Bureau of Diplomatic Security could ever have enough full-time personnel to staff the security function in Iraq. There is no alternative except through contracts."

With Blackwater, of course, there was no wait to get men on the ground, and they had only the shortest of learning curves. That was the work we all knew how to do. It was the fight that came next that blindsided us—because I learned there's another difference between the military and the contractors: We get sued.

CHAPTER 12
THE FALLUJAH FAMILIES
2005–2007

FOR YEARS FOLLOWING THE MURDERS OF WES BATALONA, SCOTT HELVENSTON, Mike Teague, and Jerry Zovko, some of their family members were lost in grief. Donna Zovko, Jerry's mother, who had been so gracious to me that night around the dining room table, was inconsolable. Over and over again she reportedly drove the forty-five miles south of Cleveland to Ohio Western Reserve National Cemetery, where we'd once stood together as her son was laid to rest, to weep at Jerry's grave. Four months after his murder, she even traveled to the Vatican, in hopes that an audience with Pope John Paul II would help provide closure. "God has accepted Jerry's soul," the Holy Father told her—yet he could do little to fill the hole left in hers.

Katy Helvenston-Wettengel, Scott's mother, had a similarly difficult time picking up the pieces. She asked those of us at Blackwater to help find her a job in Baghdad, to see the land where her son had been taken from her. Maybe that could somehow fill the void, she hoped. Unfortunately, the U.S. government had restricted civilian travel to the country unless on official state business; there was little we could do. Racked by insomnia and grief, Helvenston-Wettengel reportedly read endless news reports about the murders.

The families had previously requested any internal information Blackwater had about that fateful convoy, and the events surrounding their loved ones' deaths. It was an understandable thing to ask. Yet the press had already reported nearly everything we knew.

Suddenly, Helvenston-Wettengel decided the news accounts raised damning questions about Blackwater's policies, and the mission Scott had been sent on. She determined we must be hiding something. It was then that she reportedly suggested Donna Zovko help her scout law firms to come after us. "The lawyers we hire not only have to be mean SOBs," Helvenston-Wettengel reportedly emailed Zovko, "but they have to be wealthy, mean SOBs because this thing is not gonna go away in two months."

Soon, the phone rang at the offices of Daniel J. Callahan, a founding partner of Callahan & Blaine, a Santa Ana, California, law firm specializing in civil and business litigation. Callahan's claim to fame came just months before the Blackwater killings, when he won a $934 million jury verdict after a ten-week corporate fraud trial—the highest award ever in Orange County. He was, as Helvenston-Wettengel might have described him, a "wealthy, mean SOB."

According to a 2006 story in the *OC Weekly* newspaper, Callahan's business card boasts his being named "Attorney of the Year" in 2003 by *California Lawyer* magazine, as well as one of the "Top 10 Attorneys in the U.S." in 2004 by the *National Law Journal*. He was also a man who never seemed to shy away from a chance to raise his own profile—and in a wrongful death suit against Blackwater, the lawyer surely saw the opportunity to do just that. Whereas the killings had brought widespread visibility to the contracting industry, a landmark lawsuit against my company would have wide-ranging accountability implications for PMCs everywhere.

One can only imagine how much money Callahan suggested could be won in order to land the case. Whatever he deluded them into believing, it was enough for Helvenston-Wettengel to reportedly recruit Zovko, then the Batalonas, and finally Rhonda Teague to go along with it.

On January 5, 2005, Callahan's team filed the wrongful death lawsuit, *Helvenston et al. v. Blackwater Security,* in Wake County, North Carolina, on behalf of the families of the four deceased contractors. The suit alleges Blackwater did not provide appropriate manpower or vehicle armor for the mission into Fallujah. In addition, according to the suit, Blackwater did not give its men enough time to adequately review their route and complete risk assessments. "Had they been provided with the protections, tools and information they were promised when they signed up for their job at Blackwater, Helvenston, Teague, Zovko and Batalona would be alive today," the suit claimed. In what I've always thought was a grand irony, the case marked the only time Blackwater was ever accused of not providing *enough* firepower, or not reacting with *enough* violence in a given situation.

The families sought a jury trial, compensatory damages in excess of $10,000 each, and punitive damages "in the discretion of the jury." According to that *OC Weekly* profile, "[Callahan] says he can't wait to grill Blackwater executives in front of a jury. 'The underlying facts of this case are so hideous, and it will be on the national scene,' he says. 'I think it will be like the tobacco cases or the gun cases.'"

In reality, I felt Callahan's case was merely a combination of self-aggrandizement and unsubstantiated attacks tied openly to partisan politics. But the accuracy of the suit took a distant backseat to the lawyer's grandstanding and public pillorying of Blackwater—and, counterintuitive as it may seem, it didn't matter whether there was any truth to the allegations at all. The legalese varies a bit from state to state and country to country, but the crux of it is that statements made by parties, attorneys, and witnesses in the course of a judicial proceeding are protected—that is, those individuals can't later be sued for defamation or slander for even the most outrageous things they've said in court or written in legal documents, so long as the allegations are somehow pertinent to the issue being resolved in the proceeding.

That insulation was intended to provide protection for victims or witnesses to come forward with legitimate claims and factual statements without fear of potential legal reprisal. Since the statements will be made as part of a legal proceeding, the theory goes, the would-be defamed party has a chance to clear its name and exact ultimate vindication through the courts. Which Blackwater went on to do, repeatedly. Yet cases like Callahan's can take years to wind their way through the judicial system—and for that entire time, even the most ridiculous allegations simply sit there as fodder for critics and pseudo-pundits to seize upon. That PR damage—not the search for justice—is what spurs the periodic lawsuits alleging bizarre improprieties by celebrities, for instance. Make the story salacious enough, the hope is, and the famous figure won't even wait for the case to get through the courts—he'll just dump cash on the accuser to make the headlines go away.

But I've never backed down from a fight in my life.

Did the families of those four slain men realize then that Callahan would drag them through a bizarre, bruising legal battle that lasted more than seven years? No, I don't believe they did. They understood their loved ones' contributions to Blackwater's vital work and the way we tried to support the families of those we'd lost—even amid the legal chaos that unfolded. In fact, in March 2005, just two months before the lawsuit was filed, Blackwater held an anniversary event in Moyock, inviting the four contractors' families to be our guests. It was a way for our entire community to celebrate the lives of those we'd lost. In preparation for the occasion, Rhonda Teague wrote to our staff, thanking us for the memorial.

"You and your staff have turned a day that [my son] and I were both dreading so very much into a day we are very much looking forward to. . . . You have no idea what this means to him!"

Today, it can be hard to remember how in the aftermath of the attack Blackwater personnel became so close to those families. The lawsuit was sad and painful on every front—engaging my company in a new kind of battle that signaled the start of its second act, and the gradual erosion of its entire foundation.

Callahan had a weak case from the beginning. The lawsuit's contention of Blackwater negligence over the fact that there were four men on the escort mission instead of six fell apart because Team November 1 had required only four men for its original mission—transporting the ESS Support Services worker from Baghdad to Camp Taji. There, team leader Wes Batalona made the decision that November 1 could take on the additional job with the manpower and matériel they had, and alerted his superiors. As such, Blackwater's managers had never actually assigned anyone to the fateful mission to Camp Ridgeway.

As for having less than the standard twenty-four hours to plan and scout a route, that, too, was a result of the team's willingness to accept the new job on the fly. Our security contract stipulated that "Regency will request that ESS provide a schedule of activities and movements in need of security services at least twenty-four (24) hours in advance and for all missions of the Blackwater Protection Service Details. Emergency requirements (those with less than 24 hours' notice) will be considered but cannot always be guaranteed because of the threat level in the Iraq environment or the inability to change prior commitments." Batalona gave the emergency mission the go-ahead; then November 1 stopped for the night at Camp Fallujah, about halfway to its intended destination, around five thirty p.m. on March 30. The team had hours to consider its next moves before leaving around nine a.m. on March 31. That does not support the tale of a rushed or disorganized mission.

Further, Callahan's team made disgusting claims about Blackwater cutting corners with safety to maximize profits. "Blackwater was able to save $1.5 million in not buying armored vehicles, which they could then put in their pocket," said Marc Miles, a partner at Callahan & Blaine. The accusation that those men died because of profit margin is offensive. Moreover, as part of our deal with Regency Hotel & Hospitality Company, vehicle cost was never a consideration of ours. Regency was responsible for supplying them. The contract explicitly stated, "Upon signing this agreement, Regency will provide to Blackwater equipment for thirty-four (34) personnel to include: 12 Vehicles, Security, with protection kits."

That fact was only underscored by internal company emails that later became public. In one exchange between Tom Powell, Blackwater's operations manager in Baghdad, and Mike Rush, one of our vice presidents, Powell lamented the perils of operating in the unarmored SUVs available to Blackwater's men at the time of the Fallujah attack. He wanted to know when the far stronger vehicles would arrive. "There is no order for 'hard cars,'" Rush replied. "The contract [with Regency] only allows for 'hardening,' and yes, I realize that is not optimum.... I am including [the Regency contact] on this email since it is, in fact, up to [Regency] to fix some of the things you mentioned, particularly [supplying] reliable vehicles."

The glacial pace of providers actually *providing* the gear, weaponry, and vehicles they are obligated to is a never-ending struggle in the contracting realm—as evidenced a year later, when I bought those armored personnel carriers for the WPPS contract with my own money because State wasn't delivering acceptable SUVs in Baghdad. Further, Team November 1 entered Fallujah a day before Blackwater's security contract even officially began. When

Blackwater's men took on that mission at the end of March 2004, Regency's vehicles with protection kits simply hadn't arrived yet.

But as lawyers traded repeated motions, countersuits, appeals, and further appeals, Callahan's legal team faced larger challenges than the mere facts of the case.

Before coming on board, every Blackwater contractor and employee had to sign a service agreement that included a waiver acknowledging he could suffer serious wounding, dismemberment, and/or death during the course of his duties. That waiver stated:

> The risks include, among other things and without limitation, the
> undersigned being shot, permanently maimed and/or killed by a fire-
> arm or munitions, falling aircraft or helicopters, sniper fire, land
> mine, artillery fire, rocket-propelled grenade, truck or car bomb,
> earthquake or other natural disaster, poisoning, civil uprising, ter-
> rorist activity, hand-to-hand combat, disease, poisoning, etc., killed
> or maimed while a passenger in a helicopter or fixed-wing aircraft,
> suffering hearing loss, eye injury or loss; inhalation or contact with
> biological or chemical contaminants (whether airborne or not) and/
> or flying debris, etc.

We had signed contracts from all four men indicating they undertook those potential dangers voluntarily.

Then there was another wrinkle: Much as the families of deceased soldiers are entitled to Dependency and Indemnity Compensation and survivor benefits, widows and minor children—though not parents—of the four slain contractors had been receiving benefits under the United States Defense Base Act (DBA). Established in 1941, the DBA provides disability compensation and benefits to civilian employees, including security providers, construction workers, interpreters, medics, and others who are contracted by the government for work outside the continental United States. Some of the Fallujah families had been receiving a few thousand dollars a month under the program since the attacks. But the DBA also bars benefit recipients from filing lawsuits against companies covered by the insurance. So the plaintiffs' lawyers had to somehow argue that the DBA didn't apply in this case—and, in effect, that the families never should have received all the money from the government they'd been receiving.

Regardless, in an effort to stop the lawsuit in its tracks, Blackwater's legal team initially brought a separate argument to bear. Counselors contended that we should be insulated from these sorts of lawsuits under the sovereign immunity principle—which prevents wounded soldiers from suing the government, for instance—because contractors are considered by the Pentagon to be an arm of the Defense Department's "Total Force." Subjecting PMCs to the destabilizing wrath of tort lawsuits arising from combat zones, we said, would fundamentally weaken the ability of the commander in chief to execute the military component of American foreign policy. It was a position that struggled to gain traction, however; our legal team made appeals that went all the way to the United States Supreme Court, which ultimately declined to hear the case.

In the end, handling of the case boiled down to another crucial aspect of the service agreement. In signing it, each of the four contractors had agreed—as all our contractors had—that any disputes with my company would be settled "by binding arbitration according to the rules of the American Arbitration Association," a not-for-profit organization that resolves disputes privately, out of court. There would be no plaintiff's right to discovery in arbitration, and the contract explicitly waived "the right any of them may have to a trial by jury in respect to any litigation" arising from their work with Blackwater. That closed-door policy was crucial "in order to safeguard both our own confidential information as well as sensitive information implicating the interest of the United States at war," our legal team explained.

The plaintiffs contended they were not beholden to personal service agreements signed by their deceased relatives, but in May 2007

Senior U.S. District Judge James Fox agreed with Blackwater's position and ordered the two sides to appear before a three-member arbitration panel.

For almost a year and a half, my company paid both our side and the families' side of that arbitration process—amounting to hundreds of thousands of dollars. I was willing to do that, for a time, because we all wanted the case to be resolved. Eventually, however, the plaintiffs' refusal to contribute any money whatsoever to the process led us to stop bankrolling both sides, and the arbitrators threatened to close the case before reaching a conclusion.

Callahan's team bristled at the notion, emailing the arbitrators directly: "When [your] family members and loved ones read about the Fallujah incident in their textbooks or in the numerous news stories, and then ask you how you handled the case, will you tell them that you just threw it out because you didn't get paid?"

In June 2010, the arbitrators did just that. "While the record shows that the panel has worked extensively without compensation but is no longer willing to do so, the parties now have the case at a standstill with no prospect for improvement," they explained. "We therefore regretfully conclude that the Arbitration should be and is hereby terminated and the case is dismissed." Six months later, Judge Fox refused to send the case back to state court, and in January 2012, seven years after the lawsuit was filed, the families quietly agreed to a minimal cash settlement. Split four ways, it covered barely a fraction of the court costs.

I felt no joy in that outcome. The only sense of relief I got was in seeing the entire sordid affair finally come to an end. Apparently I wasn't alone: "It's pretty much destroyed my life," Helvenston-Wettengel said of the lawsuit.

It was a Pyrrhic victory for Blackwater. Over the duration of the drawn-out case, as Callahan faced increasingly slim odds of winning his clients the massive decision he'd surely promised them, the lawyer instead focused on manipulating public opinion, tarnishing the good we had done and the brand I had built.

In criminal cases, of course, the defendant is always assumed to be innocent. The burden falls upon the state to prove he's guilty beyond a reasonable doubt. It can be quite a hurdle to clear. In personal injury cases like the Fallujah suit, however, all the plaintiff needs is a preponderance of evidence. It's a vastly lower standard: If a judge or jury simply believes there is more than a 50 percent chance the defendant was negligent in causing injury to the plaintiff, the accuser wins. So showmanship counts as much as the facts do— in the courtroom and out—and in preparation for a jury trial that would never come, Callahan hired a PR firm that proudly boasted, "The other side is watching as the dispute takes shape in the court of public opinion. The best communication strategy will weaken the opposition's position and encourage the most favorable resolution."

That company, Washington-based Levick Strategic Communications, fancies itself a dealer in "Global High-Stakes Communications." I remember at one point looking over the firm's Web site and seeing two overarching options for potential customers: "Get Me In the News" and "Get Me Out of the News." I first heard about Richard Levick's company back in 2002, when it devised a spin campaign for a dozen Kuwaitis jailed in the military prison at Naval Station Guantánamo Bay, Cuba. In the aftermath of the 9/11 attacks, the men were accused of having ties to al-Qaeda and the Taliban; lawyers for the Kuwaitis' families insisted they were in Afghanistan performing charity work. Those lawyers hired Levick's firm to spread that message. "To be sure," Levick later explained in an article at WorkinPR.com, "the [lawyers] recognized that a top-notch legal effort would not be sufficient. The cases would have to be pled in the court of public opinion just as surely as they would be pled in a court of law."

Levick, whose firm charges as much as $40,000 per month, designed a PR strategy "to create an environment where reporters knew that this issue deserved open-minded coverage." According to Levick, it produced "literally thousands of news placements" for his clients. I was shocked by some of those stories at the time, but with them as a public cudgel, the detainees' lawyers ultimately argued for the release of ten of the men, despite objections from the U.S. military that they presented a continued threat. "You often hear lawyers and clients disclaim any attempt to directly influence juries and judges," Levick concluded. "Nonsense! PR does just that, and it does so honorably."

Five of the men, including Abdallah Salih al-Ajmi, were set free in July 2006. Then, at six fifteen a.m. on March 23, 2008, thirty-year-old al-Ajmi drove a pickup truck filled with some ten thousand pounds of explosives onto Combat Outpost Inman outside Mosul, Iraq. With a flash that left a thirty-foot-wide crater in the ground, al-Ajmi detonated a bomb that killed thirteen Iraqi soldiers and wounded more than forty more. I've always wondered how Levick felt about that.

Regardless, he clearly got one thing right. A "Drive the Narrative" section formerly on Levick's Web site read, "In a world where 80 percent of what people hear about your company is determined by others, the plaintiff's bar controls the story, the bloggers dictate the editorial calendar, and the regulators define the agenda." Accuracy doesn't have to enter into it.

The talking heads who fed the twenty-four/seven news beast said and did just about anything to make for good TV—including a ridiculous March 2008 piece of ambush journalism I believe Levick's team coordinated, in which ABC reporter Brian Ross and his cameraman jumped out at me in a parking garage as I climbed into my Chevy SUV. And Callahan seemed all for it.

Soon, leaks about the Fallujah case were everywhere. Callahan told eager reporters, "I have found the evidence concerning Blackwater's involvement in the deaths to be overwhelming and appalling." Blogs posted stories with headlines such as "Blackwater Plumbs New Depths of Shame in Fallujah Contractors Case."

As my legal team battled through the various suits and countersuits, I stumbled across one incendiary column on the blog *AlterNet*, authored by Callahan and Miles, which dramatically ratcheted up the PR battle. It was headlined "Blackwater Heavies Sue Families of Slain Employees for $10 Million in Brutal Attempt to Suppress Their Story." It provided perfect grist for the far-left Web mill, which happily reran it all over the place. The piece asserted, "Blackwater has now lifted this atrocity to a whole new level by going on the offensive and suing the families for $10 million. The families now find themselves looking down the barrel of a gun as Blackwater, armed with a war chest and politically connected attorneys, is aggressively litigating against them.... The families are simply without the financial wherewithal to defend against Blackwater. By filing suit, Blackwater is trying to wipe out the families' ability to discover the truth about Blackwater's involvement in the deaths of these four Americans and to silence them from any public comment."

It was yet another PR-driven accusation devoid of accuracy or context. I would never have sued those families, nor the estates that Batalona, Helvenston, Teague, and Zovko left to their loved ones. Reading that column was the moment that the business of that lawsuit—such that a civil suit can be considered "business"—became personal for me.

Among the details Callahan didn't include in the column was the fact that none of the four murdered men was from North Carolina, where Blackwater was headquartered. So Callahan's team had to invent jurisdictions to sue us there. To do so, he hired North Carolina–based David Kirby, the former law partner of disgraced Democratic politician John Edwards, and they established "ancillary estates" in the Tar Heel State for each of the deceased. The move didn't initially make sense to me—until it was explained that "ancillary estates" is legal jargon for entities that exist only on paper to move money around. They had no assets at all. The ancillary estates were shell companies, basically.

In an effort to stop the suit from moving forward, Blackwater countersued those shell companies, along with Richard Nordan, an associate of Kirby's who acted as administrator of the hollow estates, for violating the Blackwater service agreements those men had signed, which prevented lawsuits. We sought no damages from the families or their actual estates whatsoever.

Of course, no one at Blackwater could clarify that because by that time we were saddled with the State Department gag clause that effectively prevented us from defending ourselves. And as the case dragged on, and public opinion of my company fell further and faster, Blackwater began attracting ever greater scrutiny from Washington. The war in Iraq was becoming a viciously partisan issue, and with relentless smears about my company in the news, Blackwater practically fell into the laps of emboldened politicians. And if Callahan can be said to have done anything well in this case, it was to lean on the fact that the trial lawyers' trade association remains one of the largest donors to the Democratic Party, and then insidiously tie his civil court case into the nation's larger political debates.

Much like the absolute privilege afforded lawyers during court cases, I soon learned, legislative immunity exists for congressional statements and documents. Running the nation, the theory goes, is far too important a task for our lawmakers to worry about misspeaking or citing inaccurate statistics in the course of establishing facts and creating legislation. In fact, it's such a fundamental necessity, our Founding Fathers established a form of legislative protection in Article I, Section 6 of the United States Constitution. In what is often referred to as the "Speech or Debate Clause," the section provides in relevant part that "in all Cases, except Treason, Felony and Breach of the Peace, [senators and representatives shall] be privileged from Arrest during their Attendance at the Session of their respective Houses, and in going to and returning from the same; and for any Speech or Debate in either House, they shall not be questioned in any other Place."

Not only could Callahan make wild assertions in legal papers, advancing theories that would be parroted in the media until becoming entrenched conventional wisdom, but those same allegations could ricochet around the halls of Congress with no penalty for those who latched onto the sensationalism to score political points. Lawmakers speechifying from a bully pulpit on Capitol Hill would influence public perception far more than some judge in a court of appeals—Callahan just had to figure out how to get them to broadcast his talking points.

Democrats such as North Dakota senator Byron Dorgan and California representative Henry Waxman had previously shown themselves eager to pick through Blackwater's inner workings, though they accomplished little while in the congressional minority. But in the November 2006 elections, spurred in part by anger over the war, voters handed Democrats control of both the Senate and the House of Representatives. Nancy Pelosi, a Democrat from California, was elevated to Speaker of the House. And a month after the election, Pelosi—along with Waxman and Dorgan—received a letter from Callahan in which he decried "deplorable conduct by war profiteers such as Blackwater" and said the actions of my "extremely Republican" company "led to the death of at least four American citizens—all in the name of corporate greed."

I found it conspicuous that neither the chairs of the House and Senate Armed Services Committees, which have authority over the Pentagon's budget, nor the chairs of the House International Relations Committee or the Senate Foreign Relations Committee, which oversee State Department funds, received that letter. Then again, it was clear by now this wasn't really about profits—at least not my own.

Callahan told Pelosi, Waxman, and Dorgan (along with Nevada senator Harry Reid, the new Senate majority leader, and Maryland representative Chris Van Hollen, the new chairman of the Democratic Congressional Campaign Committee, who also received the letter) of his "precedent-setting lawsuit concerning Blackwater's wrongful conduct." He pledged to expose the "lack of accountability for private security contractors operating in Iraq." Callahan concluded with this request:

> As American citizens, we hereby petition you to initiate, support, and continue the Congressional investigations into war profiteering and specifically Blackwater's conduct. Now that there has been a shift in power in Congress, we are hopeful that your investigation, as well as the investigations by Senator Dorgan and Congressman Waxman, will be taken seriously by these extremely Republican companies, such as Blackwater, who have been uncooperative to date, and that these investigations will be fruitful and meaningful. To the extent that we can provide any assistance to you or these Congressional committees, we will do so to the extent permitted by law.
>
> We look forward to the New Direction of America, and to your dedication to putting an end to the fleecing of the American taxpayers and death of its citizens in the name of war profiteers such as Blackwater.

Waxman was already primed. For the better part of a decade, the then sixty-seven-year-old congressman had served as the ranking Democrat on the House Committee on Oversight and Government Reform, the mission of which is to "work tirelessly, in partnership with citizen-watchdogs, to deliver the facts to the American people and bring genuine reform to the federal bureaucracy." With the victory in the midterm elections, Waxman became chairman and head "muckraker," a designation included in seemingly every profile of the Los Angeles native. Now the man at the forefront of using an unpopular war for political gain was eager to wield his newfound subpoena power.

Within weeks of receiving Callahan's letter, I was told that Waxman's committee would hold a hearing to pick apart the layers of subcontracts under KBR's LOGCAP contract with the Army, "with a particular emphasis on the Blackwater company." That February 7, 2007, hearing, "Iraqi Reconstruction: Reliance on Private Military Contractors and Status Report," was ostensibly focused on escalating war costs and "sorting out overhead, subcontracts, sub-subcontracts, profit, and performance" among PMCs, the congressman said.

But before Waxman had even finished his opening statement at that hearing, things veered toward a familiar, unrelated refrain: "Today four family members of the four murdered Blackwater employees will share their testimony with us," he said. "They believe Blackwater sent their relatives into Fallujah unprepared and without armored vehicles, a rear gunner for each vehicle, or heavy automatic weapons to defend against attacks. Their experience tells them that tax dollars never reached the security personnel on the ground. They believe that the money for protective equipment took a backseat to the multiple layers of contractor profits."

One of our company representatives, general counsel Andrew Howell, agreed to appear at the hearing. Yet we found it revealing that the day before Howell's appearance, Waxman canceled another panel scheduled for the same day. That one would have included auditors from the Government Accountability Office, Defense Contract Audit Agency, and Special Inspector General's office, all of whom could have addressed the practical questions of government spending Waxman purported to be interested in. We weren't alone: "I [am concerned] that plaintiff's lawyers pursuing civil litigation in this matter against one of our scheduled witnesses for Wednesday's hearing have attempted to use this committee and this hearing to advance their private litigation," committee member Lynn Westmoreland, a Republican from Georgia, wrote to Waxman upon hearing of the cancellations. "The official business of the committee should be to provide oversight of government activities, not promote particular private interests. The plaintiffs will have their day in court; but the American people deserve to have these matters treated independently of private lawsuits."

It was little use. My company had become a full-fledged political lightning rod—far too valuable to Democrats for any sort of independent or impartial review. So only two panels remained for the February 7 show trial—the first consisting entirely of the families suing us. They began by reading a comprehensive description of grievances they acknowledged had been crafted by Callahan. "One question I have is [about] the opening statement," California Republican Darrell Issa said to them during the hearing. "Who wrote it? . . . I asked because it did appear as though it was written by an attorney who had obviously slipped in a lot of things that they believe would be facts in the lawsuit now pending."

The day's other panel contained Blackwater's Howell, along with representatives from the Army and contractors, including Regency and KBR, who had the unenviable task of enduring a witch hunt that had nothing to do with them.

The whole show ultimately proved fruitless for the inquisitors—as I knew it would. There was no dark underbelly to my company for them to uncover. Yet the politicians were adamant about trying to appease the masses—they knew Blackwater had already been found guilty in the court of public opinion. We were "mercenaries," people said. We were "cowboys." We were paid too much and beholden to no one—Bush's private army, run by a Roman Catholic war profiteer.

I began to wonder how much public pillorying one company could really withstand. With the combination of private lawsuits, congressional investigations, relentless demands to increase the size of our workforce overseas, and the cascading PR fallout at home, a perfect storm was swirling. That storm touched down seven months later, in a crowded Baghdad traffic circle known as Nisour Square.

CHAPTER 13
NISOUR SQUARE
2007

Sunday, September 16, 2007.
Just shy of noon in sweaty western Baghdad.

WITH A THUNDERCLAP AND A SIXTY-FOOT-HIGH WALL OF FLAMES, A CAR BOMB exploded in the city's affluent al-Mansour district, flipping and crumpling a half dozen sedans outside what was locally known as the "Izdihar compound." Inside that fortified complex—one of Baghdad's largest beyond the Green Zone—Kerry Pelzman, director of USAID's capacity-building office in Iraq, had been meeting with local counterparts about USAID's years-long project to bolster the Iraqi private sector and create jobs there. The ten-year USAID veteran had recently transferred into Iraq after two years directing health and education ministries across Central Asia. She was vital to the USAID mission in Baghdad. She had arrived at the Izdihar compound under the protection of Blackwater's Team 4—and it suddenly seemed that we weren't the only ones who knew she was there.

Even before the explosion, my men had been on heightened alert that day. By late 2007, according to a National Intelligence Estimate I'd read, Iraq had descended into all-out "civil war"—except for one clarification: That designation didn't capture the true misery on the ground. "I believe that there are essentially four wars going on in Iraq," Defense Secretary Robert Gates said at the time. "One is Shia-on-Shia, principally in the south; the second is sectarian conflict, principally in Baghdad; third is the insurgency; and fourth is al-Qaeda." Since January, the State Department had counted more than 54,230 attacks throughout Iraq—more than two hundred per day—and by the time of the Izdihar compound explosion, nobody could agree on just how many civilians, Iraqi security forces, and coalition troops were being massacred. Blackwater's contractors understood that letting their guards down while on duty, even for a moment, could be fatal.

Another concern we had that day was the growing string of insurgent attacks tied to the start of Ramadan, the holy ninth month of the Islamic calendar. In 2007, Ramadan began on September 13, and in the days leading up to the blast outside Izdihar, militants had staged a number of sophisticated ambushes against Blackwater's diplomatic security convoys. They'd shot down one of our helicopters with a rocket-propelled grenade, then waited with automatic weapons to ambush the rescue team that came for the passengers and crew. (Thankfully, all eight people involved survived.) Then, the next day, dozens of insurgents attacked one of our motorcades, resulting in a bloody firefight as Blackwater's men fled with their protectees to safety. That was followed by a midweek attack from an explosively formed penetrator (EFP) along Route Irish—the bomb destroyed the engine of one of our armored vehicles, sending our men to the hospital—and two days later we endured another highway ambush with small-arms fire. In just over three years of WPPS duty, Blackwater had seen twenty-three of its contractors killed in the line of duty—and for the men safeguarding Pelzman, the threat of becoming number twenty-four was all too real.

When the blast rang out, everyone's schedule changed. Typically, after an explosion like that, Blackwater's men would "hardpoint" the principal, hunkering Pelzman down in the most secure area they could find for fifteen or twenty minutes, until the situation stabilized and they could make a rapid exit. On the other hand, we'd recently seen a developing trend in attacks wherein initial explosions served as mere decoys for deadlier blasts that followed, capitalizing on the chaos. That vulnerability was compounded by the fact that as soon as the bomb went off outside the meeting location, all the Iraqi guards nearby seemed to flee. So, not sure what might be coming next, and definitely not wanting to be there to find out, Blackwater's men made the call to evacuate the USAID worker.

The security team hustled her into a black armored Suburban waiting outside. Pelzman wouldn't be out of danger until her motorcade of SUVs reached the nearest entrance to the Green Zone, three miles away. Fearing a kidnapping attempt might be under way, the men at Blackwater's operations center dispatched a support team convoy of heavily armored gun trucks to meet Pelzman's motorcade at Izdihar compound. Those gun trucks could bulldoze a path in front of the SUVs, if it came to that. Further, at the request of the State Department's regional security officer, we sent an additional armored convoy, code-named "Raven 23," to block off a crucial busy intersection in advance of Pelzman's speeding motorcade.

At approximately 12:08 p.m., the nineteen men of Raven 23 entered that intersection, officially called Nisour Square—which is actually anything but. The "square" is, in reality, a crowded traffic circle with a tangle of entrances and exits at something approximating its corners, where pedestrians scamper through and traffic cops make a feeble attempt at maintaining order. We knew all too well that insurgents see those traffic circles the same way deer hunters see trail bottlenecks—they're obvious locations for an ambush. It was crucial that Pelzman's guards be able to get her through the intersection as quickly as possible.

Raven 23's four armored vehicles drove into Nisour Square from the east and then turned left, "counterflow" to the traffic. They fanned out to wall off the southwestern and southeastern entrances to the circle.

By this point, my company's contractor database had grown so large, I didn't know all of the men on that particular team person-ally. I have learned much about their backgrounds and their reputa-tions since that day, however—and I am proud that they worked for me. Among them was Donald Ball, an Eagle Scout and decorated Marine who had been a squad leader in three grueling tours in Iraq. He was the rear turret gunner of Raven 23's first vehicle—a position akin to drawing the short straw. Handling the heaviest machine gun is little consolation to taking on the most dangerous job, practically mounted on top of an armored vehicle on a sweltering day while everyone else remains cocooned in the steel and air-conditioning below. Yet Ball could handle it; prior to joining Blackwater, he had been awarded the Navy and Marine Corps Achievement Medal for maintaining focus during a mission despite encountering "numer-ous improvised explosive devices and small arm attacks."

Former Marine Evan Liberty served as driver of the convoy's third vehicle. Liberty had served with what was then known as the Marine Security Guard Battalion (now the Marine Corps Embassy Security Group) in Egypt and in Latin America. The decorated Ma-rine had risen to the rank of sergeant of the guard, in charge of a de-tachment of twenty-four Marine embassy guards. His background made him well suited to the work we were doing in Iraq.

Paul Slough, meanwhile, was turret gunner of that same vehicle. After enlisting in the Army in 1999, Slough (pronounced "Slow") did a tour with the 3rd Infantry Division, conducting security patrols with an international peacekeeping force in Bosnia before being honorably discharged in 2002. He earned the Army's Commenda-tion and Good Conduct medals, then signed up with the Texas Na-tional Guard back home, deploying to Iraq in 2005. Slough joined my company in 2006 at the age of twenty-nine.

Dustin Heard was the rear turret gunner in the fourth Raven 23 vehicle. The twenty-seven-year-old Texas native had enlisted in the Marine Corps at nineteen. He served in Bahrain, then Kuwait, then near Karbala, in southern Iraq, as part of a team that recovered downed pilots and aircraft. After earning several commendations and awards, Heard was honorably discharged in 2004, at which point he signed up with Blackwater. While he was serving with my company, Embassy Baghdad presented him with a certificate of appreciation for "outstanding professionalism."

The men of Raven 23 were armed with M4 assault rifles, belt-fed machine guns, and 9-mm Glock pistols. As the team entered Nisour Square, Ali Khalaf, an Iraqi traffic officer in a crisp blue button-down and black slacks, hopped out from his guard shack at the southern tip of the circle and appeared to wave for traffic to halt. Blackwater's men established their positions.

No sooner had they done so, however, than a white Kia sedan approached Nisour Square from the south, driving straight toward the third and fourth trucks in our convoy. As my men would later describe it, the Kia's twenty-year-old driver, Ahmed Haithem Ahmed Al Rubia'y, paid no attention to warnings to stop. He could not possibly have not seen the armored vehicles, or the armed men, positioned directly in his path. "I and others were yelling and using hand signals for the car to stop," Slough later said, "and the driver looked directly at me and kept moving toward our motorcade."

Believing the Kia represented yet another car bomb, and fearing for his own life as well as the lives of his men, Slough was out of time to check off the varying degrees of force response. As the car drew closer, he leveled his machine gun at the Kia's windshield, and fired.

Throughout Blackwater's history, perhaps no single issue has been more misunderstood, or led to more misdirected invective, than the question of contractors' "rules of engagement"—effectively the necessary response gradations before lethal force is authorized. The standard sound bite goes something like this, from Robert Fisk of the *Independent*: "How do we explain now the armies of truculent, often ill-disciplined mercenaries now roaming Iraq on behalf of the Anglo-American occupation authorities? . . . They have no rules of engagement and many of them drink too much." That theme has been parroted over and over, in various forms and forums—making it more salacious and more ill-informed only seems to draw more attention. "There are no rules of engagement [for contractors in Iraq], no restrictions on the use of deadly force," inveterate Blackwater critic Jeremy Scahill once told a conference on globalization and culture. They're told, "Just keep our people safe no matter how many civilians you have to gun down, and enforce the gospel of the free market."

It is true that while working as contractors for the State Department or CIA in Iraq, Blackwater was not beholden to the Defense Department's rules of engagement, which detail the force responses permitted for soldiers in military operations. But anyone who asserts that my men had no parameters for when they could fire their weapons is pushing an agenda without regard to the facts. Which are these:

Each WPPS contractor was required to follow Embassy Baghdad's "escalation of force" policy, which outlined the appropriate response continuum in the face of threats. Assistant Secretary of State for Diplomatic Security Richard Griffin told Congress in 2007:

> This "escalation of force" policy utilizes a seven-step process that must be utilized as appropriate under the circumstances: (1) English/Arabic visual warning signs on vehicles; (2) hand/verbal warning signs; (3) use of bright lights; (4) use of pen flares; (5) weapon pointed at offending vehicle; (6) shots fired into engine block of vehicle; and (7) shots fired into windshield of vehicle. It should be noted that deadly force can be immediately applied provided that it is necessary under the specific situation's circumstances.

Further, as a condition of working the WPPS, all of Blackwater's men signed a written acknowledgment that obligated them to follow both the Bureau of Diplomatic Security's blanket Deadly Force and Firearms Policy and then Embassy Baghdad's site-specific Mission Firearms Policy. At the outset, the embassy's policy clearly lays out "Principles on Use of Deadly Force" (emphasis in the original):

The United States Department of State recognizes and respects the integrity and paramount value of all human life. Consistent with that primary value, but beyond the scope of the principles articulated here, is the commitment by the State Department and the United States Mission Baghdad to take all reasonable steps to prevent the need to use deadly force. The touchstone of Embassy Baghdad policy regarding the use of deadly force is *necessity*. The use of deadly force must be objectively reasonable under all the circumstances known to the individual at the time.

The embassy policy in place in 2007 listed two "permissible uses" for deadly force: First, it says, "The necessity to use deadly force arises when all other available means of preventing imminent and grave danger to a specific individual or other person have failed or would be likely to fail. Thus, employing deadly force is permissible when there is no safe alternative to using such force and without the use of deadly force, the individual or others would face imminent and grave danger." The second point acknowledges, "Determining whether deadly force is necessary may involve instantaneous decisions that encompass many factors, such as the likelihood that the subject will use deadly force on the individual or others if such force is not used by the individual."

As for the steps leading up to deadly force, the Mission Firearms Policy also clarifies something for which Blackwater's men were continually criticized in the public: the issue of warning shots, and of firing at cars that got too close to our motorcades.

Warning shots are not authorized. At no time will a weapon be fired into the ground or air as a warning to stop a threat. Warning shots may pose dangers to others in the vicinity of where the shot was fired.

Shooting at a vehicle is an authorized use of the appropriate level of force to mitigate a threat. In order to ensure a safe separation from motorcade and suspected or likely threat, shots may be fired into the vehicle's engine block as needed to prohibit a threat from entering into an area where the protective detail would be exposed to an attack. If at all feasible, other warnings, visible, verbal and combination, will be used before the use of these shots. If the vehicle continues to be a threat after shooting into the engine block, the next level of deadly force is authorized to mitigate the threat. Employees must use their discretion at the number of rounds fired into the engine block to stop the threat.

Blackwater's application of those mandates was reflected in one oft-cited statistic: From June 2005 to June 2007, my company had 195 documented episodes in which our men fired their weapons. A few critics have contended that statistic doesn't include some hypothetical number of uncounted incidents—though those people clearly aren't familiar with State Department incident reporting protocol. Any time a shot was fired by one of Blackwater's men, it had to be called in by radio and confirmed in the debrief that happens after every mission. State issued ammunition to Blackwater's men, and rounds of ammunition were counted. Anyone who'd fired his weapon and *not* reported it would have lost his job immediately—as would any of his team members who lied to protect him.

At least some of those shootings resulted in fatalities—though, admittedly, we don't have the exact numbers on it. My men were guards, not investigators. Sticking around to analyze a shooting would have been directly counter to our mission to keep the principals away from threats. "We shot to kill and didn't stop to check a pulse," one former Blackwater contractor said.

It practically goes without saying that approach earned us no friends among Iraqi civilians, or the emergent government agencies representing them. In February 2007, for instance, a Blackwater sniper on the rooftop of the Ministry of Justice, in which a U.S. diplomat had a meeting, faced incoming small-arms fire and responded by killing three potential threats on a nearby balcony. An Iraqi police report described Blackwater's shootings as "an act of terrorism," yet an internal State Department review found the contractor's defensive, well-aimed shots justified and "within the approved rules."

Three months later, one of my men fatally wounded the driver of a maroon sedan who failed to keep a safe distance from a Blackwater convoy passing by the Iraqi Ministry of Interior. After the driver refused to follow our gunners' hand signals and their yelling "*Kiff!*"— "Stop!" in Arabic—Blackwater's men first shot his radiator, and only after that failed to stop him put bullets into his windshield. The legitimate shooting led to an armed standoff between the contractors and ministry forces, ultimately resolved only by officers from a passing military convoy. The shooting "could undermine a lot of the cordial relationships that have been built up over the past four years," Matthew Degn, an American adviser to the Interior Ministry, told the *Washington Post* at the time. "There's a lot of angry people up here right now."

And then there was the shooting on a highway east of Kirkuk, in northern Iraq. The security convoy, protecting employees of the U.S. Army Corps of Engineers, was approached "at a high rate of speed" by an orange-and-white taxi, according to a Corps statement. The contractors ultimately fired into the vehicle, wounding three Iraqi civilians. Speculation abounded regarding more of Blackwater's "cowboy" ways. The only problem? My men weren't anywhere near Kirkuk that day. The shooters were from British firm Erinys International. But by late 2007, even though there were some 170 private security companies operating in Iraq, any time a contractor fired a weapon people just assumed it was Blackwater.

As my company's critics are quick to point out, those 195 shootings by Blackwater were indeed more than the combined number by DynCorp and Triple Canopy, the other two companies on the WPPS II contract. Which sounds damning—without context. The fuller picture is that Blackwater carried out sixteen thousand personal security detail missions in Iraq over that same two-year time frame, so those 195 incidents represented shots fired on only 1.2 percent of our missions. Nearly 99 percent of the time, we did not fire our weapons at all.

And while I grasp the temptation to compare Blackwater to those other firms, my company held down twice as much WPPS work as those two combined as well. The people who wrote the rule book—and made sure we obeyed it—certainly didn't seem to have a problem with our approach. "[Blackwater's behavior] is obviously condoned by State and it's what State expects, because they have contract oversight," Jack Holly, a retired Marine colonel who oversaw several private security firms as director of logistics for the U.S. Army Corps of Engineers, told the *Washington Post* in 2007. "If they didn't like it, they would change it."

On the morning of the Izdihar compound blast, just like every other morning, Blackwater's men received a premission brief on their assignments for the day and the latest intelligence. Those briefs were detailed down to the seat each team member would take in their respective vehicles and what their individual responsibilities were. State's regional security officer reiterated to our men that morning the rules of engagement and the use of force continuum—which were obeyed that day.

In the years since September 16, 2007, it has become popular to focus on what Blackwater's men might have recognized, or should have known, or could have done differently in the midst of armed conflict. Those arguments, as old as war itself, are easy to make now. But I wasn't there then. And I will not second-guess the split-second decisions of my men. The exact details of what unfolded in Nisour Square remain the subject of ongoing litigation and intense debate in the media. The description of events here is re-created from a number of government investigations, State Department radio logs, photographic evidence, news reports, and the sworn statements of Blackwater's men, whom to this day I have no reason to doubt.

It's possible that in the face of Raven 23's contractors waving him down, Al Rubia'y simply stepped on the gas instead of the brakes—that's one hypothesis. But for reasons we will never know, the white

Kia didn't stop. Finally, believing Blackwater's men were in grave and imminent danger, Slough fired a single bullet through the sedan's windshield, hitting the driver in his forehead. Given more time to investigate the potential threat, it's possible Slough would have noticed that the twenty-year-old wasn't alone in the vehicle, or that he wasn't talking to himself, or other characteristics that might have demonstrated that Al Rubia'y wasn't a bomber, but rather a medical school student driving his mother across town.

Moments after Al Rubia'y was struck, Mehasin Muhsin Kadhum, the woman in the white sedan, began screaming for help. The forty-six-year-old pathologist cradled her son's lifeless body. Ali Khalaf, the traffic officer, sprinted to the vehicle and reached into the driver's side of the car. He, too, was screaming. The Kia, with its automatic transmission—and, potentially, Al Rubia'y's right foot still resting on the accelerator—continued to roll toward Blackwater's convoy. *Is the cop a threat, too?* my men wondered. *Is he pushing the car toward us?*

Just ten days before, the Independent Commission on the Security Forces of Iraq had reported to Congress what Blackwater's men had known for years: Iraqi security forces were so corrupt, "the Ministry of Interior (MoI) is a ministry in name only," said commission chair and former Marine Corps general James L. Jones. "Sectarianism and corruption are pervasive in the MoI and cripple the ministry's ability to accomplish its mission to provide internal security for Iraqi citizens." We didn't trust anyone in those blue police shirts.

Suddenly, my men in Nisour Square saw muzzle flashes spark in the distance. AK-47 rounds pinged off the side of the convoy vehicles. *"Contact! Contact! Contact!"* The radio call from Raven 23 sliced through the din at State's tactical operations center (TOC) center in the Green Zone. "I started receiving small-arms fire from the shack approximately fifty meters behind the car," Slough later said. "I then engaged the individuals where the muzzle flashes came from." He began shooting back. The crowded traffic circle was suddenly the scene of a full-fledged firefight.

As Slough aimed into the distance, a second traffic cop ran to the white Kia. Jeremy Ridgeway, a Blackwater turret gunner on the fourth armored truck, could see that car still creeping closer. Everyone was screaming. That threat wasn't gone. So Ridgeway took aim at the vehicle and fired multiple rounds from his M4 assault rifle into the windshield, killing Kadhum instantly. More Blackwater men joined in, firing repeatedly at the sedan in hopes of stopping it.

The traffic cops fled back to their operations shed; some of Raven 23's gunners followed them in their sights while another shot a grenade at the Kia. The round exploded under the passenger compartment, blowing it off the ground. The blast ignited the fuel lines and engulfed the car in flames.

More muzzle flashes came from around the circle, from uniformed Iraqis and those in civilian clothes. By that time, both insurgents and Iraqi police carried AK-47s. Were those blue shirts taking aim at our convoy undercover enemies? Were they legitimate officers, fearing they'd been caught in a firefight with rogue contractors? My men fired back, the brittle crackle of their M4s mixing in with yelling and the sounds of shattering windshields. "Blackwater air support advised of small-arms fire at Nisour Square!" the men radioed in. "Raven 23 reports Iraqi police shooting at convoy!"

Incoming AK-47 shots bounced off the street and notched divots in the sides of Blackwater's white armored trucks. Their training demanded my men get off the X—get clear of the fight—and Raven 23 attempted to do just that. But crucially, in a detail that has been absent from most mainstream recounting of that day, a round from an insurgent rifle skipped off the pavement beneath the convoy's lead armored truck and severed its coolant hose. That vehicle was a repurposed money transfer vehicle, much like you'd find outside a bank, provided to us by the State Department. Its armor had been upgraded, but those vehicles were never designed for combat operations and their fragile radiator components below were not protected.

Suddenly, coolant gushed out into the traffic circle, pooling around the 5.56-mm brass shell casings spraying out from the Blackwater guns. The driver in Raven 23's wounded lead vehicle cranked the ignition, but the truck refused to start. Its electronic control module, the modern computer system that monitors engine performance on all heavy trucks, measured unsafe conditions for the vehicle's operation. "The team returned defensive fire and attempted to drive out of the initial ambush site," acknowledged the State Department's initial incident spot report (which was written by a Blackwater man in the operations center, but approved by State's deputy regional security officer before release). "However," the report continued, "the team command BearCat vehicle was disabled during the attack and could not continue."

More machine-gun fire cracked against the sides of Blackwater's trucks. The convoy radioed Pelzman's evac team, insisting they avoid the square. Members of Raven 23 leaped out into the street to attach tow chains to the stricken vehicle.

With added urgency, fellow team members aimed defensive return fire wherever they saw muzzle flashes. Civilians balled up in their cars, crouching behind the seats and covering their children. A blue Volkswagen sedan peeled into a U-turn south of the circle, only to have its back windshield shot out. The vehicle careened into a nearby bus stand and came to a sudden halt, blood splattered across its interior.

Nick Slatten, a Blackwater sniper from the third armored vehicle, spied two shooters in the distant tree line and fired twice, hitting one of them. From the rear vehicle, Dustin Heard fired as many as ten rounds at a gunman beyond the Kia, striking but not stopping him. Heard switched to his grenade launcher and fired a round that exploded with terrible force.

One of our Little Birds arrived overhead to offer better visuals just as the tow chains had been set. Raven 23 headed for the northwest corner of the square, our convoy gunners firing at perceived threats as the motorcade finally dragged itself off the X and eventually broke contact altogether.

Blackwater's men estimated some eight to ten aggressors had fired at the convoy during those chaotic few minutes in the traffic circle. None of Raven 23's team members were injured. The destruction the convoy left behind, however, was absolute: Trees, electric poles, and structures at the southern end of the square had been riddled with bullets. Car upon car had been savaged. More than three dozen Iraqi civilians had been shot, eleven of them killed. (Only later would Iraqi authorities claim the casualty toll had risen to seventeen.) The dead reportedly ranged in age from nine to fifty-five, some hit in the back as they attempted to flee the scene, presumably mistaken for retreating insurgents. It was one of the bloodiest incidents of the Iraq War involving security contractors—and quickly became the most publicized.

I was at home with my family when I first heard about the shooting. An email came through from another company executive mentioning there'd been an incident. Details were still being gathered, I was told, but I should prepare for a long week. In reality, the shooting set off an international whirlwind the likes of which I never could have imagined. It quickly became clear that, by late 2007, it wasn't just the insurgents who had bull's-eyes on my men.

Soon after Raven 23 arrived back in the Green Zone, the Diplomatic Security Service conducted interviews with each of the nineteen team members. Per protocol established in a memorandum, "WPPS On-Duty Discharge of Firearm Reporting Procedures," written by State regional security officer Mark Hunter, any Blackwater personnel involved in a shooting incident had to report immediately to the TOC in the palace for a debriefing. As with the Christmas Eve incident from the year before, those interviews—and the sworn written statement each of the men submitted afterward—were covered under the Garrity warning. That warning read (emphasis mine):

I, _____, hereby make the following statement at the request of _____, who has been identified to me as a Special Agent of the U.S. Department of State, Diplomatic Security Service. I understand that this statement is made in furtherance of an official administrative inquiry regarding potential misconduct or improper performance of official duties and that *disciplinary action, including dismissal from the Department's Worldwide Personnel Protective Services contract, may be undertaken if I refuse to provide this statement or fail to do so fully and truthfully. I further understand that neither my statements nor any information or evidence gained by reason of my statements can be used against me in a criminal proceeding,* except that if I knowingly and willfully provide false statements or information, I may be criminally prosecuted for that action under 18 United States Code, Section 1001.

But that was the last thing about the investigation to follow established protocol. Those WPPS reporting procedures allowed State to question an individual, but it was unheard of for the department's personnel to interview every member of a unit following a shooting. DipSec agent Ted Carpenter, who conducted those interviews, would later testify that this was the first time he'd ever been directed to speak to each team member. When he subsequently reviewed the investigations into other shooting incidents, Carpenter found the case files "consisted mainly of the statements of those involved that had fired their weapon, an after-action report by the team leader, and maybe a statement from another teammate in the detail." It seemed evident to my men that State personnel were merely fishing for details to fit the narrative they'd already mapped out.

Meanwhile, dozens of Iraqi National Police had flooded into the traffic circle at Nisour Square immediately after the convoy's departure to collect evidence and launch an investigation of their own. Within thirty minutes of the shootings, those blue shirts had been joined by U.S. Army colonel David Boslego, who'd been at the Iraqi police headquarters when the firefight erupted. By one thirty p.m., Lieutenant Colonel Michael Tarsa, the battalion commander overseeing military operations in that area of Baghdad, had also arrived on the scene.

In sharp contrast to the events my men described, the military vividly outlined for the media what it said was a one-sided fight. "It had every indication of an excessive shooting," Tarsa told the *Washington Post*. The lieutenant colonel added, "I did not see anything that indicated [the contractors] were fired upon." The military report concluded there was "no enemy activity involved" and described the shootings as a "criminal event." It's safe to say that my men, and I, disagree with that assessment.

Two days after the shoot-out, State's DipSec agents interviewed more than a dozen Iraqis—many of them police officers posted at the traffic circle—who claimed to have seen everything. That same day, the members of Raven 23 were told to submit written statements to State regarding their actions in Nisour Square—and Slough, Slatten, Ball, and Heard began the first round of what would be repeated questioning by various government agents.

Practically overnight, confidential sworn statements from convoy members were leaked—in part or in full—to a media ravenous for dirt on the latest Blackwater scandal. Headlines blared, "Blackwater Massacre Spotlights Mercenary Role in Iraq." Bloggers wondered, "Will Mass Murder in Nisour Square Slow the Growth of Blackwater?"

Meanwhile, amid the intense scrutiny, three of the men on the convoy—Adam Frost, Matt Murphy, and Mark Mealy—confided that they were upset about the actions of their team members that day. One report said a member of Raven 23 had even yelled "No! No! No!" in an effort to stop the firing. It's also true, however, that those memories were colored by the dramatic media coverage. Years later a D.C. Circuit judge would rule, "The witnesses that the government relied on most heavily before the grand jury—Raven 23 members Adam Frost, Matthew Murphy and Mark Mealy—admitted to having read these news reports, and it soon became apparent that parts of their testimony may have been tainted by their exposure."

Four days after the shooting, DipSec agents finally inspected the traffic circle, focusing intently on the areas Blackwater's men had identified as locations of opposing fire. Contrary to the military and Iraqi police findings, "We searched in these areas and collected what appeared to be AK-47 shell casings," agent Carpenter later said. "Photographs of the area were taken to include bullet strikes and the AK-47 shell casings that were collected." Back at Blackwater's base, we also took pictures of our armored vehicles pockmarked from enemy fire—proof that the convoy had been under direct attack.

However, as stipulated in the WPPS, we had to keep those vehicles free of damage at all times. Raven 23's armored trucks had to be back on the streets immediately. That meant fixing the radiator of the lead vehicle, adding a fresh coat of matte paint to the vehicles—and effectively destroying evidence in an ongoing investigation. The State Department RSO instructed us to do just that. So we did.

Soon, State asked the FBI to take over its investigation into the shooting, and by early October roughly a dozen FBI investigators were on the ground in Baghdad, on "a fact-finding mission to determine whether any of the Blackwater employees had engaged in activity in violation of American laws," as the *New York Times* described it. The FBI interviewed more than seventy-five Iraqi witnesses and victims identified by Iraqi police, and conducted dozens of interviews of my men. Of course, whenever they ventured outside the Green Zone, those State Department–associated investigators needed protection. So in a bitter irony, the FBI agents investigating Blackwater were initially going to be escorted by Blackwater guards. (The agency ultimately made other arrangements.)

In the end, the government's forensic scientists were unable to determine whether the .30-caliber bullets collected in Nisour Square were fired from our M4s or insurgent AK-47s. "FBI scientists were unable to match bullets from a deadly 2007 shooting in Iraq to guns carried by guards for U.S. government contractor Blackwater Worldwide, according to laboratory reports that leave open the possibility that insurgents also fired in the crowded intersection," read the lead to one Associated Press story about the research. At the FBI's lab, however, they did discover a bullet that had become lodged in the grille of the radiator from Raven 23's lead vehicle during the shooting—the same enemy round that had skipped off the pavement beneath the truck and split its coolant hose, disabling the vehicle.

Still, the Justice Department eventually charged Ball, Heard, Liberty, Slatten, and Slough each with fourteen counts of voluntary manslaughter, twenty counts of attempted manslaughter, and the use and discharge of a firearm during a crime of violence. (Investigators concluded that three of the killings—the pair in the Kia and a civilian standing nearby—could have been a legitimate response to perceived threats.)

The charges against Slatten were later dropped. For reasons I still don't understand, Jeremy Ridgeway, the lead turret gunner in the fourth vehicle, pleaded guilty to one count of manslaughter, along with attempting to commit murder and aiding and abetting. He agreed to testify against his fellow convoy members.

Upon hearing of the charges—and Ridgeway's plea—I released a statement saying that we at Blackwater were "extremely disappointed and surprised to learn that an individual independent contractor has said he committed wrongdoing related to his activities on September 16, 2007." We remained fully behind the indicted men, we insisted, because "these individuals acted within the rules set forth for them by the government and . . . no criminal violations occurred."

Beyond the individual charges, however, neither my company nor I was charged with any wrongdoing—which infuriated congressional Democrats hungry for blood. "While it is important to hold these individual contractors accountable for their actions, we must also hold Blackwater accountable for creating a culture that breeds this type of reckless and illegal behavior," Representative Schakowsky said in a statement. "These contractors could spend the rest of their lives in jail if they are convicted, but Blackwater will probably not even receive a slap on the wrist for its role in this and other incidents."

That wasn't the only response from Washington. Shortly after the shooting, the newly Democratic-controlled House of Representatives moved swiftly to approve a bill to bring all U.S. government contractors in Iraq under the jurisdiction of American criminal law. Contractors operating under the Defense Department, existing law held, could be charged with federal crimes under the Military Extraterritorial Jurisdiction Act (MEJA), but for employees of companies like Blackwater who had been hired by other agencies, the oversight was far less certain. So the MEJA Expansion and Enforcement Act of 2007, sponsored by North Carolina Democrat David Price, sought to extend MEJA to all contractors in war zones. "Just because there are deficiencies in the law, and there certainly are," Price said at the time, "that can't serve as an excuse for criminal actions like [the Nisour Square incident] to be unpunished."

Despite the Bush White House insisting the bill would have "unintended and intolerable consequences for crucial and necessary national security activities and operations," it passed the House by a vote of 389 to 30 before ultimately withering on the legislative vine.

Certain senators capitalized on the chance to grandstand. When Price's bill made headlines, then senator and presidential hopeful Barack Obama followed a few days later with his own Security Contractor Accountability Act of 2007. The bill, a reboot of his earlier proposed Transparency and Accountability in Military and Security Contracting Act of 2007, which had the same goal of expanding MEJA, followed in its predecessor's footsteps and went nowhere.

Not to be outdone, in early 2008 Hillary Clinton, then a Democratic senator from New York, went one step further with an all-out assault on contractors. Along with Independent senator Bernie Sanders from Vermont, she cosponsored a bill called the Stop Outsourcing Security Act. The impractical legislation would have required that only military personnel—and not "private mercenary firms," as she described them—could provide security services for State Department missions in Iraq. "From this war's very beginning, this administration has permitted thousands of heavily armed military contractors to march through Iraq without any law or court to rein them in or hold them accountable," Clinton's office said in a statement. "These private security contractors have been reckless and have compromised our mission in Iraq. The time to show these contractors the door is long past due."

Overnight, Blackwater became useful as more than a simple political whipping boy. Now my company had been turned into a full-fledged presidential campaign issue.

Many things never sat right with me about the charges from Nisour Square. Most of all, this: The thirty-five-count indictment against my men represented the first prosecution under MEJA ever filed against non–Defense Department contractors. There had been plenty of earlier contractor shootings in Iraq and Afghanistan the government could have trotted out for public spectacle, had the Justice Department wanted to. I still don't think Blackwater's men ever should have been charged at all.

So why go after my men? Why then? The answer, I believe, is that they were sacrificed by the State Department.

In a charged interview days after the shoot-out, Iraqi prime minister Nouri al-Maliki contended that the Nisour Square incident was nothing short of a direct challenge to his nation's independence. "The Iraqi government is responsible for its citizens, and it cannot be accepted for a security company to carry out a killing," he told the Associated Press. "There are serious challenges to the sovereignty of Iraq." He added: "We have coordinated with the American side to establish a joint committee to ascertain the facts and hold accountable" those responsible. That American side was represented by Condoleezza Rice, then secretary of state, who called al-Maliki to personally express regret about the shooting. She assured him of "a fair and transparent investigation into this incident" and that those responsible would be punished.

By that time, however, everyone involved knew the essential and difficult role Blackwater played in State's work in Iraq. After the shooting, the department placated the Iraqis by immediately shutting down land missions outside the Green Zone, thus keeping the perceived Blackwater menace off the streets of Baghdad. Except, when we didn't run, the State Department didn't run. Grounding us benched U.S. diplomats. So that lockdown lasted exactly three days.

Even the Iraqi government, which by that time reviled us, didn't want us to actually *leave*. "If Blackwater left at this moment, it might leave a security gap because most of the embassies and most of the foreign organizations that are working in Iraq" rely on its contractors, Tahseen al-Sheikhly, a spokesman for the Iraqi security forces, conceded at a news conference soon after Nisour Square. "This will create a security imbalance."

Additionally, upset as they were, the Iraqis had no authority to punish us. Shortly after the incident, Interior Ministry spokesman Major General Abdul-Karim Khalaf made global headlines when he insisted, "We have revoked Blackwater's license to operate in Iraq. As of now they are not allowed to operate anywhere in the Republic of Iraq. The investigation is ongoing, and all those responsible for Sunday's killing will be referred to Iraqi justice." But that was smoke and mirrors: Blackwater didn't have a license from the Interior Ministry to be revoked. Months before Nisour Square, our license renewal had been held up by repeated demands for bribes from within the crooked ministry. At the time, State's regional security officer told us to simply carry on without one—we worked for the State Department, after all.

That focus on licenses and Iraqi consent for contractors to operate within the country gave the Interior Ministry a moment of leverage, however. By the start of 2008, American diplomats had a far larger problem to sort out than determining what happened in Nisour Square, and solving it relied on Iraqi cooperation.

Back in June 2004, as Paul Bremer's CPA prepared to hand over power to the Iraqi Interim Government, the United Nations Security Council adopted a resolution reaffirming permission for the multinational military force to remain in the country "at the request of the incoming Interim Government of Iraq." All of the CPA directives—including the much discussed Order 17 regarding contractor "immunity"—had carried over as a legal framework for the sovereign nation. But the resolution was set to expire on December 31, 2008. And in order for U.S. troops to remain in Iraq beyond that, a status of forces agreement, or SOFA, had to be forged between the two nations.

Each of the one hundred or so SOFAs between the United States and countries in which our military remains for long-term deployments is unique, ranging in length from less than three pages (our 2002 SOFA with East Timor, for instance) to more than 150 (our 1966 SOFA with South Korea, which also contains more than thirty annexes). They cover things as diverse as criminal and civil jurisdiction for soldiers, taxes and fees, carrying of weapons, use of radio frequencies, and customs regulations. There is tremendous flexibility for bargaining between the host country and the State and Defense Department personnel who negotiate SOFAs before the president signs them. And invariably, according to the Congressional Research Service, "The issue most commonly addressed in a SOFA is the legal protection from prosecution that will be afforded U.S. personnel while present in a foreign country." That includes contractors—and the moment I read that, I knew my men were in trouble.

From the outset of the tense SOFA negotiations in Iraq, State and the DoD looked to fulfill President Bush's mandate for a military presence that would last "years," ensuring stability in the country and preventing undue influence from extremists and neighboring Syria and Iran. American representatives reportedly pushed for U.S. access to more than fifty military bases, the right for Americans to detain terror suspects without prior Iraqi approval, control over Iraqi airspace—and continued legal immunity for their civilian contractors.

On the other side of the debate, Iraqi radicals like Muqtada al-Sadr—and his supporters in Iran—blasted the United States as a "cancer that has spread and must be removed," and pressured al-Maliki to accept nothing less than the complete withdrawal of American forces. That got the prime minister's attention: The initial U.S.

proposal would "deeply affect Iraqi sovereignty," al-Maliki told reporters, "and this is something we can never accept."

When it came to the contractors, State made a handful of public gestures to show the Iraqis that its guards would be held more accountable. The department pledged to embed one of their own Diplomatic Security agents in each WPPS mission motorcade (never mind that there were only thirty-six total DipSec agents in Baghdad at the time), to record all radio transmissions, and to install cameras in each vehicle. We found that third suggestion ironic because a false accusation about Blackwater brutality more than two years prior had prompted us to ask State for permission to install cameras on board our trucks. We knew video footage of our missions would exonerate us almost every time against the myriad wild stories people told, and my men had even identified the "dash-hound" system—the same one used in many police cars—as a cost-effective option. Yet a State Department official in Washington shot down the idea in May 2005 because he said the department's lawyers "had some issues" with the cameras.

Beyond those public gestures, however, State grasped that cameras and radio records weren't going to satisfy an affronted Iraqi government during SOFA negotiations. An internal department report obtained by the *Washington Times* noted that "since [Nisour Square], print and broadcast media have referred to Blackwater USA and its personnel as 'mercenaries privatizing war, war-dogs, trigger happy shooters, soldiers of fortune, guns-for-hire.'" It added, "almost all global observers expressed anger that Blackwater—and other private security firms—can operate in a grey legal area as a 'private army' because... the U.S. does not have a formal Status of Forces Agreement" with Iraq. More and more, State personnel seemed to recognize that bias against my company meant the "fair and transparent investigation" Rice had promised the prime minister would likely have to be anything but.

Finally, in November 2008, Ambassador Ryan Crocker and Iraqi foreign minister Hoshyar Zebari signed the twenty-four-page

"Agreement Between the United States of America and Republic of Iraq On the Withdrawal of United States Forces from Iraq and the Organization of Their Activities during Their Temporary Presence in Iraq." I believe to this day that the Nisour Square charges against Blackwater's men were a coordinated bargaining chip. I don't find it a coincidence that "the Justice Department ha[d] been considering manslaughter and assault charges against the guards for weeks," according to reports, yet no indictments were actually handed down until immediately after the Presidency Council of Iraq officially approved the SOFA on December 4, 2008.

President Bush signed the agreement as one of his final acts in office. As of January 1, 2009, the U.S. military would be allowed to keep as many as 130,000 troops in Iraq until December 31, 2011—and the Iraqis were granted primary jurisdiction over American contractors operating in their country. And there were about to be many more of them.

As the DoD-led military mission fully transitioned to a State-led diplomatic effort, the war-torn nation hadn't exactly found much in the way of stability. "Terrorist and insurgent groups are less active but still adept; the Iraqi army continues to develop but is not yet capable of deterring regional actors; and strong ethnic tensions remain along Iraq's disputed internal boundaries," read an ominous assessment from the Senate Foreign Relations Committee. "Although a government has finally been formed, it remains to be seen how cohesive and stable it will be." The committee added: "The U.S. embassy and certain satellite sites, such as the forward operating base outside Mosul, are under daily threat from mortar and rocket fire."

With the withdrawal bearing down, it became clear to State that, without military support, the security problems the department would face in Iraq were not only profound, but also unheard of. The borderline panic was predictable. "Secure ground and air movements within Iraq, essential to DoS' current and proposed provincial presence, are now possible only because of U.S. military capabilities and availability of support," State undersecretary of management Patrick Kennedy wrote to his counterpart at the Department of Defense. "We will continue to have a critical need for logistical and life support of a magnitude and scale of complexity that is unprecedented in the history of the Department of State."

To help the diplomats achieve their mission in Iraq, that Senate Foreign Relations Committee, chaired by Democrat John Kerry, recommended Congress provide a budget for the obvious: more contractors. The math was pretty straightforward. Without the State Department hiring fifty-five hundred private security personnel, along with thousands more general "life support" contractors who would provide food, health care, and aviation services to the federal employees stationed at embassies and outposts across Iraq for the foreseeable future, U.S. combat troops simply could not be brought home. It was still a war zone, after all. Someone had to stand guard.

Meanwhile, back home in Washington, my men and I were gearing up for a different sort of battle.

CHAPTER 14
COLD AND TIMID SOULS
2007

SEPTEMBER 20, 2007, WAS A HECTIC DAY IN MCLEAN, VIRGINIA—
particularly for our lawyers. Everyone on my team was still trying to
make heads or tails of the news from Nisour Square days earlier. And
we weren't the only ones. The shooting had barely stopped when
another letter arrived at our offices from Congressman Waxman,
announcing a new hearing on Blackwater in front of the Committee
on Oversight and Government Reform. Apparently sensing that February show trial on contractor cost-effectiveness hadn't landed the
haymaker he'd intended, Waxman saw in Nisour Square a new flank
to attack. "The hearing will focus on the mission and performance of
Blackwater USA and its affiliated companies in Iraq and Afghanistan," read my invitation to testify. "One question that will be exam-
ined is whether the government's heavy reliance on private security
contractors is serving U.S. interests in Iraq. Another question will
be whether the specific conduct of your company has advanced or
impeded U.S. efforts." I stared at that letter for quite a while.

I knew that Waxman had long been known for getting his

man—as long as it fit his agenda. I remembered how in 1994 the seven CEOs of Big Tobacco earned their place in infamy before him, testifying that "nicotine is not addictive." His committee room was where Valerie Plame spoke for the first time, in March 2007, after her role as a CIA undercover officer had been revealed to columnist Robert Novak by then deputy secretary of state Richard Armitage. The next month, Waxman grilled former defense secretary Donald Rumsfeld about the cover-up following soldier Pat Tillman's death by friendly fire. I knew that in July 2007 Waxman had merely mentioned an impending hearing on "FEMA's toxic trailers," as he called them, and the disaster relief agency promptly announced a study into formaldehyde levels in the temporary housing it had set up for Hurricane Katrina victims two years earlier.

Clearly, *Time* magazine had been prescient in a 2006 profile of the new committee chairman: "Waxman is hardly an equal-opportunity muckraker," the magazine reported. "Republicans and industry groups say his investigatory zeal is limited to conservative targets: He spent the Clinton years trying to fend off congressional investigations, including the ones into the White House's questionable campaign fundraising practices, and once led a Democratic walkout when Republicans released a report on the firing of White House travel-office workers. While Waxman promises what he calls oversight, the Republicans say it'll be more like a witch hunt." Now I was the target of his hunt.

All the negative attention over the past few years had only entrenched my reluctance with public appearances; I preferred to travel incognito and simply do the jobs our government clients asked for. It wasn't even unusual for me to cover my face around swarming photographers in an effort to guard my privacy and that of my family. I always preferred a low profile. But by late 2007 the company I'd built from scratch was being ground down by the plate tectonics of political battles in Washington. It was clear that if I didn't take a stand for the company now, I might never get another chance.

As I looked at the letter from Waxman's committee, a friend

reminded me of Theodore Roosevelt's wonderful speech at the Sorbonne in Paris a century ago:

> It is not the critic who counts; not the man who points out how the strong man stumbles or where the doer of deeds could have done better. The credit belongs to the man who is actually in the arena, whose face is marred by dust and sweat and blood, who strives valiantly, who errs and comes up short again and again, because there is no effort without error or shortcoming, but who knows the great enthusiasms, the great devotions, who spends himself for a worthy cause; who, at the best, knows, in the end, the triumph of high achievement, and who, at the worst, if he fails, at least he fails while daring greatly, so that his place shall never be with those cold and timid souls who knew neither victory nor defeat.

I decided that, on behalf of everyone connected to Blackwater, I would testify. It wouldn't be one of our general counsels this time. I knew that I would never again be able to operate in the shadows. If Congress really wanted to take a shot at us, it was time for me to step into the ring.

Yet even that wasn't so simple.

Other Prince Group officials had wondered aloud if I should testify, worrying I might lash out at politicians who condescended to me about my company's performance. They were joking. Mostly. State, on the other hand, was legitimately terrified of the operational secrets I could divulge—specifically, the fact that everything Blackwater's men did in Iraq was by State's direct command. Because of this fear, Waxman's invitation wasn't the only correspondence we received that late September day. No sooner had the congressional invitation arrived in our Virginia offices than Fred Roitz, Blackwater's top compliance officer, heard from State Department contracting officer Kiazan Moneypenny.

Moneypenny practically attempted to derail the entire investigation. "This letter serves to advise Blackwater that the U.S.

Department of State requires strict adherence to the provisions of [the WPPS] pertaining to contract records and the disclosure of information," Moneypenny's correspondence read. She cited the contract's order against unapproved media coverage, then concluded:

> It is plain from the cited clause that all documents and information generated in the course of performance of [the WPPS] are fully subject to the control of the Department. I hereby direct Blackwater to make no disclosure of documents or information generated under [the contract] unless such disclosure has been authorized in writing by the Contracting Officer.

She was basically demanding we offer no background documents to Waxman's committee, and that I appear before Congress, on national TV, and say effectively nothing.

And still that wasn't the strangest request that came to our offices that same day. Soon after, Daniel Callahan, the lawyer representing the four Fallujah families and the one who seemed to be drafting the playbook for these congressional inquiries, reached out to my personal counsel at Prince Group.

That counselor, Joseph Schmitz, had been with my company for two years. He had previously served as the Pentagon's inspector general, from 2002 to 2005, heading an office of 1,250 military and civilian personnel tasked with preventing waste and fraud. Schmitz came to work for me afterward, both as a lawyer and as the chief operating officer of Prince Group, which oversaw both Blackwater and Prince Manufacturing, back in Michigan. He sat in the office next to mine on the eighth floor at 1650 Tysons Boulevard, in McLean, so I basically heard about it the moment Callahan called Schmitz out of the blue with a settlement offer.

I feel quite confident it was not dumb luck that the very afternoon a Democratic California politician asked me to appear before his congressional committee, a California trial lawyer reappeared with a settlement attempt. In that call, Callahan insisted Blackwater could "bury" its bad press "by paying $20 million . . . consisting of $5 million per family."

Callahan, we understood, was representing those Fallujah families for a contingency fee, which generally runs about 25 percent of any settlement or 30 percent of any trial award. After years of a fruitless legal battle with my company, a $5 million payoff must have sounded great to Callahan.

I began October 2, 2007, with mass at our parish in McLean. My mother, Elsa, back in Michigan, began it with a prayer.

I had no experience with these sorts of congressional appearances, but it was obvious I was in for a grilling. To prepare, I'd picked through each internal incident report since Blackwater began its work in Iraq. I'd pored over the WPPS training requirements for our men in Moyock, and the tactical operation requirements for our contractors abroad. We brought on BKSH & Associates Worldwide—a subsidiary of PR megafirm Burson-Marsteller—to drill me on all manner of attacks that might come from the politicians. For almost a week, Robert Tappan, a former State Department senior public affairs official then working for BSKH, and his team had staged mock hearings to steady me for the inquisition.

The night before my appearance, I had received calls of support from two men who had been influential in my life. The first was Chuck Colson, the former White House special counsel who in 1970 acted as Richard Nixon's "political point man," as the president described him, then spent seven months in federal prison for obstruction of justice in the Watergate scandal. "I went to prison voluntarily," Colson would later say. "I deserved it." There, he had a remarkable turnaround, launching Prison Fellowship Ministries and devoting the final four decades of his life preaching to those behind bars. He was something of a mentor for me.

The other call of support came from Oliver North, the Marine famous for his role in President Ronald Reagan's Iran-Contra scandal.

In the mid-1980s, administration officials had secretly facilitated the sale of arms to Iranians for the release of American hostages and cash, then quietly diverted some of the funds to Nicaragua to bankroll the Contra rebel groups rising up against their Sandinista government. "You're a SEAL," North told me. "I'm a Marine and I testified something like forty-five times. You can handle one." Those calls meant the world to me.

When I arrived at the Rayburn House Office Building just before ten a.m., the line outside Room 2154 snaked all the way down the white marble hallway. I entered the chamber surrounded by a team of lawyers and advisers, including Gary Jackson, who'd flown up from Moyock for the event. Vast blue carpet stretched up to two rows of wooden rostrums, and behind them dozens of seats for the committee members. I sat a few feet in front of them, alone behind a massive brown table featuring a simple white paper nametag that read, "MR. PRINCE."

In a detail that seemed to show up in every news account of the day, I wore a tailored blue suit, a starched white shirt, and a red tie— perhaps surprising those who apparently thought I might appear before Congress in a SEAL combat uniform. (I picked up that blue suit a few days earlier at Neiman Marcus; it was the very lightest-weight one they had in the store. I nearly choked when I saw the price tag, but my advisers had told me how the temperature in the room would climb thanks to the klieg lights for TV cameras and all the bodies cramming in. I wasn't going to let anyone see me sweat.)

Directly behind me that morning sat Blackwater attorney Stephen Ryan, partner and head of the Government Strategies and Government Contracts practice groups at the law firm McDermott Will & Emery. Two rows behind him sat Donna Zovko and other Fallujah family members: Rhonda Teague, June Batalona, and her daughter, Kristal. Zovko would later tell a reporter for the Cleveland *Plain Dealer* that I looked like a different man than the one she'd first met three years earlier—"like life had taken a toll on him." She was probably right.

At least I was newly freer to speak my mind in front of Waxman's committee. A few days after the State Department sent its first salvo to Blackwater, Moneypenny bowed to congressional criticism with a second letter that softened the department's stance. "I understand that [Blackwater has] received certain requests for documents and/ or information from the House Committee on Oversight and Government Reform," she wrote us on September 25, 2007. "[State] has no objection to Blackwater providing unclassified documents to the committee in response to its requests. To the extent that any unclassified documents raise concerns about disclosure of privacy information, sensitive security/operational information, or proprietary data, we ask that you identify those concerns to the Committee when providing such documents to the Committee so that they can be properly handled and protected by Committee staff."

Ironically, no one at the hearing was able to discuss the event that had sparked the entire gathering. The day before I appeared, the FBI had launched its investigation into the shooting at Nisour Square. Some critics contended that timing couldn't have been accidental and that someone was trying to keep the case out of the news. I saw something different: Once the FBI was drawn into that investigation, it seemed clear my men were in trouble. I've always figured that had the FBI stayed out, allowing me to lay out our complete case for their innocence, it would have been harder for my men to be prosecuted. Or persecuted.

With Nisour Square off the hearing agenda, Waxman was forced to include in his opening statement this awkward addendum: "This morning, the Justice Department sent a letter to the committee asking that in light of this development the committee not take testimony at this time about the events of September sixteenth."

That left the committee members with little to pick through but long-standing grievances and misinformation about Blackwater and our work—not that they weren't eager to do it. "The last point I want to make is directed to the families of the Blackwater employees killed in Fallujah . . . some of whom are here today," Waxman said to conclude his opening statement. "I know many of you believe that Blackwater has been unaccountable to anyone in our government. I want you to know that Blackwater will be accountable today!"

The chairman, as always, earned high marks for showmanship. It was that sort of rhetorical flourish that soon after prompted the *Washington Post* to regularly award satirical "Waxman of the Week" honors to any lawmaker who "takes congressional oversight duties to the next level" and "maximiz[es] publicity for his committee." On that day, however, his committee struggled to bring much substance along with its style.

For nearly four hours, as I rolled a white ballpoint pen in my hands, lawmakers stumbled through one misconception after another.

"We really have a remarkably unprecedented experiment going on in the United States today by having private military contractors," Waxman said. Except we had literally centuries of evidence that it wasn't unprecedented.

"We have to question in this hearing whether [Blackwater] created a shadow military of mercenary forces that are not accountable to the U.S. government or to anyone else," said Maryland Democrat Elijah Cummings. Except Blackwater hadn't done that.

"I am . . . troubled that taxpayers have been taken for a ride by paying six times the cost of a U.S. soldier for Blackwater contractors," said Missouri Democrat William Lacy Clay. Except that hadn't happened, either.

"What you did was you took away [Andrew Moonen's] bonuses, July Fourth, completion bonus, Christmas bonus, he paid his own way home, and he couldn't work for you anymore," said New Hampshire Democrat Paul Hodes regarding the Christmas Eve shooting. "Is that your idea, Mr. Prince, of corporate accountability?" Indeed it was.

(Following the hearing, Stewart Riley, Moonen's attorney, sent a letter to the committee complaining of the accusatory tone of the lawmakers. "People are assuming that a murder has been committed by someone who hasn't even been charged," Riley later told a

Seattle newspaper. "Where is the presumption of innocence?" In 2010, the Department of Justice decided not to seek an indictment of Moonen for the Baghdad shooting.)

Repeatedly, lawmakers fumbled through their allotted few minutes of questioning for me. D.C. Democrat Eleanor Holmes Norton asked me about Blackwater's vacation and retirement plans. Diane Watson, a Democrat from California, randomly lit into right-wing radio personality Rush Limbaugh, and anyone else who "called our soldiers, [those] who have been critical of the experience in Iraq, 'phony' soldiers."

"I am offended," she declared, "and you should be offended, too."

I had no clue how to respond to that.

I should stress my respect for our nation's lawmakers and the vast array of issues they are called to weigh in on on even a single day. In the weeks before I appeared on Capitol Hill, Waxman's committee had conducted hearings on everything from CIA leaks to diabetes drugs—so it almost goes without saying that I would know more about the PMC industry than anyone on that panel. But time and again I watched some congressional staffer dart into the room and slide a page of prepared questions in front of a representative who seemed to have no clue what he or she was about to read. What became clear as I corrected repeated misinformation was that not only were some committee members not grasping my answers, they didn't even understand their own questions.

"The hearing revealed a fascinating, but also disturbing, lack of awareness in Congress about the private military industry," wrote the Brookings Institution's Peter W. Singer, who attended the session. "[Politicians] on both sides repeatedly struggled with the most basic facts and issues that surround the over 160,000-person contractor force in Iraq: Everything from the number and roles of contractors to their status and accountability, or lack thereof. It was quite clear that this was the first time that many had been forced to think much about the issue."

• • •

There were, however, a few charges I was glad to finally respond to—largely involving money, that incessant headline generator. And if the politicians could tie it to tragedy, that only bolstered their grandstanding.

Back on November 27, 2004, one of Presidential Airways' CASA C212 airplanes, N960BW—known as "Blackwater 61"—had departed Bagram Airfield, fifty miles north of Kabul, Afghanistan. The plane was headed to Farah, one of the country's provincial capitals, some 450 miles southwest. This required navigating the giant peaks of the Hindu Kush—a name that translates as "Hindu Killer."

Coming two months after Presidential won the $34.8 million contract to shuttle troops and supplies across the country, the CASA was loaded with four hundred pounds of 81-mm mortar illumination rounds, as well as two Army passengers: Chief Warrant Officer 2 Travis Grogan and Specialist Harley Miller. At the last moment, I was told in the days that followed, the aircraft was flagged down as it taxied toward Runway 3, at which point Army lieutenant colonel Michael McMahon climbed aboard.

McMahon, the commander of Task Force Saber, which oversaw reconstruction efforts in the western part of Afghanistan, was reportedly racing back to his troops. Just after seven thirty a.m., Blackwater 61 flew away from Bagram and climbed to ten thousand feet above sea level.

In the years since that flight, I've learned much about the men aboard the aircraft that morning. I've been impressed by their backgrounds. The captain, thirty-seven-year-old Noel English, had extensive mountain flying experience. English held an airline transport pilot certificate and more than fifty-seven hundred total flight hours—nearly seven hundred in CASA C212s, largely as a bush pilot for Village Air Cargo in Anchorage, Alaska.

Loren "Butch" Hammer, the thirty-five-year-old copilot, had

more than twenty-two hundred total flight hours, much of it earned through years spent dropping smoke jumpers on wildfires throughout the peaks and valleys of the western United States. He'd been first officer on those flights, also in CASAs, which translated perfectly to the sort of low-altitude maneuvering his teams would be doing for Presidential.

Blackwater flight mechanic Melvin Rowe, forty-three, strapped himself into the cockpit jump seat for that flight to Farah. He wasn't required crew, but he'd been in Afghanistan the longest of the three, and an extra set of eyes for navigation guidance never hurt in the Hindu Kush.

Both English and Hammer had been hired within about a week of our signing the Pentagon contract. English had arrived in the country on November 14, earning just over thirty flight hours in his two weeks there; Hammer had arrived the same day, and had only three fewer flight hours in theater.

As they considered their route through the mountains to Farah, the most traditional path would have taken the aircraft thirty nautical miles southwest through the Kabul valley, then west.

Shortly after takeoff, Blackwater 61 didn't turn to the south, instead banking northwest, then ducking down into a gouge in the mountains, the Bamiyan valley. The weather that morning was pristine: clear blue skies and some thirty-nine degrees Fahrenheit on the ground back in Bagram. It would be visual flight rules all the way—no tricky instrument navigation necessary. If the men were going to choose a day to pick out a new route, that was it.

"I hope I'm goin' in the right valley," English said, according to the plane's cockpit voice recorder.

"That one or this one?" Hammer replied.

"I'm just gonna go up this one."

"Well, we've never—or at least I've never—done this Farah [trip]," Hammer said.

"We'll just see where this leads."

Where that valley led was a box canyon eighty miles west of

Bagram Airfield, with fourteen-thousand-foot peaks on both sides of the plane, and soon, in front of the plane as well. Not that that was necessarily cause for concern. "OK, we're comin' up to a box here," English said. "I think this valley might peter out right up here."

The aircraft had left Bagram's radar service area—and presumably, the men had dropped down to skirt the countryside as we did on all those low-altitude flights, hoping not to attract attention from insurgents. English appears to have had every confidence that, even in a worst-case scenario, the canyon was wide enough for the CASA C212 to simply swing a 180-degree turn and retrace its path back out.

"Yeah, [the map] shows us, uh, you got about twelve—I don't know, thirty?—miles of higher altitude [over the peaks], then there's another valley in the general direction that we're going," Hammer said. English understood: "It was good while it lasted," he said.

English clearly figured that, at some point, he would climb to clear those peaks. For the time being, though, the thirty-seven-year-old seems to have let his mind wander to other things, with the voice recorder revealing the pilots chatted about rock music. He was enjoying himself. "I swear to God," English blurted out, "they wouldn't pay me if they knew how much fun this was!"

Whether the pilots lost track of their exact location, or didn't pay enough attention to the CASA's maximum climb rate with that much cargo, or simply got wrapped up in the excitement of the flight, I can't say. Before long, however, I do know their conversation took on a very different tone as mountains rose in front of the plane—and the CASA wasn't climbing fast enough to clear them.

"OK—yeah, you're ..." Rowe said. "Uh ..."

"Yeah," Hammer said, "let's turn around."

"Yeah, drop a quarter flaps," English said.

But the mountain continued rising to meet them.

"Yeah, you need to, uh, make a decision," Rowe said. The sound of heavy breathing began filling the cockpit voice recorder.

"God—[*expletive*]!" English said.

The CASA was climbing as fast as possible; English simultaneously craned it into a fierce left turn in hopes of turning around. The plane's stall warning system screamed out in the background; the plane was pitched back at too steep an angle and the wings were threatening to stop generating lift. There, stalling would likely mean tumbling into a mountainside. Pitching the nose back down could have ended the stall threat—but also would have cut into the crucial climb rate.

"Call it off—help him out!" Rowe shouted. "Call off his airspeed for him, Butch!"

"You got ninety-five [knots]," Hammer said. "Ninety-five!"

"Oh, God!" English muttered. The stall warning screamed out again. "Oh, [*expletive*]!"

"We're goin' down!" Rowe said.

"God!"

"God!"

About thirty minutes after takeoff, the aircraft likely stalled during its climbing turn. Investigators found that Blackwater 61 had impacted the 16,580-foot Mount Baba approximately two thousand feet below its peak. The CASA's right wing and engine were shorn off; the plane seems to have cartwheeled and skidded for nearly five hundred feet before coming to rest on its left side, the left wing folded beneath the fuselage, which itself was broken forward of the main landing gear. English and Hammer were thrown from the plane, their bodies discovered 150 feet in front of the cockpit wreckage. Rowe's remains were found outside the plane's bulkhead; Grogan's and McMahon's bodies were found still strapped in their seats.

Investigators later speculated that Miller could have survived on that mountainside for as long as ten hours after the crash. One hypothesis is that despite a broken rib and significant internal bleeding, the twenty-one-year-old had climbed from the wreckage. A cigarette butt was found nearby, as was a metal ladder leaning against the fuselage, as if someone had climbed on top of the wreckage and looked around. An opened Swiss Army daypack was found on the ground near the fuselage; it's possible Miller had flipped through the pilots' maps. Two frozen urine stains were found in the snow nearby.

Inside the fuselage, a rescue team later found that someone had grabbed the water bladder from a CamelBak. An open Meal, Ready-to-Eat was discovered not far away. They found Miller's remains on an unrolled sleeping bag; he was lying down on his stomach facing the front of the fuselage, with his hands under his head.

It was only when a passenger waiting for the plane's return flight out of Farah asked about Blackwater 61's progress—five hours after the plane's disappearance, at one thirty p.m.—that the military realized there might be a problem. After a number of increasingly frantic phone calls to nearby bases in hopes of locating the aircraft, the Joint Search and Rescue Center (JSRC) was notified of the lost flight around three fifteen p.m. JSRC planes were in the air soon after—some eight hours after Blackwater 61 went down. But rescuers initially searched the more traditional route for a Bagram-Farah flight, finally picking up the downed plane's emergency locator transmitter twenty-five nautical miles north about twenty-four hours later. I was heartsick as my men in Bagram sent back constant word of severe weather that kept responders at bay for two more days—and of a possible rescue mission that evolved into one of recovery.

Soon, an investigation conducted by the Army's Collateral Investigation Board (CIB) blamed the accident, in part, on a lack of corporate oversight—a verdict with which we at Blackwater and Presidential vehemently disagreed. Presidential said as much at the time, releasing a statement that the CIB report "was concluded in only two weeks and contains numerous errors, misstatements, and unfounded assumptions."

One significant problem, we pointed out, was a deep conflict of interest: One of the two lead investigators appointed by the CIB was Lieutenant Colonel John Lynch, who had previously served under Lieutenant Colonel McMahon for years. In 2003, Lynch had even succeeded McMahon as executive officer of the 25th Combat Aviation Brigade at Wheeler Army Airfield in Hawaii. Lynch, who never visited the crash site himself, was hardly an impartial observer.

Another problem was the inherent difficulty of preserving and studying the wreckage. A Special Forces mountain team and a pararescue team aboard massive CH47 Chinook helicopters finally reached the mountainside debris field some forty-nine hours after Blackwater 61 went down. Those personnel estimated nearly two feet of snow had fallen at the crash site since the accident, so before collecting remains and the cockpit voice recorder, a CH47 hovered over the site for approximately ten minutes to blow away the snow with its rotor wash. But the rotor wash from a Chinook travels at roughly a hundred miles per hour, meaning the rescue team basically hit the crash site with a hurricane before beginning their operation. Was debris relocated by doing that? Was evidence destroyed? It's impossible to know what valuable investigative material might have been lost or contaminated.

Following the CIB report, the National Transportation Safety Board (NTSB) followed up with a damning, half-baked investigation of its own. The board's findings are often treated as gospel by lawmakers and the media—yet in the case of Blackwater 61, they were as flawed as the CIB report, and equally critical of my company. In fact, there was no way they *couldn't* be.

The problem with the NTSB's report was simple. For more than three decades, the heart of the agency's analytical process has been its "go" teams—as many as a dozen specialists who "begin the investigation of a major accident at the accident scene, as quickly as possible," according to the board, "assembling the broad spectrum of technical expertise that is needed to solve complex transportation safety problems." But those aviation go teams respond only to accidents on U.S. territory or in international waters. That meant that for its investigation into Blackwater 61, a crucial site visit was missing. Instead, "the bulk of the so-called investigative work that the NTSB conducted was listening to the [cockpit voice recorder] and reading through the Army's collateral board investigation," Peter

Goelz, a former NTSB managing director and consultant for Presidential, said in 2007.

Twice Presidential filed detailed petitions with the NTSB insisting that it had based its findings almost entirely on a deeply flawed military report. Still, our entreaties fell on deaf ears. And the families of the three soldiers used those reports to anchor a lawsuit against Blackwater, claiming that a variety of company actions (or inactions) had led to their loved ones' deaths.

When added to the accusations in the Fallujah lawsuit, the soldiers' families' claims of corporate negligence further emboldened Waxman and his committee for my appearance before them. A memo the chairman circulated to other committee members before my 2007 appearance concluded, "According to government investigative reports and other documents obtained by the Committee"—those largely being the plaintiff's legal claims—"the crash and the deaths of the crew and passengers were caused by a combination of reckless conduct by the Blackwater pilots and multiple mistakes by Blackwater."

Even three years after the crash, however, there were a number of unanswered questions about that day that defied such easy explanation, beginning with why the pilots ultimately chose the route they did. Their communication with Bagram ground control prior to take-off was recorded by the controllers, and clearly showed the Blackwater team's original intent: "Bagram Ground, Blackwater Six One ready for taxi—uh, one-seven-zero departure at one-zero-thousand." The pilots were planning to depart the airfield and fly at a heading of 170 degrees on the compass dial—practically due south—at one-zero-thousand, or ten thousand, feet of altitude. Yet when the plane took off five minutes later, Blackwater 61 headed in the opposite direction.

Only one key event transpired between those ground communications and the change in the pilots' flight path: They picked up Lieutenant Colonel McMahon.

Limitations of the CASA's cockpit recorder—it only recorded the final thirty minutes of sound, so there is no record of conversations prior to takeoff—mean we'll never know for sure what influence, if any, the lieutenant colonel had on the pilots' choice of route that day. McMahon would not have been able to command the contractors to do anything, but the pilots had already gone out of their way to stop for him at the last minute, and I'm confident that any requests he might have made concerning the route would have been deeply influential to contractors looking to best serve their customer.

What we do know is that the 3rd Squadron, 4th Cavalry McMahon commanded had initially been sent to southern Afghanistan to supervise "reconstruction and educational initiatives in Kandahar Province," according to the squadron's Web site. Just weeks before the fateful November flight, however, rival Afghan warlords began battling in the western city of Herat—and McMahon's troopers had been sent to halt the hostilities. "Task Force Saber remained in the area to disarm the militias, to successfully secure polling sites for the October national presidential elections and to conduct operations to block Taliban infiltration of Regional Command West," according to the Web site. The revised, northerly route Blackwater 61 took would have flown the men directly over the new area McMahon's men patrolled.

With all the lingering uncertainty about the events of the day, I acknowledged the obvious in front of Waxman's committee: "Anytime you have an accident, it's an accident," I said. "Something could have been done better." Clearly, that started with the men in the cockpit needing to be more aware of their surroundings.

Nonetheless, the idea that an instance of what may well have been pilot error was somehow indicative of larger corporate malfeasance simply doesn't make sense. According to one report, Richard Pere, the president of our aviation division, put it much more candidly in private conversation. In one oft-cited quote from a *60 Minutes* segment about the crash, Kevin McBride, a fellow Blackwater pilot in Afghanistan, recalled, "Richard Pere pulled me into his office. He says, 'Have you seen the cockpit voice recording transcript?' I said, 'No.' He says, 'You can't believe it. These guys are talking about

X-Wing *Star Wars* fighters and this and that. They were just having a good old time, and they flew into the [*expletive*] mountain.'" Asked why Pere might have said all that, McBride responded, "I don't think he could believe it himself."

Pere has since insisted to me that he has no recollection of any conversation like that occurring. But, regardless, all of us in the company agreed that a pair of pilots misjudging the clearance in a dangerous mountain pass was no reflection on the way we ran the business.

Presidential was suspended for one month after the accident while the Army's investigation ran its course. Then, the day the suspension was lifted, our aviation officials spent four hours answering questions about our policies in front of a military board, briefing me when it was done. The next morning, the board cleared my men for cargo flights in Afghanistan, and a week later we were reinstated to fly passengers in the war zone. We carried a general across country that very day.

By the time I appeared in front of Waxman's committee, Blackwater was flying a thousand missions a month for the DoD. And just days earlier, the Defense Department had renewed and expanded our contract with a new four-year, $92 million deal for aviation services in Afghanistan, Kyrgyzstan, Pakistan, and Uzbekistan. "We looked at their flight record. They had one accident," a military official told the *Washington Post*. "You as a consumer don't cancel your flight with American Airlines, for example, because they have one crash. I don't think we'd do that here."

In front of the TV cameras on Capitol Hill, Waxman sounded incredulous that we continued earning business after one mishap. "I want to see whether you are getting a stick as well as all these carrots," he said. But Presidential's otherwise stellar performance record aside, there was another key factor Waxman failed to take into account: The military couldn't have done the job without us. "We were hired to fill that void because . . . it is a different kind of airlift mission going in and out of the very short strips in Afghanistan," I told the committee. "We are filling that gap because these strips are too small for C17s. They are too small for C130s. [My men] are going in and out of places that the military can't get to with existing aircraft they have. That is why we are doing that mission."

If Waxman took exception to the money Blackwater had coming in, other congressmen preferred to focus on the money we spent—specifically on something known as "solatia," Blackwater's expression of condolences for civilians caught up in the horrors of war.

People are often surprised when I explain the practice to them, but it isn't new. Since the Korean War in 1950, the Pentagon has quietly handed out cash—primarily in two forms, condolences and solatia—to families of innocent foreign nationals hurt during our military actions. There's no formal international standard or obligation for it, but there is a strong moral value in helping victims and their families try to make the best of a terrible situation. There's also a tactical value: Accidents happen, the Pentagon knows, and unresolved deaths at the hands of U.S. forces obviously makes a population sympathetic to enemy efforts. Those payments were just the sort of tool the military looked to as it tried to win those hearts and minds our politicians talked about during the war.

Beginning in 2003, Congress approved approximately $180 million for something known as the Commander's Emergency Response Program, or CERP. That fund actually began with a lucky accident: Soon after driving Saddam Hussein from Baghdad, soldiers in the 3rd Infantry Division found $700 million in U.S. cash stashed in a hole in the wall of one of his palaces. The American government and CPA designated 25 percent of it for CERP. Congress re-upped the funds, supplemented by additional allotments from the UN, at about the same amount for each year of the war.

Lawmakers had originally intended for commanders to spend it on food distribution projects, water and sanitation projects, educational initiatives, and other needs of the local communities. What those funds were largely going toward, however, was making amends with the families of innocent Iraqis or Afghans killed or wounded in U.S. combat operations. "Where we think we have been wrong or have created unnecessary civilian deaths," Marine Corps commandant General James Conway told PBS, "[we] certainly do the right thing early on with the families, attempt to provide them compensation or solatia payments to acknowledge our potential wrongdoing. It's not an admission of guilt. It's an admission of the fact that a civilian has been killed and we have been involved."

The two types of payment varied only slightly. If condolence outlays were more an official expression of U.S. sympathy for a death, solatia offerings were more in line with local customs that call for an instant, token bit of restitution to make a bad situation right. In many Muslim cultures, the speedy acknowledgment of their loss was far more important than the money. "We . . . see sort of a unique thing that takes place in the culture," Conway said. "There is this almost acceptance, [which] I don't think would be as true in a Western nation, that says, 'Well, *inshallah*'—it's God's will—'that these things happen. It's unfortunate. We certainly regret the loss of our family members, but we must move on.'"

Critics have fixated on the amounts of the payments, some arguing they are too small, some too large. However, the Pentagon, not Blackwater, actually set general price guidelines: $2,500 for accidental death or significant property damage; $1,500 for disabling injuries or disfigurement; and about $200 for minor injuries. However, the amounts were a bit more fluid when commanders paid on the spot from the cash in their unit operations and maintenance accounts, which are a bit like the petty cash funds in an office. One GAO report, "The Department of Defense's Use of Solatia and Condolence Payments in Iraq and Afghanistan," even offered this example of the unfortunate math: "Two members of the same family are killed in a car hit by U.S. forces. The family could receive a maximum of $7,500 in CERP condolence payments ($2,500 for each death and up to $2,500 for vehicle damage)."

The blogosphere inevitably responded with headlines such as "How Much It Costs to Kill Someone in Afghanistan"; the Department of Defense could merely concede that war is a nasty business. "The Army does not target civilians," Major Anne D. Edgecomb, an Army spokeswoman, told the *New York Times* in 2007. "Sadly, however, the enemy's tactics in Iraq and Afghanistan unnecessarily endanger innocent civilians."

These payments became so common that by the time I appeared before Waxman's committee, the Pentagon itself estimated $42.4 million in condolences had been distributed since the start of 2005. That would have equaled a full $2,500 payout in nearly seventeen thousand cases.

As I explained to the committee, Blackwater responded to civilian deaths just as the DoD does, by way of the State Department's Claims and Condolence Payment Program. State generally instructed contractors to provide the same $2,500 for instances of death, significant injury, or major property damage, but those numbers shifted based on the facts of individual cases.

We followed State's lead to determine appropriate sums, at times paying as much as $20,000 (to the family of the man Moonen shot). At no point were we trying to put a dollar value on anyone's life, and the recipients did not accept our gestures as such.

The members on Waxman's committee struggled to wrap their heads around the issue, initially framing a gesture of sympathy as something else entirely. "What I'm concerned about is the lack of accountability," declared Representative Danny Davis, a Democrat from Illinois. "If one of our soldiers shoots an innocent Iraqi, he or she can face a military court martial. But when a Blackwater guard does this, the State Department helps arrange a payout to help the problem go away."

I did my best to set the record straight: "That [payment] is similar to what DoD does," I replied, "what the Army does if there is an accidental death from whether it's an aerial bomb, [or] a tank backs over somebody's car or injures someone. There is compensation paid to try to make amends, but that was done through the State Department. That was not paid to try to hush it up or cover it up. That's part of the regular course of action."

Then the politicians attacked the practice from a different angle. Whereas Davis was angry we paid families at all, Representative Bruce Braley, a Democrat from Iowa, left logic behind to claim we weren't paying these families enough. "Did you feel that [$20,000] was a satisfactory level of compensation for the loss of that individual?" he asked me about the guard Moonen shot. "If you . . . look at the U.S. life table, you will find that somebody your age in this country has a life expectancy of forty years. So if you were to take that [incorrect Blackwater contractor pay] rate of $1,222 a day, multiply it times 365 days a year, multiply it by a forty-year life expectancy, you would get a total lifetime earnings payout of $17,841,200. You would agree with me that pales in comparison to a payment of either $15,000 or $20,000."

Braley's thought process caught me off guard. "Your calculations there don't make any sense to me," I finally said. I didn't think it was unreasonable to debate the appropriate amount for condolence payments. Unfortunately, the members of Congress weren't prepared for just how cold-blooded the State Department's math could be.

In the days following the Christmas Eve shooting, Blackwater's management team had multiple discussions with State about how much to offer the vice president's guard's family. A gesture too small could understandably be insulting—particularly for a decedent with a political connection—and Patricia A. Butenis, the chargé d'affaires at Embassy Baghdad, suggested a solatium as high as $250,000. But in a country riven by war, desperation pushes people toward awful ends. The precedent of financial windfall for injury or even death, our State Department contacts said, could have dramatically unintended consequences.

On December 26, 2006, a special agent in the State Department's Office of High Threat Protection sent an email to a coworker, referencing the "crazy sums" of solatia suggested by Butenis. "Originally she mentioned $250,000 and later, $100,000," that agent wrote. "Of course, I think that a sum this high will set a terrible precedent. This could cause incidents with people trying to get killed by [Blackwater's] guys to financially guarantee their families' future." War is a nasty business.

Democrat Stephen Lynch, a representative from Massachusetts, read aloud the email at the hearing—prompting shock from lawmakers whose worldviews seemed limited to the sprawling marble of the Capitol Complex. Again incorrectly conflating solatia with hush money, Lynch said to me, "It would help the credibility of [your] company to have an independent inspector general reviewing these cases instead of having the State Department basically make you pay up $5,000 every time."

Lynch was cut off for exceeding his allotted time before I was able to respond. Given the chance, though, I would have reiterated that tragic accidents happen in war zones—as the DoD knows all too well. Blackwater, like the Pentagon, I would have said, offers those condolences to acknowledge a sad situation and help everyone move on. And I would have read the conclusion of that internal State Department email regarding the Christmas Eve shooting, which Lynch did not:

"This was an unfortunate event but we feel that it doesn't reflect on the overall Blackwater performance," the note said. "They do an exceptional job under very challenging circumstances. We would like to help them resolve this so that we can continue with our protective mission."

By the time clocks in the hearing room struck two p.m., the committee members were throwing practically anything at the wall to see what might stick. There was no coordinated flow or grander arc to the lawmakers' questions; rather, the hearing consisted of scattershot individual set pieces that didn't necessarily connect to anything else discussed.

I saw that the party lines were exact. Democrats asked me if Blackwater poached manpower from the military ranks (we didn't); they asked if I encouraged greater legal oversight of PMCs (I did); they asked about the crash of Blackwater 61. Republicans praised our extraordinary performance record. Lynn Westmoreland, the Republican representative from Georgia, added, "There is a party in Congress that does not like companies who show a profit. . . . They do not understand someone who is an entrepreneur and offers a valuable service that is above its competitors and that is based at a competitive price." Even after hours of questions, the collective keyhole glimpses into the industry—and my life—did little to illuminate nuanced issues.

Then Republican Darrell Issa changed tack by discussing my sister Elisabeth and her political leanings. In 1980, Betsy married Dick DeVos, who soon became vice president—and later president—of Amway International. My sister went on to be elected chair of the Michigan Republican Party; in 2006, her husband was the Republican Party candidate for the state's governorship. "Isn't it true that your family—at least that part of the family—are very well-known Republicans?" Issa asked.

"Yes," I said.

Of course, it wasn't just them: From the time of my first political donation during college until I appeared before Congress, I had personally given about $235,000 to Republican causes. My parents were conservative, my siblings were conservative, I was conservative—none of us hid that. Issa, a Republican himself, was looking to characterize the Blackwater attacks from the opposite side of the aisle as partisan bickering: "Wouldn't it be fair to say that [Blackwater] is easily identified as a Republican-leaning company?" he asked.

Regardless of which politician is asking the question, suggesting that my company's billion-dollar growth was somehow tied to who my family votes for was lazy logic.

Despite the narrative hammered into the public consciousness (and apparently the minds of our politicians), it wasn't conservatism that somehow built my business. Over and over, across presidential administrations, the government had come to us. From the aftermath of the shootings in Columbine, to training sailors after the bombing of the *Cole*, to the CIA needing guards at makeshift bases in Afghanistan, to the Pentagon needing a shield around Bremer, to the State Department needing a battalion for its diplomats, to jobs far beyond that, U.S. agencies had repeatedly reached out to Blackwater with urgent needs, regardless of who sat in the Oval Office.

My company held more than fifty different U.S. government contracts by the time I appeared before Congress, bringing in some $600 million a year. We hired two thousand contractors at any given time for jobs in twenty different countries. Just ten years after a handful of us had cleared a swath of the Great Dismal Swamp, my company had grown to include a fleet of forty aircraft, the armored personnel carrier production line, the 183-foot repurposed NOAA ship—and we had plenty more ideas in the pipeline. We guarded everything from CIA bases in Afghanistan to the Missile Defense Agency's anti-ICBM radar installation in northern Japan, while still training more than twenty-five thousand men and women each year back home in Moyock. That included not only this country's most elite forces, but those of other countries as well, such as the Taiwanese National Security Bureau's special protection service, which guards its president.

By late 2007, my company made news whenever we earned work— as when the Pentagon's Counter-Narcoterrorism Technology Program Office asked us to compete against contracting giants Lockheed Martin, Northrop Grumman, and Raytheon for parts of a $15 billion deal to battle terrorists with drug trade ties. We even made news if we didn't get a job—as tragically detailed soon after the hearing, when Pakistani prime minister Benazir Bhutto requested our protective services upon returning to her homeland after eight years in exile. (Sadly, President Pervez Musharraf refused. "It's an insult and a humiliation for Pakistan, its police, its army," he said. "Nobody takes this humiliation that we have to get Blackwater and all. What the hell?" Two months after Musharraf's refusal, the first woman prime minister of an Islamic state was murdered in Rawalpindi. A UN investigation found that "Ms. Bhutto's assassination could have been prevented if adequate security measures had been taken.")

"Blackwater's not a partisan company," I shot back at the committee. "We execute the mission given us, whether it is training Navy sailors or protecting State Department personnel."

The government came to us because Blackwater did what it couldn't do, didn't know how to do—or, just as often, simply didn't want to do. Representative Diane Watson, the Democrat from California, came closest to hitting on that issue during the hearing. "You have been paid over one billion dollars," she said, "and will continue to be paid so that you can buy the helicopters that are shot down. And so, my question to you: Are we going to have to continue to privatize because [soldiers] are not training to do what you do?"

My mind raced in a dozen directions at once—starting with an unequivocal yes: Blackwater would likely continue to fill those capability gaps for the military and the State Department. But the answer to the question Watson *didn't* ask—the same one politicians have gladly ignored for years—is just as crucial to the discussion: What gaps do we fill for *them*?

Politicians claim they want to get rid of contractors? I'd have been happy to see them send to Iraq more than the 135,000 troops Donald Rumsfeld had planned for. Even post-"surge," in 2007, the 165,000-strong U.S. force couldn't match the 180,000 PMCs on the ground there. Do lawmakers really expect the secretary of defense to declare on TV that his plan was wrong, and that generals below him were right to fight for more soldiers—and that future generals should continue risking their careers by publicly questioning their superiors?

Are those same politicians ready for more dead soldiers, and all the scrutiny that comes with it? Because by the time I appeared before Congress, the Department of Labor had counted more than a thousand contractors killed and thirteen thousand wounded in Iraq and Afghanistan. And the media never fought to take photos of those coffins being off-loaded at Dover Air Force Base in Delaware.

And where would the Department of Defense find all those troops, anyway? That would require Congress demanding a full-scale call-up of the reserves and the National Guard, tearing apart families, fighting a war with grad students, schoolteachers, and office managers—and ending those politicians' reelection campaigns in one fell swoop. Or maybe they'd rather have NATO allies put boots on the ground—and then force the Pentagon to cede major operational control to the UN in exchange for its contributions to an unpopular war. (Never mind the question of reinstating the draft—an idea so absurd today that it qualifies as a punch line on Capitol Hill.)

Or the politicians could just continue sending contractors like Blackwater. We were, after all, part of what then CENTCOM head Admiral William Fallon once gruffly referred to as the government's "surrogate army." We offered the real savings those politicians cared about.

Finally, I looked up at the rows of wooden rostrums, and Waxman's hungry committee. "Are we going to have to continue to privatize?" Representative Watson had asked me. I aimed for the bottom line. "If the government doesn't want us to do this," I said at last, "we'll go do something else."

When my testimony was done, I grabbed the "MR. PRINCE" nameplate from in front of me and stashed it in my pocket. That souvenir sits today on my desk at home.

CHAPTER 15

A NIGHTMARE AND
A MIRACLE

2005–2008

LEAVING CAPITOL HILL AFTER THE HEARING, I FINALLY WOLFED DOWN THE
PowerBar my lawyers insisted I not actually eat on national TV. On
one of the most frustrating days of my career, I was struck by the coincidence that about the last time I'd been in D.C. had produced the
proudest moment of my work with Blackwater, just two miles from
those klieg lights.

Earlier in 2007, I had spoken at the National War College, on Fort
Lesley J. McNair, which sits at the confluence of the Potomac and
Anacostia Rivers at the southern tip of Washington. The college is
part of the National Defense University, where midlevel officers in
each service—as well as the State Department and other federal
agencies—prepare for likely promotions into command roles. I had
been invited to give a talk about leadership. After that speech, I was
approached by a full-bird Army colonel who had just returned from
Iraq. He had overseen a brigade there, he said—as many as five thousand soldiers. "I want you to know," he told me, "as my guys drove
through Baghdad, on the top of the dashboards in their Humvees

was a piece of paper with Blackwater's call signs and radio frequencies." They knew, the colonel said, that in a crisis my men would always come for them, no matter what.

It was actually a sentiment I'd heard before—though never from someone with the Army's silver eagle emblems on his shoulders. During our time in Iraq, Blackwater's men and women rescued, treated, or medevaced more than forty U.S. soldiers, Marines, and government officials.

We did so dozens more times during security work in Afghanistan—including coming to the aid of Senators Joe Biden, Chuck Hagel, and John Kerry and a three-star general after their helicopter made an emergency landing in the perilous Hindu Kush. Amid a sudden, blinding snowstorm, their chopper pilot opted to set down instead of continuing the flight. An Army force was dispatched to collect the men, but the troops became disoriented in their quest to locate the helicopter. Blackwater's men plowed through, regardless of the potential danger, arriving first on the scene to evacuate them all back to Bagram Airfield. "If you want to know where al-Qaeda lives, you want to know where [Osama] bin Laden is, come back to Afghanistan with me," Biden said during a 2008 campaign stop. "Come back to the area where my helicopter was forced down, with a three-star general and three senators at 10,500 feet in the middle of those mountains. I can tell you where they are." Those grateful passengers—including President Obama's future vice president, a future secretary of state, and future secretary of defense—even posed for a quick photo at the makeshift landing site before being escorted away.

Blackwater's men responded to fires, mortar attacks, and suicide bombings that destroyed entire sections of neighborhoods. During one mission in October 2006 two of our Little Birds were returning to base after a State escort mission when our men spotted an Army motorcade that had just been hit with an EFP. Soldiers were splayed out on the ground around the shattered convoy. The first helicopter, with medic Mark York aboard, peeled off for a spontaneous landing at the site; the other Little Bird hovered overhead, providing cover.

York began triage on the ground, loading the most seriously wounded into the helicopter—and guaranteeing there was no further room for him. As his chopper lifted off and headed for a combat surgical hospital in the Green Zone, York hunkered down at the attack site and waited for Blackwater reinforcements to arrive. The Army said Blackwater's men saved five soldiers that day.

No one associated with my company was looking for awards, or commendations, or fawning magazine profiles. For us, the ultimate gratification came from hearing a simple thank-you from people such as that colonel. That sentiment said everything I wanted to hear about what my company had become, and what it could be.

Still, I feel it is important to recognize here a few remarkable stories about what Blackwater's contractors have done. Because as I left Washington after my appearance before Congress, I thought about the politicians in that hearing room who thought we were cowboys and mercenaries. I thought about the men and women getting shot at seven thousand miles away who called us heroes. I knew whose opinions would generate more headlines.

And it took no more than a few hours after my testimony for another distress call from our troops to sound in our Baghdad operations center.

At ten a.m. local time on October 3, the day after my testimony before Congress, Poland's ambassador to Iraq climbed into a reinforced Toyota Land Cruiser in the affluent Karrada district of eastern Baghdad. Edward Pietrzyk's white SUV was surrounded by two more Toyotas, full of his Polish special forces protective detail. The motorcade drove away from the Polish embassy, then turned the corner to navigate palm-lined back streets as they made their way to the city center. The convoy made it two hundred yards.

A first roadside bomb scorched the vehicles and stopped the motorcade in its tracks. Then two more bombs, detonated moments after the vehicles stopped, blew the wheels off the cars and engulfed them all in a fifteen-foot-high fireball. Then two dozen insurgents swarmed upon the burning wreckage.

Pietrzyk's guards responded valiantly. Bloodied and shaken—initial reports described the men as sustaining "massive wounds" and some even missing limbs—they pulled the injured ambassador from his SUV and burst into a nearby household for cover. The reasons for the attack were never fully clear, but Poland had been an ardent supporter of the U.S. mission in Iraq from the outset. Twenty Poles had been killed in the four years since they first assisted the American invasion of Iraq; on October 3, Bartosz Orzechowski, one of Pietrzyk's guards, became the twenty-first. The ambassador seemed destined to be next.

Battling insurgents from the house, the security detail contacted State's tactical operations center in urgent distress. American soldiers would come, the RSO told them, but the canopy of streetlights and electrical wires in the neighborhood attack zone made landing a military chopper there impossible. Ground troops couldn't reach them in time. So the U.S. embassy radioed Blackwater's operations office with a request: *Get there now.*

Our quick reaction force was off the ground moments later. Three minutes after takeoff, pilot Dan Laguna, who, like many with Blackwater Aviation had spent his military career with the Army's 160th Special Operations Aviation Regiment, picked out the red plume from a smoke grenade that signaled his landing spot. Laguna bent his helicopter into a steep turn above the narrow street; the special tethers we'd developed known as "monkey harnesses" were the only things that kept Laguna's door gunners connected to the aircraft. The pilot knifed between arcing streetlights that would have splintered his rotor blades, then set the helicopter down on the rubble strewn across the cratered gray roadway.

At the sound of the incoming aerial support, insurgents scattered into the alleyways between the three-story beige buildings. On the ground, Blackwater's door gunners unclasped their harnesses and fanned out in a perimeter for the evacuation team. Another Little

Bird followed at the landing site; a larger Blackwater Bell 412 chopper hovered overhead. Pietrzyk's blackened SUV was crumpled against the yellow-and-white-painted curb.

Our men found the barrel-chested ambassador wearing little more than a dirty white T-shirt. In the house, his guards had torn off his suit and the right leg of his pants—all but his diplomatic ID, which still hung around his neck. The fifty-seven-year-old had been burned over 20 percent of his body and had sustained internal injuries as flames shot into his nose and mouth and down his respiratory tract. His leg, hands, and head were heavily bandaged, but he was alert, and he could move.

Together, Blackwater's men and Pietrzyk's guards formed a huddle of helmets and Kevlar vests, rushing the ambassador to Laguna's chopper. Pietrzyk and Orzechowski were loaded into that Little Bird; other injured guards climbed into the second helicopter. Laguna flew the ambassador to a U.S. military hospital in the Green Zone, where Pietrzyk was stabilized before being flown to Ramstein Air Base in Germany, and ultimately to a hospital in Gryfice, in northern Poland, where he was placed in an artificial coma for two weeks. "The patient is unable to breathe and was put on a respirator," the head of the Gryfice hospital told a Polish newspaper. "His state is very serious and his prognosis is very cautious."

I used any contacts I could find in Poland to keep track of the ambassador's progress. Pietrzyk underwent extensive surgery, but the indomitable former general of all land forces in Poland refused to succumb to his injuries.

Poland's foreign minister soon released a statement noting how Blackwater's team "undoubtedly saved the lives of the Polish ambassador, Mr. Edward Pietrzyk, and his personnel, trapped in a deadly ambush." (Orzechowski, the fallen guard, was posthumously decorated with his country's Commander's Cross of the Order of Military Cross and promoted to the rank of second lieutenant.) The ambassador was back in Baghdad a mere three months later—immediately insisting Blackwater's men appear with him for a medal ceremony at the Polish embassy, which had since been moved into the Green Zone.

On January 25, 2008, surrounded by U.S. Ambassador Ryan Crocker and the commander of the Multi-National Force in Iraq, General David Petraeus, Pietrzyk pinned a Silver Star on Laguna's chest. Fellow Blackwater contractors Frank Paul, Rick Stout, Abe Bronn, John Nussbaum, Paul Chopra, Dick Aanerud, Hoyt Fraiser, Brian Perlis, Clint Matoon, Josh Kinny, Brian O'Malley, Daniel Pray, Wilson Mc-Kiethan, Nathan Pohl, Anthony Sanganetti, Scott Bruggemann, and Ali Murjan were honored with Bronze Stars for their heroism. It was the first time Poland bestowed the medals upon foreigners since World War II. "I'm here because of you, the people who are proudly carrying the name 'Black Waters,'" an emotional Pietrzyk said in his halting English. "My family—my wife, Anna Alicja, both my sons, Jan and Nicolas, and myself—we will always remember the Americans who came in a few decisive minutes to the proper place."

I'm filled with pride when I see photos from that ceremony. I used to look at them when the rhetoric about my company became too heated and the PR battle seemed to get completely out of hand. By late 2007, that was happening a lot—including on the very day my men rescued Pietrzyk. That afternoon, Iraqi prime minister Nouri al-Maliki opened his weekly Wednesday press conference by declaring, "The kind of accusations leveled against [Blackwater] means it is not fit to work in Iraq!"

I don't know if he'd heard about the ambassador's evacuation earlier that day. I doubt it would have mattered. The public portrayal of my company had long since lost any nuance or more than one dimension. But I never forgot the mandate my father had left me with—and those of us at Blackwater would never stop trying to be a force for good in the world.

Back in late August 2005, Presidential Airways took delivery of a twin-engine Aérospatiale SA330 Puma utility helicopter. Blackwater's aviation arm was just over a year old at that point, and Richard Pere knew that an all-weather chopper that could haul seven thousand pounds of cargo would come in handy at some point. No one realized it would be less than a week later.

On August 29, Hurricane Katrina made landfall on the Gulf Coast. Wind speeds over 140 miles per hour lashed at southeastern Louisiana. More than an inch of rain fell each hour. Soon, the storm surge breached levees in and around New Orleans in dozens of places, and 75 percent of the city was plunged underwater. The phone rang that Monday while I was out on a training trip; it was Pere, calling from Presidential's headquarters in Florida. We were both hearing the news.

"We have this Puma," he said.

"Send it," I blurted out. He didn't even have to ask the question.

Pere called the Coast Guard, the National Guard, and the Red Cross with an offer to donate the services of a helicopter and crew. That call was a bit of a formality; the Puma was already in the air by the time the Coast Guard gladly said yes. Blackwater's volunteers arrived in New Orleans before FEMA, the National Guard, the Red Cross, or any other disaster relief organization. From Moyock, Gary Jackson and Ana Bundy put fifty additional contractors on a pair of our cargo planes to the Gulf, augmenting the team from Florida. Less than thirty-six hours after Katrina's landfall, Blackwater had more than one hundred men in the area.

Together, those men soon moved eleven tons of supplies around the region and rescued 121 stranded people. For two weeks, the Puma flew missions for the Coast Guard, providing roughly a million dollars in aviation services, shuttling tons of food, fresh water, and other supplies around the region. All we asked was that the Coast Guard cover the cost of our fuel. "Every aircraft we had was committed, and it wasn't enough. I couldn't find anyone who could give us more," Coast Guard commander Todd Campbell, who directed much of the rescue operation, told the *Virginian-Pilot* newspaper. "Just the way [Blackwater's men] walked in, with confidence in their faces—they weren't rattled one bit by what was going on. They just listened to what we wanted and went out and did it." As Bill Mathews, Blackwater's executive vice president at the time, explained to the newspaper, "We ran to the fire because it was burning." It was what we'd always done.

Soon, of course, the mission on the ground shifted. Within days of the storm, more than fifteen hundred people were dead. Looting in New Orleans began almost instantly—some life sustaining, much of it merely opportunistic. The stories that filtered out of the city were surreal: rampant lawlessness, police officers shot, residents fearing for their lives. I couldn't believe it when New Orleans police superintendent Edwin P. Compass III appeared on *Oprah* soon after the storm and said, "The tourists are walking around there, and as soon as these individuals see them, they're being preyed upon. They are beating, they are raping them in the streets."

The echoes of anarchy from foreign war zones I'd seen were unmistakable. "This place is going to look like Little Somalia," Brigadier General Gary Jones, commander of the Louisiana National Guard's Joint Task Force, told the *Army Times* days after Katrina hit. Jones said he was preparing hundreds of armed troops to literally pacify New Orleans. "We're going to go out and take this city back," he declared. "This will be a combat operation to get this city under control."

Thankfully, almost none of the stories turned out to be true. History has clarified that the vast majority of those tales were sensationalist speculation. Yet at the time, mere rumors of crime drove the action on the ground. The city was seemingly in ruins. The bodies floating down flooded streets were very real. "The only difference between here and Iraq is there are no roadside bombs," fifty-six-year-old Dan Boelens, who had twice been to Iraq with Blackwater before joining our team in New Orleans, told the *Grand Rapids Press* newspaper. "It's like a Third World country. You just can't believe this is America." Citizens there could be forgiven for believing practically anything—though I wish that hadn't included the crazy stories about us that would follow.

In the midst of what they believed was a "breakdown in social order," CNN hired British security company AKE Group—the same firm that protects CNN's reporters in Iraq—to safeguard its teams in New Orleans. NBC News hired armed guards for its personnel there; ABC and CBS followed suit. Soon, local businesses, major corporations, even private home owners were reaching out to us as well. Blackwater had an outsize reputation, after all, which some of those people might not have liked—until it was their property that needed protection. And suddenly it wasn't just volunteer work we were doing in the Gulf Coast. "The calls came flooding in," Chris Taylor, our vice president for strategic initiatives at the time, told the *Washington Post*. "It's not something that we went down and tried to develop."

Some of our men worked a security detail for BellSouth, whose workers went neighborhood to neighborhood trying to restore the city's telecommunications infrastructure. Others guarded banks, industrial sites, power plants, petrochemical facilities—even the brick warehouse outside Baton Rouge where a local Disaster Mortuary Operational Response Team had set up a temporary morgue. We protected priceless art at museums, and family heirlooms in private homes. Down in the French Quarter, Blackwater safeguarded the historic Chateau LeMoyne hotel—almost by accident. "I was scared to death coming back into the Quarter after the storm," hotel general manager Kathleen Young said at the time. "And then I got here, and there were two Blackwater guys camped out in my lobby. Nothing was touched. They stayed with me for weeks, and I never saw anyone challenge them."

We soon had teams assigned to five hotels, including the Sheraton New Orleans, also in the French Quarter. City police were too inundated to protect the Canal Street mainstay—much less the fifteen hundred customers stranded inside, as well as the staff's movements outside the building—so Starwood Hotels & Resorts Worldwide, which owns Sheraton, contacted us. On September 2, the day after Starwood called, we had a team in place at the hotel. "They treated it as if that was their job—and they were personable," Kevin Regan, then Starwood's regional vice president for the Southeast, said. "They were not guys that you'd think would be like G.I. Joe or something like that."

Some of Blackwater's ardent critics—and conspiracy theorists—couldn't resist the comparison, however. "According to [one account], mercenaries from Blackwater USA are rumbling through the New Orleans streets, armed to the teeth and in full battle gear," read one silly report. "I have been told by contacts in Louisiana that there were extrajudicial slayings going on at the hands of the police and/or Blackwater and/or the National Guard in New Orleans," read another.

Still another, "Blackwater—What If Our Mercenaries Turn On Us?," was penned by Chris Hedges. Hedges, who spent fifteen years as a foreign correspondent with the *New York Times* and was even part of its 2002 Pulitzer-winning team for terrorism coverage, is a surprising candidate to have devolved so far into conspiracy theory lunacy—yet he has fully embraced his latest turn. "Communist and fascist movements during the last century each built rogue paramilitary forces," he wrote in that post. "The appearance of Blackwater fighters, heavily armed and wearing their trademark black uniforms, patrolling the streets of New Orleans in the aftermath of Hurricane Katrina, may be a grim taste of the future."

To support their arguments, many online pundits pointed to an August 30, 2005, Reuters news photo that showed a half dozen black-clad men with machine guns and sidearms, some in wraparound sunglasses, making their way through downtown New Orleans. But those critics apparently never even bothered to read the photo's caption.

The photo of "Blackwater fighters" in their "trademark black uniforms" is actually of a New Orleans police SWAT team on patrol. Our men in the Gulf typically wore beige polo shirts with our logo on the chest, and green pants.

Beyond that, critics who believe that I somehow turned a natural disaster into a grand business opportunity show a grasp of history as faulty as their supposed photographic evidence. Contractor use—across industries—always spikes after a natural disaster. And following Katrina, private firms from around the world poured into New Orleans as multiple government agencies geared up to hand out well over $100 billion on relief and rebuilding projects.

The Army Corps of Engineers hired companies from Florida, California, and Minnesota to remove debris. Then, the *Chicago Tribune* reported, ambulance crews from California, mold removal specialists from North Carolina, and disaster consultants from Texas arrived on the scene. Reporters found that the Navy paid Kellogg Brown & Root, one of the massive contractors on the ground in Iraq, $16.6 million for damage assessments on naval facilities in New Orleans and power restoration projects at three Mississippi facilities. For emergency housing, FEMA awarded no-bid contracts to Bechtel, Fluor, Shaw Group, and CH2M Hill to provide trailers or mobile homes for as many as twenty thousand displaced people. (Those were the same "toxic trailers" Waxman's committee would later investigate.)

Blackwater found security work in the city—though we were hardly the only ones. Along with the PMCs protecting reporting teams in New Orleans, the British company ArmorGroup International sent about fifty employees to the Gulf Coast. Texas firm Instinctive Shooting International stationed guards outside Audubon Place, a gated community of multimillion-dollar homes near Tulane University.

Then, amid the flurry of stability and reconstruction efforts, the Department of Homeland Security (DHS) came to us with an urgent and compelling need to safeguard FEMA facilities and personnel. In the face of dramatic hardships and staggering losses, the agency had reason to believe New Orleans residents might vent their frustrations on beleaguered agency staffers. "We used to go out in T-shirts with a big 'FEMA' across the back," Gary Marratta, an agency security coordinator, said at the time. "We don't do that anymore—ever since this one guy told me, 'You know, that space between the 'E' and the 'M' makes a pretty good target.'" Homeland Security's Federal Protective Service (FPS) unit offered no help—those men stayed out of the most dangerous areas of New Orleans because they "deemed the situation unsafe."

That Homeland Security contract paid Blackwater $33.3 million through the end of 2005 for security at FEMA field offices and disaster response centers and for its medical assistance teams throughout Louisiana. Almost immediately, we funneled roughly seven hundred contractors into the city; we charged $950 per staff day for them. "FPS considered this the best value to the government and believed that Blackwater Security's past performance under other contracts and current performance under contracts with the Department of State demonstrated its capability to perform under the conditions of this contract," Matt Jadacki, then the Special Inspector General for Gulf Coast Hurricane Recovery, wrote in a DHS memo. Homeland Security reserved the option to extend that contract indefinitely—and it did. Within a year, some sixteen hundred Blackwater contractors had rotated through the Gulf Coast, and DHS had paid us nearly $75 million.

It's true that based on the dramatic stories coming out of New Orleans, our men initially arrived for security details in body armor, with pistols strapped to their legs and shotguns or M4 carbines in hand. It's also true that with SWAT teams, Louisiana Department of Natural Resources forces, and fifty thousand heavily armed National Guard troops roaming the city, carrying a weapon hardly made Blackwater personnel stand out. What did make our men stand out was their training to view violence as only a last resort; each of our contractors carried an ID card listing on the back the six escalating steps of permissible force outlined by the Department of Justice—our rules of engagement.

Happily, none of our contractors had to reference that training. Our men never fired a single shot in New Orleans. And upon assessing the reality of the threats, or lack thereof, we gladly toned down the daunting silhouette. "This is not the occupation of Louisiana," Andy Veal, one of our Katrina zone supervisors, said at the time. "This is Americans helping fellow Americans."

One of my favorite stories about my company's men helping their fellow Americans came nearly a year after Hurricane Katrina—in a West African country most people can't find on a map, outside a city whose name many Americans can't even pronounce. In July 2006, nearly six thousand miles away from New Orleans, a Presidential Airways medevac flight lifted off from Burkina Faso's capital of Ouagadougou—which we all just called "Waga"—and picked its way through the storm clouds gathering north, across the border in Mali.

A year earlier, the U.S. government had launched its Trans-Sahara Counterterrorism Partnership, a State Department–led initiative designed to thwart extremist organizations across West and North Africa. The goal was to train units from seven Saharan nations—Burkina Faso, Chad, Mali, Mauritania, Niger, Nigeria, and Senegal—in critical counterterrorism tactics. Those trainers, sent in by the Defense Department's U.S. Africa Command, were American special ops personnel. Presidential's airmen were also in Burkina Faso thanks to that DoD command, on a competitively won contract to provide fixed-wing airlift support for those trainers. Presidential's pilots flew our telltale CASA C212s.

The flights out there on the edge of the desert were pretty straightforward, our site manager, David Dalrymple, told me—except for some of the landings. "On one early mission in Mali to support folks working up there, I had to land on a homemade desert runway to deliver the supplies," he remembers today. "I had the coordinates for where the runway was supposed to be, but when I got there, it was just a dirt strip with dirt on either side of it. I could barely see it until I got right on top of it." Once he set down, Dalrymple made sure to walk that sandy strip and take GPS readings for both ends—he told me they'd simply been labeled with a handful of rocks—and jotted them down for future use.

That information became crucial only a few days later, when a late afternoon distress call rang out from fellow Presidential pilot Eric Humphries. Humphries and a small company team had flown the same resupply route into Mali for the special ops trainers, but while on the ground they got drilled by one of the semiregular squalls that tear through Mali during the rainy season. "Those squall lines are preceded by hundred-mile-per-hour winds," Dalrymple says. "They just eat up everything in their path."

As the July storm churned through the Malian outpost, it pushed Humphries's CASA some fifty feet sideways across the runway ramp, blowing out a tire and causing the whole plane to lurch so violently it cracked a wingtip against the ground. Humphries was grounded.

Meanwhile, the rural training camp bore the true brunt of the storm. Tents were ripped from the ground and flung downwind; temporary structures were obliterated. When the storm subsided, Humphries could see that one person had been killed. Other men, including American soldiers, were trapped beneath the collapsed structures; it was clear to him that many had sustained severe injuries. He radioed back to Dalrymple: These men needed a medevac *now.*

The site manager in Ouagadougou climbed into the pilot's seat of a CASA outfitted with litters and trauma equipment. With him was first officer Jessie Laraux, combat medic Eric Hansen, and crew chief and mechanic Robert Manness. It was a ninety-minute flight to the Malian outpost, the men knew, and likely to be lengthened by weaving around storm cells on the way. The team also figured they had only ninety minutes of sunlight left. Finding that dirt runway in the fading light would only get harder with every passing minute. Presidential's men got off the ground and charged north.

Twenty minutes outside the Malian camp, the crew in the air got a call from Humphries on the ground. "The wind is picking up again," he warned them. "The sand is really whipping around. I can hardly see anything." Darkness was settling across the region, and something like a sandstorm was about to kneecap the visibility of the plane's landing lights. *It was hard enough finding this thing in the daylight,* Dalrymple thought.

Humphries sprang into action. He sprinted away from the landing area to find the commander of the Malian unit being trained at the outpost. "We need lights!" he shouted.

Soon, a dozen green Humvees rumbled toward the runway, spreading out to flank both sides of the 2,500-foot strip. Sand crackled against the sides of the trucks. The Malian drivers trained their headlights on the stretch of dirt Dalrymple would be shooting for. One last truck pulled to the far end of the runway, just beyond the rocks; that driver flipped on his flashing red gumball so Dalrymple had a cue when to stop.

The Presidential crew took two passes over the landing area to fully grasp the layout below—one doesn't often touch down in a nighttime outback snowglobe. But on the third pass, Dalrymple brought the CASA down confidently, and soon rolled to a halt in the aircraft parking area.

Manness, the mechanic, unloaded the jacks and spare tire and went to work on Humphries's grounded aircraft. Dalrymple confirmed with the Malian commander: Two critical patients and one deceased soldier needed transport back to Ouagadougou. As he stood there, he remembers, the sand was being blown around so hard, "it felt like needles hitting you."

Manness quickly estimated it would take a day to make Humphries's CASA flyable again. Dalrymple decided to keep those two men in Mali; he then turned to help load the wounded, plus a few extra sets of hands, onto his plane for the return leg back to Ouagadougou. Taking off by Humvee headlight, the site leader counted a first officer, two medics, two critical patients, one walking wounded, and one dead-on-arrival aboard his plane. The whole aircraft smelled like copper from all the blood, Dalrymple told me.

Ninety minutes later, the CASA touched down in Ouagadougou.

The work wasn't done, though. Hansen, the medic, immediately dialed an Army surgeon at Landstuhl Regional Medical Center in Germany. One of the critical special ops patients he'd been tending to needed an emergency splenectomy, Hansen said, and the medic needed to be talked through the procedure. Then he needed to find a place to operate. "That local hospital . . ." Dalrymple remembers. "I mean, I can't describe it. It was as sanitary as they could make it—but in no way was it sanitary at all."

Furthermore, Hansen realized, that makeshift emergency room had little in the way of drugs. Presidential's men later told me they pooled whatever cash they had on hand, then literally ran down the street to the local pharmacy to buy Schedule III narcotics while Hansen and the local doctor sliced off the soldier's shirt and began their work. Hansen assisted the procedure the entire way.

Back in Virginia, I was gratified to hear that both of the patients on that flight survived. So, apparently, was everyone in Ouagadougou, who got a firsthand look at just how far those contractors would go to help someone in need. "We'd only been in the country for four or five days when the rescue happened," Dalrymple says. "I think the locals kind of put us up on a pedestal after that one." The special forces soldier Hansen operated on made a full recovery—and word of the men's work traveled fast.

A week later, at a ceremony in Virginia, I ran into William McRaven, then a two-star admiral well on his way to becoming the four-star commander of U.S. Special Operations Command he is today. He threw his arms around me and gave me a bear hug.

"I heard your guys did some sporty flying out in Mali the other day," he said. "Thank you."

"Glad to help," I said. "We've got some sporty pilots."

In late 2006, we had decided the time was right to establish training facilities in other parts of the country, to reach military and law enforcement units that couldn't travel to the Moyock campus. My team opened an eighty-acre site outside of Mount Carroll, Illinois, in a far northwestern piece of that state known as the Driftless Area. It became Blackwater North. Then our plans for a Blackwater West took us to Southern California and an 824-acre plot of land forty-five miles southeast of San Diego, in a little town called Potrero.

I loved the fact that, with the exception of a few modern conveniences—including its two restaurants and a general store—the 850-person community had changed little since it was first settled in 1868. We saw bobcats and mule deer on our visits to the area, and hawks and golden eagles perched in hundred-year-old oak trees.

For Blackwater's purposes, an old chicken and cattle range in that broad valley we found off State Route 94 was perfect. We envisioned standing up a dozen shooting ranges and laying down a giant driving track and a helipad. It would be within reach for customers all along the West Coast—including twenty thousand sailors at Naval Base San Diego, the SEAL teams at Naval Amphibious Base Coronado, and about fifty-five thousand combined Marines at nearby Camp Pendleton, Air Station Miramar, and Air Ground Combat Center Twentynine Palms. And perhaps even more important for the vision I had for Blackwater's future, there was the border.

Potrero's nearest municipal neighbor was Tecate, just an eight-minute drive south into Mexico. And as far back as May 2005, when Gary Jackson had appeared before the House Homeland Security Subcommittee on Management, Integration, and Oversight, I had been interested in doing for U.S. Customs and Border Protection (CBP) what Blackwater had done for other agencies.

We knew that the few weeks of training Congress had been authorizing cost more for a single guard than it would have cost one of those representatives to put his or her child through four years at Harvard. So we'd drafted the outline of an eighteen-week course that would enable CBP to add two thousand new agents to its ranks, for a fraction of the cost. "Just as the private sector has responded in

moving mail and packages around the world in a more efficient manner, so too can Blackwater respond to the CBP's emergent and compelling training needs," Jackson told Congress.

There was no border contract in place when we looked to build in
Potrero, but we'd been successful in the past by creating supply before there was demand. It was a niche worth preparing for, and that
meant infrastructure.

In December 2006, Potrero's seven-member planning group—
which had little actual authority, as approval would ultimately have
to come from San Diego County's Board of Supervisors—voted unan-
imously to approve the project. The planning group shared Blackwater's vision, and saw in our proposed facility an economic wellspring
for a town where 25 percent of the population lived in poverty.

The citizens of Potrero saw it very differently.

Within a few months, three hundred residents had signed a peti-
tion opposing our expansion there. Green T-shirts and red bumper
stickers declaring "Stop Blackwater" were a common sight. Residents
of Potrero said at those Blackwater rallies that they feared all the live
ammunition in an area predisposed to wildfires. They objected to the
potential noise, the possible impact on the local wildlife, and the increased traffic that would stream through the valley.

Reading between the lines, however, I understood that, by that
time, voters in Potrero mostly just objected to the Iraq War—and to
the cartoonishly evil image that surrounded my company. Soon,
those voters went so far as to recall five of the planning board's members, electing in their place staunchly anti-Blackwater candidates to
derail our bid for expansion.

It was a humbling experience for all of us. Yet as frustrating as I
found their reasons for opposing us, I couldn't help but respect a
community coming together and embracing America's democratic
process. They didn't want to have anything to do with us. I accepted
that message.

And then Southern California caught on fire.

On October 20, 2007, the first of nearly two dozen blazes began raging in Angeles National Forest. Soon, half a million acres were destroyed. Nearly one million residents were forced to flee their homes—the largest evacuation in California history. The inferno was visible from space.

The next day, the Harris fire—one of eight in San Diego County alone—began on Harris Ranch Road in Potrero. Ninety thousand acres in and around the quiet mountain town were engulfed. More than 450 structures were incinerated; eight people perished. Food, fuel, and other basic necessities dwindled. Power in the town was gone—and with it, water for the many residents who relied on electric pumps for their wells. Bumper stickers be damned, none of us at Blackwater were going to let that community suffer if there was anything we could do to help it.

Many of our contractors were firefighters, or otherwise had experience at disaster sites. We immediately sent a rapid response team to Potrero, and within days they were clearing and flattening ground in nearby Barrett Junction for a massive relief center. Then came ten thousand pounds of gear: sleeping bags, clothing, children's toys, microwave ovens, and more.

Three beige tents—one for single women, one for single men, one for families, each with lighting and air-conditioning—offered shelter for two hundred displaced residents. A fourth tent was set up with TVs and DVD players. Nearby trailers offered shower and laundry facilities.

As we coordinated the buildup of the relief center, another organization, the Churches of Christ Disaster Response Team, from West Melbourne, Florida, sent personnel to run the site and organize meals. Blackwater donated all the materials and supplies for the tent city for ninety days, helping residents of Potrero get back on their feet. Even the ones who seemed to misread the situation: "They're just trying to show a good face for the community, but it's all a ploy. It's all a game," resident Don Lytle told KBPS, San Diego's public radio station. "[Blackwater is] just trying to be the community's heroes."

Once our three months of relief work in Barrett Junction was done, my company left for good. We withdrew our proposal for a campus there, saying at the time it was a matter of decibel levels at the shooting ranges and fearing those might not fit within county regulations. But everyone understood the additional reality. Potrero's residents didn't want us there. So Blackwater West found a home in a different part of San Diego County.

Still, I look back on Potrero as a success story for my company. I've always been proud that ours were some of the first boots on the ground to help those men and women in a time of crisis—at a time when expansion plans and business prospects didn't have anything to do with it. No one delivering children's toys to a scorched valley cared about some hypothetical contract we might one day sign with Border Patrol. "I'm going to continue [this relief work] even through that kind of ridicule because it is the right thing to do," Brian Bonfiglio, Blackwater West's vice president, said from Barrett Junction as fires raged in the hills surrounding the town. "This is something we've always done. This is what we do."

I've always felt those months we spent in Potrero offered just a glimpse of what a Blackwater humanitarian mission could have looked like. Because it's also true the people in my company had skill sets far beyond any sort of typical aid worker—and one of my favorite company stories comes from a place far more distant than Southern California.

Three months after the Harris fire, I got a call from Michigan about a situation unfolding eight thousand miles away. Three college students from Grand Rapids, I was told, had been sent to far western Kenya as part of an international aid team from Set Free Ministries. The students—sisters Brittanie and Aubrie Vander Mey, then twenty-one and nineteen, respectively, and their friend Jamie Cook, then twenty—had planned to spend two months in Kimilili, 180 miles west of Nairobi, caring for orphans with HIV and AIDS at the Omwabini medical center.

I knew that foreign aid workers were a common sight in the East African nation. Kenya has long had strong social and cultural bonds with the West and—particularly when compared to neighbors Uganda, Sudan, Ethiopia, and Somalia—had to that point been a relative model of stability in the region.

But that all changed on December 30, 2007. Three days after a hotly contested presidential election, Party of National Unity incumbent Mwai Kibaki was declared the winner amid reports of major vote tampering. He was promptly sworn in that very evening, and the country immediately descended into violent rebellion, with members of Kibaki's dominant Kikuyu ethnic group battling protesting Luos, who supported presidential rival Raila Odinga.

Within weeks, more than 1,150 people were dead. Some 350,000 across the country were driven from their homes. According to intelligence reports we were getting, crimes against humanity were ghastly. Men, women, and girls were being forcibly circumcised and raped by the warring factions. And on January 1, 2008, a few miles outside Kimilili, rebels set upon a church in which Kikuyu citizens were seeking refuge. The angry mob doused the refugees' blankets and mattresses with gasoline, stacked them in front of the doors to the church, and burned the building to the ground. As many as fifty women and children were killed.

By the time I heard about the situation, those three college girls—too blond to blend in—were hiding out in the Set Free Ministries' orphanage, praying the warring factions didn't enter their compound. Escape was far too risky; the few roads out of nearby Kimilili were blocked by heavily armed militias. A handful of Masai warriors guarded the orphanage, but had violence come to that doorstep, the results could have been unthinkable.

Dean Vander Mey, Brittanie and Aubrie's father and the ministry's executive director, was beside himself. He had looked into chartering a helicopter to grab the girls, I was told, but had no luck. He had pleaded to his local officials, international aid organizations, and members of Congress for help. He got nowhere. "They said, 'Stay safe; don't move,'" Vander Mey recalled. "That's what they were telling us [to tell our daughters]: 'You're in harm's way, but don't move.'" Phone calls with his children got more wrenching with each passing news report. "They were scared, and I said, 'Honey, I don't know what to do.'"

Finally, living thirty miles outside Holland, Michigan, Vander Mey remembered that he had relatives who might know some of my relatives. Soon, we were on the phone together—and then I was on the phone to Kabul, Afghanistan. I would invade hell itself if my children's lives were in danger, and my team at Blackwater was determined to help those families bring their children home. Richard Pere, our aviation head, called Ricky "C. T." Chambers.

A former FBI special agent, "Chocolate Thunder"—he's as imposing as the nickname suggests—had been the lead bureau investigator for the 1997 embassy bombings in Nairobi and Dar es Salaam. He knew the area well. By early 2008, C.T. was also Blackwater's regional director of training in Afghanistan for our various narcotics interdiction contracts and border police training programs. Chambers immediately found a flight to Nairobi.

From there, he and a small team rented a tiny plane and organized a humanitarian snatch-and-grab mission. They flew themselves to a dirt airstrip outside of Kimilili, quickly snuck into the outpost, and hurried the women and other missionaries back to the plane—and then back to Nairobi. Two days later, the girls' commercial flight touched down at the Gerald R. Ford International Airport in Grand Rapids. I heard from friends back in Michigan when local news teams broadcast the girls racing hand in hand down the jet bridge, back into the arms of their waiting parents.

The girls' families offered us money as thanks. We wouldn't accept it. In fact, the only time cash came up was when Chambers called his boss and asked if it was all right to upgrade to first class for his flight back to Kabul. "It's been a long week," he said. We happily agreed.

• • •

All of these incidents—Katrina, Ouagadougou, Potrero, the Kenya rescue—were deeply connected with my faith. For some reason, many people are aware of my embrace of Christianity but somehow can't imagine me as being capable of charity. In reality, my faith has informed every aspect of my life. While I've made mistakes, I've also learned about grace—and one of the biggest lessons of grace involved an experience with my own growing family.

A year after Joan's death, I married Joanna. It was the right thing to do, I felt, in spite of the wrong I had done during my first marriage. I wanted to be a father for our son Rafe, who was born shortly after Joan's death. Soon after the wedding, our second son, Jack, was born. And finally, Joanna and I were blessed with a third boy, Charles Donovan Prince, in 2007. While I sensed God's influence and grace in my life through all of our children, it was through Charlie that I really sensed his hand.

In late September 2008, little Charlie managed to wedge himself through the back door of our Virginia home. I was on a site visit in Afghanistan at the time; Joanna was out of the house at a shopping mall. Our nanny had just finished bathing Charlie in the kitchen, and she turned her head for a moment to check on the other children. Like that, the one-year-old slipped out the door and went to play by the pool. He tumbled in.

Charlie was floating there motionless when Christian, my oldest son, then twelve, found him a short time later. Christian dove and pulled him out, then performed the CPR he'd just learned through a Red Cross certification program at Blackwater. Sophia called 911 and family friends, somehow remaining calm amid the frantic scene until an ambulance arrived to take Charlie to the hospital.

My cell phone rang at two a.m. in Kabul. A crowd had gathered in the hospital; Joanna was beside herself. I scrapped my original travel plans, which had called for a stopover in Pakistan for the weekend, and within minutes was on a plane home. I have virtually no recollection of that fifteen-hour flight—I was so consumed by the fear of losing my son, I hardly breathed.

And then, when I burst through the door of our home, I saw a strange thing: Charlie was smiling. He had his normal coloring back, and was alert, and generally looked exactly the way he had when I'd left for the trip a few days before. They'd discharged him from the hospital, and there was ultimately no residual damage from the accident whatsoever. "God was clearly never going to let Charlie die," friends said. "But I suppose everything happens for a reason."

Later, I flipped on the news—and nearly dropped the remote control: At eight p.m. Islamabad time, right when I had originally planned to be checking into the Marriott hotel there, terrorists had driven a six-wheeled truck loaded with thirteen hundred pounds of explosives up to its front gates. "The biggest explosion in Pakistani history," as government investigators described it, destroyed the building, killing 53 and wounding more than 260 others. Christian had saved Charlie's life. I believe Charlie saved mine.

Today, my face lights up when I tell people about the Citizen Award that Christian earned from the Fairfax County Fire and Rescue Department for his actions that day and about Sophia's grace under pressure that reminds me so much of her mom.

I feel a similar pride in the way our Blackwater family was able to rescue others—everyone from soldiers to disaster victims to stranded aid workers. About 175 in all, if I had to guess. It's not something we tracked. "Blackwater has been really wonderful," Don Vander Mey, grandfather to Brittanie and Aubrie, told his local newspaper after the girls' safe return to Michigan. "They've been getting a lot of negative publicity lately but they did something that no one else could."

Dean Vander Mey described the whole situation slightly differently: "It's been a nightmare and a miracle," he said. I know the feeling.

CHAPTER 16

THE DOWNFALL

2009–2010

AS 2009 DAWNED, BLACKWATER FELT MORE LIKE A NIGHTMARE THAN A miracle, and the company's end seemed almost inevitable.

On January 1 of that year, the new status of forces agreement between the United States and Iraq went into effect; in one of their inaugural acts of sovereignty, Iraqi officials declared they would not issue my company a license for our continued operation in the country. "They presented their request, and we rejected it," Alaa al-Taia, an Interior Ministry official, told the *New York Times*.

Under State's guidance, we hadn't previously needed that license. But after the agreement, we were told by the department, Iraqi permission for us to be there was important. The Iraqis wouldn't grant it. "There are many marks against this company, specifically that they have a bad history and have been involved in the killing of so many civilians." With the new SOFA, Interior Ministry spokesman Major General Abdul-Karim Khalaf declared that military contractors "will be under the authority of the Iraqi government, and those companies that don't have licenses, such as Blackwater, should leave Iraq immediately."

Considering compliance with State Department contract requirements was at the heart of so many of our troubles in Iraq, the department did conspicuously little to champion our cause. That part still burns, even today. Maybe it's naive, or maybe just idealistic, but I've always believed in loyalty and dedication to a team. Clearly, our program managers at State didn't feel the same way.

Our security work for the department, eligible for annual review under the WPPS II, was set to be reupped in early May 2009. But I learned two days after the Interior Ministry's decision that State had made a decision of its own: Blackwater was done in Iraq. Triple Canopy would take over our work. Any question of us running further security missions in Baghdad, a senior U.S. official said at the time, was "basically a moot point because they were not going to be allowed to operate in Iraq anyway."

With that, some 50 percent of my company's revenue was about to vanish. I read about it on a blog before State had the courtesy to tell us personally.

It was the culmination of what had, over the past year, become an increasingly acrimonious relationship with the department. As Blackwater was publicly dragged through the mud, State couldn't stay entirely clean. Rather than focus on our perfect success record, State dwelled on any negative press we generated, and how it might reflect on them. Department personnel were guilty by—or simply of—association with us, they felt, and in the months following my appearance on Capitol Hill, there was more mud than ever.

The IRS, for instance, dug into our accounting practices for classifying our men on the ground as "independent contractors" instead of "employees"; Waxman promptly issued a press release, which would be distributed widely, accusing us of tax evasion. We were practically a test run for the left-wing bureaucracy siccing the IRS on opponents. (Our accounting practices were entirely within the law, though in our fourteen-page response to the accusations, one note was ignored by the chairman: "As Blackwater continues to co-operate with the Committee's review," we wrote, "it respectfully re-quests that the Committee afford the attached [explanation] the same level of public attention and consideration that the Committee afforded the letter you released on October 22, 2007.")

News from years earlier somehow shot back into the light. In 2005, two employees in our armory—Kenneth Cashwell and Wil-liam "Max" Grumiaux—had been caught by Blackwater's own inter-nal investigators falsifying paperwork. They had been stealing guns intended for our overseas contractors and selling them on the black market.

At the time, we'd immediately called in the FBI and Bureau of Al-cohol, Tobacco, Firearms and Explosives to crack down on anyone in Moyock associated with the crime. But even that backfired: Fac-ing as much as a decade in prison and fines up to $250,000, Cashwell and Grumiaux bargained down to three years' probation and a thousand-dollar fine by agreeing to testify against us in any future firearms cases involving Blackwater. "I'm sorry for what I've done," Grumiaux said of his crimes. "I feel like I've dishonored myself, hav-ing served in the military, and that's a burden I'll have to bear for the rest of my life."

That two-year-old story somehow broke following my appear-ance on Capitol Hill; only at the very bottom of those news reports did sentences like this appear: "Federal officials confirmed in 2005, when the men were fired, that Blackwater came forward and asked authorities for help."

By that point, even innocuous things about my company gener-ated fanciful headlines. For instance, at one point we purchased a single-propeller Embraer EMB-314 Super Tucano attack plane de-signed mainly for border patrol and counterinsurgency operations. The Brazilian aircraft, which was built as a training device and subject to all the standard import regulations for that type of equip-ment, offered us a perfect way to expand our Moyock capabilities, in exactly the way that Navy "ship in a box" had years earlier. Almost predictably, however, our buying a single fighter trainer was immediately trumpeted online as, "Blackwater is building its own air force of 'ground attack planes' and just bought a fleet of 'Super Tucano light combat aircraft from the Brazilian manufacturer Embraer.'"

As if that wasn't bizarre enough, one of our contractors in Baghdad then engaged in another deadly shooting—this time of a dog. Its name was apparently Hentish. It had been a mainstay at the housing of *New York Times* reporters. I was told the shooter, one of our K9 handlers, had been sweeping the newspaper's area of the compound before a visit from U.S. embassy personnel, when Hentish—a feral canine that had come to rely on the table scraps reporters fed him— became territorial and attacked our bomb-sniffing dog. After several unsuccessful attempts to separate the animals, and not wanting to see an extremely valuable Blackwater asset hurt by what amounted to a wild animal, the handler had no choice but to use his pistol to eliminate the threat. "Blackwater Shoots the *New York Times*' Dog," read the next day's headlines—and soon State was making multiple follow-up visits to the compound to investigate. "They took the incident very seriously," the *New York Times* reported.

In the early part of 2009, I couldn't go twenty-four hours without hearing some conspiracy theory about some evil thing my company was purportedly doing—and for many people, the theories seemed as plausible as the facts. At the very least, they further colored the interpretation of our work and the State Department's objectives in Baghdad. It was exhausting.

In a climate one pro-Blackwater blogger described as "a heady cocktail of fear, ignorance and paranoia," columnists such as Frank Rich of the *New York Times* piled on. When Charles D. Riechers, a head procurement officer in the Air Force, committed suicide after a reporter detailed his taking a phony position at contractor Commonwealth Research Institute for a little quick cash—"I really didn't do anything for CRI," Riechers admitted; "I got a paycheck from them"—Rich wrote: "As it happens, [Riechers] was only about three degrees of separation from Blackwater." In reality, Riechers had no relationship whatsoever with my company—yet through efforts like that, the name Blackwater somehow became synonymous with corruption.

At the extreme end of the spectrum, one frequently updated blog that always provided me with a little gallows humor was called *All You Need Is a Crazy Rich Guy with a Private Army*. Created by New Zealander Evelyn Gilbert, the site wore its mission on its sleeve: "The premise of this blog [is] that Erik Prince, who started the mercenary firm called Blackwater, may very well have provided the crew responsible for the 9/11 attacks."

It wasn't exactly a surprise to me that State Department personnel weren't thrilled with the realities inherent in the job they asked us to do. They didn't like the aggressive driving. They didn't like the shootings, or the idea that our department-mandated tactics had the potential to undermine their nation-building efforts. According to one report, Jessica Gans, a consultant to the department in Iraq during our time there, told the *Los Angeles Times* that she bristled at seeing "heavily armed contract guards frighten Iraqi civilians and destroy their property."

I could handle those broadsides. But the hypocrisy of the situation grated on me when those same critics acknowledged what happened as soon as they left the Green Zone—at which point, as one U.S. official described it, "You want the biggest, meanest guys in the world protecting you."

For years Blackwater's ability to achieve its performance standards spoke louder to department administrators than news reports—the product of a simple philosophy I'd used to build our business: "Make yourself indispensable, and you'll always have work." Amid the fallout from Nisour Square, however, State clearly began to reassess things. "During the late summer and fall of 2007, actions by Blackwater WPPS management personnel ... caused the program office to lose confidence in their credibility and management ability," wrote Paul Isaac, the contracting officer for State's

Overseas Protective Operations–High Threat Protective Division, in a July 2008 internal evaluation.

So in January 2009, days after Barack Obama was sworn in as president and Hillary Clinton was appointed the new secretary of state—both of whom had campaigned to end the use of private security contractors—the department came for Blackwater's jugular by canceling our WPPS II work.

But as that contract was coming to a sudden halt, the new Democratic administration soon learned the same lesson as its predecessor: "Indispensable" means exactly that. In the years since we'd first won the major Baghdad component of the security work—job responsibilities technically known as Task Order 6—we'd picked up a pair of additional task orders: Task Order 8, for protective service details in Hillah, Najaf, and Karbala, south of Baghdad; and Task Order 10, State's official adoption of our aerial support to include search and rescue capabilities, medevacs, and our quick reaction forces.

Our work for State in Baghdad might end in May 2009, but Task Order 8 south of the city wouldn't expire until August, eight months after Iraq's Interior Ministry told us to leave the country entirely. And State was so fearful of the sudden loss of our aircraft, they actually renegotiated a new Task Order 10 contract with us days after they dealt the devastating financial blow to my company. It was going to take the department the better part of a year, State told us, to find a new firm to provide Blackwater's aviation capabilities. So under the new terms, our aviation specialists would remain in the country until September, and State would pay us an additional $22.2 million.

By late 2009, when Blackwater finally concluded four years of myriad WPPS II duties in Iraq, the State Department had paid us more than one billion dollars for our work.

The same month Iraq refused us an operating license, our five contractors from Nisour Square pleaded not guilty in court to fourteen counts of manslaughter and twenty counts of attempted manslaughter. The court case made headlines everywhere—I knew the last thing we needed at that point was to give anyone anything *legitimate* to complain about. Then, just as Blackwater security teams on the ground pulled out of Baghdad, two of our contractors engaged in a new shooting incident in Afghanistan's capital.

On May 5, 2009, two men working for one of our company subsidiaries, Paravant, got into a shoot-out as they escorted three Afghan interpreters through Kabul to a taxi stand a few miles from the contractors' base. Soon, contractors Christopher Drotleff and Justin Cannon were charged under the Military Extraterritorial Jurisdiction Act with numerous offenses, including involuntary manslaughter and attempted murder.

And then the anger hit me. I was aghast at the contractors' recklessness—and furious about what it could mean back in Moyock. As if State's ire in Iraq wasn't damaging enough to everything we'd built at Blackwater, our team now had a new shooting to deal with in another major country of operation.

We'd put that Paravant offshoot in Afghanistan on a subcontract with Raytheon Technical Services Company. Even if our security work slowed in Iraq, I knew, the Afghan theater still offered ample business opportunities for us. It was the best chance we had to keep the company afloat. As part of rebuilding efforts aimed to allow coalition forces to withdraw from Afghanistan, NATO had set personnel benchmarks for the Afghan National Police (ANP) and Afghan National Army (ANA): 160,000 trained ANP members, and 240,000 capable ANA soldiers by the end of 2013. The United States was spearheading those training efforts, preparing to spend more than $9 billion in 2010 alone to develop those forces. Making sure we were part of that was a key step to steadying my company's footing.

Raytheon had been awarded a ten-year, $11.2 billion contract from the U.S. Army "to consolidate operations and maintenance, systems integration and engineering support services for the Army's live, virtual and constructive training systems" in Afghanistan. In less convoluted terms, Raytheon had to make sure the ANA quickly got up to snuff. They came to us, offering Paravant a subcontract worth $25 million to put the actual training personnel on the ground in Kabul and to teach Afghanistan's nascent army the basics.

When I say "basics," I mean that many members of the ANA reported from tribal areas that had never seen indoor plumbing or electricity. Our instructors teaching "Intro to Toilet Use" isn't a joke—and I certainly don't mean it as a knock on the Afghans. Those men, and a handful of women who traded burkas for camouflage, took extraordinary pride in helping to stabilize their nation. In my site visits there, I saw a level of passion for the job that I've rarely witnessed elsewhere.

That came through in the results: Every six weeks, some thirteen hundred ANA members graduated Paravant's training program with skills unparalleled by other units in the Afghan army. I remember sitting in Kabul's diesel-choked traffic jams in a battered local SUV, watching pickup trucks roll by full of Afghan soldiers holding their weapons with trigger fingers straightened and firmly pressed against the receiver. They'd been trained well. I took nearly as much pride in that as they did.

Drotleff and Cannon were among our instructors on that assignment. Those site visits showed me the quality of their work. It quickly became clear to the team in Moyock that our trouble in Afghanistan didn't have anything to do with how our contractors did their jobs, but rather with what some of those men did when they *weren't* working.

I was livid. My company had stretched itself increasingly thin to fill all our contracts, juggling some seven hundred employees in North Carolina, twelve hundred contractors on security details in Iraq and Afghanistan, one hundred contractors on aviation services in those two countries, and two hundred additional contractors to train the Afghan Border Police and Narcotics Interdiction Unit. The new ANA training work had meant about seventy-five more contractors in Afghanistan—who were suddenly managing to shoot people. Blackwater was facing more scrutiny than ever, and *this* was how they responded? I wouldn't have it. I fired virtually everyone involved in the incident.

If there was one silver lining, it was that in each of the theaters in which Blackwater operated, our actual job performance remained exemplary. By September 2009, we had trained more than 38,000 ANA soldiers, with reviews showing our contractors "were outstanding, flexible, and delivered a quality service. [Raytheon] consistently reported . . . that Paravant's efforts were achieving over a 90 percent qualification rate for the ANA soldiers." That was on top of the 3,700 Afghan Border Police personnel we trained, and the 5,700 Narcotics Interdiction Unit officers.

Back home, we continued to train military, state, and local law enforcement personnel at our three U.S. campuses—roughly twenty thousand men and women in 2009 alone. Regardless of the storm clouds gathering, that track record would keep us in business. My company could survive even with State curtailing our work, but we had to tighten our internal operations—and figure out how to lower a profile that had become undeniably toxic.

Blackwater's branding had, in the past, gone through minor corporate cleanups. After Katrina, the gunned-up, black-clad warriors on our Web site were joined by information about the humanitarian work we were capable of. We ran ads featuring starving infants being spoon-fed, with this text: "Now that we are aware of many atrocities on this earth, those of us who enjoy secure, peaceful, and free lives are called upon to help share that promise with the world. Through selfless commitment and compassion for all people, Blackwater works to make a difference in the world and provide hope to those who still live in desperate times."

Then, following the shooting in Nisour Square, our original logo—once described by the *New York Times* as "a bear's paw print in a red crosshairs, under lettering that looks to have been ripped from a fifth of Jim Beam"—was toned down to reduce the visual impact of the rifle scope and lessen the menacing skeletal image of the bear paw. We'd become more *"Fortune* 500" than "gun show." We dropped the Blackwater name from our logo altogether; by late 2007, we'd become entirely recognizable to the people who wanted to find us.

Still, by 2009, it was clear an updated logo wouldn't do much in the face of years of harsh press. I couldn't shake the unsettling lesson that this nation was no meritocracy after all. Clearly, the most able didn't always end up on top—not when so many people seemed eager to drag us down. So if the PR nightmare was going to doom Blackwater, then "Blackwater" had to go.

We instituted a months-long search for a new corporate identity, considering all sorts of branding. Ultimately, our executives voted to rename the company "Xe Services," which means . . . nothing. Which was exactly the point.

Pronounced "zee," Xe is the periodic symbol for the chemical element xenon, a colorless, odorless gas found in trace amounts in the earth's atmosphere. You'd never know it was there unless someone pointed it out. That was the new, understated direction for the company. We pledged to get back to our training center roots, expand our instructional programs, and disappear into the background. The main Moyock campus was also renamed: "Blackwater Lodge and Training Center" became the simpler "U.S. Training Center, Incorporated."

Pundits pegged our renaming as damage control, and cheered what they perceived as the company's death rattle. Blackwater's makeover was "not a direct result of a loss of contract, but certainly that is an aspect of our work that we feel we were defined by," we said publicly at the time. Critics saw it as a symbolic victory against military contractors in general. That's because they thought the rebranding was our idea.

In reality, Jennifer Joy may have been the first to specifically ask about a name change. Joy was a manager at Raytheon overseeing the ANA training in Afghanistan. When Jim Sierawski, then a vice president at Blackwater, first reached out to her about our competing for the subcontract, "Ms. Joy expressed some level of concern about having the Blackwater name appear on [Raytheon's] approved list of vendors for the [training] contract," we told Congress in 2010. "Mr. Sierawksi recalls Ms. Joy asking if Blackwater had considered changing its name."

I wasn't thrilled with the idea. But if customers like Raytheon wanted that built-in deniability—a way to hire us while also being able to later claim, "We didn't know it was Blackwater!"—I thought it best to let them have it. Regardless of what the paperwork said, everyone at the company knew where we stood. Literally. I knew that in the lobby of our Moyock headquarters the twenty-foot-wide name "Blackwater" remained cast in the concrete floor.

Soon "Paravant" was born to land the ANA work, and we leaned more heavily than ever on our network of some three dozen affiliates and subsidiaries to help secure business. Blackwater always had various offshoots—Backup Training Corporation offered computer-based law enforcement training courses, for instance; Pelagian Maritime oversaw applications for our repurposed research vessel; E&J Holdings was the branch that managed our real estate acquisition, including expansions at the Moyock campus. That series of offshoots became only more valuable as the Blackwater name became radioactive. Soon, we were earning repeat government business through Presidential Airways, Greystone, Constellation Consulting Group, GSD Manufacturing, Raven Development Group, and more.

It limited our visibility—though, from a legal standpoint, it also limited our liability in each arena. Blackwater simply followed the lead of other major contractors that create offshoots to compete for various business opportunities. Northrop Grumman has equally mysterious-sounding subsidiaries, such as Litton Industries, TRW Inc., Teledyne Ryan Aeronautical, and Logicon Corporation; Lockheed Martin oversees nearly twenty divisions, including Advanced Marine Systems, CADAM Inc., and Metier Management Systems along with its raft of missile, space, and aeronautical firms. Critics attacked us for using "fronts" and "shell companies"—but there was no grand secret there: I owned them all. And the majority of them were even registered to 850 Puddin Ridge Road in Moyock—the same well-known address as Blackwater's headquarters.

Our customers all knew whom they were hiring—and that went for the State Department, which, like other clients, issued us clear and unambiguous verbal guidance that shedding our company name was best for everyone involved. Because regardless of what was happening in Iraq, State suddenly needed our help in Afghanistan—and beyond.

On March 27, 2009, President Obama stood at a podium in Room 450 of the Dwight D. Eisenhower Executive Office Building in Washington. Over his right shoulder was Secretary of State Hillary Clinton; over his left, Defense Secretary Robert Gates. "Today, I am announcing a comprehensive new strategy for Afghanistan and Pakistan," the president said.

In the eight years since the United States had invaded Afghanistan, stability there had moved at a glacial pace, to the extent it moved forward at all. Taliban suicide bombings continued seemingly at will in the fledgling democracy. Insurgent aggression had prevented enough voter registration that the country's landmark presidential elections, scheduled for May 2009, had to be pushed back three months. The United States had just come off its deadliest year of the war there, with 155 service members killed in 2008. In 2009, it only got worse.

As part of that "new strategy," the Obama administration pledged to push an additional twenty-one thousand troops into Afghanistan, following that later in the year with a pledge for another twelve thousand, ultimately more than doubling the Bush administration's force in the failing war effort. But President Obama included an additional component that he said differentiated this approach from that of his predecessor: "This push must be joined by a dramatic increase in our civilian effort," he said. "To advance security, opportunity, and justice—not just in Kabul, but from the bottom up in the provinces—we need agricultural specialists and educators, engineers and lawyers." The "civilian surge," as it came to be known, would send hundreds of people to the country under the State Department's guidance—and someone had to keep them safe. As soon as I heard President Obama's speech, I knew what that plan might mean for our newly rebranded firm.

Since 2005, Blackwater had provided protection details for U. S. Ambassador to Afghanistan Karl Eikenberry, Embassy Kabul personnel, visiting diplomats and congressional delegations, and USAID under Task Order 4 of the WPPS II. We had conducted 2,730 protection missions across Afghanistan in 2008 alone, earning all of the $174 million State paid us for the work. "During the entire time USTC [U.S. Training Center] has operated in Afghanistan, no one under USTC's protection has been injured or killed, and there have been no incidents involving the use of deadly force," a 2009 performance audit by State's inspector general found. "The representatives [protected by the contractors] reported that USTC employees are professional, make them feel secure, and are respectful to both officials under chief of mission authority and their Afghan counterparts."

Facing a civilian surge that closely mirrored the security mess State had previously found in Iraq, the department, and its new secretary, Hillary Clinton, found the same solution: They awarded our U.S. Training Center an eighteen-month contract worth $120 million for static and protective security services at consulates being built in Herat and Mazar-i-Sharif. That served as a stopgap until State could complete its new global, third-generation WPPS contract in 2010. Bad press in Iraq be damned; State's mission in Afghanistan needed the most capable PMCs it could find, as soon as they could get there.

Expanding our existing work in the country to additional consulates made sense for everybody—except our detractors on Capitol Hill, including the Commission on Wartime Contracting in Iraq and

Afghanistan. "Of course, the concern is whether in Afghanistan, where the mission is most critical right now, we might have in the future the same kind of incident that we saw in Iraq," Clark Kent Ervin, a panel commissioner appointed by Democrat Nancy Pelosi, said during a hearing three days later. Charlene Lamb, State's deputy assistant secretary for international programs, replied that "past performance played an incredible amount" in determining whether or not to award us that contract. She added: "In this case, with this specific award, Xe is the only company of our three under the WPPS II contract currently operating in Afghanistan. Their infrastructure is there already."

My company again seemed to be finding its stride. With that contract locked down, our next piece of business with State generated even more headlines. In August 2010, the department leveled an enormous fine against my company: $42 million, for 288 instances of Arms Export Control Act (AECA) and International Traffic in Arms Regulations (ITAR) violations between 2003 and 2009. But *not* for any of the reasons the average person might expect.

ITAR and AECA work in concert to regulate the export of defense goods and services, as well as technical data—everything from training programs to guided missiles—to foreign entities. The enforcement of those laws falls under the purview of State, though bureaucratic machismo enters the picture when the Departments of Commerce and the Treasury throw their weight around on various items. Most commonly, that happens with gear classified as "dual use" or with goods having both a commercial and a military application.

Zip ties are a perfect example. The flimsy ones are useful for tying off trash bags (commercial use); heavy-duty ones can be used by law enforcement agents as impromptu handcuffs (military use). To send a box of plastic zip ties to our teams training Afghanistan's new counternarcotics police, we had to submit a half-inch-thick application package to State for its sign-off on our exporting defense and training goods; then we had to resubmit the application to the Commerce Department because zip ties are a dual-use item. Failure to spend literally weeks securing both approvals made our exporting a box of those plastic strips a violation of ITAR, if something far less dramatic than what one might generally think of when it comes to international arms smuggling.

In 2009 alone, those three government export agencies processed 130,000 applications from U.S. companies, many of which were zip tie–style overlaps. The model was so onerous, in 2012 the U.S. government launched a wide-ranging Export Control Reform Initiative to create a single licensing agency that is "transparent, predictable, and timely," according to the State Department. But it certainly wasn't that way when we first ramped up Blackwater's operations abroad and had to make sure our teams were equipped to do their jobs successfully.

I remember instances when approvals from one department would take six weeks, yet we were ordered to begin work overseas within thirty days. It left us in a precarious position with things like body armor, weapon optical sights, and other gear. And in those moments, we chose to move forward with the crucial missions in the field and provided our men and women with the weapons, protections, and other tools they needed to do their jobs and advance U.S. interests.

The majority of our violations, however, didn't involve tangible matériel at all but rather came from our exporting intellectual property.

AECA and ITAR enforcers work hard to ensure that no bad actors receive the same valuable training as U.S. personnel and its allies. Blackwater ran afoul of those regulations by not securing timely approval for training even friendly foreign contingents, including military and law enforcement units from Canada, for example, and improperly providing background biographical information on some of the thousands of men and women abroad we had been approved to train each year. (Among the violations was training snipers from Taiwan's National Security Bureau, which State concluded "had potential national security implications," as well as training an Afghan border patrol official who happened to be a native of Iran.)

Further, we ran into intellectual property issues when we employed a pair of consultants from Volvo in Sweden for our Grizzly armored personnel carrier development program. We hadn't secured the proper approvals first, and therefore were "providing [them] unauthorized access to ITAR-controlled technology," according to the State Department.

The $42 million consent agreement we ultimately signed came after a three-year investigation into our work by agents from the Departments of Defense, Justice, State, Homeland Security, Treasury, and Commerce, as well as the FBI and the CIA's inspector general's office—and after a lengthy negotiation process on our end. At the time, ours was the highest ITAR settlement ever, eclipsing the $32 million settlement paid by Hughes Electronics Corporation and Boeing in 2003 for providing long-range rocket data and defense services to the Chinese government.

I was deeply offended by having to pay nearly 10 percent of our annual revenue in fines, particularly because, unlike selling secrets to the Chinese, State publicly acknowledged, "These violations did not involve sensitive technologies or cause a known harm to national security. The Department notes that many of the alleged ITAR violations occurred while Xe was providing services in support of U.S. Government programs and military operations abroad." Two years later, in 2012, I was disgusted when United Technologies Corporation (UTC) resolved more than five hundred ITAR violations for delivering to Chinese authorities the extremely sensitive software allowing their military competitor to develop its first attack helicopter. UTC agreed to pay a $55 million settlement, or about 0.08 percent of its $64 billion annual revenue.

Blackwater had gotten hung up in the red tape, and then hung out to dry at the bargaining table. But we'd made sure to negotiate a few crucial things into that settlement, which I knew were vital to the company's survival in the long run.

Since December 2008, the government had been denying most of our export applications, which had hobbled our ability to pursue contracts abroad. (No one will hire a contractor to do a job if it can't actually get the tools to the job site.) With the settlement, those denials were lifted.

The agreement also ruled out criminal charges arising from any of those violations, which could have brought a suspension of our ability to work for the government, regardless of whether there was any validity to the charges. Any convictions on hypothetical charges could have meant a complete debarment from pursuing U.S. government contracts, and likely my company's collapse.

So we paid off State and turned our attention to landing the next contract—which was right around the corner. Because even as it scolded us, the department never dared turn its back on us entirely. With the fine out of the way, we were awarded work under its third iteration of the WPPS contract the very next month.

In September 2010, State split up its five-year, $10 billion WPPS III, which the department renamed simply the WPS, or Worldwide Protective Services contract, among eight separate firms: Aegis Defence Services, DynCorp International, EOD Technology, Global Strategies Group, International Development Solutions, SOC, Torres International Services, and Triple Canopy. This time, State was ensuring that no single provider would have the massive sway we did during the WPPS II.

The name Blackwater—or, rather, our affiliates—didn't appear on State's winners' list. It didn't even show up among the sixty-one firms on the "Interested Vendors List" from which the department chose the winners. But we were certainly there—and State knew it—buried in the background of the company International Development Solutions (IDS), a brand-new joint venture launched between our U.S. Training Center and fellow Virginia-based contractor Kaseman.

IDS won Task Order 2 of the WPS, an ongoing $84 million deal to provide security in Israel's volatile West Bank, largely protecting motorcades from the U.S. consulate in Jerusalem. The task order called for forty-six full-time contractors to safeguard the presidential

envoys and staff who make up the U.S. contingent of the Middle East
Quartet, representatives from the United States, the European
Union, the Russian Federation, and the United Nations who are
slowly mediating the region's fragile peace process.

When, one month after awarding us the contract, State confirmed Blackwater's ties to IDS, and the work it would be doing in Je-
rusalem suddenly came to light, it brought with it the criticism I'd
come to expect at home. But harsh words also came from a new corner abroad: "We emphasize that our Palestinian land is not an arena
for the criminals of that infamous company," read an outraged statement from Hamas, the Sunni Muslim extremist group that State
designated a "Foreign Terrorist Organization" back in 1997 and
which in 2006 was elected the majority in the Palestinian parlia-
ment. I took a measure of pride in that one. I'm not sure whether a
person can really gauge the quality of his work by the enemies he's
made, but if I somehow upset Hamas, and the Taliban, and Henry
Waxman, I must have done something right.

Even as we straightened ourselves in the boardroom, the jackals
continued stalking us in the courtroom. Days after the Nisour
Square shooting, State had reached out directly to some of the
victims with condolence payments of as much as $12,500 for
those killed—a rare instance when the department didn't coordinate
payments from the contractor, underscoring the severity of the
situation. "It's not an admission of culpability," U.S. embassy
spokeswoman Mirembe Nantongo said at the time, "and this is in no
way a waiver of future claims [against Blackwater]." Unfortunately,
thanks to Susan Burke, a Washington D.C. personal injury lawyer,
and her partnership with Michael Ratner at the New York–based
Center for Constitutional Rights (CCR), those claims would come en
masse.

Burke and Ratner made a perfect match. CCR was cofounded in
1966 by William Kunstler, a self-described "radical lawyer" perhaps

best known for convincing the Supreme Court in 1989 that flag burning should be legal. "I am a double agent," Kunstler once bragged to
the *New York Times,* "working within the system to bring down the
system." That viewpoint led him to defend a series of questionable-at-best characters later in his career, including "a drug dealer
who shot six policemen, a fifteen-year-old accused (and later exonerated) in the notorious gang rape and beating of a jogger in New York's
Central Park, an Islamist militant accused of assassinating Jewish
leader Rabbi Meir Kahane, several of the defendants in the 1993
World Trade Center bombing and Mafia don John Gotti," according
to the description of a documentary his daughters later put together
about his life. "We wanted all of his clients to be innocent and all
of his cases to be battles for justice and freedom," Emily Kunstler
said. "But at some point, we thought he had stopped standing for
anything worth fighting for."

Soon after Kunstler's death, Michael Ratner took over as president of CCR and brought the same slant to the modern battlefield,
"filing countless cases on behalf of [those] swept up in the so-called
War on Terror," according to the center's Web site. "On June 12, 2008,
CCR helped win a historic Supreme Court victory in *Boumediene vs.
Bush,* securing the right for the men at Guantánamo and other non-
citizens to challenge the legality of their detention through habeas
proceedings in federal courts." Ratner was clear about his approach
to national security during an interview with the weekly *Socialist
Worker* newspaper in 2006: "When I started doing my work in this
area after 9/11, I thought we were moving toward a police state," he
said. "We have arrived."

Burke, meanwhile, had shifted directions after years spent in
corporate litigation, and in 2008 began successfully suing the Pentagon and private military contractors over various alleged abuses.
When a furious Iraqi government recommended Blackwater pay out
$136 million to compensate the Nisour Square victims—$8 million
for each Iraqi killed—Burke and CCR jumped at the chance to profit
from the war in their own way.

Soon after my appearance on Capitol Hill, the legal team hit us with the lawsuit *Estate of Himoud Saed Abtan, et al. v. Prince, et al.,* filed on behalf of what grew to be more than sixty victims or their estates. Burke described me as a "modern-day merchant of death." Her legal team wrote in the complaint that "Blackwater created and fostered a culture of lawlessness amongst its employees, encouraging them to act in the company's financial interests at the expense of innocent human life." They alleged that I, and my company, were liable under the federal Alien Tort Statute for committing war crimes and summary execution, among other things.

But Burke wasn't done. Over the next few years, she would spearhead more than a half dozen additional lawsuits against me and Blackwater, accusing us of ever more salacious and ridiculous things.

It started with an allegation of fraud for overcharging the government on contracts, brought by former Blackwater employees Brad and Melan Davis. That suit included such false assertions as Blackwater allegedly placing a Filipina prostitute in Afghanistan on our payroll as part of our team's "Morale Welfare Recreation." (The judge threw out that allegation before it even went to the jury.) The Davises were hardly battling troubled consciences, however; they sued us under the False Claims Act, which allows whistle-blowers to collect as much as 25 percent of recovered damages.

Then another Burke-led suit brought by four Iraqis alleged that "Mr. Prince was well aware that his men, including his top executives in Moyock, North Carolina, viewed shooting innocent Iraqis as sport." It added, "Those who killed and wounded innocent Iraqis tended to rise higher in Mr. Prince's organization than those who abided by the rule of law." In a further bizarre addition, the lawsuit alleged that one of Blackwater's employees had photographed company executive Ana Bundy packaging illegal weapons for shipment to Iraq, and then, the lawyers claimed, the employee mysteriously died soon after. "Discovery is needed to ascertain whether Mr. Prince directly or indirectly participated in the events leading to the death of the young man who photographed executive Anna [*sic*]

Bundy," the complaint read. "One employee commented to the young man that such photographs 'are what get people killed.'"

It was clear to me that some lofty quest for justice was hardly the point of those various suits. They all seemed to ultimately seek "punitive damages in an amount sufficient to strip Mr. Prince of the substantial revenue he earned from his pattern of constant misconduct and callous disregard for human life."

I'd never imagined that being a successful entrepreneur could mean spending so much time in the courtroom. Each time, the rafts of salacious allegations quickly fell apart in front of a judge or jury, and they were dismissed. To cite one example, the trial judge threw out all but one count of the Davis fraud suit because there was no evidence to support their sensational claims. The one remaining count was thrown out by the jury as it found no liability by my company. In fact, we were even awarded costs for years of legal fees related to the case. Yet more than any other factor, the effort it took to defend my company against outlandish, money-grubbing lawsuits such as that one hindered our ability to serve our clients effectively. By 2010, I was shelling out $2 million per month in legal bills. And though the trial lawyers couldn't cripple us financially, their accusations had impacts in other ways, never failing to light up a news cycle.

Burke did achieve one small judicial success: After more than two years of repeated motions filed on both sides of the Nisour Square suit, we settled with seven of the Iraqi families in January 2010. I'm not at liberty to discuss the terms, but the Associated Press reported that estates of the deceased each received $100,000; the wounded $30,000. "We are pleased that the original settlement has been affirmed by the plaintiffs," one of our attorneys, Peter White, said at the time. "This enables Xe's new management to move the company forward free of the costs and distraction of ongoing litigation, and provides some compensation to Iraqi families."

Yet after years of getting nowhere in her pursuit of us, it appears Burke's team resorted to questionable tactics to secure even that. Just days after the settlement, those plaintiffs asked the Iraqi government to step in and try to nullify the deal because, they said, they felt pressured and deceived by their lawyers. Three separate Iraqis said the American attorneys pressured them into signing the agreement with fanciful stories of an impending Xe bankruptcy, and my supposed arrest. "They told me Blackwater was about to go into bankruptcy, that their manager will be sent to prison and the government will confiscate all their assets," Mahdi Abdul Khodr told the *Los Angeles Times*. Another plaintiff, Fawzia Sharif, said, "I feel I was deceived by them. They told me the company is going to go bankrupt and this was my last chance. But now I wonder, how could this happen to such a big company?"

The settlement stood, however. Two years after that, a settlement was reached with families of six other Nisour Square victims in a separate suit, for similarly modest amounts. Gradually, we hoped, Blackwater might be putting its darkest days behind it.

Unfortunately, by that time, every business process we conducted was placed under a microscope, from our contractor hiring process to the second-guessing of our compliance process. In Moyock, we understood that saving the company meant taking even more drastic measures than changing our name and settling lawsuits. As part of those measures, Gary Jackson, my dear friend and the man who built Blackwater with me, decided it was best for him to retire.

Jackson and I had always shared a singular focus for growing the company—I had vision; he was a natural at putting together business plans. He did that so well, his leadership was championed in the *Harvard Business Review* alongside the CEO of Nokia, executives at Coca-Cola, Ernst & Young, and more: "I constantly push for the 80 percent solution that is executable now over the 100 percent solution we might be able to devise in another three weeks," he said. Under his management, Blackwater grew so fast that in 2006 *Fast Company* magazine named him one of their "Fast 50," a collection of the "people in business, technology, government, the arts, and beyond who are writing the history of the next 10 years." "Blackwater, based in the tiny town of Moyock, North Carolina, has become one of the largest private-security companies in Iraq and the world," they wrote. "Given the statistics . . . on military privatization, president Gary Jackson is in for a very strong (and long) decade." My friend was joined on that list by Bill Gates of Microsoft, DuPont CEO Charles Holliday, Bill Clinton, and other luminaries.

Together, Jackson and I were relentless, a pair of former Navy SEALs building an empire contract by contract. Any disagreements we had were always respectful. He once instituted a "fifteen-minute pissed-off rule" that I loved: Employees—and executives, for that matter—were allowed fifteen minutes to be furious about some company decision they disagreed with, and then it was back to work. Jackson and I were a perfect business fit, but it grew to be more than that. We'd become family. He'd been there for me during Joan's illness, and my marriage to Joanna, and together we'd weathered the storms from Fallujah and Nisour Square and the hearings on Capitol Hill. Blackwater never would have become the company it did without his guidance. He loved it as much as I did, even as it grew ever larger, plowing forward and picking up steam and becoming harder and harder to control. In order for Xe to forge a new path, the company needed someone who could fill his large shoes.

Shortly after changing our company's name, I hired Joseph Yorio to be its new president. The Jeannette, Pennsylvania, native had an elite military background, having served ten years with the Army's 10th Mountain Division, the 1st Ranger Battalion, and the 7th and 11th Special Forces Groups. But he also brought with him equally valuable experience in multinational corporations, having been an executive at paper distributor Unisource Worldwide, the office products firm Corporate Express, and shipping company DHL. That was experience neither Jackson nor I had ever been able to fall back on.

Yorio was joined at the top by Xe's new chief operating officer and executive vice president, Danielle Esposito. She had been with the company for nearly a decade, and I knew she had the talent and familiarity with our operations to help smooth what was going to be a major transition. Together, Esposito and Yorio tightened down the internal procedures to make the company more acceptable to those in Washington.

In a matter of months, nine vice presidents—half of the total—and sixteen directors left the company. Some were asked to go; others resigned because they didn't agree with Yorio's vision for the company or because they'd had enough of the public inquisitions. Yorio and Esposito expanded certification and compliance programs, acknowledging, "In previous years, the company export compliance program was inadequate to address the regulatory requirements for exports of equipment in support of U.S. Government missions." They brought on a new general counsel, Christian Bonat, who had during the first Obama administration been senior counsel to the Defense Department's General Counsel, providing policy advice on matters of litigation and legislation. They introduced an anonymous, worldwide whistle-blower hotline operated by an independent third party in multiple languages, including various Afghan dialects.

Then the new team instituted a new governance structure at Xe that included a board of directors. It was a far different approach from the way I'd always done things, though I knew "Blackwater" had entered a new era and I begrudgingly endorsed the change. "The company must work to address past, and to prevent future, errors in order to move forward," the management team said.

Finally, I knew there was one last Blackwater holdover who had to go. Me.

It remains difficult to describe how hard that decision was for me, and what leaving the company, under those circumstances, truly felt like. For all the incredible things we accomplished, I can't help but reflect on all that Blackwater never got to do on my watch: the humanitarian and peacekeeping work we could have revolutionized if only we'd been granted the authority to match the funding and the willpower that we brought to the table. I'd wanted to privatize firefighting, and then I wanted to create a national sort of talent agency for police forces to draw upon in times of crisis. We were never at a lack for ideas. Walking away from people who felt like family was hard enough; walking away when what we were building together seemed only half done was heartbreaking.

Twelve years after carving the foundation of my company in the North Carolina swampland, I resigned as Blackwater's CEO, taking on the honorary title of chairman of the new board of directors. I no longer had any involvement in day-to-day operations. "It is with pride in our many accomplishments and confidence in Xe's future that I announce my resignation as the company's Chief Executive Officer," I wrote in an internal email to the staff. "I feel like a proud parent. I have looked after this company since its infancy and I am now sending it off to college." I was effectively done with Blackwater.

It soon became clear, however, that the Justice Department wasn't done with us.

In April 2010, a fifteen-count indictment was issued against Jackson, former executive vice president William Mathews, former general counsel Andrew Howell, former firearms manager Ronald Slezak, and former vice president Ana Bundy, alleging the employees falsified paperwork and gave false statements while improperly possessing and distributing firearms. The charges were especially galling because the factual bases for the prosecution arose from Blackwater's use of the very weapons that were destined for use in overseas missions on behalf of the agency.

The allegations largely revolved around seventeen AK-47s and seventeen Bushmaster M4 machine guns registered to the Camden County Sheriff's Office—yet purchased by, and stored at, Blackwater's armory—and five guns we gifted to Jordan's King Abdullah II at the CIA's request during a royal visit to our Moyock campus in March 2005. Justice then added a damning catchall count asserting the combined allegations showed my employees "did knowingly combine, conspire, confederate and agree to commit offenses against the United States."

The individual charges brought with them potential prison sentences that lasted decades apiece, along with fines up to $250,000. The government strong-armed our senior executives in hopes they might cough up something illegal about the man those investigators were really after. The Justice Department surely hoped one of them would say something to implicate me directly. To the prosecutors' disappointment, there was nothing of the sort to be said.

However, some courageous former government officials did come forward, exposing the government's role in all the conduct of the indictment. After almost three years of wondering whether they were going to spend decades in jail, the five former Blackwater employees were basically exonerated. Soon after defense counsel had provided declarations by former government officials stating that the CIA had asked Blackwater to do the very acts its employees were being prosecuted for, the government dismissed the case against the three of them, and allowed the other two to plead to a one count bookkeeping misdemeanor, resulting in no prison time.

What's more, I was impressed by the way everyone on Blackwater's team stuck to the confidentiality requirements in our government contracts, even when it would have benefited them personally not to. In one interview with the Raleigh *News & Observer*, for instance, Jackson was asked why the sheriff and his nineteen deputies in sleepy Camden County would hatch an agreement with Blackwater to procure seventeen "primitive military rifles," as the indictment described them, which "have little or no application for law enforcement agencies within the United States." Jackson equivocated. "Because they needed guns, I imagine," he finally said.

The pretty obvious truth was that the deputies didn't need AK-47s—we did. But we couldn't publicly explain what was happening behind the scenes. The same was true for King Abdullah's visit to Moyock, and for Blackwater's many shadowy missions that have only been hinted at in the press or speculated about online. Beyond the Defense Department work that launched our company and the State Department work that made us famous, we had for years filled contracts for the organization known in military circles as the "OGA"—the Other Government Agency. The CIA. We never talked about that work—and unfortunately still can't.

CHAPTER 17
THE NEXT REINVENTION
2011–Present

ON THE MORNING OF MY FORTY-SECOND BIRTHDAY, I GOT A CALL FROM MY mother. "Happy birthday," she said. "Remember, your dad was forty-two when he had his first attack." The men in my family don't tend to grow old.

I think about that sometimes, when I see my teenage kids dig through the refrigerator in the kitchen, or hear them talk about summer plans, or even joke about the latest boy to approach one of my daughters at the beach. ("*Please* don't be scary!" my daughters tell me whenever a boy comes to the house to pick them up. "Don't worry," I say. "I'll just sit over there and clean a few guns.") I wonder about the future whenever there's tightness in my chest when I deal with lawyers and legacy problems from my time with Blackwater. It reminds me of the last time I saw my father, at Sophia's baptism, and about sitting at her mother's bedside when she died at the age of thirty-three.

It makes me think about my life's work. Because when it comes to Blackwater, if I had it all to do over again, I'm not sure I would. At the very least, I'd be more selective in the federal departments I worked for. Otherwise, I might just send a note back to 1998 and tell myself to go start my own manufacturing business. Or do something else entirely in a different part of the world—anything, anyplace.

I'm still haunted by an incident that involved my accountant: As he escorted a veteran IRS agent around my farm during yet another tax audit, the officer mentioned how in twenty-five years of handling high-profile tax cases, he had "never been under so much pressure to *get* someone as to *get* Erik Prince." I'm just not sure what good I gained from the path I chose, or what part of America it is that craves that sort of relentless political persecution.

In March 2010, I sold Aviation Worldwide Services—including subsidiary Presidential Airways—to AAR Corporation, a multipurpose logistics provider based outside Chicago that was looking to increase its services for the defense industry. Our fleet had grown to include seventy-three aircraft and some seven hundred men. The deal was for $200 million. "Since 2005," AAR said in a press release at the time, "Presidential had flown more than 70,000 missions worldwide, transported 270,000 personnel, and delivered 50 million pounds of cargo and mail."

Then, soon after, I put Blackwater—or, officially, Xe Services—up for sale. I could barely tell the executives in Moyock without choking up. "After three and a half years of an assault by some of the bureaucracy, a sort of proctology exam brought on by some in Congress," I said then, "it's time to hang it up." It felt like losing a loved one yet again.

In a little over a decade, my company had risen from a soggy patch of Carolina swamp ground to gross some $2 billion. I personally earned only a typical executive salary from the work, and pushed all the company earnings right back into helping Blackwater grow, expanding its facilities and capabilities to better serve future clients. At the height of its influence, in 2007, Blackwater had nearly twenty-five hundred contractors deployed in almost a dozen countries, and a database of some fifty thousand former special forces troops, soldiers, and retired law enforcement agents we could call upon for training and security contracts. Thanks to the relentless assault by politicians and parasitic trial lawyers, the business was valued at less than it had been worth in 2004.

Critics may have questioned my company's tactics, but to this day no one has ever doubted our results: In some fifty thousand completed personal security detail missions, we never suffered a single loss of life or serious injury to those in our care.

Sadly, the same can't be said of our contractors, forty-one of whom gave their lives serving a mission they believed in, helping the United States advance its interests abroad. Other Blackwater contractors sustained life-changing injuries while on the job. To say that they came away from the fight far worse off than I have is almost to trivialize what those words mean.

I check in periodically to a Facebook page called "Small Victories." The posts there are written by Derrick Wright, a former Army Ranger, then wilderness survival instructor, then Blackwater team leader for a high-threat protective detail in Baghdad. He's always been an overachiever, and today that page is a poignant chronicle of his latest mission: Wright's recovery from a traumatic brain injury suffered during a rocket attack on Blackwater's Green Zone housing in April 2007.

With telltale dry wit that made it through the blast unscathed, Wright says simply: "I got my brains blown out." He's open about how the shrapnel from the explosion that night shattered his skull, and riddled his left knee, back, and neck with shards of metal that ripped through his bedroom wall. Blackwater team members sweeping the complex after the blast found him collapsed on the floor of his room in a puddle of blood and cerebral fluid that was leaking from the gaping wound near his forehead. "That's what I've heard, anyway," he says. "The last thing I remember about that night is getting one shoe on before the rocket hit. There's a full month of my memory that's just gone."

Within minutes of the attack, word of the damage had made it back to our offices in Virginia. I'd been told Wright was effectively brain-dead.

As Blackwater medics in Baghdad stabilized him and loaded Wright into a transport plane, back in the States we sent an employee to Austin, Texas, to pick up his wife, Cindy, and accompany her to the Army's Landstuhl Regional Medical Center in Germany, where Derrick was flown in hopes of saving his life. Her itinerary brought Cindy through Virginia, and I remember meeting her in our offices there. I thought about Joan, and losing my own spouse; Cindy and I cried together. We prayed.

And miraculously, those surgeons did save him. Soon enough, Derrick was awake and alert; everyone at Blackwater celebrated when we heard that he'd squeezed Cindy's hand. Soon, he was flown back to a hospital in San Antonio, and ultimately headed home—to a house he could no longer navigate in a wheelchair, seemingly endless rehabilitation, and a lifetime of learning how to be the "new Derrick," as he calls it: a former high-threat specialist who now has double vision; a former Ranger who says he struggles cognitively to keep up when there's too much happening around him; a former wilderness survival guide who speaks eloquently about his more recent satisfaction in deciphering his hometown bus map.

When the initial whirlwind of recovery had subsided, I was proud to hire Wright again, and bring him back to Blackwater to work in our Moyock documents department. It was important to me to help the Wrights however I could, from paying to remodel their home to offering a little professional stability. Unfortunately, Wright was not going to be kept on after the sale of the company, although he soon landed a position at a local museum back in Texas, where he can be closer to home, and his wife and three children. He hopes to become a motivational speaker, and there's no doubt he has much wisdom to impart.

"I look back at 'the event' as sort of a do-over," Wright says now.

"It forced me to step back and look at my priorities. It really opened my eyes to the friends and family I've got around me." I'm incredibly moved that with all he's been through, Wright freely volunteers, "I will always think of being a Blackwater protective team leader in Baghdad as the best job I've ever had."

I'm inspired when I think about the dedication of the men and women who came to work at my company. I loved collaborating with them in Moyock, and visiting our teams in the field. Together, we accomplished more than any of us could have ever anticipated. I remember opening the newspaper one morning and seeing a photo of a U.S. soldier sitting alone on a desolate Afghan mountain ridgeline. He was reading his mail. I loved that Blackwater had delivered it to him. That single image seemed to sum up so much about what my company was capable of.

Today, people ask me what happened—when it felt like things started to come apart. It began, I suppose, with the explosive growth. As the contracts rolled in and the requests kept coming, all of us ran hard to help our customers accomplish their missions. Not just to fulfill our contract, I kept reminding our contractors, but to accomplish the mission. There's a difference.

For those customers, delivery time was perhaps the most crucial metric, so the 80 percent solutions Jackson championed, involving repurposed aircraft, and used armored vehicles, and most any other choice that avoided the military's overwrought supersolutions, were absolutely the right ones. Doing our jobs at home meant that our men in dangerous places could do theirs. That meant people stayed alive. We got unlucky with a few bad hires, but perspective is important: We oversaw thousands of human beings, not machines. Even turbine engines, with only a handful of moving parts, break down now and then. And this is war. Blackwater's men didn't exactly operate in a place where people tracked the days since the last accident.

Then Nisour Square happened. The damage Blackwater sustained after losing four men in Fallujah, as wide ranging as it was, was surmountable. But that shoot-out in the square was the blasting cap that sent a shock wave through the company, through the judicial system, and, most important, through a Democratic Party hell-bent on attacking the Bush administration over an unpopular war. There, it detonated the media's massive secondary attack.

Most members of Congress didn't know very much about security contracting or the realities of armed conflict, but they did know Blackwater was owned by a religious military man from a prominent conservative family. They knew my company was wildly successful thanks to hard work, not any sort of earmarked federal funds. For the politicians and their bureaucratic henchmen, performance doesn't matter at the end of the day, just politics, and I represented everything Democrats loathed. So they tore the company down, and they burned their witch. "This isn't just about broken laws or wasted tax revenues," then presidential contender Barack Obama announced at a 2007 campaign stop in Iowa City. "This is about our claims to moral leadership in the world. We cannot win a fight for hearts and minds when we outsource critical missions to unaccountable contractors."

Of course, within our government's bureaucracy, only the names on the office doors ever really change. Since his election, President Obama's embrace of contractors has flown directly in the face of his campaign rhetoric.

After early token gestures toward reforming transparency and oversight in the PMC industry, he promptly flooded Iraq with more hired guns in order to bring U.S. men and women in uniform home. "The last American soldier[s] will cross the border out of Iraq with their heads held high, proud of their success," President Obama said in October 2011. "That is how America's military efforts in Iraq will end." What he neglected to mention was that in their place the U.S. government left a contractor footprint the size of an Army division, which will remain for the foreseeable future. The United States hasn't left Iraq; only the troops have. "The Obama administration is about to see a major surge of contractors there in Iraq . . . as the military goes away," Representative Jason Chaffetz, a Republican from Utah, said at a 2011 hearing of the Committee on Oversight and

Government Reform. "Are we just playing a little bit of a shell game here?"

I remember reading about the last of those roughly 40,000 U.S. troops being withdrawn on December 18, 2011, when a caravan of a hundred military vehicles wound across southern Iraq into Kuwait in the dead of night. I knew it was the State Department that was truly left hanging by their departure; by 2011, State relied upon military personnel for fourteen critical security-related functions, as well as "logistical support, food and fuel, and about 1,000 other detailed tasks," according to the Commission on Wartime Contracting in Iraq and Afghanistan. Looking ahead, the State Department's total manpower in Iraq is soon expected to reach 17,000 people spread throughout Embassy Baghdad, and nearly a dozen consulates and branch offices in the country. All but about 1,750 of whom will be contractors. (Roughly 5,500 of them will do the private security work Blackwater perfected.)

I can't help but note the irony that when facing that prospect, Secretary of State Hillary Clinton proved just as unwilling as President Obama to back up her campaign promises to curtail contractor use. I also find it interesting that the public has heard very little about the new "war profiteers" who took Blackwater's place, and how intentional that decision seems to be.

After theatrically exploding its relationship with Blackwater in 2009, Clinton's State Department handed our security work in Baghdad over to Triple Canopy, in a five-year contract worth $977 million. My company bore the brunt of public negativity in Baghdad, but make no mistake: Triple Canopy, which had some two thousand men in Iraq during the height of the war working for a range of clients, was hardly beyond reproach.

Triple Canopy's contractors bartered alcohol for guns and other gear from U.S. troops, according to a former company manager, then added to their personal arsenals with weapons purchased on the Iraqi black market, which may well have funded the exact people they were in Iraq to protect against. ("Who are we [financially] supporting in doing that?" Ronald Boline, the former Triple Canopy manager, said in a lawsuit deposition in June 2007. "We're supporting people who are trying to kill Americans, is the logical conclusion.") Triple Canopy officials denied that the company had done anything wrong.

In another ugly, disputed incident from 2007, three Triple Canopy contractors in Baghdad said their team leader wrapped up an airport run mission briefing with the off-hand comment, "I want to kill somebody today." When asked by a team member why, he allegedly replied, "Because I'm going on vacation tomorrow. That's a long time, buddy." A few hours later, according to the contractors on that mission, their team leader sprayed bullets into the windshields of two Iraqi vehicles on Route Irish. The contractors remember him saying, "That didn't happen, understand?" (The team leader denied the allegations.) But Triple Canopy wasn't Blackwater; the general public never heard very much about those stories.

Today, having seen no appreciable shift in the "transparency and accountability needed for good governance" that President Obama had pledged to achieve, there are many who remain skeptical about how the new contracting gold rush will play out in Iraq and, soon, in Afghanistan, when U.S. troops withdraw from that theater by the end of 2014. "We're very, very worried," Dov Zakheim, a member of the Commission on Wartime Contracting, told Congress. "I can give you the worst-case [scenario]. The worst case is you have another Nisour Square thing, which is to say . . . everything spins out of control."

My wild ride with Blackwater came to an end in December 2010. Six months after I put it up for sale, Xe Services was purchased by USTC Holdings, a Los Angeles–based investor consortium led by private equity firms Forté Capital Advisors and Manhattan Growth Partners.

Soon after, a headhunter recruited Ted Wright, then the president of a business unit at enormous contractor KBR, to be Xe's new CEO. He quickly began remaking Blackwater in that company's image, changing more than 80 percent of the instructors we'd had in Moyock and moving the company's Tysons Corner offices inside the Beltway, to Arlington, Virginia. He hired a New York–based public relations firm to rebrand the company again: Xe Services became

ACADEMI. Wright said the company's new goal was to be more "boring." For a while, it seemed as if every time I opened the newspaper, he was ripping me or the previous management team.

Nonetheless, some of ACADEMI's strategic moves have seemed like familiar steps along the trail we originally blazed. Under Wright, the company has expanded its training programs across Mexico, Africa, and Central Asia, and taken on a $17.6 million contract to provide intelligence analysis for the Department of Defense's Counter-Narcoterrorism Technology Program in Afghanistan.

Then, in May 2012, ACADEMI quietly bought out International Development Solutions, the firm Xe partnered with in order to win the West Bank portion of State's latest WPS contract. Getting back in the department's good graces will require changing "the culture" of the company, Wright told AOL's *Defense* blog at the time—though he also acknowledged the same difficulties we ran into. In telling the site that all ACADEMI contractors would have to sign a new corporate code of conduct, for instance, he posed this hypothetical about a worker overseas: "He's got a gun in his hand, he's doing a dangerous job—how do you control him? I can't. He's 8,000 miles away. What I can do is give him a code of conduct."

I nearly shouted at my computer screen when I read that. "Blackwater's men *all* signed codes of conduct!" I wanted to yell. "It was the size of a *book*!"

How much Wright's particular paperwork will rein in that handful of contractors who make bad decisions remains to be seen. But if and when Wright can convince State to embrace the current incarnation of Blackwater, the new CEO imagines the company heading right back to where the previous ownership left off: "I think eventually, we're going to get a license," he told the *Wall Street Journal*. "We're going to do business in Iraq."

In truth, I think it's a smart plan. Government clients would be wise to accept them. The situation on the ground in Iraq—and in similar war zones around the world—is crying out for innovations by private enterprise. Blackwater clearly proved how well entrepreneurs can fill gaps in military capabilities. What the U.S. government needs to do now is incorporate PMCs for jobs far beyond mail carriers and bodyguards. It's the surest way to bring sanity back to our defense spending.

The United States spent more than $800 billion for the nine-year Iraq War, for instance, yet the idea of success there seems as intangible as ever. Within days of the United States withdrawing its troops at the end of 2011, Shia prime minister Nouri al-Maliki arrested the bodyguards protecting his vice president, Tariq al-Hashemi, a Sunni; al-Maliki accused them of spearheading a Green Zone car bombing intended to assassinate him. Al-Hashemi, wanted in connection with the plot, fled to Turkey—at which time his fellow Sunni lawmakers boycotted the Iraqi parliament for a month. By late 2012, al-Hashemi had been sentenced in absentia to death by hanging. Al-Maliki had drawn closer to the Shias in the hornet's nest that is the Iranian capital of Tehran.

Frustrations in Iraq spilled into the streets as supporters launched new waves of sectarian violence. The prospect of civil war there still looms large on the horizon—I suspect Sunni radicals won't stop until al-Maliki is gone—raising the possibility that international forces could be drawn *back* into the quagmire. It's hard to argue that the United States "won" anything of real value in the conflict, and that's important for more than just discussions of strategy.

One doesn't have to have launched a business to understand that while the military has made great strides in minimizing the human toll of conflict, the Pentagon's sense of fiscal responsibility has gone in exactly the opposite direction. The United States pours out more on defense—almost $700 billion a year—than the next nineteen countries combined, some 40 percent of which goes to overhead costs. Some estimates peg the secretive number of American military bases abroad at 900 (others suggest it's closer to six hundred), with American troops stationed in some 150 countries. And that doesn't include another $80 billion spent each year by government intelligence organizations.

I still regularly see examples of misguided big-war thinking today: In the decade after the attacks of 9/11, for instance, the DoD added a hundred new admirals and generals to its ranks—bringing the total to nearly a thousand. The Navy now has more admirals (331 as of May 2012, according to the U. S. Naval Institute) than ships for them to command (282). And in 2010, then defense secretary Robert Gates said that an internal DoD review found that "in some cases the gap between me and an action officer may be as high as thirty layers." (*Newsweek* pointed out that in 1948, when the Cold War began, the secretary of defense had a deputy and a three-man staff that oversaw fifty employees. Gates's twenty-six political appointees ran a staff of three thousand, and he was a defense secretary who *reined in* excesses.)

Since 1995, the Government Accountability Office has designated the DoD's financial management "high risk," thanks to weak oversight that "adversely affect[s] DoD's ability to control costs; ensure basic accountability; anticipate future costs and claims on the budget; measure performance; maintain funds control; prevent and detect fraud, waste, and abuse; [and] address pressing management issues." An organization with twenty-five hundred lines in its budget can't react and adapt to changing dynamics in Iraq, Afghanistan, or anywhere else. Pentagon spending has morphed into a crushing burden on the national budget that will only worsen until politicians—mostly Republicans—finally acknowledge they have to explore cheaper, better, smarter ways of using not only our military, but also the multinational peacekeeping alternatives.

We're clearly not there yet: In 2013, a wave of automatic cuts commonly known as "sequestration" went into effect, aiming to whack back defense spending that more than doubled in the decade after 9/11 (from $294 billion to $716 billion). California Republican representative Howard "Buck" McKeon, the chairman of the House Armed Services Committee, warned the upcoming cuts would be "crippling." Former defense secretary Leon Panetta predicted it would be "doomsday." In reality, the Pentagon's $34 billion budget cut meant that 650,000 civilian DoD employees were initially scheduled to take eleven unpaid furlough days in 2013—which was eventually cut to six. Otherwise, the hysteria was clearly overblown.

And that only underscores the obvious. Slashing the defense budget—by 40 percent or more—should be a key component of any future budget agreements. The government needs to seriously tighten belts across the board, and that includes Pentagon spending. If those committee members would like a starting point for where to cut, how about choirs and sports sponsorships?

According to a 2012 bipartisan initiative between Representatives Jack Kingston, a Georgia Republican, and Betty McCollum, a Democrat from Minnesota, the Pentagon has spent more than $1.5 billion on military music over the past four years, including choirs and bands. The representatives added that the DoD is planning to spend $388 million on 140 military bands and more than 5,000 full-time professional musicians in 2013.

Additionally, they pointed out, the Pentagon will spend more than $70 million in taxpayer money this fiscal year to sponsor NASCAR and IndyCar teams, professional bass fishing, and ultimate fighting. A May 2012 USA Today article detailed that "in fiscal year 2012, the National Guard [was] contacted by more than 24,800 individuals interested in joining because of the racing sponsorship." Of those, only twenty were qualified candidates. None joined.

That sounds like typical DoD inefficiency to me. In everything we did, Blackwater demonstrated how an organization could achieve a maximum return on investment. We filled contracts the way auto manufacturers run production lines—the way I read about in The Machine That Changed the World: The Story of Lean Production by James Womack, Daniel Jones, and Daniel Roos. We created a linear flow in which "materials," or contractors, came in one end, were processed, then came out the end as a finished product delivered to the customer.

I'd picked up that book after Joan and I got home from one trip to Europe. At one point we'd been driving on the autobahn in Germany when a white flash appeared in my rearview mirror. In the blink of an eye, the car blew past us. It was a West German Mercedes S500 moving so fast it seemed ready to take off. Then, suddenly, the driver stood on his brakes: In front of him, a clunky East German Trabant—a car auto critic Dan Neil once described as "a hollow lie . . . constructed of recycled worthlessness"—changed lanes and cut off the Mercedes, nearly causing a massive pileup.

When I later set out to build the training facility, the metaphor from that day was clear to me: What got created under monolithic government control was dramatically inferior to what came from a free-market company whose very survival was pinned to the quality of its work. I told my men to think like Mercedes, and we turned Blackwater into a self-contained machine that could recruit, vet, equip, train, deploy, and support all manner of men to accomplish some of the most difficult missions in the world, all for a fraction of what the DoD typically spent.

The Pentagon is a far larger animal than Blackwater, of course, but that doesn't mean it shouldn't be run with an eye toward efficiency. Why fly cargo drops in Afghanistan with expensive bombers that can land only at select improved airstrips? Our durable little CASA C212 turboprops were cheaper and far more practical. Why allow politics to continue to influence procurement? Two decades after the infamous $640 toilet seats of the 1980s, backroom deals are still common. As just one example, in 2009 Republican representative Harold Rogers of Kentucky earmarked funds for "leakproof" drip pans for Black Hawk helicopters costing $17,000 apiece—which were made by Phoenix Products, one of his donors' companies. An out-of-state competitor of the well-connected company estimated those pans should cost about $2,500 each.

When I see advertisements in military trade journals that don't detail how fast, strong, or lethal a new weapon is, but rather how many congressional districts it's made in, I know there's something fundamentally wrong with the system. That reckless procurement process has repeatedly been revised since its introduction in 1971, yet there's a long way to go. "With good financial oversight," retired vice admiral Jack Shanahan once told CBS News, "we could find $48 billion in loose change in that building, without having to hit the taxpayers."

I also believe that multinational efforts would benefit from similar innovation. Private contractors would be a welcome alternative to the hundred thousand blue-helmeted United Nations peacekeepers who deployed to more than a dozen locations around the world in 2012, to the tune of $7 billion, some 20 percent of which was paid by U.S. taxpayers. Less than 150 of those UN troops are Americans, however; ten thousand of them are from Bangladesh, followed by similar numbers of Pakistani and Indian forces, all of whose home countries treat the international organization almost like a get-rich-quick scheme. The soldiers they send are poorly trained, poorly equipped, and then billed out for the UN's flat rate of $1,028 per soldier per month, paid to the home country. I've seen those sending nations then pay the soldiers a few dollars a day and pocket the rest.

The costs have spiraled so much, the UN now pays about $525 million a year to run its peacekeeping mission in Liberia, which eclipses the country's entire $459 million annual national budget. Elsewhere on the continent, a seventeen-thousand-man UN protection force in the Democratic Republic of Congo put up little resistance in late 2012 as rebels seized the major city of Goma. Those ineffectual peacekeepers were part of the UN's MONUSCO program, whose entire mission is to stabilize the Congo—and who can't seem to deliver results with a $1.4 billion annual operating budget.

How successful would entrepreneurs be in replacing those blue helmets? I remember being a SEAL and hearing about the answer as it was happening.

In 1995, after four years of crushing civil war, the government of Sierra Leone turned to South African company Executive Outcomes to help battle the Revolutionary United Front, or RUF. Immediately, two hundred contractors whipped Sierra Leone's inept military forces into shape, then combined manpower to assault RUF positions. Mineral mining camps that had been rebel strongholds were returned to the government; ten months after Executive Outcomes was hired, RUF agreed to sign a peace accord and cease hostilities. Two hundred contractors brought the war to a full stop. I've been told Executive Outcomes charged about $36 million, a fraction of what the UN would have spent.

Soon after, Sierra Leone held its first democratic elections in more than two decades. And then the PMC's impact was drawn into even starker relief: The U.S. State Department helped broker peace talks between the new government and RUF; as a condition of the talks and a show of good faith to the RUF, State insisted the contractor leave the country entirely. Executive Outcomes complied. Four months later, rebels overthrew the new democratic government and began the killing anew. The UN responded by sending thousands of peacekeepers, many of whom were taken hostage by the crazed rebels.

I understand that PMCs won't ever replace our military, or UN peacekeeping forces—nor should they. But today, the outdated business approaches at those institutions simply cost American taxpayers too much. The United States has effectively priced itself out of the next war.

The common excuse to continue stiff-arming contractors is that the roles I'm describing aren't "inherently governmental." It's time for politicians to come up with a better argument. I've watched that line in the sand shift far too much for it to act as any sort of standard. Forty years ago, for instance, no one would have imagined that NASA would now rely upon a private contractor, SpaceX—which developed, built, and operates its own rocket and spacecraft—to resupply the International Space Station. But it does, and it's time for the Pentagon to follow NASA's lead. It's time to embrace the beauty of private enterprise, which is specifically that it doesn't behave like the government.

I will be curious to see where ACADEMI goes from here. I haven't set foot on the Moyock campus in years, yet I still pay close attention to the industry, and the news, just as I always have. Tragedies still unfold that have the potential to alter our thinking about diplomatic security, while simultaneously underscoring the quality of the work my company once did.

Unfortunately, the latest example came just after nine thirty p.m. on September 11, 2012, in eastern Libya, when a horde of militants swarmed the U.S. diplomatic mission in Benghazi.

Perhaps because of its status as a temporary establishment, as opposed to an official embassy or consulate, there were no U.S. Marines stationed outside that mission. Instead, the security for the walled compound was provided by a small team of government-sanctioned Libyan militia members, along with a half dozen or so hired guns from British security contractor Blue Mountain Group. Inside the compound, the protection of the diplomats was the responsibility of three members of State's long-standing Bureau of Diplomatic Security (DS).

That bureau hadn't seen any grand rise in its numbers since Blackwater was first called upon to help ease their workload a decade earlier, however, and getting by with only three DS agents in Benghazi felt awfully thin to some on the ground. Eric Nordstrom, State's regional security officer in Libya until shortly before the Benghazi attack, later told Congress that he'd requested as many as a dozen DS personnel there but had been told by his superiors that he was "asking for the sun, the moon, and the stars."

"It's not the hardships; it's not the gunfire; it's not the threats. It's dealing and fighting against the people, programs, and personnel who are supposed to be supporting me," a frustrated Nordstrom told Congress. "For me, the Taliban is on the inside of the building."

For a frontier post like Libya, I find it unconscionable that those diplomats were dependent mostly upon local security services. Even before that night, security in the compound—which consisted of a rented villa and two outbuildings surrounded by vast orchards—had clearly been on the minds of the few diplomats stationed there. Benghazi had been a hotbed of rebellion in the uprising against dictator Muammar Gaddafi a year earlier, and by late 2012 Libya's second largest city had become a safe haven for radical militias. They clearly knew the Americans were in their midst: The State Department documented some fifty "security incidents" at the Benghazi consulate between July 2011 and July 2012, and in June 2012 an attacker placed a bomb on the compound's perimeter wall, blowing a twelve-foot-wide hole in it that was described as "big enough for forty men to go through."

It turned out there were five DS agents at the mission in Benghazi on the night of September 11, because Ambassador J. Christopher Stevens had arrived from the U.S. embassy in the Libyan capital of Tripoli, along with his own pair of DS agents. He was there at the behest of Secretary Clinton, who, on the May 2012 day she swore Stevens in as ambassador, asked him to make Benghazi a permanent outpost. Stevens had to schedule his trip to Benghazi in mid-September, as he had to submit a report requesting the funds for carrying out Clinton's directive before September 30, the end of the fiscal year. Around nine p.m. on September 11, he retired to his bedroom in the compound's yellow-walled Villa C, which housed the living quarters and a small safe room in case of attack.

Less than an hour later, there was an explosion. Then Libyan guards manning the compound's tactical operations center in one of the outbuildings saw militants streaming through the compound's main gates with all manner of weapons. Three of the five DS agents rushed to the outbuilding to collect guns and other gear; a fourth DS agent was in the

TOC when the attack began; the final DS agent guided Stevens and State information officer Sean Smith to the safe room in Villa C.

One of those State security officers called over to a nearby government annex, located roughly a mile southeast of the consulate. "The compound is under attack," he said. "People are moving through the gates." The CIA reportedly scrambled a six-man security team, which drove two vehicles to the firefight. They picked up an agency translator and three Libyan volunteers en route.

The compound's TOC was soon overrun by the attackers. It's not clear whether the local guards did much of anything to stop them. I had a friend visit the compound the day after the incident, who reported a distinct lack of pockmarks and impact points on the walls or bullet casings on the ground. The fact that so few shots had been fired strongly suggests to me that the guards fled.

Being a rental property, the villa housing the ambassador had never been designed to withstand an assault by a militia. There were no bulletproof windows or other advanced protections. The only defensive positions outside it were two low walls of sandbags. Soon the rebels were inside that building, too, torching the furniture, and then the villa itself.

Smoke filled the bathroom where Stevens, Smith, and the DS agent, Scott Strickland, were taking cover—so Strickland improvised. He forced his way out an emergency escape window, and collapsed to the patio below. Realizing that Stevens and Smith had not followed him out, the agent made repeated trips back through the window to the safe soon in search of them, until the heat and smoke shut him out entirely.

Strickland scrambled up to the roof to radio the other agents. Three of them arrived back at Villa C in one of their armored cars, but as agents reentered the residence, they were able to locate only Smith. He was already dead of smoke inhalation.

Shortly before ten thirty p.m. those CIA personnel arrived at the compound, opening fire upon the militants beyond the front gate. After clearing a path to Villa C, they, too, joined the search for

Ambassador Stevens, but were repeatedly driven back by the inferno and more small-arms fire from the attackers.

Soon, shooting at the compound slowed enough for State's men to load into the armored vehicle with Smith's body and escape the scene. The CIA personnel directed them to the government annex a mile away; then they made one last fruitless sweep for Stevens before fighting their way out of the compound and back to the annex themselves. There, they all ran into the second wave of the night's plotted assault.

At the annex, some three dozen CIA and DS personnel came under mortar attack by militants who had lain in wait for them to return. The Americans rushed to the rear building of the compound farthest away from the roadway; there, two security contractors— Tyrone Woods and Glen Doherty, who had just arrived as part of an agency backup team flown in from Tripoli—ran up to the roof to engage the attackers. Soon, a series of mortar rounds crashed down onto the building, erupting on the rooftop and killing the two men.

Finally, by five thirty a.m., the attack was over. Roughly thirty Americans from the annex packed into vehicles and headed for the Benghazi airport. Also by that time, looters had ransacked Villa C at the State Department complex, where they stumbled upon the body of the ambassador, who, it appears in video evidence, was still alive. Some of those looters drove him to Benghazi Medical Center, but doctors there found him unresponsive. He, too, had died of smoke inhalation.

Libyans brought his body to the airport, where CIA personnel flew it back to Tripoli. The fifty-two-year-old was the first U.S. ambassador killed while on duty since 1979.

In the weeks after the killings, it was suggested that State had some sort of agreement with the CIA personnel down the road to provide manpower as a security fallback at State's diplomatic mission. Confusion about those responsibilities may have played a part in the security failures that night. One thing seems clear to me, however: The Obama administration's view of threats, and the appropriate response to them, has prompted dangerously lax security at diplomatic outposts around the world—and because of that, four Americans came home in caskets. Say what you will about Blackwater's operational tactics, but with our men on duty, no secretary of state ever had to appear at Dover or Andrews Air Force Base to receive the bodies of fallen diplomats.

In 2010, fed up with an endless drip of frivolous lawsuits and years of bad press, I relocated to Abu Dhabi, United Arab Emirates, with my four oldest children and our giant South African Boerboel, Ezra. Some speculated I was trying to escape the long arm of U.S. law. Congresswoman Jan Schakowsky reportedly even told the UK's *Independent*, "If Mr. Prince had not emigrated to the United Arab Emirates, which does not have an extradition agreement with the U.S., he too would now be facing prosecution."

That's just more derogatory noise; and false. I remain a Virginia resident and taxpayer and do not fail to exercise my right to vote. I flew all the way back to vote in person at the Middleburg Town Hall last November. Maybe someday the voters will get it right again. I have a home in Abu Dhabi because it is convenient. I'm working now with a private equity start-up, financing agriculture, energy, and mining projects in Africa, the Middle East, and other difficult parts of the world. It harnesses the logistics coordination I've always done well, and I get to eat dinner with my family at night. Just the way my father tried so hard to do.

I still come back to the United States regularly, to ski in Colorado, and see my three youngest boys, who live with their mother. (My divorce from Joanna was perhaps inevitable.) And I always like being back at the farm in Virginia. The shooting range on the hill is still there, full of old Blackwater targets and one of Jim Dehart's mini-BEAR training systems. It all still works when we throw the switch on the circuit breaker box, though it's used mostly by my teenagers now. Seeing it all set up is rather bittersweet for me. More bitter, I think, than sweet.

The brand name, however, lives on. As part of the sale of my company, I kept ownership of the Blackwater trademark and bear paw logo. It's a polarizing brand, I know—but it's still got a proud following in some quarters.

The ultimate irony there is that as I look forward, it's possible I actually could build another training facility and explore more security work. I often hear from old friends who say, "Just do it again! Get the band back together, and we'll make a new Blackwater!" There will never stop being a demand for that expertise, but I don't know that I see it happening. That's got nothing to do with business; it's personal. The loss of my father rocked me; then, after Joan's death, I put emotional walls up that probably haven't ever fully come back down. Seeing the company I'd built torn down for no reason was almost too much to bear.

The way the Blackwater story ended still gnaws at me. I'm no hero. The world knows all too well about my mistakes. But I was never meant to play the villain.

I take some solace knowing that, in the end, history will judge me and all that we accomplished at Blackwater. Perhaps children someday will read about us the way I read about cowboys, and battling pirates on the high seas, and Claire Chennault leading those Flying Tigers. Maybe someday people will grasp that Blackwater's legacy is far more than shootings—that it also includes the shelters we set up in Afghanistan to house orphans and widows driven from their homes. Maybe they'll understand that it was precisely my deep faith that made me insist on building mosques at our bases overseas, so our neighbors would have a place to practice their own faith.

Perhaps something in my journey will inspire a child in the Heartland the way I'd been inspired, and he'll also dedicate his life to being a force for good in the world. I have to look no further than a village in upstate New York to know that I've achieved that.

There, in 2006, in a peaceful suburban neighborhood just north of Schenectady, I funded the Joan Nicole Prince Home. It's a place where terminally ill patients without private housing can stay and find peace during their final days. There's a stone path that circles a meditation garden outside the two-story home, and a collection of purple hydrangeas bloom by the back porch.

Today, that charitable organization has its own board of directors; I'm not attached to its operation in any discernible way. I don't want to risk having my name affect the tremendous work the men and women there do. That part is hard, but regardless of how rarely I visit, I know that above the fireplace in the living room there's a portrait of Joan smiling down. And beneath it on the mantel are small sculptures that remind me of the porcelain Lladró figurines I bought her for our first Christmas together—back before there was any inheritance, or cancer, or Blackwater.

It remains to be seen what my future might hold. Tomorrow is one less day than I've got now, and only God knows how many more I'll have. But in the meantime, I'm enjoying a quieter life. I had a small Hobie Cat delivered to our home in Abu Dhabi shortly after my family relocated. The kids are still learning their way around the fiberglass catamaran, the same way I once poked around with our Boston Whaler back in Michigan. But most every day in Abu Dhabi is a good day to skim across the bay, catching the next gust of wind and teaching my own children to feel at home on the water.

THE CIA AND ERIK PRINCE

by Max Boot

This is the chapter the CIA wouldn't want you to read.

Originally, Erik Prince had written a chapter for this book on his relationship with the CIA. But precisely because he did have a close relationship with the CIA, he was bound under the terms of his nondisclosure agreement to submit his manuscript for approval to the CIA's Publications Review Board, which is charged with excising any classified information (and which often takes its charge so zealously that it deletes even commonly available information that any reader of Wikipedia can access in seconds). By the time the CIA's censors were through, there were so many deletions that Prince and his publishers decided that the chapter as written was unsalvageable. So the publisher asked me to write this afterword, which provides the essential information about Prince's dealings with the CIA based solely on publicly available reports. In so doing I have not had access to any classified material, nor have I spoken to Prince, with whom I have no personal or business relationship. In fact, I have met him only once—when,

*years ago, he gave me a tour of the Blackwater facility in North
Carolina, a tour he has given to numerous other writers and journalists over the years. Where he is quoted below, the quotations
come from previously published media accounts.*

*What follows is written not from Prince's own perspective or
that of a defender of his but rather from the perspective of a dis-
interested observer trying to provide the most accurate depiction
possible based on what is publicly known—which, needless to say,
is not the entire story. Only those with access to the CIA's own
highly classified files know everything that went on, and possibly
not even them, given the proclivity of government officials to
avoid writing down the most sensitive information in their possession. This, however, is my best attempt to summarize what
those of us on the outside know about what went on between Erik
Prince and the CIA.*

> **—Max Boot, Jeane J. Kirkpatrick Senior Fellow in National
> Security Studies at the Council on Foreign Relations and
> author of five books, most recently *Invisible Armies: An
> Epic History of Guerrilla Warfare from Ancient Times to
> the Present* (Liveright, 2013)**

WHEN ON SEPTEMBER 11, 2001, AL-QAEDA OPERATIVES FLEW HIJACKED
aircraft into the World Trade Center and the Pentagon, the United
States was plunged into a war against a shadowy network for which
it was not well prepared. This very lack of preparation created a
business opportunity for Blackwater and other private sector firms
that stepped forward to assist the armed forces and intelligence
agencies that had been tasked with fighting a difficult and unfamiliar
war on terror.

The U.S. armed forces had spent much of the previous, post–Gulf
War decade focusing on high-tech conventional operations that fell
into the category "network-centric warfare"—an approach better

suited to obliterating Saddam Hussein's tanks in the deserts of Iraq than locating and killing individual terrorists hiding among a civilian population. The military's special mission units, such as Delta Force, were better prepared to hunt terrorists in the shadows, but this was a role they had seldom been called upon to undertake by risk-averse politicians in Washington fearful of another "Black Hawk Down." General Peter Schoomaker, a former Army chief of staff and commander of the U.S. Special Operations Command, lamented: "Special Operations was never given the mission. It was very, very frustrating. It was like having a brand-new Ferrari in the garage, and nobody wants to race it because you might dent the fender."

For its part, the CIA, the nation's premier agency for human intelligence (i.e., espionage), had seen a precipitous decline of its covert action capabilities since the heady days of the 1960s, when it had waged a "secret war" in Laos, or even the 1980s, when it had supplied the mujahideen with the weapons that helped to evict the Red Army from Afghanistan. The CIA had maintained tenuous relations with some of the former mujahideen now reassembled as the Northern Alliance, a rebel group fighting the Taliban extremists and their al-Qaeda allies for control of Afghanistan. But there were no CIA officers permanently stationed in the Taliban's Afghanistan or Saddam Hussein's Iraq. Because the United States did not have diplomatic relations with either country, it lacked embassies that could provide a platform and cover for CIA operatives posing as diplomats.

The National Clandestine Service, the CIA division responsible for human espionage, had withered as a result of post–Cold War budget cuts. The Special Activities Division (SAD), the euphemistically named unit within the Clandestine Service responsible for paramilitary operations, had shrunk even more. In November 2001, Bob Woodward reported in the *Washington Post* that the SAD—an appropriate acronym under the circumstances—had just "150 fighters, pilots and specialists," equivalent to just one company-sized formation in the army.

But, however small, the Special Activities Division still had the ability to punch above its weight class. By the time Woodward wrote those words, the Special Activities operatives and the Army's Special Forces "A-teams" had already established a presence on the ground in Afghanistan, long before the more ponderous conventional military forces could arrive on the scene. The CIA's Jawbreaker team had been the first to arrive, on September 26, 2001, in a Russian-built, CIA-operated helicopter, carrying millions of dollars in cash to buy off Northern Alliance warlords. The A-teams, commonly known as Green Berets, arrived a few weeks later, carrying sophisticated communications equipment to enable them to call in air strikes. It was a potent combination of capabilities that rapidly enhanced the striking power of the Northern Alliance and brought to an end Taliban control of Afghanistan.

While the special operations forces provided military capabilities the CIA did not have, the CIA's paramilitaries, most of them former special operations soldiers themselves, showed that they could deploy faster and with fewer constraints than their uniformed counterparts. That's because the CIA operates under Title 50 of the U.S. Code, which authorizes covert actions based on a presidential finding, whereas the military operates under Title 10 war-fighting authority, which brings with it more public and congressional scrutiny—and a more ponderous chain of command. Military missions are often "clandestine," meaning that the element of secrecy is employed to preserve tactical surprise, but the operation is then generally acknowledged to have been carried out by the U.S. armed forces. The CIA, by contrast, is empowered to carry out "covert" operations, which are defined under U.S. law as designed "to influence political, economic, or military conditions abroad, where it is intended that the role of the United States Government will not be apparent or acknowledged publicly." In other words, CIA covert actions are designed to have "deniability," which actions by the uniformed military naturally lack. (There are some instances of military special operators operating in plain clothes, but these are relatively rare.)

The CIA also brought, theoretically at least, greater regional expertise and experience in dealing with prickly foreigners—and a greater willingness to undertake dangerous missions without all of the support infrastructure demanded by the military (such as having nearby quick reaction forces and search and rescue forces on call). The very first American killed in Afghanistan after 9/11 was Johnny "Mike" Spann, a member of the Special Activities Division, who was slain on November 25, 2001, during the uprising at the Qala-i-Jangi prison in the north.

For both the CIA and the special operations forces—which shared a common origin in the World War II–era Office of Strategic Services founded by Erik Prince's hero, "Wild Bill" Donovan—the toppling of the Taliban in the fall of 2001 was their finest hour. But their job was not done with the capture of Kabul and the installation of Hamid Karzai as a Western-backed alternative to the Taliban. The Taliban and al-Qaeda had been defeated but not annihilated. Both sought and found refuge across the border in Pakistan, and they began to regroup to stage fresh attacks. It was imperative, from Washington's standpoint, to keep after these extremists, and that, in turn, required dramatically beefing up American intelligence capabilities in Afghanistan and the tribal regions of Pakistan.

In the wake of the 9/11 attacks, the CIA began to hire thousands of new employees to wage the global war on terror. Many were young and inexperienced, and most were hired as intelligence collectors or intelligence analysts—not as paramilitaries. Yet collecting intelligence in a chaotic country like Afghanistan, or later Iraq, was not like collecting intelligence in Eastern Europe during the Cold War. In those days the CIA's primary adversary was the KGB, a rival intelligence service that played by common rules. Both sides sought to stymie the other's intelligence-gathering efforts, but each side recognized the other's diplomatic immunity. CIA officers might be arrested in Russia, but if so they would be expelled, not killed. (It was a different story for local "assets" recruited by the CIA—as traitors to the Motherland, they would face execution or lengthy prison terms.)

The Taliban and al-Qaeda, by contrast, did not play by the rules of "civilized" espionage. They targeted for death any Westerners they could find, whether troops, aid workers, journalists, diplomats, or spies. Post-Taliban Afghanistan remained a lawless land where attacks from the Taliban, or common criminals, posed a lethal threat to any CIA operatives intent on gathering information.

Unfortunately, the CIA did not have enough of its own paramilitaries to protect its case officers as they gathered intelligence, recruited Afghan allies, and orchestrated raids on al-Qaeda and Taliban targets. In 2004, an article in *Foreign Affairs* referred to "600–700 covert operators" on the CIA's payroll (the actual figure is classified), a substantial increase from the total of 150 cited by Bob Woodward three years earlier but still inadequate to meeting surging demand for their services. The strain only grew when the United States invaded Iraq in the spring of 2003. Now the CIA had two wars to wage. The CIA tried to make up some of the shortfall by borrowing special operations forces from the military, a procedure known as "sheep dipping." But the Special Activities Division was still overstretched and so, too, was the Global Response Staff, whose specific mission was providing protective services to the Clandestine Service abroad.

Enter Blackwater, which was about to expand its operations from simply training military and police personnel at its sprawling complex in Moyock, North Carolina, to deploying its own employees to defend and facilitate America's growing presence in Afghanistan and then Iraq. This was part of a growing trend of the U.S. government relying more on private contractors to wage wars. In the Gulf War there had been approximately one contractor for every sixty service personnel; in Iraq and Afghanistan, after a long period of downsizing in the military's active-duty end strength, the figure was closer to one to one, meaning that if a hundred thousand troops deployed, a hundred thousand contractors would follow to support them. The figures for the intelligence services were classified but undoubtedly similar.

In 2010 the *Washington Post* reported, for example, that out of 854,000 people with top secret clearances, 265,000 of them were contractors, making up roughly a third of the intelligence community's entire workforce. At the CIA alone, the *Post* reported, there were 10,000 contractors from 114 different firms.

Blackwater was only one of many private companies that stepped forward to fill this surging demand, and it was far from the biggest. (The *Washington Post* reports, for instance, that "revenue from General Dynamics' intelligence- and information-related divisions, where the majority of its top-secret work is done, climbed to $10 billion in the second quarter of 2009, up from $2.4 billion in 2000.") "You have to remember where CIA was after 9/11," said Pete Hoekstra, a retired congressman who chaired the House Intelligence Committee from 2004 to 2006 and later served as its ranking member. "They were gutted in the 1990s. They were sending raw recruits into Afghanistan and other dangerous places. They were looking for skills and capabilities, and they had to go to outside contractors like Blackwater to make sure they could accomplish their mission."

Prince recalls that he was eager to help defend America after 9/11. He applied to join the Special Activities Division, and he says he was fully vetted but turned down on the grounds that he lacked sufficient "field experience," presumably because his stint in the SEALs had been relatively brief.

Prince did not give up easily. He did not have extensive contacts at the CIA, but he did know "Buzzy" Krongard, the CIA's executive director, whose son had been, like Prince, a Navy SEAL. He recounts approaching Krongard and, through him, putting the CIA in touch with sources on the ground in Afghanistan. According to Prince's own account in this book, which has not been reported elsewhere, his initial contact with Afghanistan came through a friend, Charlie Santos, who was an employee of a Saudi-based oil company and who also happened to be a friend of the important Afghan warlord Abdul Rashid Dostum. Prince says he put Santos in touch with the CIA, thereby facilitating a direct link between the CIA and Dostum that proved invaluable in the fall of 2001. From the start, then, Blackwater was involved not only in protective services, its signature initiative, but also in intelligence gathering—a less publicized role.

Blackwater's role with the CIA was soon to grow substantially. Early in 2002 Blackwater received a contract to guard the CIA's new station in Kabul, supposedly a secret location but widely known to be located in the Ariana Hotel downtown near the U.S. embassy and the multinational military command. Prince says that he himself was among the first guards on the scene and helped to establish the template for a Blackwater protective detail, creating tactics, techniques, and procedures that would be employed before long on a much wider scale across Afghanistan and Iraq.

To do the day-to-day work, Blackwater recruited primarily from veterans of the U.S. military's special operations forces. The men working with the CIA had to be specially vetted to a higher standard than run-of-the-mill guards, including through the use of polygraph tests. Those who met the CIA's demanding standards were employed by a subsidiary known as Blackwater Select. They were paid $550 per day and received more flexibility than they had known in the more hierarchical and rule-ridden culture of the armed forces. They could even hope to cadge a drink after going off duty—the CIA's "Talibar" was one of the few legal sources of booze in a strictly Islamic country where the U.S. military was prohibited from imbibing even on its own bases.

Because Blackwater kept the Kabul station safe, it won the CIA's trust and was awarded additional contracts to protect more CIA bases that were springing up around southern and eastern Afghanistan—the heartland of the Taliban. Not only did Blackwater deploy teams of guards to each base; aircraft belonging to its aviation arm, Presidential Airways, helped to supply these CIA bases along with military bases. Blackwater flew thousands of supply sorties, its aircraft going low to parachute supplies into remote outposts. This expanding Blackwater role was covert, in line with all CIA activities; it received publicity only when things went wrong.

Things went as wrong as they possibly could have on December 30, 2009, at Forward Operating Base Chapman, a CIA enclave located in the eastern Afghan province of Khost, just a few miles from the Pakistan border. The CIA's chief of base there, Jennifer Matthews, along with a number of her subordinates and a Jordanian intelligence officer, had gathered to welcome Humam Khalil Abu-Mulal al-Balawi, a Jordanian doctor and jihadist whom the CIA and Jordanian intelligence believed had been recruited to penetrate al-Qaeda's top echelon. In reality al-Balawi had been "turned" by al-Qaeda into a triple agent—and a suicide bomber. Rather than meeting with his CIA contacts, al-Balawi blew them up with a suicide vest hidden under his robes. Nine people were killed, not counting al-Balawi, making this the CIA's worst loss of life since the bombing of the U.S. embassy in Beirut in 1983.

Among those killed were two employees of Xe Services, as Blackwater was then known: a forty-six-year-old former Green Beret named Dane Paresi, who had previously won a Bronze Star for his heroism in Afghanistan, and a thirty-five-year-old former SEAL named Jeremy Wise. The fact that al-Balawi was able to set off his bomb in the presence of Blackwater security guards might indicate that Paresi and Wise had failed at their jobs, but postbombing inquiries exonerated them of any wrongdoing or negligence.

The most detailed account of the attacks, *The Triple Agent* by the Pulitzer Prize–winning *Washington Post* reporter Joby Warrick, depicts Paresi and Wise as being more alive to the danger posed by al-Balawi than some of their complacent CIA colleagues, who insisted that he be allowed on the base without once being searched. "Paresi," Warrick writes, "was highly skeptical of the security plan the officers had rehearsed, and he had said so, sharing his concerns with both his [Blackwater] supervisor back in Virginia and the CIA's security chief in Khost, Scott Roberson [who was also killed in the blast]."

Warrick adds that Paresi, who was "known for his unflappable calm and his Zen-like insistence on looking after the small details,"

was willing to speak up when the decisions of his superiors "exasperated him" but he "also understood his place"—"he had a family to
feed and would do his job, even if he didn't like it."

When the day came, Paresi and Wise did their jobs well, even if
they could not stop al-Balawi's suicide attack. Warrick recounts that
the two men "had instinctively raised their guns when Balawi balked
at exiting on their side of the car" and had "watched with growing
alarm as Balawi hobbled around the vehicle, one hand grasping the
crutch and the other hidden ominously under his shawl." The two
men shouted in unison: "Hands up! Get your hand out of your clothing!" Instead al-Balawi detonated his vest.

The CIA subsequently honored Paresi and Wise by adding stars
for them to its memorial wall, which honors CIA employees killed in
the line of duty, even though, as contractors, they were not eligible
for burial in Arlington National Cemetery. Indeed many other attacks against CIA officers in Iraq and Afghanistan were thwarted by
Blackwater, which, despite its propensity to generate controversy,
had an exemplary record of safeguarding the "principals" under its
care—as the U.S. government implicitly acknowledged by repeatedly
renewing Blackwater's contracts for protective services.

Blackwater's responsibilities did not end at the perimeter of CIA
bases where they provided "static" security. By 2005, with insurgencies growing in both Afghanistan and Iraq, the CIA mandated that
its officers not venture outside headquarters in Kabul and Baghdad
without a personal security detail. Blackwater provided teams of
bodyguards who would accompany CIA officers on all of their missions. Inevitably, because Blackwater employees were experienced
veterans of the special operations forces, they became closely involved in both mission planning and execution. Indeed young CIA
officers would have been negligent if they had not asked grizzled veterans of Delta Force about the best way to carry out an operation.
Blackwater personnel wound up going well beyond a narrowly defensive role to take part in "snatch and grab" missions on an almost
nightly basis. Sometimes the contractors operated in conjunction

with secretive military special mission units. They and their CIA colleagues also worked with "strike forces" made up of locally recruited fighters. Hand-picked Blackwater employees also provided security for the transportation of detainees to CIA "black sites" for interrogation and detention.

A former Blackwater official told the *New York Times* that their personnel "were supposed to be the outer layer of the onion, out on the perimeter" but instead had become "the drivers and the gunslingers" on CIA missions. A retired CIA officer explained to the *Washington Post*: "There was no bench strength with either the CIA or Special Forces, so sometimes they would turn to contractors, who often had lots of the same skills."

The transformation of Blackwater's role had occurred with the full support of—indeed at the request of—the CIA personnel on the ground even if agency superiors in Washington were not always aware of the enhanced role being played by contractors in the field. Erik Prince says he never knew everything his men did, either, because they operated under the cloak of secrecy, but he repeatedly encouraged them to do "whatever it takes" to help their CIA clients. "Several former Blackwater guards" told the *New York Times* "that their involvement in the operations became so routine that the lines supposedly dividing the Central Intelligence Agency, the military and Blackwater became blurred." "A former top CIA officer" added: "It became a very brotherly relationship. There was a feeling that Blackwater eventually became an extension of the agency."

This was not the only area where the dividing line between CIA and Blackwater blurred. Prince hired a series of high-level CIA officials to work at Blackwater, most notably J. Cofer Black, the flamboyant former head of the CIA's Counterterrorism Center, famous for assuring President George W. Bush after 9/11 that, by the time the CIA was done, Osama bin Laden and his confederates "would have flies walking across their eyeballs." Others included Enrique "Ric" Prado, former chief of operations at the Counterterrorism Center, and Robert "Rob" Richer, former associate deputy director of the National Clandestine Service. According to Pulitzer Prize–winning journalist Mark Mazzetti, Prince also "regularly invited top CIA officers to the Kentucky Derby, or down to Blackwater's headquarters, in eastern North Carolina's Great Dismal Swamp, for a day of shooting at the company's expansive training grounds."

The new hires from the CIA helped Prince start the new subsidiary Total Intelligence Solutions, designed to provide risk assessment for companies doing business overseas. They also helped Blackwater land more contracts from the intelligence community. There was nothing nefarious about this; it was standard operating procedure in Washington, where both former CIA director J. James Woolsey and future director of national intelligence James Clapper, for instance, went to work for Booz Allen Hamilton, a much larger contractor than Blackwater.

One of the contracts Blackwater won was to operate the drones that the CIA flew over Pakistan from bases in both Pakistan and Afghanistan. The most famous of these was the Predator, known in its armed and updated configuration as the Reaper, but there were also other, less publicized drones, some of them built specially for stealth. Armed with Hellfire missiles and five-hundred-pound laser-guided bombs, the drones were at the cutting edge of the war on terror. They had first been used after the September 11 attacks, and their employment had dramatically expanded under the Obama administration. According to the Web site *Long War Journal,* a project of the nonprofit Foundation for the Defense of Democracies and considered an essential source for drone strike statistics, the number of U.S. drone strikes in Pakistan grew from 35 in 2008 to 53 in 2009 and 117 in 2010, most of them taking place in North and South Waziristan, strongholds of the Haqqani network and both the Afghan and Pakistani Taliban. The drone strikes have been criticized for stoking resentment of the United States, but they also undoubtedly disrupted al-Qaeda plots and made it harder for that organization to regroup.

The drones could be remotely piloted, and their munitions fired, by CIA personnel sitting in the United States; contractors would not be responsible for deciding whom the U.S. government would blow up. But someone had to be on the ground to recover, service, and arm the aircraft. Blackwater—or, more accurately, Xe Services—won a contract to do just that; the deal also included guarding the drone bases, the biggest one being in Jalalabad, Afghanistan, which would be the launch site of the SEAL Team raid that killed Osama bin Laden. Blackwater personnel traveled to Nellis Air Force Base in Nevada, home of the Air Force's remotely piloted vehicle program, to be trained in their tasks. Thus, just as Blackwater had been crucial for President Bush's war on terror, so it proved indispensable for President Obama's continuation of that struggle against al-Qaeda, notwithstanding the hostility against Blackwater exhibited by some of the president's supporters.

CIA director Leon Panetta finally terminated Xe's drone operations contract in 2009, after leaks to the *New York Times* sparked controversy about the company's role in carrying out "inherently governmental functions" such as conducting offensive military and intelligence operations. (The U.S. armed forces continue to rely on other contractors to service aircraft in the field.)

While voiding the Predator contract, in June 2010 Panetta renewed Xe's contract to continue providing security for CIA operatives in the field. To get that work, worth an estimated $100 million, Xe beat out in competitive bidding two other contractors, DynCorp and Triple Canopy, which had shared the work of protecting State Department personnel in Iraq.

Unsurprisingly, the new CIA contract drew criticism from Representative Jan Schakowsky, who complained, "I am continually and increasingly mystified by this relationship. To engage with a company that is such a chronic, repeat offender is reckless." However, Panetta publicly defended the decision, saying Blackwater had "cleaned up its act." A government official explained to the *Washington Post*, on the condition of anonymity, why the firm had beaten out its competitors: "Blackwater has undergone some serious changes. They've had to if they want to survive. They've had to prove to the government that they're a responsible outfit. Having satisfied every legal requirement, they have the right to compete for contracts. They have people who do good work, at times in some very dangerous places. Nobody should forget that, either."

The murkiest part of Blackwater's relationship with the CIA concerns its involvement in what has been described as a "secret program to locate and assassinate top operatives of Al Qaeda." The program dated back to the early post-9/11 days, when Ric Prado, then still with the CIA, worked to develop a capability to deploy small teams to kill or capture wanted terrorists.

Although countless movies have depicted the CIA as having legions of assassins at its beck and call, the reality is otherwise. The CIA's capacity for lethal action had been shut down after the Church Committee hearings of the 1970s exposed plots against Fidel Castro, Patrice Lumumba, and other world leaders. President Gerald Ford subsequently issued an executive order forbidding assassinations.

Prado was eager to reconstitute that capability after 9/11, in order to augment the hunting of terrorists that was being conducted by the U.S. armed forces and by both military and CIA aircraft. All of this was fully legal. Both the Authorization for the Use of Military Force passed by Congress on September 14, 2001, and an executive order signed by President Bush authorized killing al-Qaeda members just as the military killed other enemy combatants.

To train the new CIA direct-action team, made up initially of full-time agency employees, Prado turned to Blackwater. "Wary of attracting undue attention," Adam Ciralsky reported in *Vanity Fair*, "the team practiced not at the company's North Carolina compound but at Prince's own domain, an hour outside Washington, D.C. The property looks like an outpost of the landed gentry, with pastures and horses, but also features less traditional accents, such as an indoor firing range."

The direct action team's targets reportedly included Mamoun Darkazanli, an al-Qaeda financier living in Hamburg, and A. Q. Khan, the rogue Pakistani scientist who's helped the nuclear weapons programs of Iran, Libya, and North Korea. CIA teams were said to have deployed to track Darkazanli in Germany and Khan in Dubai, but senior officials in Washington never authorized pulling the trigger. Apparently they were willing to kill terrorists with bombs and missiles—but not with sniper's bullets.

After Prado joined Blackwater in 2004, he tried to resuscitate the program, this time relying heavily on Prince for help. By this time Prince had already been recruited by the CIA as a vetted "asset"—a process that occurred in 2004 and required high-level approval and the generation of a "201" (personnel) file. This did not make Prince an employee of the CIA but designated him as a trusted individual who worked on behalf of the agency. This designation has been typically conferred on foreigners stealing their own country's secrets on behalf of the United States, but sometimes it is conferred on Americans who possess unusual talents, resources, and contacts to help the CIA. Howard Hughes, for example, had been recruited as an agency asset in 1974 to build a ship known as the *Glomar Explorer* that would allow the CIA to salvage a sunken Russian submarine.

In similar fashion, Prince could mobilize his extensive resources, and Blackwater's, to help the CIA achieve its mission. "I was looking at creating a small, focused capability," Prince later explained, "just like ['Wild Bill'] Donovan did years ago." Indeed Donovan was famous for recruiting well-connected individuals such as Allen Dulles and Julia Child, who could use their private sector experience for the OSS's benefit; the CIA followed a similar swashbuckling template in its early days before becoming heavily bureaucratized. Prince's recruitment was, thus, a throwback to the CIA's early days.

Much of what Prince did he did on "spec," fronting his own money to help the CIA, much as his father had developed products for Detroit's automakers on his own initiative. "I grew up around the auto industry," Prince later explained. "Customers would say to my dad, 'We have this need.' He would then use his own money to create prototypes to fulfill those needs. He took the 'If you build it, they will come' approach."

One of the initiatives that Prince and Prado quietly developed, out of sight not only of the general public but also of most of their Blackwater colleagues, was a private network of foreign spies. "According to two sources familiar with his work," *Vanity Fair* reported, "Prince was developing unconventional means of penetrating 'hard target' countries—where the C.I.A. has great difficulty working either because there are no stations from which to operate or because local intelligence services have the wherewithal to frustrate the agency's designs." In pitching his services to the Drug Enforcement Administration in October 2007, Prado wrote, "We have a rapidly growing, worldwide network of folks that can do everything from surveillance to ground truth to disruption operations. These are all foreign nationals so deniability is built in and is a big plus."

Publicly available details of what this "worldwide network" actually did are hard to come by, but *Vanity Fair* reported that "he and a team of foreign nationals helped find and fix a target in October 2008, then left the finishing to others. 'In Syria,' he says, 'we did the signals intelligence to geo-locate the bad guys in a very denied area.' Subsequently, a U.S. Special Forces team launched a helicopter-borne assault to hunt down al-Qaeda middleman Abu Ghadiyah. Ghadiyah, whose real name is Badran Turki Hishan Al-Mazidih, was said to have been killed along with six others."

Prince also embraced Prado's proposal to set up teams to kill terrorist leaders. In so doing Prince was apparently acting in his private capacity as a CIA asset rather than as the owner of Blackwater. Apparently neither Cofer Black nor Rob Richer took part in this plan. Prince later explained to *Vanity Fair*: "We were building a unilateral, unattributable capability. If it went bad, we weren't expecting the chief of station, the ambassador, or anyone to bail us out."

Yet while the capability to carry out these missions was developed, it was never utilized. In 2006 the CIA pulled the plug because of what Prince described as "institutional osteoporosis." By this time, with the CIA's "enhanced interrogation" programs already a matter of international controversy, there were few volunteers in the CIA's ranks to push forward with an "assassination" program that could expose its participants to negative publicity and even prosecution.

"I put myself and my company at the CIA's disposal for some very risky missions," Prince later said. One of the risks he ran was public exposure. In June 2009, CIA director Leon Panetta briefed the House and Senate Intelligence Committees on the already canceled covert action program to kill terrorists and named Prince and Blackwater as participants. It took only a few weeks for the news to leak, with the *Wall Street Journal*, the *New York Times*, and the *Washington Post* running headlines breathlessly reporting, as the *Post* put it, "CIA Hired Firm for Assassin Program." Immediately thereafter came the *New York Times'* revelations about Blackwater's role in the Predator program.

Prince was livid and understandably so—his cover had been blown. "The left complained about how [CIA operative] Valerie Plame was compromised for political reasons," he later told *Vanity Fair*. "A special prosecutor [was even] appointed. Well, what happened to me was worse. People acting for political reasons disclosed not only the existence of a very sensitive program but my name along with it." The CIA sent a referral of the case to the Justice Department, but, unlike in the case of Valerie Plame, no special counsel was appointed to investigate the matter and no one was ever prosecuted for leaking this highly classified information.

His outing as a CIA asset resulted, Prince says, in his being put on an al-Qaeda hit list, forcing him and his family to take extensive security precautions. All of the uproar around Blackwater also resulted in legal repercussions.

The prosecution began in 2008 when agents from the Bureau of Alcohol, Tobacco, Firearms, and Explosives, their guns drawn, raided Blackwater's Moyock compound to execute a federal search warrant. ATF agents had been regular visitors to the facility in the past; Blackwater was a registered federal firearms dealer and had to comply with numerous state and federal regulations. Now, in what Prince denounced as a "cartoonish show of force," the ATF agents were looking for evidence that Blackwater had skirted the law. The agents hauled away seventeen Romanian-made AK-47s and seventeen Bushmaster M4 rifles.

Federal prosecutors subsequently filed a raft of felony charges against five former Blackwater employees, including former president Gary Jackson, former executive vice president William Mathews, and former general counsel Andrew Howell. The federal indictment, filed in April 2010 in the Eastern District of North Carolina, charged that "defendants conspired to commit offenses against the United States, including making false statements in records of a federally licensed firearms dealer, possessing machine guns and unregistered firearms, and obstructing justice."

The charges stemmed from three separate incidents. First, the defendants were accused of using the Camden County Sheriff's Department to arrange "straw purchases" of automatic weapons (the M4s and AK-47s), which could be possessed lawfully only by law enforcement agencies. Second, the defendants were accused of giving King Abdullah II of Jordan a gift of several firearms (an M4, a Remington shotgun, and several Glock pistols, all engraved with the Blackwater logo) when the king visited the Blackwater facility on March 19, 2005, and subsequently falsifying paperwork to cover up the transfer. Third, the defendants were accused of overseeing the shortening by Blackwater's armorers of 227 long rifles into short-barrel rifles "without registering the weapons as such." The fact that some of the weapons in question were shipped to Iraq in sacks of dog food caught the attention of reporters; Blackwater explained that the subterfuge was necessary to prevent the weapons from being pilfered by corrupt foreign customs agents.

One Blackwater employee, Gary Flannelly, had previously pleaded guilty to making false statements on a federal firearms form, but the five defendants in this case denied they had done anything wrong and fought back in court with the company's support. The heart of their defense was that in all it did Blackwater was acting as a proxy for the CIA and the United States government. In support of this argument, Blackwater submitted depositions from former senior CIA officials, including Buzzy Krongard, as well as various emails, memos, photos, and other documents. It even came out that the CIA had its own secure telephone line and SCIF, or sensitive compartmented information facility, at Blackwater's headquarters for the handling of classified information.

One of Blackwater's defense documents said that "the CIA routinely used Blackwater in missions throughout the world. These efforts were made under written and unwritten contracts and through informal requests. On many occasions, the CIA paid Blackwater nothing for its assistance. Blackwater also employed CIA officers and agents, and provided cover to CIA agents and officers operating in covert and clandestine assignments. In many respects Blackwater, or at least portions of Blackwater, was an extension of the CIA."

Among the myriad duties that Blackwater performed for the CIA, Blackwater executives said, was providing guns to Jordan's King Abdullah II. The king had visited Blackwater headquarters along with CIA officials, but the CIA had forgotten to supply gifts for him and asked Blackwater to provide them instead.

The defense was convincing enough—and, from the government's standpoint, embarrassing enough—that Thomas G. Walker, the U.S. Attorney for the Eastern District of North Carolina, eventually agreed to drop all the felony charges. On February 21, 2013, the *New York Times* reported: "The federal government's three-year prosecution of five former officials of Blackwater Worldwide virtually collapsed on Thursday after charges against three of the officials were dismissed and the other two agreed to plead guilty to reduced misdemeanor charges with no jail time." The only guilty pleas the government secured came from former Blackwater president Gary Jackson and former executive vice president William Mathews. They pled guilty to a misdemeanor charge of faulty record keeping and agreed to three years of probation, four months of home confinement, and a fine of $5,000.

This was an ignominious end to such a high-profile case.

Blackwater's critics could take solace from the fact that in 2010 the firm, after admitting "numerous mistakes" in its adherence to export control laws, had reached an agreement with the State Department to pay a $42 million civil penalty. Subsequently, in August 2012, Blackwater reached a settlement with the Justice Department to pay $7.5 million more in civil fines to settle charges that the company, by then ACADEMI, had been guilty of "unauthorized sales of satellite phones in Sudan; unauthorized military training provided to foreign governments, including Canada's; illegal possession of automatic weapons; and other violations." But all attempts to bring serious criminal charges against the firm and its employees had collapsed, in no small part because Blackwater had become so inextricably intertwined with the war-fighting functions of the United States government—including the CIA.

ACKNOWLEDGMENTS

BLACKWATER, AND THIS BOOK ABOUT IT, WOULD NEVER HAVE BECOME WHAT they did without the assistance of dozens of people. First and foremost, I want to thank Ken Viera, Jim Dehart, and everyone else who helped launch a small business in the swamp back in 1997. And I want to thank Gary Jackson: I may have been the idea guy, but he translated concept into action and took the business from a few men in a swamp to an efficient global machine. He's one of the finest friends I've ever known.

I also want to thank Richard Pere and team who joined us and built out the finest aviation operation since Air America. His editing skills on this manuscript were as sharp as his piloting skills.

I'm grateful to all the former Blackwater employees and contractors who agreed to speak about their time with the company, and the terrific things we accomplished. I owe a debt of gratitude to the people and patriots of Moyock, North Carolina, who embraced the company, and my team's mission there. I still enjoy seeing people in our bear-paw-branded apparel wherever in the world I spot them.

Thanks to Adrian Zackheim, Bria Sandford, and the rest of the team at Portfolio/Penguin, who took on this project and worked tirelessly to convert a manuscript into a book on a highly accelerated schedule. And to David Kuhn and others at Kuhn Projects for making that connection in the first place. I want to truly thank and recognize Davin Coburn for giving coherent voice to my thoughts and recollections. Without your prose the book would not be what it is today. I also want to thank Dr. Mike Waller, who recorded and researched many of the events recounted in this book. Thanks also to Joe and Victoria for watching my back like guardian angels.

For her love, support, and guidance at every step of this project, I am forever indebted to Stacy DeLuke. I would like to thank all seven of my kids for their patience in putting up with their dad's stress, travel, and frequent absence. I love you all more than you can imagine.

Thanks to my parents, Ed and Elsa Prince, for giving me a great formation and foundation to build upon. I especially want to thank my dad because his risk and subsequent success allowed me to take my own risks and forge the man I am today.

NOTES

INTRODUCTION

1 *At eleven p.m., eighteen cars*: Frank Gallagher, "A First-Person Account of a Vehicle Ambush," *Security Driver Magazine*, April 2013.

1 *Especially not on the "Highway of Death"*: Oliver Poole, "Baghdad's Highway of Death 'Now Safe,'" *Telegraph*, December 10, 2005.

1 *insurgents had effectively owned*: Paul McGeough, "The World's Most Dangerous Road," *Sydney Morning Herald*, June 8, 2005.

1 *State Department would ultimately outlaw its personnel*: Julian E. Barnes, "Road with a Bad Rep," *U.S. News & World Report*, February 20, 2005.

1 *Shortly before eleven p.m.*: Frank Gallagher, "A First-Person Account of a Vehicle Ambush," *Security Driver Magazine*, April 2013.

2 *"Needless to say, some of the radio traffic"*: Ibid.

2 *the Coalition Provisional Authority leader and his right-hand man*: L. Paul Bremer III, *My Year in Iraq* (New York: Simon & Schuster, 2006), p. 245.

2 *"We promised to have a cup of mead"*: Frank Gallagher, "A First-Person Account of a Vehicle Ambush," *Security Driver Magazine*, April 2013.

2 *Gallagher . . . wrapped his fingers*: L. Paul Bremer III, *My Year in Iraq* (New York: Simon & Schuster, 2006), p. 246.

2 *a call from a Blackwater bird*: Frank Gallagher, "A First-Person Account of a Vehicle Ambush," *Security Driver Magazine*, April 2013.

3 *The lead and follow armored cars*: Ibid.

3 *he later learned had been an AK-47 round*: Ibid.

3   *an improvised explosive device (IED) rocked*: L. Paul Bremer III, *My Year in Iraq* (New York: Simon & Schuster, 2006), p. 246.

3   *"We'd been ambushed"*: Ibid.

3   *"Tuna! Tuna! Tuna!"*: Frank Gallagher, "A First-Person Account of a Vehicle Ambush," *Security Driver Magazine*, April 2013.

3   *One of the trailing Suburbans pulled*: Ibid.

3   *"I asked for a casualty report"*: Ibid.

3   *The stench of explosives lingered*: L. Paul Bremer III, *My Year in Iraq* (New York: Simon & Schuster, 2006), p. 246.

4   *We became the ultimate tool*: Bill Sizemore and Joanne Kimberlin, "Blackwater: On the Front Lines," *Virginian-Pilot*, July 25, 2006.

4   *Blackwater was slagged as the face of military evil*: John Fasano, "Blackwater Gets the Shaft," *Tactical Life*, May 12, 2010.

4   *Gun-toting bullies for hire*: Nina Burleigh, "Bullies Ascendant," *AlterNet*, October 31, 2004.

CHAPTER 1: MY FATHER'S SON

10   *he struck out to create Prince Manufacturing*: Unless otherwise noted, the history of Prince Manufacturing is drawn from personal time working at the company and extensive conversations with family members about its history.

11   *David Swietlik . . . once told*: "Hoover's Company Profiles: BuhlerPrince, Inc.," www.answers.com/topic/idraprince-inc, captured February 26, 2013.

11   *Seven years after its founding*: George Dila, "Downtown Needs Visionary, Gutsy Leader," *Ludington Daily News*, March 18, 2003.

12   *"It was then, while he lay"*: Letter from Gary L. Bauer and the Family Research Council, April 13, 1995, www.iclnet.org/pub/resources/text/frc/frc-msn.9504 .txt, captured February 26, 2013.

12   *a town named Holland*: "Holland, Michigan: Our History," www.holland.org /about-holland/our-history/, captured February 26, 2013.

14   *In the 1980s their aid helped revitalize*: Phil Tanis, "Ed Prince and Emilie (Prince) Wierda Interview," Hope College Oral History Project, August 1985.

14   *George H. W. Bush toured the center*: Myron Kukla, "Evergreen Commons Senior Center Turns 25," *Grand Rapids Press*, April 4, 2010.

14   *launch the Family Research Council*: Letter from Gary L. Bauer and the Family Research Council, April 13, 1995, www.iclnet.org/pub/resources/text/frc/frc -msn.9504.txt, captured February 26, 2013.

16   *President Reagan gave a speech*: Ronald Reagan, "What Ever Happened to Free Enterprise?," Hillsdale College, November 10, 1977.

19   *Today, Rohrabacher is serving his thirteenth term*: U.S. Congress biography of Dana Rohrabacher, rohrabacher.house.gov/biography, captured February 26, 2013.

19   *He also helped create the Reagan Doctrine*: Ibid.

19   *"Freedom is not the sole prerogative"*: Ronald Reagan, "Address Before a Joint Session of the Congress on the State of the Union," February 6, 1985, at American Presidency Project, www.presidency.ucsb.edu/ws/?pid=38069, captured February 26, 2013.

20 *Behrends, then a Marine reserve major*: Crowell & Moring biography of Paul Behrends, www.crowell.com/professionals/paul-behrends, captured February 26, 2013.

20 *Nicaraguan Association for Human Rights believed*: Ilan Berman and J. Michael Waller, *Dismantling Tyranny: Transitioning Beyond Totalitarian Regimes* (New York: Rowman & Littlefield, 2005), p. 107.

22 *"Because of its particularly challenging requirements"*: Navy SEAL BUD/S Training Stages Overview, www.sealswcc.com/navy-seals-buds-training -stages-overview.aspx#.UUnq4hmtIvc, captured February 27, 2013.

24 *"You felt in a way like you were part"*: Letter from Gary L. Bauer and the Family Research Council, April 13, 1995, www.iclnet.org/pub/resources/text/frc/frc -msn.9504.txt, captured February 26, 2013.

24 *"Ed Prince was not an empire builder"*: Ibid.

25 *sold the Prince Automotive unit*: U.S. Securities and Exchange Commission File No. 1-5097, July 19, 1996.

26 *Edgar D. Prince Technical Campus*: Johnson Controls, www.johnsoncontrols .com/content/us/en/products/automotive_experience/our-approach/global -leadership/Holland.html, captured February 27, 2013.

CHAPTER 2: THE GREAT DISMAL SWAMP

27 *SEAL Team 8 had just wrapped*: Ryan C. Henderson, "Crossing the Rubicon," *NATO Review*, Autumn 2005.

28 *Our military complex ramps up*: Max Boot, "Overspending the Peace Dividend," *Los Angeles Times*, January 8, 2012; John J. Gargan, "To Defend a Nation: An Overview of Downsizing and the U.S. Military," *M@n@gement* 2, no. 3, 1999.

28 *"Soviet Union is no longer the threat"*: "Report on the Bottom-Up Review," U.S. Defense Department, October 1993.

28 *the peacekeeping failure in Bosnia*: Ryan C. Henderson, "Crossing the Rubicon," *NATO Review*, Autumn 2005.

28 *Both men were accused*: The Prosecutor of the Tribunal against Radovan Karadzic and Ratko Mladic, filed November 16, 1995.

29 *Dutch UN Protection Force did little*: UN General Assembly, *Report of the Secretary-General Pursuant to General Assembly Resolution 53/35: The Fall of Srebrenica*, November 15, 1999.

29 *Kofi Annan admitted*: "U.N. Blames Serbs, Itself for Massacre in Bosnian Enclave," Associated Press, November 16, 1999.

29 *Defense Department's spending cuts had reduced*: "The Report of the Quadrennial Defense Review," U.S. Defense Department, May 1997.

29 *More than a hundred military bases*: Josh Kirschenbaum and Lorraine Giordano, "Employment Analysis of East Bay Military Base Civilian Employees," University of California, Institute of Urban and Regional Development, 1998.

33 *the midst of the largest military-industrial complex*: "Military Families and Personnel," Ready Hampton Roads, readyhamptonroads.org/Citizens/Military -FamiliesandPersonnel.aspx, captured February 27, 2013.

CHAPTER 3: COLUMBINE, THE *COLE*, AND CANCER

40 *the country's first law enforcement*: "U.S. Coast Guard Aviation History: Coast Guard Helicopter Interdiction Tactical Squadron," U.S. Coast Guard, 2004.

40 *Coast Guard estimated it was stopping less*: Ibid.

40 *Just after eleven a.m. on Tuesday, April 20*: "Columbine High School shootings," *Encyclopaedia Britannica*, www.britannica.com/EBchecked/topic/1528263/Columbine-High-School-shootings, captured August 2, 2013.

41 *In one of the worst school shootings*: Columbine Memorial, www.columbinememorial.org/, captured August 2, 2013.

41 *the public fixated on potential causes*: Susan Greene, "Backward, Forward on Columbine," *Denver Post*, March 22, 2009.

41 *We noticed that more than seventy-five police*: David Kohn, "What Really Happened at Columbine?," CBS News, April 29, 2009.

41 *a reported one thousand personnel*: "Managing the Incident," Jefferson County, Colorado, Sheriff, http://www.operationaltachics.org media Columbine%20Article.pdf.

41 *the passing of teacher Dave Sanders*: Dave Olinger, "911 Tapes Tell Tale of Chaos," *Denver Post*, May 21, 2000.

41 *the National Tactical Officers Association*: "NTOA History," National Tactical Officers Association, www.ntoa.org/about.html, captured August 2, 2013.

41 *We called the massive structure*: "Mock NC School Helps Train Lawmen Across Nation," Associated Press, March 31, 2000.

42 *In September 1999, the NTOA sent*: Jon Frank, "Firearms Training Centers on Schools Under Assault," *Virginian-Pilot*, October 4, 1999.

42 *As a reporter once described our work*: Mark Hemingway, "Warriors for Hire: Blackwater USA and the Rise of the Private Military Contractors," *Weekly Standard*, December 18, 2006.

42 *"There was no back-slapping"*: Michelle Gotthelf, "Police Response a Matter of Debate," APB News, April 17, 2000.

43 *The USS Cole is a billion-dollar warship*: David Briscoe, "Profile of the USS *Cole*," ABC News, October 13, 2000.

43 *In August 2000, the destroyer sailed*: R. W. Rogers, "Danger in Even 'Routine' Missions," *Daily Press*, October 13, 2000.

43 *a deployment with the U.S. 5th Fleet*: "USS *Cole* Makes First 5th Fleet Port Call Since Terrorist Attack," Navy NewsStand, October 3, 2006.

43 *Two months later, as the ship refueled*: "Command Investigation into the Actions of USS *Cole* (IDDG 67) in Preparing for and Undertaking a Brief Stop for Fuel at Bandar at Tawahi (Aden Harbor), Aden, Yemen, on or about 12 October 2000," U.S. Navy, www.history.navy.mil/Special%20Highlights/USSCole/REPORT/INVESTRPT.pdf, captured August 2, 2013.

43 *Then the duo set off a blast equivalent*: Richard Miniter, *Losing Bin Laden* (New York: Regnery, 2004), p. 216.

43 *Seventeen sailors were killed*: Ibid., p. 218.

43 *Petty Officer John Washak*: Thomas E. Ricks and Steve Vogel, "*Cole* Sailors on Sentry Duty Did Not Have Ammunition in Their Guns," *Washington Post*, November 14, 2000.

44 *The report concluded that the* Cole's: Yonah Alexander and Tyler B. Richardson, *Terror on the High Seas* (Santa Barbara, CA: Praeger, 2009), p. 116.

44 *In his statement to the JAG report*: "USS *Cole* Briefing—Secretary of Defense William S. Cohen," U.S. Department of Defense, January 19, 2001.

44 *"With those surveys . . . the Navy is basically saying"*: Author interview with Fred Roitz, July 2013.

46 *In May 2001, Admiral Vern Clark*: "Lessons Learned from the Attack on the U.S.S. *Cole*," Hearing Before the Committee on Armed Services, U.S. Senate, May 3, 2001.

47 *Earnings at Prince Machine had quadrupled*: "Hoover's Company Profiles: BuhlerPrince, Inc.," www.answers.com/topic/idraprince-inc, captured February 26, 2013.

CHAPTER 4: THE RISE OF BLACKWATER

50 *two senior colonels in China's People's Liberation Army*: Qiao Liang and Wang Xiangsui, *Unrestricted Warfare* (Beijing: PLA Literature and Arts Publishing, February 1999).

50 *The book advocated*: "Unrestricted Warfare," www.cryptome.org/cuw.htm #Preface, captured August 2, 2013.

50 *President George W. Bush's national security team*: "Bush Adds Clinton Holdover to Security Team," Associated Press, October 1, 2001.

51 *the ethnic Uzbek worked for a time*: John F. Burns, "Afghan Fights Islamic Tide," *New York Times*, October 14, 1996.

51 *Dostum rose to the rank of army general*: Tim Weiner, "The Commander: Rebel with Long Career of Picking Fights (and Sides)," *New York Times*, November 10, 2001.

51 *By 1997, thanks in large part to his willingness*: Ibid.

51 *Its main city was Mazar-i-Sharif*: Tim McGirk, "Inside Karzai's Campaign," *Time*, October 4, 2004.

51 *Dostum was ousted*: Roy Allison and Lena Jonson, *Central Asian Security* (Washington D.C.: Brookings Institution Press, 2001), p. 113.

51 *Dostum was forced into exile*: Brian Glyn Williams, "Dostum: Afghanistan's Exiled Warlord," *Foreign Policy*, August 10, 2009.

52 *The return was possible thanks*: Brian Glyn Williams, "General Dostum and the Mazar i Sharif Campaign: New Light on the Role of Northern Alliance Warlords in Operation Enduring Freedom," *Small Wars & Insurgencies* 21, December 8, 2010.

52 *Massoud, known as the "Lion of Panjshir"*: Steve Coll, "Flawed Ally Was Hunt's Best Hope," *Washington Post*, February 23, 2004.

52 *Massoud was killed by a pair of Arab suicide bombers*: Ibid.

52 *There was only one U.S. contact*: Ahmed Rashid, *Taliban: Islam, Oil and the New Great Game in Central Asia* (London: I. B. Tauris, 2008), p. 171.

52 *Delta had sent Santos to negotiate the building*: Ibid.

53 *the agency cast aside roughly a thousand paid informants*: Mark Matthews, "CIA Debates Merits of Bad Spies," *Baltimore Sun*, March 4, 1997.

53 *higher-ups at the CIA had been urging*: Gary C. Schroen, *First In* (New York: Ballantine, 2005), p. 15.

53 *Bush had publicly insisted the military campaign*: Susan Baer and David L. Greene, "'Face of Terror Not True Faith of Islam,' Bush Declares," *Baltimore Sun*, September 18, 2001.

53 *These factors swayed CIA planners*: Gary C. Schroen, *First In* (New York: Ballantine, 2005), p. 16.

54 *small teams of CIA operatives and Army Special Forces*: Ibid.

54 *Even Massoud had financed his rebel alliance*: Steve Coll, "Flawed Ally Was Hunt's Best Hope," *Washington Post*, February 23, 2004.

54 *CIA's seven-man Northern Afghanistan Liaison Team*: Leigh Neville, *Special Operations Forces in Afghanistan* (Oxford: Osprey, 2008), p. 6.

54 *"I don't want bin Laden and his thugs"*: Gary C. Schroen, *First In* (New York: Ballantine, 2005), p. 32.

55 *Operation Enduring Freedom began*: Donna Miles, "Obama Marks 10 Years of U.S. Service in Afghanistan," American Forces Press Service, October 7, 2011.

55 *The Army's first twelve-man Special Forces*: "Joint Special Operations Task Force—North (JSOTF-N): 'Task Force Dagger,'" www.globalsecurity.org/military/agency/dod/jsotf-n-af.htm, captured August 2, 2013.

55 *Two days later, a second A-team*: Dwight Jon Zimmerman, "21st Century Horse Soldiers—Special Operations Forces and Operation Enduring Freedom," *The Year in Special Operations, 2011–2012*.

55 *"the Flintstones meets the Jetsons"*: "War Stories," PBS *Frontline*, www.pbs.org/wgbh/pages/frontline/shows/campaign/ground/warstories.html, captured August 2, 2013.

55 *They called in such ferocious air strikes*: Ibid.

55 *In the early morning darkness*: Romesh Ratnesar, "The Afghan Way of War," *Time*, November 11, 2001.

55 *Task Force Dagger retook control*: "Operation Enduring Freedom: October 2001–March 2002," www.history.army.mil/brochures/Afghanistan/Operation%20Enduring%20Freedom.htm#intro, captured August 2, 2013.

56 *Nearly two-thirds of the country changed hands*: Bob Woodward, *State of Denial: Bush at War, Part III* (New York: Simon & Schuster, 2006), p. 130.

56 *"I asked for a few Americans"*: "Heroes on Horseback," *Iowa Alumni Magazine*, October 2009.

57 *"The only concern we had"*: Jeremy Scahill, "Blackwater's Brothers," *Nation*, December 3, 2007.

CHAPTER 5: INHERENTLY TRADITIONAL

59 *his speculation on the distance to reach*: "All About Christopher Columbus," www.scholastic.com/teachers/article/all-about-christopher-columbus-1451-1506, captured August 2, 2013.

59 *Finally, at the start of 1492*: Washington Irving, *The Life and Voyages of Christopher Columbus*.

59 *With the Capitulations of Santa Fe*: "Santa Fe Capitulations," UNESCO, www.unesco.org/new/en/communication-and-information/flagship-project-activities/memory-of-the-world/register/full-list-of-registered-heritage/registered-heritage-page-8/santa-fe-capitulations/, captured August 2, 2013.

60 *He also wanted options on future business ventures*: "1492: An Ongoing Voyage," U.S. Library of Congress, www.loc.gov/exhibits/1492/columbus.html, captured August 2, 2013.

60 *The* Niña, Pinta, *and* Santa María *arrived*: "Today in History: October 12," U.S. Library of Congress, http://memory.loc.gov/ammem/today/oct12.html, captured August 2, 2013.

60 *at its four corners are additional statues*: "Lafayette Square Historic District," U.S. National Park Service, www.nps.gov/nr/travel/wash/dc30.htm, captured August 2, 2013.

60 *In 1607, for instance, Captain John Smith*: "A True Relation by Captain John Smith, 1608," American Journeys, www.americanjourneys.org/aj-074/sum mary/, captured August 2, 2013.

61 *The company intended to mine for gold*: Wesley Frank Craven, *The Virginia Company of London, 1606–1624*, http://www.gutenberg.org/files/28555 /28555-h/28555-h.htm.

61 *as aggressive as a wolverine*: "A True Relation by Captain John Smith, 1608," American Journeys, www.americanjourneys.org/aj-074/summary/, captured August 2, 2013.

61 *He explored the bay area*: "Virginia Discovered and Described: John Smith's Map of Virginia and Its Derivatives," Library of Virginia, March 2007.

61 *The pale-faced PMC with the fiery red beard*: "History of Jamestown: Pocahontas," http://apva.org/rediscovery/page.php?page_id=26, captured August 2, 2013.

61 *In 1614, Smith mapped the northern*: "Captain John Smith," U.S. National Park Service, www.nps.gov/jame/historyculture/life-of-john-smith.htm, captured August 2, 2013.

61 *Council for New England, previously known*: "Exploring the New World, Part 2," www2.lib.virginia.edu/exhibits/mellon/expNWp2.html, captured August 2, 2013.

62 *a military contractor hired by the pilgrims*: "Myles Standish," *Encyclopaedia Britannica*, www.britannica.com/EBchecked/topic/563091/Myles-Standish, captured August 2, 2013.

62 *one of the forty-one signers*: "Mayflower and the Mayflower Compact," Plimoth Plantation, www.plimoth.org/learn/just-kids/homework-help/mayflower-and -mayflower-compact, captured August 2, 2013.

62 *Approved by Governor John Hancock in 1780*: "The History of the Arms and Great Seal of the Commonwealth of Massachusetts," www.sec.state.ma.us/pre /presea/sealhis.htm, captured August 2, 2013.

62 *That coat of arms shows an Algonquian*: Ibid.

62 *"a professional soldier hired to train"*: "Today in Guard History: December 21, 1620," National Guard, www.nationalguard.mil/news/todayinhistory/decem ber.aspx, captured August 2, 2013.

62 *trusted the private sector's ability to provide solutions*: Marc Lindemann, "Civilian Contractors Under Military Law," *Parameters*, Autumn 2007.

63 *a skilled Polish freedom fighter with an expertise in artillery*: "Tadeusz Kosciuszko: A Man of Unwavering Principle," Institute of World Politics, www.iwp .edu/programs/page/tadeusz-kosciuszko-a-man-of-unwavering-principle, captured August 2, 2013.

63 *The fortifications he built*: Ibid.

63 *Prussian officer Baron Friedrich Wilhelm von Steuben*: "Friedrich Wilhelm von Steuben," Bergen County Historical Society, www.bergencountyhistory.org /Pages/gnsteuben.html, captured August 2, 2013.

63 *the French aristocrat the Marquis de Lafayette*: James R. Gaines, "Washington and Lafayette," *Smithsonian*, September 2007.

63 *"pushy French teenager"*: Ibid.

63 *and today there are some two dozen towns or cities*: "America Celebrates 250th Birthday of the Marquis de Lafayette," Academy Communications, August 15, 2007.

63 *Comte Jean de Rochambeau was sent*: "Yorktown Battlefield: Comte de Rocham-
    beau," U.S. National Park Service, www.nps.gov/york/historyculture/rocham
    beaubio.htm, captured August 2, 2013.

63 *"I cannot but acknowledge the infinite obligations"*: "From George Washington to
    Thomas McKean, 12 October 1781," U.S. National Archives, http://founders
    .archives.gov/documents/Washington/99-01-02-07143, captured August 2, 2013.

64 *So powerful was the Royal Navy*: Henry Lawrence Swinburne, *The Royal Navy*.

64 *The Continental Navy, such as there was one*: D. H. T. Shippey, "Patriots in Hell,"
    Breed's Hill Institute, 2008.

64 *proposed a turnkey solution*: Michael A. Palmer, "The Navy: The Continental Pe-
    riod, 1775–1780," Naval History and Heritage Command, www.history.navy
    .mil/history/history2.htm, captured August 2, 2013.

64 *Suddenly the twelve hundred guns*: D. H. T. Shippey, "Patriots in Hell," Breed's
    Hill Institute, 2008.

64 *Congress printed blank commissions*: "To Form a More Perfect Union," U.S. Library
    of Congress, http://memory.loc.gov/ammem/collections/continental/orgwar
    .html, captured August 2, 2013.

64 *By the end of the war, privateers*: D. H. T. Shippey, "Patriots in Hell," Breed's Hill
    Institute, 2008.

65 *Privateers again took to the high seas*: "Privateering in the War of 1812," www
    .eighteentwelve.ca/?q=eng/Topic/66, captured August 2, 2013.

65 *Lincoln relied upon the Pinkerton National Detective Agency*: "History," Pinker-
    ton, www.pinkerton.com/history, captured August 2, 2013.

65 *George McClellan soon hired the Scottish immigrant*: Ibid.

65 *"developing a different view of espionage"*: "Intelligence in the Civil War," Cen-
    tral Intelligence Agency, https://www.cia.gov/library/publications/additional
    -publications/civil-war/p11.htm, captured August 2, 2013.

65 *colloquially known Escadrille Américaine*: "Escadrille Américaine," National
    Museum of the U.S. Air Force, www.nationalmuseum.af.mil/factsheets/fact
    sheet.asp?id=687, captured August 2, 2013.

65 *Roosevelt sent retired U.S. Army Air Corps captain*: "Maj. Gen. Claire Lee
    Chennault," National Museum of the U.S. Air Force, www.nationalmuseum.af
    .mil/factsheets/factsheet.asp?id=1338, captured August 2, 2013.

66 *three squadrons commanded by Chennault*: Bob Bergin, "Claire Lee Chennault
    and the Problem of Intelligence in China," *Studies in Intelligence* 54, no. 2, June
    2010.

66 *"In the councils of government, we must guard"*: "Eisenhower: Farewell Address,
    1961," PBS American Experience, www.pbs.org/wgbh/americanexperience
    /features/primary-resources/eisenhower-farewell/, captured August 2, 2013.

66 *"At a time when all too many forces"*: Deborah C. Kidwell, "Public War, Private
    Fight? The United States and Private Military Companies," Combat Studies In-
    stitute, 2005.

67 *PMCs operate in more than fifty*: David Isenberg, "Security for Sale," *Asia Times*,
    August 14, 2003.

67 *"LOGCAP provides contingency support"*: Colonel Scott S. Haraburda, Lieuten-
    ant Colonel Frances A. Bloom, and Major Robert T. Keck, "Contracting Agility
    in LOGCAP—Kuwait," *Army Logistician*, July–August 2009.

67 *During the first Gulf War, PMCs made up*: Stephen Lendman, "Outsourcing War:
    The Rise of Private Military Contractors," *SteveLendmanBlog*, January 19,

2010, http://sjlendman.blogspot.com/2010/01/outsourcing-war-rise-of-private.html, captured August 19, 2013.

67 *But the DoD wanted a larger presence*: Leslie Wayne, "America's For-Profit Secret Army," *New York Times*, October 13, 2002.

67 *DoD contracts with PMCs grew*: "Statement of David M. Walker, Comptroller General of the United States, Before the Subcommittee on Readiness, Committee on Armed Services," U.S. House of Representatives, March 11, 2008.

68 *described as the first contractor wars*: Moshe Schwartz, "Department of Defense Contractors in Iraq and Afghanistan: Background and Analysis," Congressional Research Service, July 2, 2010.

68 *The vast majority of the DoD's PMCs*: Ibid.

68 *four key components of the DoD's "Total Force"*: "Quadrennial Defense Review Report," U.S. Defense Department, February 6, 2006.

68 *During the first Gulf War, the Army*: Leslie Wayne, "America's For-Profit Secret Army," *New York Times*, October 13, 2002.

68 *the Army could still only meet recruiting benchmarks*: "Military Accepting More Ex-Cons," Associated Press, February 14, 2007.

68 *offering $20,000 bonuses for recruits*: Karoun Demirjian, "Army Is Offering a Quick $20,000," *Chicago Tribune*, August 4, 2007.

68 *Only 71 percent of Army recruits that year*: Susanne M. Schafer, "Army Opens Prep School for Dropouts to Fill Ranks," *USA Today*, August 27, 2008.

68 *"We cannot operate without private security"*: James Risen, "Iraq Contractor in Shooting Case Makes Comeback," *New York Times*, May 10, 2008.

69 *"We're never going to war"*: Nir Rosen, "Security Contractors: Riding Shotgun with Our Shadow Army in Iraq," *Mother Jones*, April 24, 2007.

69 *in Obama's first year in office*: Bill Moyers Journal, June 5, 2009.

69 *efforts by the DoD to "reduce the number"*: "Quadrennial Defense Review Report," U.S. Defense Department, February 2010.

69 *Yet it also clearly states*: Ibid.

69 *But of the thousands of contractors*: "Shadow Force: Private Security Contractors in Iraq," David Isenberg speech, February 16, 2009.

70 *"contractors are required to be armed"*: Moshe Schwartz, "Department of Defense Contractors in Iraq and Afghanistan: Background and Analysis," Congressional Research Service, July 2, 2010.

70 *"Privatizing the ultimate sacrifice"*: Rob Nordland, "Risks of Afghan War Shift from Soldiers to Contractors," *New York Times*, February 11, 2012.

70 *"inherently governmental functions"*: Yana Kunichoff, "Extent of Blackwater and CIA Collaboration Uncovered," *Truthout*, December 11, 2009.

71 *"now the equivalent of a new service"*: Daniel Goure, "2010 QDR Means More Work for Support Contractors," *Early Warning* blog, January 29, 2010.

CHAPTER 6: BREMER AND THE BUSINESS MODEL

72 *He issued this ultimatum*: "Bush: 'Leave Iraq Within 48 hours,'" CNN, www.cnn.com/2003/WORLD/meast/03/17/sprj.irq.bush.transcript/, captured August 3, 2013.

72 *March 20 dawned in Baghdad*: Catherine Marie Dale, "Operation Iraqi Freedom: Strategies, Approaches, Results, and Issues for Congress," Congressional Research Service, February 22, 2008.

72 *by April 9, U.S. troops would secure*: Ibid.

73 *the United States captured Tikrit*: Alex Spillius, "Fall of Tikrit Ends the War," *Telegraph*, April 15, 2003.

73 *his infamous "Mission Accomplished" speech*: "Bush Makes Historic Speech Aboard Warship," CNN, www.cnn.com/2003/US/05/01/bush.transcript/, captured August 3, 2013.

73 *"Major combat operations in Iraq have ended"*: Ibid.

73 *Iraq War plan delivered to President Bush*: "Top Secret Polo Step," National Security Archive, www.gwu.edu/~nsarchiv/NSAEBB/NSAEBB214/, captured August 3, 2013.

73 *Afghan Interim Authority had appointed*: "President Hamid Karzai," Embassy of the Islamic Republic of Afghanistan, www.afghanembassy.com.pl/cms/en /goverment/hamid-karzai, captured August 3, 2013.

73 *"While we at CENTCOM were executing the war plan"*: Tommy Franks, *American Soldier* (New York: Regan, 2004), p. 441.

74 *"There was a commonly held belief"*: Ibid., p. 526.

74 *State Department officials believed*: Thomas E. Ricks and Karen DeYoung, "For U.S., the Goal Is Now 'Iraqi Solutions,'" *Washington Post*, January 19, 2008.

74 *a December 2002 memo titled "A Perfect Storm"*: Ibid.

74 *"When you hit this thing, it's like a crystal glass"*: "Hard Lessons: The Iraq Reconstruction Experience," Office of the Special Inspector General for Iraq Reconstruction, February 2, 2009.

74 *a 2009 report by the Special Inspector General*: Ibid.

75 *"In a military compound under nominal guard by U.S. soldiers"*: Ibid.

75 *Iraqis were not, in fact, greeting U.S. forces as liberators*: Susan Page, "Confronting Iraq," *USA Today*, April 1, 2003.

75 *Into that chaos stepped Bremer*: "Ambassador Paul Bremer Named as Presidential Envoy to Iraq," U.S. Department of State, http://iipdigital.usembassy.gov /st/english/texttrans/2003/05/20030506161121ynnedd0.7209436.html #axzz2b0n70Zq8, captured May 6, 2013.

75 *sweeping directive by Secretary of Defense Donald Rumsfeld*: "Hard Lessons: The Iraq Reconstruction Experience," Office of the Special Inspector General for Iraq Reconstruction, February 2, 2009.

75 *The safety of the ambassador in Baghdad*: "Frank Gallagher," *Security Driver Magazine*, http://securitydriver.com/04/frank-gallagher/, captured August 3, 2013.

76 *"with no government, no electricity, and no functioning security"*: "Hard Lessons: The Iraq Reconstruction Experience," Office of the Special Inspector General for Iraq Reconstruction, February 2, 2009.

76 *one of Hussein's final acts of power*: David Blair, "Saddam Empties Iraq's Jails," *Telegraph*, October 21, 2002.

76 *disbanded Iraq's entire military*: James P. Pfiffner, "US Blunders in Iraq: De-Baathification and Disbanding the Army," *Intelligence and National Security* 25, no. 1, February 2010.

76 *CPA wasn't big on severance packages*: Ibid.

76 *"additional enemies of the Coalition"*: "Hard Lessons: The Iraq Reconstruction Experience," Office of the Special Inspector General for Iraq Reconstruction, February 2, 2009.

77 *"I slept with earplugs"*: Bill Powell, "The CEO of Iraq, Paul Bremer, Has Landed the World's Toughest Job. Can He Pull It Off?," *Fortune*, August 11, 2003.

77 *Early that month, a car bomb had destroyed*: "Significant Terrorist Incidents 1961–2003," U.S. Department of State, http://2001-2009.state.gov/r/pa/ho /pubs/fs/5902.htm, captured August 3, 2013.

77 *Less than two weeks later*: "Final Report of the Independent Panel to Review Detention Operations," U.S. Defense Department, August 2004.

77 *set fire to a major pipeline*: Jamie Wilson, "Iraq Hit by Fresh Attack on Oil Pipeline," *Guardian*, August 17, 2003.

77 *Sergio Vieira de Mello, the UN's top envoy in Iraq*: Jesse Singal, Christine Lim, and M. J. Stephey, "August 2003: United in Grief," *Time*, March 19, 2010.

77 *at the end of August, a car bomb exploded*: "Mosque Bombing," CBS News, www .cbsnews.com/2300-500145_162-570797.html, captured August 3, 2013.

77 *"we had certainly been losing soldiers"*: "Interview: L. Paul Bremer III," PBS *Frontline*, www.pbs.org/wgbh/pages/frontline/yeariniraq/interviews/bremer .html, captured February 26, 2013.

77 *in the three months since major combat operations ended*: "Iraq Coalition Casualties: Fatalities by Year and Month," iCasualties, www.icasualties.org/Iraq /ByMonth.aspx, captured August 3, 2013.

78 *"most threatened American official anywhere in the world"*: L. Paul Bremer III, *My Year in Iraq* (New York: Simon & Schuster, 2006), p. 151.

78 *Pentagon awarded my company*: Kelley Beaucar Vlahos, "Hired Guns," *American Conservative*, November 19, 2007.

78 *"They needed men around him really fast"*: Author interview with Fred Roitz, July 2013.

78 *Blackwater initially provided a thirty-six-man team*: Frank Gallagher, "A First-Person Account of a Vehicle Ambush," *Security Driver Magazine*, April 2013.

78 *Bremer had first met Gallagher*: L. Paul Bremer III, *My Year in Iraq* (New York: Simon & Schuster, 2006), p. 152.

79 *Pentagon contract gave us a scant*: Author interview with Richard Pere, December 2012.

79 *packed the Little Birds into the cargo hold*: Ibid.

80 *"lots of room for an assassin"*: L. Paul Bremer III, *My Year in Iraq* (New York: Simon & Schuster, 2006), p. 151.

81 *"We in the al-Qaeda organization will guarantee"*: "CIA Says Bin Laden Likely Behind Bounty Offer," NBC News, www.nbcnews.com/id/4917940/ns/world _news-mideast_n_africa/t/cia-says-bin-laden-likely-behind-bounty-offer /#.Uf53CFO9zUY, captured August 3, 2013.

81 *those close to Bremer found bounties on their heads*: Robert Young Pelton, *Licensed to Kill* (New York: Random House, 2006), p. 110.

81 *On the morning of June 28, 2004, after a brief ceremony*: L. Paul Bremer III, *My Year in Iraq* (New York: Simon & Schuster, 2006), p. 395.

81 *Blackwater's team waited until the crowds cleared*: Ibid.

82 *UN had largely pulled out*: "UN Role in Iraq," Global Policy Forum, www .globalpolicy.org/political-issues-in-iraq/un-role-in-iraq.html, captured August 3, 2013.

82 *this great description in a piece*: Roy Batty, "Rock Stars of Baghdad," Military .com, February 8, 2007.

CHAPTER 7: THE EXPANSION PLAN

88 *The 82nd Airborne had been on long patrol*: Author interview with Richard Pere, December 2012.

88 *littered with the roadside remnants*: Bill Roggio, "Pakistan Shuts Down NATO Supply Line Through the Khyber Pass," *Long War Journal*, December 30, 2008.

88 *thirty miles west of the pass was Tora Bora*: "Tora Bora Revisited: How We Failed to Get Bid Laden and Why It Matters Today," Senate Committee on Foreign Relations, November 30, 2009.

88 *"The tyranny of distance and terrain"*: N. D. Hooker Jr., "Operation Enduring Freedom X: CJTF-82 and the Future of COIN," *Joint Force Quarterly*, Fourth Quarter 2011.

89 *miles of paved road in the entire country*: "USAID Spends $3.4 Billion on Assistance Programs in Afghanistan," U.S. Agency for International Development, http://iipdigital.usembassy.gov/st/english/article/2008/04/20080401144535 xjsnommis0.9323084.html#axzz2b0n70Zq8, captured August 3, 2013.

90 *Air Force solicitation of competitively bid contract*: "Contracts for Monday, September 20, 2004," U.S. Defense Department, www.defense.gov/contracts /contract.aspx?contractid=2850, captured August 3, 2013.

90 *more than the combined total*: "Blackwater Timeline," *Virginian-Pilot*, http:// hamptonroads.com/2006/07/blackwater-timeline, captured August 3, 2013.

91 *In 2001, Blackwater earned some $735,000*: "Blackwater USA," Hearing Before the Committee on Oversight and Government Reform, U.S. House of Representatives, October 2, 2007.

91 *In 2002, that increased to $3.4 million*: Ibid.

92 *trained Afghan border agents and narcotics officers*: Mark Sedra and Cyrus Hodes, "The Search for Security in Post-Taliban Afghanistan," International Institute for Strategic Studies, October 30, 2007.

92 *State even asked us to train security personnel*: Rick Skwiot, "On the Firing Line: The Blackwater Training Center," *Port Folio Weekly*, 2010.

93 *The airships have been used for defense*: "Airship Types in the Postwar Period," Naval History and Heritage Command, www.history.navy.mil/download /lta-10.pdf, captured August 3, 2013.

94 *defense spending on unmanned aerial vehicles*: Harlan Geer and Christopher Bolkcom, "Unmanned Aerial Vehicles: Background and Issues for Congress," Congressional Research Service, November 21, 2005.

94 *"The problem is if it really does work"*: David Macaulay, "Blackwater USA Hires Ford Workers to Build New APC," *Daily Advance*, February 20, 2007.

95 *government procurement spending rose by 86 percent*: "Dollars, Not Sense: Government Contracting Under the Bush Administration," Committee on Oversight and Government Reform, U.S. House of Representatives, June 2006.

95 *By 2005, the federal government spent a record*: Ibid.

95 *"In 2000, the Defense Department spent $133.5 billion"*: Ibid.

95 *Five years later, the department's contract spending*: Ibid.

96 *"The incentive for businesses in a regular free market"*: Ibid.

96 *according to the report, "nearly half was spent"*: Ibid.

97 *"the largest part of our appropriations"*: Phillip Ewing, "McCain: LCS Shows Spending Out of Control," *Navy Times*, September 29, 2008.

97 *roughly 70 percent of the federal government's expenditures*: "Dollars, Not Sense: Government Contracting Under the Bush Administration," Committee on Oversight and Government Reform, U.S. House of Representatives, June 2006.

97 *At the top of the cost-plus list*: Ibid.

97 *The heroic landing by the three members*: Glenn Pew, "DHL Airbus A300 Struck by Missile, Baghdad," AVweb.com, February 10, 2008.

98 *The man who would one day become vice chairman*: Kevin McMurray, "Cofer Black, Out of the Shadows," *Men's Journal*, October 17, 2008.

98 *labeling the country a "state sponsor of terrorism"*: "State Sponsors of Terrorism," U.S. Department of State, www.state.gov/j/ct/rls/crt/2011/195547.htm, captured August 3, 2012.

98 *perhaps the most famous terrorist of his time*: Kevin McMurray, "Cofer Black, Out of the Shadows," *Men's Journal*, October 17, 2008.

99 *moved from Ibn Khaldoun hospital*: John Follain, *Jackal* (New York: Arcade, 1998), p. 217.

99 *In reality, the police were cooperating with Black's team*: Ibid., p. 218.

99 *Black's appointment as CIA task force chief*: "Biography: Cofer J. Black," U.S. Department of State, http://2001-2009.state.gov/outofdate/bios/b/15367.htm, captured August 3, 2013.

99 *George Tenet circulated a memo*: Jeffrey Smith and Walter Pincus, "Tenet Leaves Legacy of Big Successes, but Also Big Failures," *Washington Post*, June 4, 2004.

99 *bin Laden had discovered Black*: Mark Bowden, "The Dark Art of Interrogation," *Atlantic*, October 1, 2003.

99 *intelligence personnel countersurveilling*: Steve Coll, *Ghost Wars* (New York: Penguin, 2004), p. 271.

100 *U.S. ambassador to Sudan complained*: Ibid.

100 *"He had a reputation as a bit of a cowboy"*: Ned Zeman, David Wise, David Rose, and Bryan Burrough, "The Path to 9/11," *Vanity Fair*, November 2004.

100 *At the start of the decade, government agencies*: Tim Shorrock, *Spies for Hire* (New York: Simon & Schuster, 2008), p. 19.

101 *By 2003, a snowballing dependence on contractors*: Ibid.

101 *Even the VIP lot was full*: Suzanne Simons, *Master of War* (New York: HarperCollins, 2009), p. 150.

102 *"Cofer can open doors"*: Dana Hedgpeth, "Blackwater's Owner Has Spies for Hire," *Washington Post*, November 3, 2007.

102 *"We've got more generals per square foot"*: Esther Schrader, "U.S. Companies Hired to Train Foreign Armies," *Los Angeles Times*, "April 14, 2002.

103 *Black's son was a lieutenant in the Army*: Kevin McMurray, "Cofer Black, Out of the Shadows," *Men's Journal*, October 17, 2008.

103 *FOB Tillman sat along Afghanistan's rugged*: Quil Lawrence, "For U.S. Troops, Fighting Starts at Afghan Border," NPR, December 13, 2011.

103 *"The reason I came to Blackwater was its mission"*: Kevin McMurray, "Cofer Black, Out of the Shadows," *Men's Journal*, October 17, 2008.

CHAPTER 8: FALLUJAH

104 *Pentagon rotated in and out*: Lawrence J. Korb, Sean E. Duggan, and Peter M. Juul, "How to Redeploy," Center for American Progress, August 2008.

104 *"a logistics feat that will rival any in history"*: "Defense Department Operational Update Briefing," U.S. Defense Department, www.defense.gov/transcripts /transcript.aspx?transcriptid=2788, captured August 2, 2013.

104 *That turbulence, Defense Secretary Donald Rumsfeld added*: Ibid.

104 *attacks across Iraq numbered in the dozens per day*: Michael E. O'Hanlon and Jason H. Campbell, "Iraq Index," Brookings Institution, October 1, 2007.

104 *More than two hundred American troops had been killed*: "Iraq Coalition Casualties: Fatalities by Year and Month," iCasualties, www.icasualties.org/Iraq /ByMonth.aspx, captured August 3, 2013.

105 *some 80 percent of all guerrilla attacks*: Frank Smyth, "Hasty Elections Could Divide Iraq," *Newsday*, October 7, 2004.

105 *2005 analysis by the Washington Institute for Near East Policy*: Michael Eisenstadt and Jeffrey White, "Assessing Iraq's Sunni Arab Insurgency," Washington Institute for Near East Policy, December 2005.

105 *largely left to police itself thanks to DoD planning*: Charles Swannack, "Lessons from the Sunni Triangle," Washington Institute for Near East Policy, July 20, 2004.

106 *The 82nd Airborne shot back*: "U.S. Troops Shoot Iraqi Protestors," PBS *NewsHour*, www.pbs.org/newshour/updates/shooting_04-29-03.html, captured August 3, 2013.

106 *Townspeople danced on the wreckage*: "Fifteen Killed as US Helicopter Shot Down," *Taipei Times*, November 3, 2003, http://taipeitimes.com/News/front /archives/2003/11/03/2003074408.

106 *lead contractor being paid through that massive Army LOGCAP*: Walter Pincus, "U.S. Pays Steep Price for Private Security in Iraq," *Washington Post*, October 1, 2007.

106 *the subcontracted security provider for ESS*: Ibid.

106 *a restructured deal with Regency*: Ibid.

106 *provide a squad of thirty-four men*: Ibid.

107 *"This was refused both times"*: "Private Military Contractors in Iraq: An Examination of Blackwater's Actions in Fallujah," Committee on Oversight and Government Reform, U.S. House of Representatives, September 2007.

107 *upon losing the contract, CRG promptly announced*: Blackwater Security Consulting, LLC et al. v. Nordan, Case Number 2:2006cv00049, December 20, 2006.

107 *On March 30, the four men of Blackwater Team November 1*: Blackwater's Response to "Private Military Contractors in Iraq: An Examination of Blackwater's Actions in Fallujah," Majority Staff report, October 2007.

108 *They delivered the principal without an issue*: Ibid.

108 *Could the four-man Blackwater team leave right away*: Ibid.

108 *The silver-haired forty-eight-year-old*: Kevin Dayton, "Ambush Victim from Big Island Was a Soldier's Soldier," *Honolulu Advertiser*, April 7, 2004.

108 *Batalona was part of the first invasion force*: Sean Flynn, "The Day the War Turned," *GQ*, October 2006.

108 *retired the year after, moved back to Hawaii*: Jaymes Song, "Tragedy in Iraq Shakes Community on Big Isle," *Honolulu Star-Bulletin*, April 4, 2004.

108 *took a job as a security guard*: Sean Flynn, "The Day the War Turned," *GQ*, October 2006.

108 *Zovko, a Cleveland native*: Thomas J. Sheeran, "2 Slain Civilians Memorialized," *Deseret News*, April 11, 2004.

108 *served six years, starting out as a military policeman*: "Fla. Native Among Dead Civilians," Associated Press, April 2, 2004.

108 *The Croatian-American saw action in Bosnia*: Joseph Neff and Jay Price, "Chapter 3: A Private, Driven Man," *Raleigh News & Observer*, July 28, 2004.

108 *six foot three and built . . . He spoke*: Sean Flynn, "The Day the War Turned," *GQ*, October 2006.

109 *reported to Iraq in the summer of 2003*: Joseph Neff and Jay Price, "Chapter 3: A Private, Driven Man," *Raleigh News & Observer*, July 28, 2004.

109 *In February 2004, he and Batalona signed*: Sean Flynn, "The Day the War Turned," *GQ*, October 2006.

109 *The giant Tennessean was a former Night Stalker*: Michelle E. Shaw, "Iraq Atrocity Hits Close to Home," *Tennessean*, April 2, 2004.

109 *He'd signed up just after his seventh wedding anniversary*: Ibid.

109 *"He was aware of the conditions"*: Lauren Howard, "Local Man Among Four Slain in Iraq," *Leaf-Chronicle*, April 2, 2004.

109 *donated his time to help out*: Ibid.

109 *"Mike, from the men of Task Force DAGGER"*: "Goodbye Mike Teague . . . Killed in Fallujah," http://forums.gunbroker.com/pop_printer_friendly.asp?TOPIC _ID=103270, captured August 3, 2013.

109 *Helvenston had dropped out of high school*: Sean Flynn, "The Day the War Turned," *GQ*, October 2006.

109 *the youngest SEAL in naval history*: Ibid.

109 *The Florida native was deployed by the SEALs*: "History," SPECWAROPS, www .specwarops.com/html/History.html, captured August 3, 2013.

109 *when his canopy malfunctioned during a jump*: Abby Goodnough and Michael Luo, "Families of Men Slain by Mob Focus on Their Lives, Not How They Died," *New York Times*, April 3, 2004.

110 *he started a fitness company, Amphibian Athletics*: "Blackwater Founder Implicated in Murder of Witnesses Against Them," AnandTech message board, August 6, 2009.

110 *"I'm just damn glad to be here!"*: Sean Flynn, "The Day the War Turned," *GQ*, October 2006.

110 *"His feeling was, 'If your time is up'"*: "Former GIs Were Used to Danger," Tribune News Services, April 2, 2004.

110 *November 1 didn't have the heavy-duty squad automatic weapons*: "Private Military Contractors in Iraq: An Examination of Blackwater's Actions in Fallujah," Committee on Oversight and Government Reform, U.S. House of Representatives, September 2007.

110 *The contract that Blackwater and Regency had initially signed*: Blackwater-Regency contract, "Agreement for Security Services," March 12, 2004.

111 *Earlier in 2004, nine men were killed*: Jim Michaels, "9 Die in Copter Crash in Iraq," *USA Today*, January 8, 2004.

111 *insurgents fired rocket-propelled grenades*: "Abizaid Convoy Attacked; Timing of Elections Still Uncertain," PBS *NewsHour*, February 12, 2004.

111 *A mission to Camp Ridgeway and back*: Sean Flynn, "The Day the War Turned," *GQ*, October 2006.

111 *Batalona determined that even without the fully armored vehicles*: "Consolidated Report: The 31 March 2004 Fallujah Ambush," Coalition Provisional Authority, April 2004.

112 *To avoid the city, another route*: Sean Flynn, "The Day the War Turned," *GQ*, October 2006.

113 *U.S. intelligence reports have determined*: "Post-Incident Investigation: Ambush of BSC Team 31 Mar 04 in Fallujah," Blackwater.

113 *"There's no doubt that terrorists and insurgents"*: David Barstow, "Security Firm Says Its Workers Were Lured into Iraqi Ambush," *New York Times*, April 9, 2004.

113 *"The Ministry of Interior, concerned about a pattern"*: "The Continuing Challenge of Building the Iraqi Security Forces," Committee on Armed Services, U.S. House of Representatives, 2007.

114 *One boy put his hands on the passenger-side door*: Blackwater's Response to "Private Military Contractors in Iraq: An Examination of Blackwater's Actions in Fallujah," Majority Staff report, October 2007.

114 *They spoke to two men in their thirties*: Ibid.

114 *Helvenston and Teague never even had a chance*: Ibid.

115 *one terrified ESS driver would later report*: Ibid.

115 *"There was no evidence of return fire"*: "The Continuing Challenge of Building the Iraqi Security Forces," Committee on Armed Services, U.S. House of Representatives, 2007.

115 *"Fallujah is the graveyard of Americans"*: "Violence Strike's Iraq's Sunni Triangle," Associated Press, March 31, 2004.

116 *brought to mind Somalia*: Anthony H. Cordesman, "Iraq's Evolving Insurgency: The Nature of Attacks and Patterns and Cycles in the Conflict," Center for Strategic and International Studies, February 3, 2006.

117 *"They want to frighten us out of Iraq"*: Ibid.

117 *"War is the province of danger"*: Carl von Clausewitz, *On War*.

120 *Jerry's brother, Tom Zovko, told mourners*: "Veteran Killed by Iraq Mob Is Buried," Associated Press, April 11, 2004.

122 *Joseph Neff, a reporter who would extensively cover*: Joseph Neff, "Private Military Contractors: Determining Accountability," Nieman Reports, Summer 2008.

123 *"What kind of people loot dirt?"*: Bing West, *No True Glory: A Frontline Account of the Battle for Fallujah* (New York: Bantam, 2005), p. 16.

123 *insurgents began spreading leaflets around town*: Ibid., p. 51.

123 *"Fallujah is probably our center of gravity"*: David Isenberg, "Fallujah: The First Iraqi Intifada," *Asia Times*, January 8, 2008.

124 *Conway would later explain*: Rajiv Chandrasekaran, "Key General Criticizes April Attack in Fallujah," *Washington Post*, September 13, 2004.

124 *"Somewhere out in this world"*: Colin Freeman, "Horror at Fallujah," *San Francisco Chronicle*, April 1, 2004.

124 *"deliberate, it will be precise and it will be overwhelming"*: John D. Banusiewicz, "Coalition Vows 'Deliberate' Response to Attacks," American Forces Press Service, April 1, 2004.

124 *"The president knows this is going to be bloody"*: Rajiv Chandrasekaran, *Imperial Life in the Emerald City* (New York: Random House, 2006), p. 274.

125 *a condolence letter from Ambassador Bremer's office*: "Letter from L. Paul Bremer III," PBS *Frontline*, www.pbs.org/wgbh/pages/frontline/shows/warriors/contractors/bremerletter.html, captured August 3, 2013.

125 *Operation Vigilant Resolve commenced*: Rory McCarthy, "Uneasy Truce in the City of Ghosts," *Guardian*, April 23, 2004.

125 *The 1st Battalion, 5th Marine Regiment attacked*: Thomas G. Mahnken, Thomas A. Keaney, *War in Iraq: Planning and Execution* (London: Routledge, 2007), p. 172.

125 *The 2nd Battalion, 1st Marine Regiment stormed*: Ibid.

125 *helicopters fired Hellfire missiles*: Kenneth W. Estes, "Into the Fray: U.S. Marines in the Global War on Terrorism," U.S. Marine Corps, 2011.

125 *Fighter jets flew more than a hundred sorties*: Bing West, *No True Glory: A Frontline Account of the Battle for Fallujah* (New York: Bantam, 2005), p. 225.

126 *originally built to shield their residents*: Richard S. Lowry, "Recording History Part IX—The War Never Really Ended in Fallujah," *OpFor*, January 6, 2008.

126 *bloody procession that led to the deaths of more than a dozen Marines*: "At Least 12 Marines Killed as Iraq Fighting Rages," Fox News, www.foxnews.com /story/2004/04/06/at-least-12-marines-killed-as-iraq-fighting-rages/, captured August 4, 2013.

126 *seven hundred insurgents were killed*: Gregg Zoroya, "Fallujah Brigade Tries U.S. Patience," *USA Today*, April 13, 2004.

126 *estimated total civilian deaths there*: Carter Malkasian, "Signaling Resolve, Democratization, and the First Battle of Fallujah," *Journal of Strategic Studies*, June 2006.

126 *Iraqi minister of health estimated a far smaller number*: Ibid.

126 *threatened to resign unless the ambassador initiated a cease-fire*: Carter Malkasian, "Signaling Resolve, Democratization, and the First Battle of Fallujah," *Journal of Strategic Studies*, June 2006.

127 *They pulled out of the city entirely three weeks later*: Ibid.

127 *Fallujah grew into a staging ground for insurgent attacks*: Bill Roggio, "Iraq by the Numbers: Graphing the Decrease in Violence," *Long War Journal*, December 17, 2007.

127 *largest urban battle since Hue in Vietnam in 1968*: Jim Garamone, "ScanEagle Proves Worth in Fallujah Fight," American Forces Press Service, January 11, 2005.

127 *Operation Phantom Fury soon became*: Gerri Hirshey, "Wounded, and Sharing War Stories," *New York Times*, November 11, 2007.

127 *between the two assaults on Fallujah, they unloaded*: Ann Scott Tyson, "Increased Security in Fallujah Slows Efforts to Rebuild," *Washington Post*, April 19, 2005.

127 *military officials announced that U.S. forces controlled*: "Operation Phantom Fury," *USA Today*, http://usatoday30.usatoday.com/news/graphics/phantom _fury/flash.htm, captured August 4, 2013.

127 *More than ninety soldiers died*: Dwight Jon Zimmerman and John D. Gresham, *Uncommon Valor* (New York: Macmillan, 2010), p. 240.

127 *U.S. forces left a bombed-out wasteland*: Ibid.

127 *unrelenting toxicity in the flattened city that appears to have led to a staggering rise in birth defects*: "10 Years After the Iraq War: Innocent New Lives Are Still Dying and Suffering," Human Rights Now, April 2013.

127 *Marines with 3rd Battalion*: "31 U.S. Troops Killed in Fallujah," Associated Press, November 14, 2004.

128 *"It's symbolic because the insurgents closed the bridge"*: Ibid.

128 *"Fuck you"*: "'The Warrior Class': The Blackwater Videos," *Harper's*, http://harpers.org/blog/2012/04/the-warrior-class-the-blackwater-videos/, captured August 4, 2013.

CHAPTER 9: BLACKWATER VERSUS THE MAHDI ARMY

129 *Shias made up roughly 60 percent*: Sharon Otterman, "Iraq: The Sunnis," Council on Foreign Relations, December 12, 2003.

130 *Muqtada al-Sadr, the frumpy thirty-year-old*: "Iraq's Muqtada Al-Sadr: Spoiler or Stabilizer?," International Crisis Group, July 11, 2006.

130 *al-Sadr is the son of Ayatollah*: Ibid.

130 *The third of four sons*: "Muqtada al-Sadr, Back in Business," *Economist*, www .economist.com/node/18652167, captured May 5, 2011.

130 *gunmen working for the Iraqi secret police*: Amit R. Paley, "Al-Sadr Getting Ready to Lead Iraq?," *Washington Post*, May 28, 2008.

130 *While initially dismissed by fellow religious leaders*: "Iraq's Muqtada al-Sadr: Spoiler or Stabilizer?," International Crisis Group, July 11, 2006.

130 *allegedly going so far as to orchestrate the murder*: Ibid.

131 *"The most puzzling aspect of Muqtada's ascent"*: Ibid.

131 *"His critics, and even a few of his allies"*: Ibid.

131 *"In the Najaf-Kufa area, al-Sadr's militia"*: Francis X. Kozlowksi, "U.S. Marines in Battle: An-Najaf," August 2004.

131 *"most dangerous accelerant of potentially self-sustaining"*: Reid Smith, "An Iraqi Time Bomb," *American Spectator*, June 28, 2011.

132 *"Bremer Follows in the Footsteps of Saddam"*: Rajiv Chandrasekaran and Anthony Shadid, "Fallujah and Shiite Cleric Represent a 2-Front War," *Washington Post*, April 10, 2004.

132 *transcribed a fiery sermon from al-Sadr*: Dick Camp, *Battle for the City of the Dead* (Minneapolis: Zenith, 2011), p. 27.

132 *U.S. soldiers escorted the newspaper staff*: Ibid.

132 *They held portraits of al-Sadr and chanted*: Rajiv Chandrasekaran and Anthony Shadid, "Some Say U.S. Miscalculated in Recent Iraq Moves," *Washington Post*, April 12, 2004.

132 *"important constituencies in both the Shia and Sunni"*: Ali A. Allawi, *The Occupation of Iraq* (New Haven, CT: Yale University Press, 2007), p. 266.

132 *"The Iraqi political system was on the brink"*: "Interview: L. Paul Bremer III," PBS *Frontline*, http://archive is tpm 3Wp.

133 *"The fledgling Iraqi police"*: Patrick Cockburn, *Muqtada al-Sadr and the Battle for the Future of Iraq* (New York: Scribner, 2008), p. 146.

135 *"Iraq was center stage; I wanted to contribute"*: Philip Kosnett, "My Reasons for Volunteering in Iraq," U.S. Department of State official blog, November 28, 2007.

135 *only to be fought off by his El Salvadoran escorts*: Denis Gray, "El Salvadoran Soldiers Honored for Bravery in Iraq," Associated Press, May 7, 2004.

135 *"Our union is fond of saying"*: Transcript, *Lou Dobbs Tonight*, May 3, 2004.

135 *One of those National Guardsman*: Paul Huggins, "Showing the Spirit of America," *Decatur Daily*, June 26, 2005.

136 *Corporal Lonnie Young, a burly twenty-five-year-old*: Kate Wiltrout, "Norfolk Marine Tells Story of Rooftop Fight in Iraq," *Virginian-Pilot*, September 19, 2004.

136 *The Guardsmen heard reports of potential unrest*: Paul Huggins, "Showing the Spirit of America," *Decatur Daily*, June 26, 2005.

136 *They headed for the roof*: Kate Wiltrout, "Norfolk Marine Tells Story of Rooftop Fight in Iraq," *Virginian-Pilot*, September 19, 2004.

137 *members of al-Sadr's army reportedly*: Claude Salhani, "America's Intifada?," UPI, April 5, 2004.

137 *"One of the Iraqis quickly dropped"*: "A Real-Life Account of Combat Readiness," *America's North Shore Journal*, http://northshorejournal.org/a-real-life -account-of-combat-readiness, captured August 4, 2013.

138 *"I was up there within thirty seconds"*: "Contractors in Combat: Firefight from a Rooftop in Iraq," *Virginian-Pilot*, http://hamptonroads.com/2006/07/contrac tors-combat-firefight-rooftop-iraq, captured August 4, 2013.

138 *"I stopped for a second"*: "A Real-Life Account of Combat Readiness," *America's North Shore Journal*, http://northshorejournal.org/a-real-life-account-of-combat -readiness, captured August 4, 2013.

138 *This is too surreal*: Paul Huggins, "Showing the Spirit of America," *Decatur Daily*, June 26, 2005.

139 *"You look at these people and you know"*: Ibid.

139 *Eliminate the threat*: Ibid.

139 *suddenly collapsed on the rooftop*: "A Real-Life Account of Combat Readiness," *America's North Shore Journal*, http://northshorejournal.org/a-real-life-account -of-combat-readiness, captured August 4, 2013.

139 *The sniper had hit Eddy sideways*: Ibid.

139 *Young grabbed gauze pads*: Ibid.

140 *"We came up with a plan"*: Ibid.

140 *Young dashed across the base*: Kate Wiltrout, "Norfolk Marine Tells Story of Rooftop Fight in Iraq," *Virginian-Pilot*, September 19, 2004.

140 *Blood shot out*: "A Real-Life Account of Combat Readiness," *America's North Shore Journal*, http://northshorejournal.org/a-real-life-account-of-combat-readi ness, captured August 4, 2013.

140 *"Using my index finger"*: Ibid.

140 *had hit him on his left shoulder just outside*: Ibid.

140 *"I knew that I heard the unmistakable"*: Ibid.

141 *"And if three people got shot"*: Paul Huggins, "Showing the Spirit of America," *Decatur Daily*, June 26, 2005.

141 *the question began to pound*: Ibid.

142 *"All hell is breaking loose"*: L. Paul Bremer III, *My Year in Iraq* (New York: Simon & Schuster, 2006), p. 318.

142 *"Muqtada's people are really swarming"*: Ibid.

142 *"Spanish put out an idiotic statement"*: Ibid., p. 319.

142 *The ambassador became livid*: Ibid.

144 *Together, they unfastened*: "A Real-Life Account of Combat Readiness," *America's North Shore Journal*, http://northshorejournal.org/a-real-life-account-of -combat-readiness, captured August 4, 2013.

144 *"before we put all the personal weapons"*: "SimplyDynamic," AR15.com message board, August 5, 2005, captured August 4, 2013.

145 *"I felt very nervous"*: "A Real-Life Account of Combat Readiness," *America's North Shore Journal*, http://northshorejournal.org/a-real-life-account-of-combat-readi -ness, captured August 4, 2013.

145 *In the footage*: Author copy of video; also available online at www.youtube.com /watch?v=s7TRP-d5h2Q, captured August 4, 2013.

146 *"[insurgents] were just coming straight on"*: "Danpass," AR15.com message board, October 13, 2008, captured August 4, 2013.

146 *In the video*: Author copy of video; also available online at www.youtube.com /watch?v=s7TRP-d5h2Q, captured August 4, 2013.

146 *"You could sit there"*: "Danpass," AR15.com message board, May 15, 2009, captured August 4, 2013.

146 *"That's Mahdi Army!"*: Author copy of video; available online at www.youtube .com/watch?v=s7TRP-d5h2Q, captured August 4, 2013.

147 *"they're shootin' back"*: Ibid.

147 *"Terrorize your enemy"*: John F. Burns, "7 U.S. Soldiers Die in Iraq as a Shiite Militia Rises Up," *New York Times*, April 5, 2004.

147 *Sanchez says he raced*: Ricardo S. Sanchez, *Wiser in Battle* (New York: HarperCollins, 2009), p. 339.

148 *"Without commenting at a news conference"*: Dana Priest, "Private Guards Repel Attack on U.S. Headquarters," *Washington Post*, April 6, 2004.

149 *In his book, the general writes*: Ricardo S. Sanchez, *Wiser in Battle* (New York: HarperCollins, 2009), p. 337.

149 *"Fighting everywhere"*: Ibid.

149 *"Those Blackwater and CPA guys"*: David Isenberg, "Dogs of War: Blackwater, Najaf—Take Two," UPI, May 16, 2008.

149 *"Those [Blackwater] civilians were not providing"*: Ibid.

149 *"Although the Ambassador didn't want to believe"*: Ibid.

150 *"An attack by hundreds of Iraqi militia"*: Dana Priest, "Private Guards Repel Attack on U.S. Headquarters," *Washington Post*, April 6, 2004.

150 *described it on his* Intel Dump *blog*: Phil Carter, "Blackwater Commandos in Najaf Battle," Antiwar.com, April 6, 2004.

150 *"a whole new issue in military affairs"*: David Barstow, "Security Firm Says Its Workers Were Lured into Iraqi Ambush," *New York Times*, April 9, 2004.

150 *July 2004 report by the Army's inspector general*: "Detainee Operations Inspection," Department of the Army Inspector General, July 21, 2004.

151 *"the key reason, the sole reason"*: "Iraq Commander: Abu Ghraib Ruined My Career," Associated Press, November 2, 2006.

CHAPTER 10: THE RULES OF THE ROAD

153 *"thirteen years since the American flag"*: "Ambassador Negroponte's Speech on the Occasion of the Flag-Raising Ceremony," U.S. Embassy Baghdad, June 30, 2004.

153 *"a thousand people hunkered behind sandbags"*: Jane C. Loeffler, "Fortress America," *Foreign Policy*, September 1, 2007.

153 *Americans had overseen the creation*: Richard L. Armitage, "Prepared Statement Before the Senate Committee on Foreign Relations," May 18, 2004.

154 *"develops and implements effective security"*: "About Diplomatic Security: Overview," U.S. Department of State, www.state.gov/m/ds/about/overview/, captured August 4, 2013.

154 *only about a thousand special agents*: Michael J. Courts, "Testimony Before the House Committee on Foreign Affairs," November 15, 2012.

154 *"first used PSCs in 1994"*: Jennifer K. Elsea, Moshe Schwartz, and Kennon H. Nakamura, "Private Security Contractors in Iraq: Background, Legal Status and Other Issues," Congressional Research Service, August 25, 2008.

155 *In June 2004, the State Department issued*: "Joint Audit of Blackwater Contract and Task Orders for Worldwide Personal Protective Services in Iraq," Office of the Special Inspector General for Iraq Reconstruction, June 2009.

155 *That "indefinite delivery, indefinite quantity" deal*: Samuel P. Cheadle, "Private Military Contractor Liability Under the Worldwide Personal Protective Services II Contract," *Public Contract Law Journal*, March 22, 2009.

156 *"The Government requires a favorable image"*: "Blackwater, Triple Canopy and DynCorp—Contract with the U.S. State Department: Worldwide Personal Protective Services (WPPS) Contract," author copy.

157 *"high-visibility deterrent"*: Ibid.

157 *more than five hundred servicemen had been killed*: "Iraq Coalition Casualties: Fatalities by Year and Month," iCasualties, www.icasualties.org/Iraq/ByMonth .aspx, captured August 3, 2013.

158 *More than four hundred of those*: Anthony H. Cordesman, "Iraq's Evolving Insurgency: The Nature of Attacks and Patterns and Cycles in the Conflict," Center for Strategic and International Studies, February 3, 2006.

158 *some fifty-six hundred roadside bombs*: Ibid.

159 *"one of the most visible and egregious"*: Joseph S. Smyth, "The Impact of the Buy American Act on Program Managers," *Acquisition Review Quarterly*, Fourth Quarter 2009.

162 *"tend to overreact to a lot of things"*: Sudarsan Raghavan, Joshua Partlow, and Karen DeYoung, "Blackwater Faulted in Military Reports from Shooting Scene," *Washington Post*, October 5, 2007.

163 *"I am one of the few members of Congress"*: Jan Schakowsky, "On the Issues: Contracting," http://schakowsky.house.gov/index.php?option=com_content&view =article&id=2738&Itemid=64, captured February 11, 2013.

163 *"extraordinarily professional organization"*: "Interview: Marine Col. Thomas X. Hammes (Ret.)," PBS *Frontline*, www.pbs.org/wgbh/pages/frontline/shows /warriors/interviews/hammes.html, captured August 3, 2013.

164 *"A Free Pass in Iraq"*: Tom Engelhardt, "Order 17: A Free Pass in Iraq," *Nation*, September 17, 2007.

164 *"Where Military Rules Don't Apply"*: Steve Fainaru, "Where Military Rules Don't Apply," *Washington Post*, September 20, 2007.

164 *"There is no law that restricts"*: Bassam Sebti, "The Criminals' Kick Out," www .bassamsebti.com/2007/09/criminals-kick-out.html, captured February 3, 2013.

164 *"Order 17 gave new meaning"*: Tom Engelhardt, "Order 17: A Free Pass in Iraq," *Nation*, September 17, 2007.

164 *The relevant part of that notice*: "Coalition Provisional Authority Order Number 17 (Revised)," Institute for International Law and Justice, www.iilj.org/ courses/documents/Order17.Section4.pdf, captured August 8, 2013.

165 *The CPA's public notice concluded*: "Public Notice Regarding the Status of Coalition, Foreign Liaison and Contractor Personnel," Coalition Provisional Authority, www.iraqcoalition.org/regulations/20030626_20030626_CPANOTICE _Foreign_Mission_Cir.html.pdf, captured August 8, 2013.

165 *The order states in relevant part*: "Coalition Provisional Authority Order Number 17 (Revised)," Institute for International Law and Justice, www.iilj.org /courses/documents/Order17.Section4.pdf, captured August 8, 2013.

165 *"Rape, murder, smuggling, sex abuse, child molestation"*: Mark Hemingway, "Blackwater Down," *National Review*, September 2, 2007.

166 *NATO's official parties' agreement*: "Agreement Between the Parties to the North Atlantic Treaty Regarding the Status of Their Forces," NATO, www.nato .int/cps/en/natolive/official_texts_17265.htm, captured August 8, 2013.

166 *National Defense Authorization Act added a new provision*: Uniform Code of Military Justice, www.au.af.mil/au/awc/awcgate/ucmj.htm, captured August 8, 2013.

167 *key words "or a contingency operation"*: Mark Hemingway, "Blackwater's Legal Netherworld," *National Review*, September 26, 2007.

167 *contract concerns the "Safeguarding of Information"*: "Safeguarding of Information," Statement of Work, U.S. Department of State Worldwide Personal Protective Services, contract SAQMPD-05-D1098, www.state.gov/documents /organization/136445.pdf, captured August 8, 2013.

168 *One email from Moe to Blackwater*: Suzanne Simons, *Master of War* (New York: HarperCollins, 2009), p. 166.

168 *"A Blackwater spokesman declined"*: John M. Broder and James Risen, "Blackwater Tops Firms in Iraq in Shooting Rate," *New York Times*, September 27, 2007.

168 *"They were there to assist"*: "Interview: Marine Col. Thomas X. Hammes (Ret.)," PBS *Frontline*, www.pbs.org/wgbh/pages/frontline/shows/warriors/inter views/hammes.html, captured August 8, 2013.

169 *"The contract was awarded"*: Jennifer K. Elsea, Moshe Schwartz, and Kennon H. Nakamura, "Private Security Contractors in Iraq: Background, Legal Status and Other Issues," Congressional Research Service, August 25, 2008.

169 *That cost was significant*: "Review of Diplomatic Security's Management of Personal Protective Services in Iraq," U.S. Department of State and the Broadcasting Board of Governors Offices of Inspector General, January 2009.

169 *my company brought in some $340 million*: R. J. Hillhouse, "Condi Can't Afford to Lose Blackwater," *Wired*, October 11, 2007.

170 *Blackwater's take dwarfed the payouts*: Ibid.

170 *And our manpower*: Ibid.

170 *"Security is key to establishing"*: "U.S. Embassy in Iraq," Congressional Research Service, March 11, 2005.

170 *"It was the first time a majority"*: Dana Milbank and Claudia Deane, "Poll Finds Dimmer View of Iraq War," *Washington Post*, June 8, 2005.

171 *"With the presidency and control of Congress"*: Richard Simon, "Democrats Pile on Bush," *Los Angeles Times*, November 3, 2005.

171 *the "Three Stooges"*: Jacob Weisberg, "The Three Stooges," *Slate*, March 8, 2006.

171 *"For Democrats, Many Verses, but No Chorus"*: Adam Nagourney, "For Democrats, Many Verses, but No Chorus," *New York Times*, March 6, 2006.

171 *"Democrats Struggle to Seize Opportunity"*: Shailagh Murray and Charles Babington, "Democrats Struggle to Seize Opportunity," *Washington Post*, March 7, 2006.

171 *"Democrats Vow Not to Give Up Hopelessness"*: "Democrats Vow Not to Give Up Hopelessness," *Onion*, February 27, 2006.

171 *"I don't support our troops"*: Joel Stein, "Warriors and Wusses," *Los Angeles Times*, January 24, 2006.

CHAPTER 11: CHARACTER COUNTS

173 *"Once I did a little reading"*: Hal Brown, "Blackwater Revisited," *Capitol Hill Blue*, September 18, 2007.

173 *"vigorous condemnation of immoral killers"*: Lindsey Cameron, "Private Military Companies: Their Status Under International Humanitarian Law and Its Impact on Their Regulation," *International Review of the Red Cross*, September 2006.

174 *six conditions to be satisfied*: "Protocol Additional to the Geneva Conventions of 12 August 1949, and Relating to the Protection of Victims of International Armed Conflicts (Protocol I), 8 June 1977: Article 47," International Committee of the Red Cross, www.icrc.org/ihl/WebART/470-750057, captured August 8, 2013.

175 *UN convention defines the term*: "International Convention Against the Recruitment, Use, Financing and Training of Mercenaries," United Nations, www.un.org/documents/ga/res/44/a44r034.htm, captured August 8, 2013.

175 *"I just roll my eyes"*: David Isenberg, "Civil Discourse and Private Military Contractors," *Huffington Post*, April 19, 2010.

176 *President Bush was "a dog"*: "Journalist Hurls Shoes at 'Dog' Bush," Agence France Presse, December 15, 2008.

177 *"In a perfect world"*: Julian E. Barnes, "Soul-Searching at the Secret Service," *Los Angeles Times*, December 16, 2008.

178 *"You have to be disciplined"*: Ann Scott Tyson, "Private Security Workers Living on Edge in Iraq," *Washington Post*, April 23, 2005.

178 *"I like being someplace"*: Ibid.

180 *"In certain circumstances, and when directed"*: "Physical Efficiency Battery Scores," Statement of Work, U.S. Department of State Worldwide Personal Protective Services, contract SAQMPD-05-D1098, www.state.gov/documents/organization/136439.pdf, captured August 8, 2013.

181 *American employers are affected by bad hires*: "Nearly Seven in Ten Businesses Affected by a Bad Hire in the Past Year, According to CareerBuilder Survey," CareerBuilder.com, www.careerbuilder.com/share/aboutus/pressreleasesdetail.aspx?sd=12/13/2012&id=pr730&ed=12/31/2012, captured August 8, 2013.

182 *he'd been drinking heavily*: John M. Broder, "Ex-Paratrooper Is Suspect in a Blackwater Killing," *New York Times*, October 4, 2007.

182 *Mahdi's security guards were arrested*: Sam Dagher, "Arrests in Bank Robbery Create a Rift Between Iraqi Officials," *New York Times*, August 2, 2009.

182 *He died early the next day*: Mike Carter, "Widow of Iraqi Guard Sues Seattle Man for Blackwater Shooting," March 20, 2009.

182 *"blatant and egregious" violation*: John M. Broder, "Ex-Paratrooper Is Suspect in a Blackwater Killing," *New York Times*, October 4, 2007.

183 *Gary Jackson told reporters*: Bill Sizemore, "Blackwater Supports Inquiry into Fatal Shooting," *Virginian-Pilot*, July 25, 2007.

183 *a Garrity warning*: James Risen, "Efforts to Prosecute Blackwater Are Collapsing," *New York Times*, October 20, 2010.

184 *"earn an average of about $1,000 a day"*: Sewell Chan and Karl Vick, "U.S. Vows to Find Civilians' Killers; Marines Move to Seal Off Fallujah; Army Steps Up Patrols in Baghdad," *Washington Post*, April 2, 2004.

184 *"make up to $1,000 a day"*: Jeremy Scahill, "Bush's Rent-an-Army," *Los Angeles Times*, January 25, 2007.

184 *"It's more than just salary"*: "Military Compensation: Army Benefits," GoArmy .com, www.goarmy.com/benefits/total-compensation.html, captured August 9, 2013.

184 *the Army's recent, heavy push*: "Bonuses: Earning Extra Money," GoArmy.com, www.goarmy.com/benefits/money/bonuses-earning-extra-money.html, captured August 9, 2013.

184 *Soldiers are offered as much*: "Army Announces More Ways to Earn Up to $40,000," Military.com, www.military.com/recruiting/bonus-center /resources/army-announces-more-ways-to-earn-bonuses-up-to-$40000, captured August 9, 2013.

184 *the College Loan Repayment Program*: "College Loan Repayment Program," Army-Portal.com, www.army-portal.com/benefits/clrp.html, captured August 9, 2013.

185 *The list of incentives goes on*: "Military Compensation: Army Benefits," GoArmy .com, www.goarmy.com/benefits/total-compensation.html, captured August 9, 2013.

185 *"because you could be dead the next day"*: Ann Scott Tyson, "Private Security Workers Living on Edge in Iraq," *Washington Post*, April 23, 2005.

185 *summarized the forty-four-page study*: Rick Maze, "A New Report Says You Make Twice What You Thought," *Military Times*, July 16, 2007.

186 *"While both Special Forces and military police"*: "Rebuilding Iraq: Actions Needed to Improve Use of Private Security Providers," U.S. Government Accountability Office Report to Congressional Committees, July 2005.

186 *"This similarity indicates"*: Ibid.

186 *oft-cited congressional memo about my company*: "Additional Information about Blackwater USA," Memorandum to Members of the Committee on Oversight and Government Reform, U.S. House of Representatives, October 1, 2007.

187 *as I later explained to Congress*: "Blackwater USA," Hearing Before the Committee on Oversight and Government Reform, U.S. House of Representatives, www .gpo.gov/fdsys/pkg/CHRG-110hhrg45219/pdf/CHRG-110hhrg45219.pdf, captured August 9, 2013.

187 *On top of the overhead*: Ibid.

187 *"This war has produced some of the most lavish"*: Ibid.

187 *first thorough, nonpartisan examination of the issue*: "Contractors' Support of U.S. Operations in Iraq," Congress of the United States Congressional Budget Office, August 2008.

188 *"Because of the broad level of interest"*: "Warfighter Support: A Cost Comparison of Using State Department Employees versus Contractors for Security Services in Iraq," U.S. Government Accountability Office, March 4, 2010.

188 *The report noted that by using federal employees*: Ibid.

189 *Those statistics echoed a 2007 refrain*: Patrick B. Pexton, "Gold-Plated Rambos," *Washington Post*, October 2, 2007.

CHAPTER 12: THE FALLUJAH FAMILIES

190 *she reportedly drove the forty-five miles*: Wayne Drash, "Mom: My Son Was Mutilated and I Want Answers," CNN, November 7, 2007.

190 *"God has accepted Jerry's soul"*: Andrea Simakis, "United in Grief, Two Mothers Want to Know How Their Sons Died While Working for Blackwater in Iraq," *Plain Dealer*, May 30, 2008.

191 *Racked by insomnia and grief*: Ibid.

191 *Helvenston-Wettengel reportedly read*: Ibid.

191 *highest award ever in Orange County*: Lisa Girion and Debora Vrana, "Massive Verdict for Biomedical Company," *Los Angeles Times*, September 25, 2003.

191 *business card boasts his being named*: Nick Schou, "Only Pawns in Their Game," *OC Weekly*, July 13, 2006.

192 *Callahan's team filed the wrongful death lawsuit*: Helvenston et al. v. Blackwater Security, www-tc.pbs.org/wgbh/pages/frontline////shows/warriors/contractors/complaint.pdf, captured August 9, 2013.

192 *"Had they been provided"*: Ibid.

192 *"can't wait to grill Blackwater"*: Nick Schou, "Only Pawns in Their Game," *OC Weekly*, July 13, 2006.

194 *Teague wrote to our staff*: Author's copy of the email.

194 *Our security contract stipulated*: "Article 2: Regency Responsibility," Blackwater-Regency Agreement for Security Services, http://oversight-archive.waxman.house.gov/documents/20061207151614-43671.pdf, captured August 9, 2013.

195 *"Blackwater was able to save"*: Jeremy Scahill, "Blood Is Thicker Than Blackwater," *Nation*, April 20, 2006.

195 *The contract explicitly stated*: "Appendix B: Schedule of Rates, Supplies and Services," Blackwater-Regency Agreement for Security Services, http://oversight-archive.waxman.house.gov/documents/20061207151614-43671.pdf, captured August 9, 2013.

195 *"There is no order"*: "E-mails Related to Private Security Contracting—Iraqi Reconstruction: Reliance on Private Military Contractors," www.globalsecurity.org/military/library/congress/2007_hr/070207-emails.pdf, captured August 9, 2013.

196 *That waiver stated*: "Iraqi Reconstruction: Reliance on Private Military Contractors and Status Report," Hearing Before the Committee on Oversight and Government Reform, U.S. House of Representatives, February 7, 2007.

196 *Some of the Fallujah families*: Mike Baker, "Judge: Defense Insurance Act Bars Suits Against Subcontractor Blackwater," *Insurance Journal*, February 12, 2009.

197 *"by binding arbitration"*: "Iraqi Reconstruction: Reliance on Private Military Contractors and Status Report," Hearing Before the Committee on Oversight and Government Reform, U.S. House of Representatives, February 7, 2007.

197 *"the right any of them may have"*: Ibid.

197 *That closed-door policy was crucial*: Mike Baker, "Iraq Security Contractor Countersues," *Washington Post*, January 19, 2007.

198 *my company paid both our side*: Peter Krouse, "Wrongful Death Lawsuit Against Former Blackwater USA Dismissed," *Plain Dealer*, January 26, 2011.

198 *emailing the arbitrators directly*: "Blackwater Liability Case Axed for Fee Nonpayment," Courthouse News Service, www.courthousenews.com/2011/01/25/33608.htm, captured August 9, 2013.

198 *"While the record shows"*: Helvenston et al. v. Blackwater Security dismissal, www.gvsu.edu/cms3/assets/A710F777-E74C-F8BD-F645CFB2BE41D80C/blackwater.pdf, captured August 9, 2013.

198 *"It's pretty much destroyed my life":* "Blackwater Suit Tossed 7 Years After Grisly Deaths," Associated Press, January 25, 2011.

199 *PR firm that proudly boasted:* "What We Do: Settlement Negotiations," Levick .com, http://levick.com/practices/litigation-communications, captured August 13, 2013.

199 *two overarching options for potential customers:* "What We Do," Levick.com, captured September 12, 2012.

199 *"To be sure," Levick later explained:* Richard Levick, "A Long-Term Struggle: How a Media Campaign Helped Turn the Guantánamo Tide," WorkinPR.com, http:// jmw.typepad.com/files/pr-perspective-levick-2.htm, captured August 9, 2013.

199 *Levick, whose firm charges:* Brenton Henry, "Gaming Operators to Pay for PR," *Antigua Observer*, September 28, 2012.

199 *"deserved open-minded coverage":* Richard Levick, "A Long-Term Struggle: How a Media Campaign Helped Turn the Guantánamo Tide," WorkinPR.com, http:// jmw.typepad.com/files/pr-perspective-levick-2.htm, captured August 9, 2013.

199 *"literally thousands of news placements":* Ibid.

200 *"Nonsense!":* Ibid.

200 *drove a pickup truck:* Rajiv Chandrasekaran, "A 'Ticking Time Bomb' Goes Off," *Washington Post*, February 23, 2009.

200 *detonated a bomb that killed:* Ibid.

200 *A "Drive the Narrative" section:* "Drive the Narrative," Levick.com, captured September 12, 2012.

200 *Callahan told eager reporters:* Nick Schou, "Fallujah Strikes Again!," *OC Weekly*, June 13, 2007.

200 *Blogs posted stories with headlines:* Russ Wellen, "Blackwater Plumbs New Depths of Shame in Fallujah Contractors Case," OpEdNews.com, June 8, 2007.

201 *It was headlined:* Daniel J. Callahan and Marc P. Miles, "Blackwater Heavies Sue Families of Slain Employees for $10 Million in Butal Attempt to Surpress Their Story," *AlterNet*, June 7, 2007.

201 *The piece asserted:* Ibid.

202 *referred to as the "Speech or Debate Clause":* "Article I," Illinois General Assembly, www.ilga.gov/commission/lrb/Article1.htm, captured August 9, 2013.

203 *received a letter from Callahan:* Callahan and Blaine letter to Nancy Pelosi, http://online.wsj.com/public/resources/documents/blackwater010907.pdf, captured August 9, 2013.

204 *"precedent-setting lawsuit":* Ibid.

204 *"lack of accountability for private security":* Ibid.

204 *Callahan concluded with this request:* Ibid.

204 *"work tirelessly":* "About the Committee," Committee on Oversight and Government Reform, U.S. House of Representatives, http://oversight.house.gov /about-the-committee/, captured August 9, 2013.

205 *That February 7, 2007, hearing:* "Iraqi Reconstruction: Reliance on Private Military Contractors and Status Report," Hearing Before the Committee on Oversight and Government Reform, U.S. House of Representatives, February 7, 2007.

205 *"Today four family members":* Ibid.

205 *Lynn Westmoreland . . . wrote:* Lynn A. Westmoreland letter to Henry Waxman, http://rsc.scalise.house.gov/doc/ca_021207_westmorelandblackwater.pdf, captured August 9, 2013.

206 *"One question I have"*: "Iraqi Reconstruction: Reliance on Private Military Contractors and Status Report," Hearing Before the Committee on Oversight and Government Reform, U.S. House of Representatives, February 7, 2007.

CHAPTER 13 : NISOUR SQUARE

207 *Inside that fortified complex*: Steven R. Hurst and Qassim Adbul-Zahra, "Pieces Emerge in Blackwater Shooting," *USA Today*, October 8, 2007.

207 *The ten-year USAID veteran*: "Ms. Kerry Pelzman, HLC Member," USAID India, http://mbph.in/health-leadership-council/members.html, captured August 9, 2013.

208 *"I believe that there are essentially four"*: Mark Mazzetti and David Stout, "Intelligence Report Predicts Spiraling of Violence in Iraq," *New York Times*, February 2, 2007.

211 *"I and others were yelling"*: Sworn Statement of Paul Slough, http://abcnews .go.com/images/Blotter/Gunner_blackwater_abcnews_071114.pdf, captured August 9, 2013.

211 *standard sound bite*: Robert Fisk, "New Iraq? Hooded Protest and Masked Statistics," *Independent*, March 20, 2004.

212 *"There are no rules of engagement"*: Transcript, Nazareth College Conference on Globalization and Culture, http://rochester.indymedia.org/node/6961, captured August 9, 2013.

212 *"escalation of force" policy*: "Private Security Contracting in Iraq and Afghanistan: Statement of Ambassador Richard J. Griffin," U.S. Department of State, http://2001-2009.state.gov/m/ds/rls/rm/93191.htm, captured August 9, 2013.

212 *"Principles on Use of Deadly Force"*: "Mission Firearms Policy: American Embassy—Baghdad," State, Foreign Operations, and Related Programs Appropriations for Fiscal Year 2006: Hearings Before a Subcommittee of the Committee on Appropriations, U.S. Senate, www.gpo.gov/fdsys/pkg/CHRG-109shrg99878 /pdf/CHRG-109shrg99878.pdf, captured August 9, 2013.

213 *"permissible uses"*: Ibid.

213 *second point acknowledges*: Ibid.

213 *the issue of warning shots*: Ibid.

214 *my company had 195 documented episodes*: John M. Broder, "Chief of Blackwater Defends His Employees," *New York Times*, October 3, 2007.

214 *"We shot to kill"*: Steve Fainaru, *Big Boy Rules* (Cambridge, MA: Da Capo, 2009), p. 183.

214 *An Iraqi police report*: Steve Fainaru, "How a Blackwater Sniper Fire Felled 3 Iraqi Guards," *Washington Post*, November 8, 2007.

215 *internal State Department review*: Ibid.

215 *"could undermine a lot"*: Steve Fainaru and Saad al-Izzi, "U.S. Security Contractors Open Fire in Baghdad," *Washington Post*, May 27, 2007.

215 *"at a high rate of speed"*: Andrew E. Kramer, "Security Contractors Shoot at Taxi, Wounding 3 Iraqis," *New York Times*, October 19, 2007.

215 *The contractors ultimately fired*: Steve Fainaru and Amit R. Paley, "Private Guards Fire on Taxi; Three Iraqis Hurt, Police Say," *Washington Post*, October 19, 2007.

216 *"obviously condoned by State"*: Steve Fainaru, "Where Military Rules Don't Apply," *Washington Post*, September 20, 2007.

217 *Slough fired a single bullet*: Sworn Statement of Paul Slough, http://abcnews .go.com/images/Blotter/Gunner_blackwater_abcnews_071114.pdf, captured August 9, 2013.

217 *the woman in the white sedan*: Sudarsan Raghavan, "Tracing the Paths of 5 Who Died in a Storm of Gunfire," *Washington Post*, October 4, 2007.

217 *sprinted to the vehicle and reached*: James Glanz and Alissa J. Rubin, "From Errand to Fatal Shot to Hail of Fire to 17 Deaths," *New York Times*, October 3, 2007.

217 *continued to roll toward Blackwater's convoy*: Sworn Statement of Paul Slough, http://abcnews.go.com/images/Blotter/Gunner_blackwater_abcnews_071114 .pdf, captured August 9, 2013.

217 *Iraqi security forces were so corrupt*: James L. Jones, "The Report of the Independent Commission on the Security Forces of Iraq," September 6, 2007.

217 *"Contact! Contact! Contact!"*: Jim Hanson, "The End of the Warrior Witch Hunt," *Washington Times*, January 7, 2010.

217 *"I then engaged the individuals"*: Sworn Statement of Paul Slough, http://abc news.go.com/images/Blotter/Gunner_blackwater_abcnews_071114.pdf, captured August 9, 2013.

218 *a second traffic cop ran*: Sudarsan Raghavan, "Tracing the Paths of 5 Who Died in a Storm of Gunfire," *Washington Post*, October 4, 2007.

218 *More Blackwater men joined in*: Sworn Statement of Paul Slough, http://abc news.go.com/images/Blotter/Gunner_blackwater_abcnews_071114.pdf, captured August 9, 2013.

218 *The blast ignited*: *United States of America v. Jeremy P. Ridgeway*, November 18, 2008.

218 *"Blackwater air support advised"*: Matt Apuzzo and Lara Jakes, "Blackwater Radio Logs: Guards Took Incoming Fire," *Tucson Citizen*, December 18, 2008.

218 *Incoming AK-47 shots*: Ibid.

218 *detail that has been absent*: Blackwater incident report.

219 *the truck refused to start*: Sworn Statement of Paul Slough, http://abcnews .go.com/images/Blotter/Gunner_blackwater_abcnews_071114.pdf, captured August 9, 2013.

219 *"The team returned defensive fire"*: "Spot Report—091607-01," Bureau of Diplomatic Security, U.S. Embassy Baghdad, http://i.a.cnn.net/cnn/2007 /images/09/16/17sept07.pdf, captured August 9, 2013.

219 *The convoy radioed Pelzman's evac team*: Matt Apuzzo and Lara Jakes, "Blackwater Radio Logs: Guards Took Incoming Fire," *Tucson Citizen*, December 18, 2008.

219 *A blue Volkswagen sedan*: Sudarsan Raghavan and Josh White, "Blackwater Guards Fired at Fleeing Cars, Soldiers Say," *Washington Post*, October 12, 2007.

219 *The vehicle careened*: Ibid.

219 *Nick Slatten, a Blackwater sniper*: *United States of America v. Paul A. Slough, et al.*, Criminal Action No. 08-0360 (RMU), December 31, 2009.

219 *From the rear vehicle*: Ibid.

219 *Heard switched to his grenade*: Ibid.

219 *Raven 23 headed for the northwest*: "Spot Report—091607-01," Bureau of Diplomatic Security, U.S. Embassy Baghdad, http://i.a.cnn.net/cnn/2007 /images/09/16/17sept07.pdf, captured August 9, 2013.

219 *Blackwater's men estimated*: Ibid.

220 *More than three dozen Iraqi civilians*: "Iraq: Blackwater Shootings Killed 17," Associated Press, October 7, 2007.

220 *any Blackwater personnel involved*: United States of America v. Paul A. Slough, et al., Criminal Action No. 08-0360 (RMU), December 31, 2009.

220 *were covered under the Garrity*: Ibid.

220 *That warning read*: Ibid.

221 *DipSec agent Ted Carpenter*: Ibid.

221 *Carpenter found the case files*: Ibid.

221 *those blue shirts were joined*: Ibid.

221 *Tarsa, the battalion commander*: Sudarsan Raghavan and Josh White, "Blackwater Guards Fired at Fleeing Cars, Soldiers Say," *Washington Post*, October 12, 2007.

222 *"It had every indication"*: Ibid.

222 *"I did not see anything"*: Ibid.

222 *"no enemy activity involved"*: Renee Montagne and Jackie Northam, "Blackwater Guards Given Immunity in Iraq Shooting," NPR, October 30, 2007.

222 *a "criminal event"*: Sudarsan Raghavan and Josh White, "Blackwater Guards Fired at Fleeing Cars, Soldiers Say," *Washington Post*, October 12, 2007.

222 *confidential sworn statements from convoy members*: Sworn Statement of Paul Slough, http://abcnews.go.com/images/Blotter/Gunner_blackwater_abcnews_071114.pdf, captured August 9, 2013.

222 *Headlines blared*: Ian Thompson, "Blackwater Massacre Spotlights Mercenary Role in Iraq," PSLweb.org, September 21, 2007.

222 *Bloggers wondered*: "Speed Bump: Will Mass Murder in Nisoor Square Slow the Growth of Blackwater?," *Winter Patriot* blog, http://winterpatriot.blogspot.com/2007/10/speed-bump-will-mass-murder-in-nisoor.html, captured August 9, 2013.

222 *"No! No! No!"*: James Glanz and Alissa J. Rubin, "From Errand to Fatal Shot to Hail of Fire to 17 Deaths," *New York Times*, October 3, 2007.

222 *D.C. Circuit judge would rule*: Barbara Leonard, "High Court to Consider Sealed Blackwater Filing," Courthouse News Service, November 14, 2011.

223 *"We searched in these areas"*: United States of America v. Paul A. Slough, et al., Criminal Action No. 08-0360 (RMU), December 31, 2009.

223 *"a fact-finding mission to determine"*: David M. Herszenhorn, "House's Iraq Bill Applies U.S. Laws to Contractors," *New York Times*, October 5, 2007.

223 *forensic scientists were unable to determine*: "No Forensic Match for Ammo in Blackwater Shooting," Associated Press, April 1, 2009.

223 *"FBI scientists were unable to match bullets"*: Ibid.

224 *Justice Department eventually charged*: Donna Leinwand, "Blackwater Charges: 14 Counts of Manslaughter," *USA Today*, December 9, 2008.

224 *pleaded guilty to one count*: Jason Ryan and Brian Ross, "Blackwater Guard in Secret Deal to Testify in Massacre Case," ABC News, December 8, 2008.

224 *I released a statement*: Pete Williams, "Blackwater Guards Charged," NBC News, December 8, 2008.

224 *We remained fully behind the indicted men*: Ibid.

224 *"While it is important to hold these individual"*: Jan Schakowsky, "Schakowsky Statement on Indictment of Blackwater Guards," December 8, 2008.

225 *Price said at the time*: David Johnston and John M. Broder, "F.B.I. Says Guards Killed 14 Iraqis Without Cause," *New York Times*, November 14, 2007.

225 *"unintended and intolerable consequences"*: "House Passes Bill That Would Hike Penalties for U.S. Security Contractors in Iraq," Associated Press, October 4, 2007.

225 *withering on the legislative vine*: Ibid.

225 *Security Contractor Accountability Act of 2007*: "S.2147 (110th): Security Contractor Accountability Act of 2007," GovTrack.us, www.govtrack.us/congress/bills/110/s2147, captured August 10, 2013.

225 *Transparency and Accountability in Military and Security Contracting Act of 2007*: "S.674: Transparency and Accountability in Military and Security Contracting Act of 2007," OpenCongress, www.opencongress.org/bill/110-s674/show, captured August 10, 2013.

225 *Stop Outsourcing Security Act*: "S.2398 (110th): Stop Outsourcing Security Act," GovTrack.us, www.govtrack.us/congress/bills/110/s2398, captured August 10, 2013.

225 *Clinton's office said in a statement*: David Isenberg, "Dogs of War: Round Laws, Square Holes," UPI, March 7, 2008.

226 *The thirty-five-count indictment against my men*: Department of Justice, "Five Blackwater Employees Indicted on Manslaughter and Weapons Charges for Fatal Nisur Square Shooting in Iraq," www.justice.gov/opa/pr/2008/December/08-nsd-1068.html, captured August 10, 2013.

226 *"The Iraqi government is responsible"*: John Daniszewski and Tarek El-Tablawy, "Al-Maliki: Shootings 'Cannot Be Accepted,'" *San Diego Union-Tribune*, September 24, 2007.

226 *"fair and transparent investigation"*: "Iraq Battle Was Self-Defense, Security Firm Says," CNN, September 18, 2007.

227 *"If Blackwater left at this moment"*: Alissa J. Rubin and Andrew E. Kramer, "Al-Maliki Protests Killings," *New York Times*, September 24, 2007.

227 *"We have revoked Blackwater's license"*: "Iraq Battle Was Self-Defense, Security Firm Says," CNN, September 18, 2007.

227 *"at the request of the incoming Interim Government of Iraq"*: "Security Council Endorses Formation of Sovereign Interim Government in Iraq; Welcomes End of Occupation by 30 June, Democratic Elections by January 2005," United Nations, www.un.org/News/Press/docs/2004/sc8117.doc.htm, captured August 10, 2013.

228 *SOFAs between the United States and countries*: R. Chuck Mason, "Status of Forces Agreement (SOFA): What Is It, and How Has It Been Utilized?," Congressional Research Service, March 15, 2012.

228 *"The issue most commonly addressed in a SOFA"*: Ibid.

228 *"cancer that has spread and must be removed"*: Anthony H. Cordesman and Jose Ramos, "Sadr and the Mahdi Army: Evolution, Capabilities, and a New Direction," Center for Strategic and International Studies, August 4, 2008.

229 *"deeply affect Iraqi sovereignty"*: "Maliki Says Talks on Iraq-US Pact Deadlocked," Agence France Presse, June 13, 2008.

229 *lawyers "had some issues"*: "Blackwater's 2005 Cameras Request Denied," *Washington Times*, October 23, 2007.

229 *"almost all global observers expressed anger"*: "Editorial: The Blackwater Lynching," *Washington Times*, January 7, 2010.

230 *Council Presidency of Iraq officially approved the SOFA*: "Sources: Five Blackwater Guards Charged," Associated Press, December 5, 2008.

230 *"a government has finally been formed"*: "Iraq: The Transition from a Military Mission to a Civilian-Led Effort," Report to the Members of the Senate Committee on Foreign Relations, January 31, 2011.

230 *"Secure ground and air movements"*: Ibid.

231 *across Iraq for the foreseeable future*: Anna Fifield, "Contractors Reap $138bn from Iraq War," *Financial Times*, March 18, 2013.

CHAPTER 14: COLD AND TIMID SOULS

232 *"The hearing will focus on the mission"*: Letter from Henry Waxman to Erik Prince, http://oversight-archive.waxman.house.gov/documents/20070920144454.pdf, captured August 10, 2013.

233 *"nicotine is not addictive"*: "Tobacco CEO's Statement to Congress, 1994 News Clip: 'Nicotine Is Not Addictive,'" http://senate.ucsf.edu/tobacco/executives1994congress.html, captured August 10, 2013.

233 *Valerie Plame spoke for the first time*: Andrea Seabrook, "The Public Debut of Valerie Plame Wilson," NPR, March 17, 2007.

233 *Waxman grilled former defense secretary*: Paul von Zielbauer, "Panel Queries Rumsfeld on Tillman Battle Death," *New York Times*, August 2, 2007.

233 *"FEMA's toxic trailers"*: "Committee Holds Hearing on Manufacturers of FEMA's Toxic Trailers," Committee on Oversight and Government Reform, U.S. House of Representatives, http://oversight-archive.waxman.house.gov/story.asp?id=2069, captured August 10, 2013.

233 *2006 profile of the new committee chairman*: Karen Tumulty, "The Scariest Guy in Town," *Time*, November 27, 2006.

234 *wonderful speech at the Sorbonne*: Theodore Roosevelt, "Citizenship in a Republic," speech delivered at the Sorbonne, Paris, April 23, 1910.

234 *No sooner had the congressional invitation*: Peter Spiegel, "Blackwater Told to Clear Disclosures," *Los Angeles Times*, September 26, 2007.

234 *"This letter serves to advise"*: Letter from Kiazan Moneypenny to Fred Roitz, accessible at http://iraqnam.blogspot.com/2007/09/house-oversight-committee-chair-state.html, captured August 10, 2013.

235 *It is plain from the cited clause*: Ibid.

235 *reached out to my personal counsel*: Author interview with Joseph Schmitz, July 2013.

236 *"bury" its bad press*: Robert D. Novak, "Playing Politics with Blackwater," *Washington Post*, October 8, 2007.

236 *"I went to prison voluntarily"*: Tim Weiner, "Charles W. Colson, Watergate Felon Who Became Evangelical Leader, Dies at 80," *New York Times*, April 21, 2012.

237 *"You're a SEAL"*: Author recollection.

237 *"like life had taken a toll on him"*: Andrea Simakis, "Reasons and Closure Are Elusive, Even Four Years After Four Men Died," *Plain Dealer*, May 30, 2008.

238 *"no objection to Blackwater providing unclassified documents"*: Letter from Kiazan Moneypenny to Victor Esposito, accessible at http://iraqnam.blogspot.com/2007/09/house-oversight-committee-chair-state.html, captured August 10, 2013.

238 *this awkward addendum*: "Blackwater USA," Hearing Before the Committee on Oversight and Government Reform, U.S. House of Representatives, October 2, 2007.

238 *Waxman said to conclude his opening statement*: Ibid.

239 *"Waxman of the Week" honors*: Mary Ann Akers and Paul Kane, "While Nevada Caucuses, the Senate Can Wait," *Washington Post*, January 17, 2008.

239 *"a remarkably unprecedented experiment"*: "Blackwater USA," Hearing Before the Committee on Oversight and Government Reform, U.S. House of Representatives, October 2, 2007.

239 *"We have to question in this hearing"*: Ibid.

239 *"troubled that taxpayers have been taken for a ride"*: Ibid.

239 *"Is that your idea, Mr. Prince, of corporate accountability?"*: Ibid.

240 *"Where is the presumption of innocence?"*: Rick Anderson, "Welcome Aboard Blackwater Airlines," *Seattle Weekly*, November 13, 2007.

240 *randomly lit into right-wing radio personality*: "Blackwater USA," Hearing Before the Committee on Oversight and Government Reform, U.S. House of Representatives, October 2, 2007.

240 *"I am offended"*: Ibid.

240 *"a fascinating, but also disturbing"*: P. W. Singer, "Blackwater Hearings Ain't No Superbad," *Wired*, October 2, 2007.

241 *Back on November 27, 2004*: "Aircraft Accident Brief: CASA C-212-CC, N960BW," National Transportation Safety Board, November 27, 2004.

241 *loaded with four hundred pounds*: Ibid.

241 *Chief Warrant Officer 2 Travis Grogan and Specialist Harley Miller*: "The Crash of Blackwater Flight 61," Memorandum to the Members of the Committee on Oversight and Government Reform, U.S. House of Representatives, October 2, 2007.

241 *aircraft was flagged down as it taxied*: Rick Anderson, "Welcome Aboard Blackwater Airlines," *Seattle Weekly*, November 13, 2007.

241 *Blackwater 61 flew away from Bagram*: "Aircraft Accident Brief: CASA C-212-CC, N960BW," National Transportation Safety Board, November 27, 2004.

242 *"I hope I'm goin' in the right valley"*: "Transcript: The Last Flight of Blackwater 61," *Virginian-Pilot*, http://hamptonroads.com/2006/07/transcript-last-flight -blackwater-61, captured August 10, 2013.

242 *a box canyon*: "Aircraft Accident Brief: CASA C-212-CC, N960BW," National Transportation Safety Board, November 27, 2004.

243 *"OK, we're comin' up to a box here"*: "Transcript: The Last Flight of Blackwater 61," *Virginian-Pilot*, http://hamptonroads.com/2006/07/transcript-last-flight -blackwater-61, captured August 10, 2013.

243 *"Yeah [the map] shows us"*: "The Edge of Reason: The Transcript of the Deadly Flight," *Der Spiegel*, www.spiegel.de/international/world/the-edge-of-reason -the-transcript-of-the-deadly-flight-a-509853.html, captured August 12, 2013.

243 *"It was good while it lasted"*: Ibid.

243 *"I swear to God"*: Ibid.

243 *"OK—yeah, you're"*: Ibid.

244 *"Call it off—help him out!"*: Ibid.

244 *Investigators found that Blackwater 61 had impacted*: "Aircraft Accident Brief: CASA C-212-CC, N960BW," National Transportation Safety Board, November 27, 2004.

244 *English and Hammer were thrown*: Ibid.

244 *Rowe's remains . . . strapped in their seats*: Ibid.

245 *Two frozen urine stains*: Ibid.

245 *"was concluded in only two weeks and contains numerous errors"*: Leo Shane III, "Report Blames Firm's Training, Procedures for Fatal Crash in Afghanistan," *Stars and Stripes*, October 6, 2005.

245 *a deep conflict of interest*: "Executive Summary: CASA 212, N960BW," Collateral Investigation Board, http://oversight-archive.waxman.house.gov/documents /20071012205257.pdf, captured August 12, 2013.

245 *succeeded McMahon as executive*: "Colonel John Lynch," U.S. Army Aviation Center of Excellence and Fort Rucker, www-rucker.army.mil/usaace/director ates/cdid/tcm-ra/bio/director.html, captured August 12, 2013.

246 *hovered over the site for approximately ten minutes*: "Aircraft Accident Brief: CASA C-212-CC, N960BW," National Transportation Safety Board, November 27, 2004.

246 *"begin the investigation of a major accident"*: "The Investigative Process at NTSB," National Transportation Safety Board, www.ntsb.gov/investigations /process.html, captured August 12, 2013.

246 *"The bulk of the so-called investigative work"*: Del Quentin Wilber, "A Crash's Echoes, from War Zone to Washington," *Washington Post*, October 17, 2007.

247 *A memo the chairman circulated*: "The Crash of Blackwater Flight 61," Memorandum to the Members of the Committee on Oversight and Government Reform, U.S. House of Representatives, October 2, 2007.

247 *Their communication with Bagram*: Author copy of BW61 air traffic control transcripts.

248 *"reconstruction and educational initiatives"*: "History of the 4th US Cavalry," 3/4 Cavalry Chapter, www.3-4cav.org/index.php?option=com_content&view =article&id=70, captured August 12, 2013.

248 *"Task Force Saber remained"*: Ibid.

248 *I acknowledged the obvious*: "Blackwater USA," Hearing Before the Committee on Oversight and Government Reform, U.S. House of Representatives, October 2, 2007.

248 *"Richard Pere pulled me into his office"*: "The Flight and Crash of 'Blackwater 61,'" *60 Minutes*, June 27, 2010.

249 *"I don't think he could believe it himself"*: Ibid.

249 *flying a thousand missions a month*: "Blackwater USA," Hearing Before the Committee on Oversight and Government Reform, U.S. House of Representatives, October 2, 2007.

249 *renewed and expanded our contract*: "The Crash of Blackwater Flight 61," Memorandum to the Members of the Committee on Oversight and Government Reform, U.S. House of Representatives, October 2, 2007.

249 *"I want to see"*: "Blackwater USA," Hearing Before the Committee on Oversight and Government Reform, U.S. House of Representatives, October 2, 2007.

249 *"We were hired"*: Ibid.

250 *Commander's Emergency Response Program*: "Military Operations: Actions Needed to Better Guide Project Selection for Commander's Emergency Response Program and Improve Oversight in Iraq," U.S. Government Accountability Office, June 23, 2008.

250 *began with a lucky accident*: Donald P. Wright and Timothy R. Reese, "On Point II: Transition to the New Campaign—The United States Army in Operation

Iraqi Freedom," www.globalsecurity.org/military/library/report/2008/on point/chap09-02.htm, captured August 12, 2013.

250 *American government and CPA*: Ibid.

251 *"Where we think we have been wrong"*: "Interview: Gen. James Conway," PBS *Frontline*, www.pbs.org/wgbh/pages/frontline/haditha/themes/civilians.html, captured August 12, 2013.

251 *"We . . . see sort of a unique thing"*: Ibid.

251 *this example of the unfortunate math*: "Military Operations: The Department of Defense's Use of Solatia and Condolence Payments in Iraq and Afghanistan," U.S. Government Accountability Office, May 31, 2007.

252 *The blogosphere inevitably responded*: "How Much It Costs to Kill Someone in Afghanistan," *Law in Action* blog, www.alphabetics.info/international/2012 /03/16/how-much-it-costs-to-kill-someone-in-afghanistan/, captured August 12, 2013.

252 *"The Army does not target civilians"*: Paul von Zielbauer, "Civilian Claims on U.S. Suggest the Toll of War," *New York Times*, April 12, 2007.

252 *Pentagon itself estimated $42.4 million*: Sharon Behn, "U.S. Paid $42.4 Million to Iraqis; Sum Covers 'Collateral' Damage; Number Compensated Unknown," *Washington Times*, February 27, 2008.

252 *"What I'm concerned about"*: "Blackwater USA," Hearing Before the Committee on Oversight and Government Reform, U.S. House of Representatives, October 2, 2007.

252 *"That [payment] is similar to what DoD does"*: Ibid.

253 *"Did you feel that [$20,000] was a satisfactory level"*: Ibid.

253 *"Your calculations there don't make any sense to me"*: Ibid.

253 *suggested a solatium as high as $250,000*: Ibid.

254 *"a sum this high will set a terrible precedent"*: Ibid.

254 *"It would help the credibility"*: Ibid.

254 *"This was an unfortunate event"*: Ibid.

255 *"There is a party in Congress that does not like"*: Ibid.

255 *"Isn't it true that your family"*: Ibid.

255 *"Wouldn't it be fair to say"*: Ibid.

256 *my company made news whenever we earned work*: August Cole, "Next Test for Blackwater," *Wall Street Journal*, November 13, 2007.

256 *President Pervez Musharraf refused*: Brian Till, "Could the U.S. Have Prevented Benazir Bhutto's Death?," *Atlantic*, May 23, 2011.

257 *A UN investigation found*: Ibid.

257 *"Blackwater's not a partisan company"*: "Blackwater USA," Hearing Before the Committee on Oversight and Government Reform, U.S. House of Representatives, October 2, 2007.

257 *"You have been paid over one billion dollars"*: Ibid.

257 *U.S. force couldn't match the 180,000 PMCs*: P. W. Singer, "Can't Win With 'Em, Can't Go to War Without 'Em: Private Military Contractors and Counterinsurgency," Brookings Institution, September 2007.

257 *Department of Labor had counted*: David Ivanovich, "Labor Dept.: 1,001 Civilian Workers Have Died in Iraq," *Houston Chronicle*, August 8, 2007.

258 *the government's "surrogate army"*: Mike Baker, "'Cowboy' Aggression Works for Blackwater," *Washington Post*, September 24, 2007.

258 *"Are we going to have to continue to privatize?"*: "Blackwater USA," Hearing Before the Committee on Oversight and Government Reform, U.S. House of Representatives, October 2, 2007.

258 *"we'll go do something else"*: Ibid.

CHAPTER 15: A NIGHTMARE AND A MIRACLE

260 *We did so dozens more times*: Jake Tapper and Matthew Jaffe, "The Story Behind Biden's Emergency Helicopter Landing in Afghanistan," ABC News, September 22, 2008.

260 *arriving first on the scene*: Andrew Miga, "Senators in Emergency Landing," *USA Today*, February 21, 2008.

260 *"If you want to know where al-Qaeda lives"*: Jake Tapper and Matthew Jaffe, "The Story Behind Biden's Emergency Helicopter Landing in Afghanistan," ABC News, September 22, 2008.

260 *The first helicopter, with medic*: "Five Examples of Superior/Heroic Contractor Performance," U.S. Department of State, www.thespywhobi lledme.com/the _spy_who_billed_me/2007/11/the-blackwaters.html, captured August 13, 2013.

261 *Blackwater's men saved*: Ibid.

261 *Poland's ambassador to Iraq*: Jay Price and Hussein Kadhim, "Blackwater Flies Injured Polish Diplomat to Hospital," McClatchy Newspapers, October 3, 2007.

261 *The convoy made it two hundred yards*: Ibid.

261 *Then, two more bombs*: Paul von Zielbauer, "Baghdad Bombing Wounds Polish Ambassador and Kills 2," *New York Times*, October 3, 2007.

262 *Then two dozen insurgents swarmed*: "To the Rescue," *State Magazine*, April 2008.

262 *sustaining "massive wounds"*: Jay Price and Hussein Kadhim, "Blackwater Flies Injured Polish Diplomat to Hospital," McClatchy Newspapers, October 3, 2007.

262 *The reasons for the attack were never fully clear*: Kim Curtis, "Ambush Injures Polish Diplomat in Iraq," *Washington Post*, October 3, 2007.

262 *Three minutes after takeoff*: Dan Laguna and Michael S. Wren, *You Have to Live Hard to Be Hard* (Bloomington, IN: AuthorHouse, 2010), p. 215.

262 *The pilot knifed between arcing streetlights*: Ibid.

262 *Another Little Bird followed*: Ibid.

263 *sustained internal injuries as flames shot into his nose*: "Polish Ambassador to Iraq in Coma," PressTV, http://edition.presstv.ir/detail/26033.html, captured August 13, 2013.

263 *Blackwater's men and Pietrzyk's guards*: Dan Laguna and Michael S. Wren, *You Have to Live Hard to Be Hard* (Bloomington, IN: AuthorHouse, 2010), p. 215.

263 *"The patient is unable to breathe"*: "Polish Ambassador Wounded in Iraq Fights for Life," Polskie Radio, October 5, 2007.

263 *Orzechowski, the fallen guard*: "Funeral of Bartosz Orzechowski, GPB Officer Killed in Iraq," Polish Ministry of the Interior, October 8, 2007.

264 *On January 25, 2008, surrounded by U.S. Ambassador*: Dan Laguna and Michael S. Wren, *You Have to Live Hard to Be Hard* (Bloomington, IN: AuthorHouse, 2010), p. 219.

264 *Fellow Blackwater contractors*: Ibid., p. 220.

264 *"I'm here because of you"*: Ibid., p. 218.

264 *"it is not fit to work in Iraq!"*: Kim Curtis, "Ambush Injures Polish Diplomat in Iraq," *Washington Post*, October 3, 2007.

265 *Hurricane Katrina made landfall*: Alex Graumann, Tamara Houston, Jay Lawrimore, David Levinson, Neal Lott, Sam McCown, Scott Stephens, and David Wuertz, "Hurricane Katrina: A Climatological Perspective," National Oceanic and Atmospheric Administration, October 2005.

265 *Together, those men soon moved*: Bill Sizemore, "Blackwater Employees Create a Stir in New Orleans," *Virginian-Pilot*, September 15, 2005.

265 *For two weeks, the Puma flew missions*: August Cole, "From Iraq's Green Zone to the French Quarter," *MarketWatch*, September 18, 2005.

265 *"Every aircraft we had"*: Joanne Kimberlin and Bill Sizemore, "Blackwater: On American Soil," *Virginian-Pilot*, July 27, 2006.

266 *"We ran to the fire"*: Ibid.

266 *more than fifteen hundred people were dead*: "Hurricane Katrina: A Nation Still Unprepared," Special Report of the Committee on Homeland Security and Governmental Affairs, U.S. Senate, www.gpo.gov/fdsys/pkg/CRPT-109srpt322/pdf/CRPT-109srpt322.pdf, captured August 13, 2013.

266 *"They are beating, they are raping"*: Jim Dwyer and Christopher Drew, "After Katrina, Crimes of the Imagination," *New York Times*, September 29, 2005.

266 *"This place is going to look like Little Somalia"*: Joseph R. Chenelly, "Troops Begin Combat Operations in New Orleans," *Army Times*, September 3, 2005.

266 *"We're going to go out and take this city back"*: Ibid.

266 *"The only difference between here and Iraq"*: Ted Roelofs, "Iraq or New Orleans— It's All Part of the Job for a Security Guard," *Grand Rapids Press*, September 13, 2005.

267 *CNN hired British security company*: Nichola Groom, "Private Security Firms in Demand in Katrina Chaos," Reuters, September 2, 2005.

267 *NBC News hired armed guards*: Ibid.

267 *"The calls came flooding in"*: Griff White, "Private Security Contractors Head to Gulf," *Washington Post*, September 8, 2005.

267 *"I was scared to death coming back"*: Joanne Kimberlin and Bill Sizemore, "Blackwater: On American Soil," *Virginian-Pilot*, July 27, 2006.

267 *"They treated it as if that was their job"*: August Cole, "From Iraq's Green Zone to the French Quarter," *MarketWatch*, September 18, 2005.

268 *"mercenaries from Blackwater USA"*: Larry Chin, "Private Security and Mercenary Companies Patrol New Orleans," Global Research, September 8, 2005.

268 *"extrajudicial slayings going on"*: Mac McKinney, "Explosive: Cynthia McKinney Told 5,000 Executed During Katrina," OpEdNews.com, October 1, 2008.

268 *"Communist and fascist movements during the last century"*: Chris Hedges, "What If Our Mercenaries Turn on Us?" *Common Dreams*, June 3, 2007.

269 *private firms from around the world*: Annette Haddad, "Roadblocks to Rebuilding," *Los Angeles Times*, September 4, 2005.

269 *The Army Corps of Engineers hired*: Lisa Myers, "Is Katrina Cleanup a Fleecing of America?," NBC News, June 5, 2006.

269 *ambulance crews, mold-removal specialists*: Lolly Bowean and Deborah Horan, "Waves of Outsiders Come Looking for Work," *Chicago Tribune*, September 18, 2005.

269 *the Navy paid Kellogg Brown & Root*: "DHS Agents Head to Gulf Coast," Associated Press, September 13, 2005.

269 *FEMA awarded no-bid contracts*: Ibid.; Griff Witte and Spencer S. Hsu, "Big Katrina Contractors Win More FEMA Work," *Washington Post*, August 10, 2006, www.washingtonpost.com/wp-dyn/content/article/2006/08/09/AR2006080901931.html, captured August 19, 2013; Raymond Hernandez and Eric Lipton, "In Shift, FEMA Will Seek Bids for Gulf Work," *New York Times*, October 7, 2005, www.nytimes.com/2005/10/07/politics/07home.html?_r=0, captured August 19, 2013.

269 *the British company ArmorGroup*: Griff White, "Private Security Contractors Head to Gulf," *Washington Post*, September 8, 2005.

269 *"We used to go out in T-shirts"*: Joanne Kimberlin and Bill Sizemore, "Blackwater: On American Soil," *Virginian-Pilot*, July 27, 2006.

270 *"deemed the situation unsafe"*: Michael Gaynor, "The Hurricane Katrina Catastrophe Inside Story: Mike Brown Answers My Questions," RenewAmerica.com, March 8, 2006.

270 *That Homeland Security contract paid Blackwater*: Matt Jadacki, "Management Advisory Report on Armed Guard Services Provided by Blackwater Security Consulting, LLC Under Contract HSCEFC-05-J-F00002," Office of Inspector General, March 2, 2006.

270 *Almost immediately, we funneled*: Ibid.

270 *"FPS considered this the best value"*: Ibid.

270 *Within a year, some sixteen hundred*: Joanne Kimberlin and Bill Sizemore, "Blackwater: On American Soil," *Virginian-Pilot*, July 27, 2006.

271 *"This is not the occupation of Louisiana"*: Ibid.

271 *Trans-Sahara Counterterrorism Partnership:* "Trans-Sahara Counterterrorism Partnership," U.S. Africa Command, www.africom.mil/NEWSROOM/Document/7432, captured August 13, 2013.

271 *sent in by the Defense Department's U.S. Africa Command*: Ibid.

271 *"On one early mission in Mali"*: Author interview with David Dalrymple, July 2013.

272 *"Those squall lines are preceded"*: Ibid.

272 *With him was first officer*: Ibid.

272 *"The wind is picking up again"*: Ibid.

273 *"it felt like needles hitting you"*: Ibid.

274 *"That local hospital"*: Ibid.

274 *"I think the locals kind of put us up"*: Ibid.

275 *"Just as the private sector has responded"*: Statement of Gary Jackson at the Homeland Security Subcommittee on Management, Integration, and Oversight, U.S. House of Representatives, May 24, 2005.

276 *those voters went so far as to recall*: Allison Hoffman, "Board OKing Blackwater Plan Recalled," *Washington Post*, December 12, 2007.

276 *the first of nearly two dozen blazes:* "California Fire Siege 2007: An Overview," California Department of Forestry and Fire Protection, www.fire.ca.gov/fire_protection/downloads/siege/2007/Overview_CompleteFinal.pdf, captured August 13, 2013.

277 *largest evacuation in California history*: Ibid.

277 *More than 450 structures were incinerated*: Stephen Badger, "2007 U.S. Multiple-Death Fires," *NFPA Journal*, September/October 2008.

277 *"just trying to show a good face"*: Amita Sharma, "Blackwater Provided Potrero with Relief Supplies During Fires," KPBS, October 29, 2007.

278 *We withdrew our proposal for a campus*: Miriam Raftery, "Blackwater Withdraws Plans for Camp in Potrero," *Alpine Sun*, March 13, 2008.

278 *"I'm going to continue"*: Amita Sharma, "Blackwater Provided Potrero with Relief Supplies During Fires," KPBS, October 29. 2007.

278 *"something we've always done"*: Anne Krueger, "Blackwater's Relief Efforts Win Praise of Project Foe," *San Diego Union-Tribune*, October 30, 2007.

278 *Three college students from Grand Rapids*: "Kenyan Aid Workers Expected to Land at 4:30 p.m.," *Grand Rapids Press*, January 7, 2008.

278 *The students*: Ibid.

279 *He was promptly sworn in*: Jeffrey Gettleman, "Disputed Vote Plunges Kenya into Bloodshed," *New York Times*, December 31, 2007.

279 *Some 350,000 across the country*: "2011 Human Rights Reports: Kenya," U.S. Department of State Bureau of Democracy, Human Rights, and Labor, May 24, 2012.

279 *Men, women, and girls*: Clar Ni Chonghaile, "Kenya Heads to Polls as Women Seek Justice for Violence During Last Election," *Guardian*, March 1, 2013.

279 *rebels set upon a church*: Nick Wadhams, "A Massacre in a Kenyan Church," *Time*, January 1, 2008.

279 *As many as fifty women and children*: Ibid.

279 *"Stay safe"*: Nardy Baeza Bickel, "With Blackwater's Help, Aid Workers Flee Kenya," *Grand Rapids Press*, January 6, 2007.

280 *Two days later, the girls' commercial flight*: Nardy Baeza Bickel, "Orphanage Volunteers Relieved to Be Home," *Grand Rapids Press*, January 7, 2007.

282 *driven a six-wheeled truck*: Omar Waraich, "Blast Leaves Pakistan Shaken," *Time*, September 21, 2008.

282 *"biggest explosion in Pakistani history"*: Ibid.

282 *Citizen Award*: Fairfax County Fire and Rescue Department, *Line Copy*, vol. 4, 2008.

282 *"They've been getting a lot of negative publicity"*: Nardy Baeza Bickel, "With Blackwater's Help, Aid Workers Flee Kenya," *Grand Rapids Press*, January 6, 2007.

282 *"It's been a nightmare and a miracle"*: Ibid.

CHAPTER 16: THE DOWNFALL

283 *"They presented their request"*: Timothy Williams, "U.S. Refuses to Renew Blackwater Security in Iraq," *New York Times*, February 9, 2009.

283 *"many marks against this company"*: Ibid.

284 *"basically a moot point"*: "Official: Blackwater's Iraq Security Deal Won't Be Renewed," Associated Press, January 30, 2009.

284 *The IRS . . . dug into our accounting*: "Evidence of Tax Evasion by Blackwater," Committee on Oversight and Government Reform, U.S. House of Representatives, http://oversight-archive.waxman.house.gov/story.asp?id=1562, captured August 13, 2013.

285 *"As Blackwater continues to cooperate"*: Letter from Stephen M. Ryan to Henry Waxman, www.contractormisconduct.org/ass/contractors/123/cases/825/1261/blackwater-latc-employee-misclass_blackresp.pdf, captured August 13, 2013.

285 *two employees in our armory*: "Former Blackwater Employees Sentenced to Probation, Cooperating with Federal Investigation," Associated Press, January 10, 2008.

285 *Cashwell and Grumiaux bargained down*: Ibid.

285 *"I'm sorry for what I've done"*: Ibid.

285 *"Federal officials confirmed in 2005"*: Ibid.

285 *we purchased a single-propeller Embraer*: Sharon Weinberger, "Blackwater Buying Counter-Insurgency Aircraft," *Wired*, August 27, 2007.

286 *"Blackwater is building its own air force"*: Ken Layne, "Blackwater," *Wonkette*, captured August 14, 2013.

286 *another deadly shooting—this time of a dog*: Maria Newman, "Guards Shoot Dog at Baghdad Bureau," *New York Times*, December 18, 2007.

286 *"Blackwater Shoots the* New York Times' *Dog"*: "Blackwater Shoots the *NY Times*'s Dog," *Dailykos*, www.dailykos.com/story/2007/12/18/423886/-Blackwater-Shoots-the-NY-Times-s-Dog-160, captured August 13, 2013.

286 *"They took the incident very seriously"*: Maria Newman, "Guards Shoot Dog at Baghdad Bureau," *New York Times*, December 18, 2007.

286 *"a heady cocktail of fear, ignorance and paranoia"*: "Mercenaries Buying Fleet of Star Destroyers," *White Rabbit* blog, www.blackwaterblogger.com/2007/09/supert.html, captured August 13, 2013.

286 *"I really didn't do anything"*: Frank Rich, "Suicide Is Not Painless," *New York Times*, October 21, 2007.

286 *"only about three degrees"*: Ibid.

287 *"The premise of this blog"*: "Mercenaries Will Protect the 1% and Here Is Why!," *All You Need Is a Crazy Rich Guy with a Private Army*, http://crazyrichguy.wordpress.com/2012/05/20/1037/, captured August 14, 2013.

287 *"heavily armed contract guards"*: Paul Richter, "Blackwater Warnings Got Little Attention," *Los Angeles Times*, October 7, 2007.

287 *"the biggest, meanest guys"*: Ibid.

287 *"late summer and fall of 2007"*: David Isenberg, "The State Department Tells Us How They Really Felt: Part 1," *Huffington Post*, February 17, 2012.

288 *Task Order 8 south of the city*: Matthew Lee and Mike Baker, "Blackwater Out of Iraq? No, Not Yet," *San Diego Union-Tribune*, April 20, 2009.

288 *renegotiated a new Task Order 10 contract*: Ibid.

288 *pay us an additional $22.2 million*: Ibid.

288 *paid us more than one billion*: "Joint Audit of Blackwater Contract and Task Orders for Worldwide Personal Protective Services in Iraq," Office of the Special Inspector General for Iraq Reconstruction, June 2009.

288 *five contractors from Nisour Square pleaded not guilty*: Del Quentin Wilber, "Former Blackwater Guards Plead Not Guilty," *Washington Post*, January 7, 2009.

289 *two men working*: Tim McGlone, "Defense Rests in Trial of Ex-Blackwater Contractors," *Virginian-Pilot*, March 8, 2011.

289 *Drotleff and Cannon were charged*: "Two Individuals Charged with Murder and Other Offenses Related to Shooting Death of Two Afghan Nationals in Kabul, Afghanistan," U.S. Department of Justice, www.justice.gov/usao/vae/news/2010/01/20100107cannonnr.html, captured August 15, 2013.

289 *subcontract with Raytheon*: August Cole, "War-Zone Contractors Draw Senate Scrutiny," *Wall Street Journal*, February 25, 2010.

289 *160,000 trained ANP members*: Luis Peral and Ashley J. Tellis, "Afghanistan 2011–2014 and Beyond: From Support Operations to Sustainable Peace," European Union Institute for Security Studies, June 2011.

289 *240,000 capable ANA soldiers*: Ibid.

289 *preparing to spend more than $9 billion in 2010*: "Report on Progress Toward Security and Stability in Afghanistan: United States Plan for Sustaining the Afghanistan National Security Forces," U.S. Defense Department, April 2011.

289 *Raytheon had been awarded*: Raytheon, "Warfighter Support Services," www.rayjobs.com/index.cfm?NavID=303, captured August 15, 2013.

289 *"consolidate operations and maintenance"*: Raytheon, "Warfighter FOCUS," www.raytheon.com/capabilities/idiq/mai/wff/, captured August 15, 2013.

290 *offering Paravant a subcontract worth $25 million*: Walter Pincus, "Army Contractor's Use of a Cover Name for Blackwater Angers Sen. McCaskill," *Washington Post*, March 9, 2010.

290 *never seen indoor plumbing or electricity*: Bruce Huffman, "Afghanistan First," *Defence Management Journal* 46.

290 *Every six weeks*: "New Recruits Join Afghan National Army," ISAF Joint Command, January 24, 2011.

290 *some thirteen hundred ANA members*: "Blackwater USA," Hearing Before the Committee on Oversight and Government Reform, U.S. House of Representatives, October 2, 2007.

291 *trained more than 38,650 ANA soldiers*: "Contracting in a Counterinsurgency: An Examination of the Blackwater-Paravant Contract and the Need for Oversight," Hearing Before the Committee on Armed Services, U.S. Senate, February 24, 2010.

291 *"were outstanding, flexible, and delivered"*: Ibid.

291 *on top of the 3,700 Afghan Border Police personnel*: Ibid.

291 *and the 3,700 Narcotics Interdiction Unit officers*: Ibid.

291 *roughly twenty thousand men and women in 2009*: Ibid.

291 *"we are aware of many atrocities"*: R. J. Hillhouse, "Blackwater's Identity Crisis: Ninjas or Social Workers?," *Spy Who Billed Me*, December 13, 2006.

291 *"a bear's paw print in a red crosshairs"*: Paul von Zielbauer, "Blackwater Softens Its Logo from Macho to Corporate," *New York Times*, October 22, 2007.

292 *"not a direct result of a loss of contract"*: Mike Baker, "Blackwater Dumps Tarnished Brand Name for 'Xe,'" *Salt Lake Tribune*, February 13, 2009.

292 *Joy may have been the first*: "Contracting in a Counterinsurgency: An Examination of the Blackwater-Paravant Contract and the Need for Oversight," Hearing Before the Committee on Armed Services, U.S. Senate, February 24, 2010.

293 *network of some three dozen affiliates*: James Risen and Mark Mazzetti, "30 False Fronts Won Contracts for Blackwater," *New York Times*, September 3, 2010.

294 *On March 27, 2009, President Obama stood*: "Remarks by the President on a New Strategy for Afghanistan and Pakistan," White House, March 27, 2009.

294 *"Today, I am announcing"*: Ibid.

294 *pushed back three months*: "Afghan Presidential Vote Delayed to August 20," Agence France Presse, January 30, 2009.

294 *deadliest year of the war*: Stephanie Gaskell, "Deadliest Year for U.S. Troops on Afghan Duty: 311 Killed in 2009, Up from 155 in 2008," *New York Daily News*, December 29, 2009.

294 *In 2009, it only got worse*: Ibid.

294 *an additional twenty-one thousand troops*: Gordon Lubold, "Gates: Afghanistan Surge Could Require More Than 30,000 Troops," *Christian Science Monitor*, December 3, 2009.

294 *a pledge for another twelve thousand*: Ibid.

294 *more than doubling the Bush administration's force*: Ibid.

294 *"This push must be joined"*: "Remarks by the President on a New Strategy for Afghanistan and Pakistan," White House, March 27, 2009.

295 *conducted 2,730 protection missions*: "Contracting in a Counterinsurgency: An Examination of the Blackwater-Paravant Contract and the Need for Oversight," Hearing Before the Committee on Armed Services, U.S. Senate, February 24, 2010.

295 *all of the $174 million*: "Performance Evaluation of the U.S. Training Center Contract for Personal Protective Services in Afghanistan," Middle East Regional Office of Inspector General, August 2009.

295 *2009 performance audit*: Ibid.

295 *eighteen-month contract worth $120 million*: "Blackwater Firm Gets $120M U.S. Gov't Contract," CBS News, June 19, 2010.

296 *"the concern is whether in Afghanistan"*: "Private Security Contractors in Iraq: Where Are We Going?," Commission on Wartime Contracting hearing, June 21, 2010.

296 *"Xe is the only company"*: Ibid.

296 *leveled an enormous fine against my company*: "Xe Services LLC Enters Civil Settlement of Alleged Violations of the AECA and ITAR," U.S. Department of State, www.state.gov/r/pa/prs/ps/2010/08/146215.htm, captured August 15, 2013.

297 *In 2009 alone, those three government export agencies*: "Overview of U.S. Export Control System," U.S. Department of State, www.state.gov/strategictrade/overview/, captured August 15, 2013.

297 *"transparent, predictable, and timely"*: "Licensing Police Review and Building a Single Licensing Agency," Export.gov, http://export.gov/ecr/eg_main_027616.asp, captured August 15, 2013.

297 *"potential national security implications"*: "Proposed Charging Letter," U.S. Department of State letter to Victor Esposito, www.pmddtc.state.gov/compliance/consent_agreements/pdf/Xe_PCL.pdf, captured August 15, 2013.

298 *"unauthorized access to ITAR-controlled technology"*: Ibid.

298 *eclipsing the $32 million settlement*: "Hughes Electronic Corp. and Boeing Co. Violated U.S. Export Laws on Satellite Technology," U.S. Immigrations and Customs Enforcement news release, May 22, 2008.

298 *"These violations did not involve"*: "Xe Services LLC Enters Civil Settlement of Alleged Violations of the AECA and ITAR," U.S. Department of State, www.state.gov/r/pa/prs/ps/2010/08/146215.htm, captured August 15, 2013.

298 *delivering to Chinese authorities*: "United Technologies Subsidiary Pleads Guilty to Criminal Charges for Helping China Develop New Attack Helicopter," U.S. Justice Department, June 28, 2012.

298 *UTC agreed to pay a $55 million*: Ibid.

299 *split up its five-year, $10 billion WPPS III*: "US State Department's 5-Year, $10.0B WPS Security Contract," *Defense Industry Daily*, www.defenseindustrydaily.com/US-State-Departments-5-Year-100B-WPS-Security-Contract-06594/, captured August 15, 2013.

299 *background of the company International Development Solutions*: Spencer Ackerman, "Exclusive: Blackwater Wins Piece of $10 Billion Mercenary Deal," *Wired*, October 1, 2010.

299 *IDS won Task Order 2*: "WPS Task Order 2: Solicitation No. SAQMMA10R0005," FedBizOpps.gov, https://www.fbo.gov/?s=opportunity&mode=form&tab=core &id=28770b3c4c3b645d70dfe3a01f10422a&_cview=0, captured August 15, 2013.

300 *confirmed Blackwater's ties to IDS*: Jeff Stein, "Onetime Blackwater Affiliate Scores U.S. Contract," *Washington Post*, January 7, 2011.

300 *"We emphasize that our Palestinian land is not an arena"*: Tania Kepler, "Blackwater-Related Firm to Provide 'Protective Security' in West Bank," Alternative Information Center, January 13, 2011.

300 *condolence payments of as much as $12,500*: Sudarsan Raghavan, "U.S. Offers Cash to Victims in Blackwater Incident," *Washington Post*, October 25, 2007.

300 *"It's not an admission of culpability"*: Ibid.

301 *"I am a double agent"*: Marc A. Thiessen, "The Dean of the Gitmo Bar," *Weekly Standard*, March 29, 2010.

301 *defend a series of questionable-at-best characters*: "William Kunstler, Disturbing the Universe," PBS POV, www.pbs.org/pov/disturbingtheuniverse/film _description.php, captured August 15, 2013.

301 *"We wanted all of his clients to be innocent"*: Ibid.

301 *"filing countless cases on behalf"*: "Illegal Detentions and Guantanamo," Center for Constitutional Rights, http://ccrjustice.org/illegal-detentions-and-guanta namo, captured August 15, 2013.

301 *"we were moving toward a police state"*: "They Want to Intimidate People from Dissenting," *Socialist Worker*, http://socialistworker.org/2006-1/581/581_10 _MichaelRatner.shtml, captured August 15, 2013.

301 *recommended Blackwater pay out $136 million*: "Iraq Wants Blackwater to Pay $136 Million Compensation," Reuters, www.reuters.com/article/2007/10/09 /us-iraq-blackwater-idUSYAT93808120071009, captured August 15, 2013.

302 *"modern-day merchant of death"*: Gabor Steingart, "Merchants of Death: Memo Reveals Details of Blackwater Targeted Killings Program," *Der Spiegel*, August 24, 2009.

302 *"Blackwater created and fostered a culture of lawlessness"*: "Blackwater USA Sued for Firing on Iraqi Civilians, According to Legal Team for Injured Survivor and Families of Three Killed," Center for Constitutional Rights, http://ccrjustice .org/newsroom/press-releases/blackwater-usa-sued-firing-iraqi-civilians, -according-legal-team-injured-sur, captured August 15, 2013.

302 *committing war crimes and summary execution*: "*Abtan, et al. v. Prince, et al.*," Center for Constitutional Rights, http://ccrjustice.org/ourcases/current -cases/abtan-et-al-v-blackwater-usa-et-al, captured August 15, 2013.

302 *It started with an allegation of fraud*: Mark Mazzetti, "2 Ex-Workers Accuse Blackwater Security Company of Defrauding the U.S. for Years," *New York Times*, February 10, 2010, http://www.nytimes.com/2010/02/11/us/11suit .html?_r=0, captured August 19, 2013.

302 *Blackwater allegedly placing a Filipina prostitute*: Ibid.

302 *The judge threw out that allegation*: "Jury Rules in Favor of Blackwater in Lawsuit," Associated Press, August 5, 2011, www.foxnews.com/us/2011/08/05 /jury-rules-in-favor-blackwater-in-lawsuit/, captured August 19, 2013.

302 *"Mr. Prince was well aware"*: Bill Sizemore, "Another Lawsuit Targets Founder of Blackwater," *Virginian-Pilot*, September 16, 2009.

302 *"Discovery is needed"*: "Plaintiffs' Second Amended Complaint: *Abtan, et al. v. Prince, et al.,*" Center for Constitutional Rights, www.ccrjustice.org/files /10.28.09%20Plaintiffs%27%20Second%20Amended%20Complaint.pdf, captured February 12, 2013.

303 *"punitive damages in an amount sufficient to strip Mr. Prince"*: Ibid.

303 *thew out all but one count*: Ben Vernia, "Fourth Circuit Affirms Judgment in Favor of Blackwater Subsidiary in Whistleblowers' Suit," *False Claims Counsel*, December 10, 2012.

303 *settled with seven of the Iraqi families*: David Zucchino, "Iraqis Settle Lawsuits over Blackwater Shootings," *Los Angeles Times*, January 8, 2010.

303 *estates of the deceased each received*: Ibid.

303 *"We are pleased that the original settlement"*: Ibid.

303 *Iraqi government to step in and try to nullify the deal*: Liz Sly, "Iraqis Say They Were Forced to Take Blackwater Settlement," *Los Angeles Times*, January 11, 2010.

304 *"Blackwater was about to go into bankruptcy"*: Ibid.

304 *"I feel I was deceived by them"*: Ibid.

304 *settlement was reached with families of six other Nisour Square victims*: "Blackwater Successor Settles Baghdad Shooting Suit," Associated Press, January 7, 2012.

304 *"I constantly push for the 80 percent solution"*: "Iraqi Reconstruction: Reliance on Private Military Contractors and Status Report," Hearing Before the Committee on Oversight and Government Reform, U.S. House of Representatives, February 7, 2007.

304 *named him one of their "Fast 50"*: "The 5th Annual Fast 50," *Fast Company*, www .fastcompany.com/most-innovative-companies/2006, captured August 15, 2013.

305 *"Blackwater, based in the tiny town"*: Charles Fishman, "The 5th Annual Fast 50: No. 11. Private Army," *Fast Company*, www.fastcompany.com/magazine/103 /open_11-jackson.html, captured August 15, 2013.

306 *"In previous years, the company export compliance program"*: David Isenberg, "Shaping Up Blackwater's Act," *Huffington Post*, June 29, 2010.

306 *"The company must work to address past"*: Ibid.

307 *"I announce my resignation"*: Mike Baker, "Xe Tries to Leave History of Blackwater Behind," Fox News, March 2, 2009.

307 *a fifteen-count indictment was issued against Jackson*: Eli Lake, "Exclusive: Court Docs Reveal Blackwater's Secret CIA Past," *Daily Beast*, March 14, 2013.

307 *allegations largely revolved around seventeen AK-47s and seventeen Bushmaster M4*: Ibid.

307 *"did knowingly combine, conspire, confederate and agree to commit offenses"*: Author copy of *United States of America v. Gary Jackson, William Wheeler Mathews, Jr., Andrew Howell, Ronald Slezak, Ana Bundy.*

308 *The individual charges brought with them potential prison sentences*: "Five Blackwater Employees Indicted," Federal Bureau of Investigation, April 16, 2010.

308 *"primitive military rifles"*: Author copy of *United States of America v. Gary Jackson, William Wheeler Mathews, Jr., Andrew Howell, Ronald Slezak, Ana Bundy.*

308 *"Because they needed guns, I imagine"*: Joseph Neff, "Blackwater Circumvents Weapons Laws," *Raleigh News & Observer*, June 24, 2008.

CHAPTER 17: THE NEXT REINVENTION

311 *The deal was for $200 million*: "AAR Corp. to Acquire Aviation Worldwide Services," AAR Corp., www.aarcorp.com/news/aar_aws_032510.htm, captured August 15, 2013.

311 *"Presidential had flown more"*: Ibid.

311 *"it's time to hang it up"*: Jeff Stein, "Blackwater's Prince: Congress Gave Me 'Proctology,'" *Washington Post*, June 24, 2010.

312 *Facebook page called "Small Victories"*: Derrick Wright, "Small Victories," Facebook.com, https://www.facebook.com/pages/Small-Victories/155275984537320, captured August 15, 2013.

312 *"I got my brains blown out"*: Author interview with Derrick Wright, July 2013.

312 *"That's what I've heard, anyway"*: Ibid.

313 *learning how to be the "new Derrick"*: Ibid.

313 *"I look back at 'the event' as sort of a do-over"*: Ibid.

314 *"the best job I've ever had"*: Ibid.

315 *"This is about our claims to moral leadership"*: Christine Hauser, "New Rules for Contractors Are Urged by 2 Democrats," *New York Times*, October 4, 2007.

315 *"The last American soldier[s] will cross the border out of Iraq"*: "Remarks by the President on Ending the War in Iraq," White House, www.whitehouse.gov/the-press-office/2011/10/21/remarks-president-ending-war-iraq, captured August 15, 2013.

315 *"about to see a major surge of contractors"*: Charley Keyes, "Plans for Private Contractors to Protect U.S. Diplomats in Iraq Criticized," CNN, October 4, 2011.

316 *"logistical support, food and fuel"*: David Isenberg, "The State Department Takes Charge: Be Afraid, Be Very Afraid," *Huffington Post*, September 24, 2010.

316 *total manpower in Iraq is soon expected*: Walter Pincus, "State Department Report on U.S. Withdrawal from Iraq Cites Lack of Money, Other Problems," *Washington Post*, June 3, 2011.

316 *Roughly 5,500 of them will do the private security work*: Spencer Ackerman, "The Iraq War Ain't Over, No Matter What Obama Says," *Wired*, October 21, 2011.

316 *Triple Canopy, in a five-year contract worth $977 million*: Richard Lardner, "Security Problems Uncovered at U.S. Bases in Iraq," Associated Press, April 26, 2009.

316 *Triple Canopy's contractors bartered alcohol for guns*: T. Christian Miller, "Former Iraq Security Contractors Say Firm Bought Black Market Weapons, Swapped Booze for Rockets," *ProPublica*, September 18, 2009.

316 *"Who are we [financially] supporting"*: Ibid.

317 *"I want to kill somebody today"*: Steve Fainaru, "Four Hired Guns in an Armored Truck, Bullets Flying, and a Pickup and a Taxi Brought to a Halt. Who Did the Shooting and Why?," *Washington Post*, April 15, 2007.

317 *"Because I'm going on vacation tomorrow"*: Ibid.

317 *"That didn't happen, understand?"*: Ibid.

317 *"transparency and accountability needed for good governance"*: Charles Ornstein and Hagit Limor, "Where's the Transparency That Obama Promised?," *Washington Post*, March 31, 2011.

317 *"We're very, very worried"*: "Where Is the Peace Dividend? Examining the Final Report to Congress of the Commission on Wartime Contracting," Hearing

Before the Committee on Oversight and Government Reform, U.S. House of Representatives, October 4, 2011.

318 *Wright said the company's new goal*: Nathan Hodge, "Company Once Known as Blackwater Ditches Xe for Yet Another New Name," *Wall Street Journal*, December 12, 2011.

318 *Under Wright, the company has expanded*: "USTC Tapped for Afghan Intel Work," UPI, August 17, 2011.

318 *ACADEMI quietly bought out International Development Solutions*: Sydney J. Freedberg Jr., "ACADEMI—Ex-Blackwater—Boosts State Dept. Business, Eyes Acquisitions," *Breaking Defense*, June 8, 2012.

318 *"He's got a gun in his hand"*: Ibid.

318 *"I think eventually, we're going to get a license"*: Nathan Hodge, "Company Once Known as Blackwater Ditches Xe for Yet Another New Name," *Wall Street Journal*, December 12, 2011.

319 *United States spent more than $800 billion*: Jordan Weissmann, "An $800 Billion War: The Immense Cost of Invading Iraq, in Charts," *Atlantic*, March 22, 2013.

319 *spearheading a Green Zone car bombing*: "Iraq's Sunni Vice President Tariq Al-Hashemi Sentenced to Death in Absentia," Associated Press, September 9, 2012.

319 *al-Hashemi had been sentenced in absentia to death by hanging*: Ibid.

319 *almost $700 billion a year*: "SIPRI Military Expenditure Database," Stockholm International Peace Research Institute, www.sipri.org/research/armaments/milex/milex_database, captured August 15, 2013.

319 *the next nineteen countries combined*: Ibid.

319 *some 40 percent of which goes to overhead costs*: Jim Garamone, "Gates Calls for Significant Cuts in Defense Overhead," American Forces Press Service, May 8, 2010.

319 *number of American military bases abroad*: Glenn Kessler, "Ron Paul's Strange Claim about Bases and Troops Overseas," *Washington Post*, February 9, 2012.

319 *others suggest it's closer*: Ibid.

319 *American troops stationed in some 150 countries*: "U.S. Military Personnel by Country," CNN, www.cnn.com/interactive/2012/04/us/table.military.troops/, captured August 15, 2013.

320 *added a hundred new admirals and generals*: Dina Rasor, "The Pentagon's Biggest Overrun: Way Too Many Generals," *Truthout*, January 5, 2012.

320 *Navy now has more admirals (331)*: "Sixteen Pages of Admirals," U.S. Naval Institute, http://blog.usni.org/2012/05/19/sixteen-pages-of-admirals, captured August 15, 2013.

320 *than ships for them to command (282)*: Ibid.

320 *"in some cases the gap between me and an action officer"*: John Barry and Evan Thomas, "A War Within," *Newsweek*, September 12, 2010.

320 *three-man staff that oversaw fifty employees*: Ibid.

320 *"DoD's ability to control costs"*: "DOD Financial Management," U.S. Government Accountability Office, www.gao.gov/highrisk/dod_financial_manage ment/why_did_study, captured August 15, 2013.

320 *twenty-five hundred lines in its budget*: Cheryl Pellerin, "Partners, Innovation Help Pentagon Deal with Budget Cuts," American Forces Press Service, September 5, 2012.

320 *from $294 billion to $716 billion*: "Editorial: Cut Defense Spending, but Not Mindlessly," *USA Today*, http://usatoday30.usatoday.com/news/opinion /story/2012-08-02/defense-spending-budget-Pentagon/56721082/1, captured August 15, 2013.

321 *upcoming cuts would be "crippling"*: Susan Davis, "Super-Committee Failure Forecasts Sequester Fight," *National Journal*, November 21, 2011.

321 *Panetta predicted it would be "doomsday"*: Jim Garamone, "Debt Reduction 'Sequestration' Concerns Panetta, Mullen," American Forces Press Service, August 4, 2011.

321 *scheduled to take eleven unpaid furlough days*: Matthew Hay Brown, "Pentagon Cuts Civilian Furlough Days," *Baltimore Sun*, August 6, 2013.

321 *Pentagon has spent more than $1.5 billion on military music*: "The Balancing Act," Congressional Progressive Caucus, http://cpc.grijalva.house.gov/balancing -act/, captured August 15, 2013.

321 *spend $388 million on 140 military bands*: Betty McCollum, "Military Spends Too Much on Music, Sports Promos," *Minneapolis Star Tribune*, July 17, 2012.

321 *more than 5,000 full-time professional musicians*: Ibid.

321 *Pentagon will spend more than $70 million in taxpayer money*: Ibid.

321 *"interested in joining because of the racing sponsorship"*: Dustin Long, "National Guard Urged to Prove Value of Sponsorships," July 19, 2012.

322 *"a hollow lie"*: Dan Neil, "The 50 Worst Cars of All Time: 1975 Trabant," *Time*, www.time.com/time/specials/2007/article/0,28804,1658545_1658533 _1658030,00.html, captured August 15, 2013.

322 *"leakproof" drip pans for Blackhawk helicopters*: Eric Lichtblau, "Earmark Puts $17,000 Pans on Army Craft," *New York Times*, May 18, 2012.

323 *"With good financial oversight"*: Aleen Sirgany, "The War on Waste," *CBS Evening News with Scott Pelley*, February 11, 2009.

323 *to the tune of $7 billion*: "Financing Peacekeeping," United Nations Peacekeeping, www.un.org/en/peacekeeping/operations/financing.shtml, captured August 15, 2013.

323 *20 percent of which was paid by U.S. taxpayers*: Brett D. Schaefer, "How Much Does the U.N. Cost Us?," *National Review*, September 14, 2012.

323 *Less than 150 of those UN troops*: "Fact Sheet: United Nations Peacekeeping," United Nations, www.un.org/en/peacekeeping/documents/factsheet.pdf, captured August 15, 2013.

323 *billed out for the UN's flat rate of $1,028*: "Financing Peacekeeping," United Nations Peacekeeping, www.un.org/en/peacekeeping/operations/financing .shtml, captured August 15, 2013.

323 *UN now pays about $525 million a year*: Colum Lynch, "U.S. and Europe Fight over Cuts in Peacekeeping," *Foreign Policy*, October 10, 2011.

323 *eclipses the country's entire $459 million annual budget*: Ibid.

323 *put up little resistance in late 2012*: "Congo Army Clashes with M23 Rebels Close to Eastern City of Goma," Reuters, July 14, 2013.

323 *$1.4 billion annual operating budget*: Robyn Dixon, "U.N. Force in Congo, MONUSCO, Criticized as Ineffective," December 22, 2012.

324 *Executive Outcomes to help battle the Revolutionary United Front*: James Rupert, "Diamond Hunters Fuel Africa's Brutal Wars," *Washington Post*, October 16, 1999.

324 *rebels overthrew the new democratic government and began the killing*: Ibid.

325 *hired guns from British security contractor*: Tabassum Zakaria, Susan Cornwell, and Hadeel Al Shalchi, "For Benghazi Diplomatic Security, U.S. Relied on Small British Firm," Reuters, October 17, 2012.

325 *protection of the diplomats was the responsibility of three members*: Accountability Review Board report, U.S. Department of State, www.state.gov/documents /organization/202446.pdf, captured August 15, 2013.

325 *"asking for the sun, the moon, and the stars"*: Michael R. Gordon, "Official Tells Panel a Request for Libya Was Denied," *New York Times*, October 10, 2012.

326 *"Taliban is on the inside of the building"*: Ibid.

326 *State Department documented some fifty "security incidents"*: Joseph I. Lieberman and Susan M. Collins, "Flashing Red: A Special Report on the Terrorist Attack at Benghazi," Committee on Homeland Security and Governmental Affairs, U.S. Senate, December 30, 2012.

326 *"big enough for forty men to go through"*: Eli Lake, "U.S. Consulate in Benghazi Bombed Twice in Run-Up to 9/11 Anniversary," *Daily Beast*, October 2, 2012.

326 *there were five DS agents at the mission*: Accountability Review Board report, U.S. Department of State, www.state.gov/documents/organization/202446 .pdf, captured August 15, 2013.

326 *Around nine p.m. on September 11*: Joseph I. Lieberman and Susan M. Collins, "Flashing Red: A Special Report on the Terrorist Attack at Benghazi," Committee on Homeland Security and Governmental Affairs, U.S. Senate, December 30, 2012.

326 *saw militants streaming through the compound's main gates*: Fred Burton and Samuel M. Katz, "40 Minutes in Benghazi," *Vanity Fair*, August 2013.

326 *Three of the five DS agents rushed to the outbuilding*: Joseph I. Lieberman and Susan M. Collins, "Flashing Red: A Special Report on the Terrorist Attack at Benghazi," Committee on Homeland Security and Governmental Affairs, U.S. Senate, December 30, 2012.

327 *"The compound is under attack"*: David Ignatius, "In Benghazi Timeline, CIA Errors but No Evidence of Conspiracy," *Washington Post*, November 1, 2012.

327 *CIA reportedly scrambled a six-man security team*: Ibid.

327 *drove two vehicles to the firefight*: Ibid.

327 *They picked up an agency translator and three Libyan*: Ibid.

327 *no bulletproof windows or other advanced protections*: Jill Reilly, "Safe House Where Ambassador Died Had No Marine Guard and His Body Was Missing for Five Hours: Full Scale of Chaos Surrounding Libyan Killings Revealed," *Daily Mail*, September 12, 2012.

327 *He forced his way out an emergency escape*: Accountability Review Board report, U.S. Department of State, www.state.gov/documents/organization/202446 .pdf, captured August 15, 2013.

327 *until the heat and smoke shut him out entirely*: Ibid.

327 *Shortly before ten thirty p.m. those CIA*: Joseph I. Lieberman and Susan M. Collins, "Flashing Red: A Special Report on the Terrorist Attack at Benghazi," Committee on Homeland Security and Governmental Affairs, U.S. Senate, December 30, 2012.

328 *repeatedly driven back by the inferno*: Ibid.

328 *load into the armored vehicle with Smith's body and escape*: Accountability Review Board report, U.S. Department of State, www.state.gov/documents/orga nization/202446.pdf, captured August 15, 2013.

328 *fighting their way out of the compound and back to the annex:* Ibid.

328 *The Americans rushed to the rear building:* Jennifer Griffin, "CIA Operators Were Denied Request for Help During Benghazi Attack, Sources Say," Fox News, October 26, 2012.

328 *erupting on the rooftop and killing the two men:* Ibid.

328 *packed into vehicles and headed for the Benghazi airport:* David Ignatius, "In Benghazi Timeline, CIA Errors but No Evidence of Conspiracy," *Washington Post,* November 1, 2012.

328 *in video evidence, was still alive:* "Witness: Stevens Was Breathing When Found," Associated Press, September 17, 2012.

328 *looters drove him to Benghazi Medical Center:* Ethan Chorin, "What Libya Lost," *New York Times,* September 13, 2012.

328 *Libyans brought his body to the airport:* Sharyl Attkisson, "Officials Instructed Benghazi Hospital to List Stevens as 'John Doe,'" CBS News, May 30, 2013.

328 *some sort of agreement with the CIA personnel:* Adam Entous, Siobhan Gorman, and Margaret Coker, "CIA Takes Heat for Role in Libya," *Wall Street Journal,* November 1, 2012.

329 *he too would now be facing prosecution:* Guy Adams, "Iraq Mercenaries Boss Triggers Rage with Blackwater Video Game," *Independent,* September 8, 2011.

AFTERWORD: THE CIA AND ERIK PRINCE

335 *like having a brand-new Ferrari in the garage:* Richard H. Shultz Jr., "Showstoppers," *Weekly Standard,* January 26, 2004.

335 *"150 fighters, pilots and specialists":* Bob Woodward, "Secret CIA Units Playing a Central Combat Role," *Washington Post,* November 18, 2001.

336 *"to influence political economic, or military conditions":* Jennifer D. Kibbe, "The Rise of the Shadow Warriors," *Foreign Affairs,* March/April 2004.

337 *Erik Prince's hero:* Adam Ciralsky, "Tycoon, Contractors, Soldier, Spy," *Vanity fair,* January 2010.

338 *"600–700 covert operators":* Kibbe, "Rise of Shadow Warriors."

339 *the figure was closer to one to one:* Mark Hemingway, "Warriors for Hire: Blackwater USA and the Rise of Private Military Contractors," *Weekly Standard,* December 18, 2006.

339 *there were 10,000 contractors from 114 different firms:* Dana Priest and William M. Arkin, "National Security Inc.," *Washington Post,* July 19, 2010.

339 *"revenue from General Dynamics":* Ibid.

339 *"They were gutted in the 1990s":* Eli Lake, "Court Docs Reveal Blackwater's Secret CIA Past," *Daily Beast,* March 14, 2013.

339 *Prince recalls that he was eager to help:* Ciralsky, "Tycoon, Contractor, Soldier, Spy."

339 *Prince did not give up easily:* See Chapter 4.

340 *Prince says that he himself:* Ciralsky, "Tycoon, Contractor, Soldier, Spy."

340 *Blackwater recruited primarily from veterans:* Ibid.

340 *aircraft belonging to its aviation arm:* Adam Ciralsky, "Tycoon, Contractor, Soldier, Spy," *Vanity Fair,* January 2010.

341 *"Paresi . . . was highly skeptical of the security plan":* Joby Warrick, *The Triple Agent: The Al Qaeda Mole Who Infiltrated the CIA* (New York: Doubleday, 2011), p. 162.

341 *"known for his unflappable calm and his Zen-like insistence"*: Ibid., p. 165.

342 *"exasperated him" but he "also understood his place"*: Ibid., p. 165.

342 *"Hands up!"*: Ibid., p. 8.

343 *"the drivers and the gunslingers"*: James Risen and Mark Mazzetti, "Blackwater Guards Tied to Secret C.I.A. Raids," *New York Times*, December 11, 2009.

343 *"There was no bench strength"*: R. Jeffrey Smith and Joby Warrick, "Blackwater Tied to Clandestine CIA Raids," *Washington Post*, December 11, 2009.

343 *encouraged them to do "whatever it takes"*: James Risen and Mark Mazzetti, "Blackwater Guards Tied to Secret C.I.A. Raids," *New York Times*, December 11, 2009.

343 *"the military and Blackwater became blurred"*: Ibid.

343 *"It became a very brotherly relationship"*: Ibid.

343 *"would have flies walking across their eyeballs"*: Mark Mazzetti, *The Way of the Knife: The CIA, a Secret Army, and a War at the Ends of the Earth* (New York: Penguin Press, 2013), p. 12.

344 *"regularly invited top CIA officers to the Kentucky Derby"*: Ibid., p. 122.

344 *number of U.S. drone strikes in Pakistan*: Bill Roggio and Alexander Mayer, "Charting the Data for US Airstrikes in Pakistan, 2004–2013," *Long War Journal*, www.longwarjournal.org/pakistan-strikes.php, captured August 19, 2013.

345 *Blackwater personnel traveled to Nellis Air Force Base*: James Risen and Mark Mazzetti, "C.I.A. Said to Use Outsiders to Put Bombs on Drones," *New York Times*, August 21, 2009.

345 *Panetta finally terminated Blackwater's drone operations contract*: Mark Mazzetti, "Blackwater Loses a Job for the C.I.A.," *New York Times*, December 12, 2009.

345 *"continually and increasingly mystified by this relationship"*: James Risen and Mark Mazzetti, "30 False Fronts Won Contracts for Blackwater," *New York Times*, September 3, 2010.

345 *Blackwater had "cleaned up its act"*: Ibid.

345 *"undergone some serious changes"*: Jeff Stein, "CIA Gives Blackwater Firm New $100 Million Contract," *Washington Post*, June 23, 2010.

346 *"secret program to locate and assassinate top operatives"*: Mark Mazzetti, "CIA Sought Blackwater's Help to Kill Jihadists," *New York Times*, August 20, 2009.

346 *"Wary of attracting undue attention"*: Adam Ciralsky, "Tycoon, Contractor, Soldier, Spy," *Vanity Fair*, January 2010.

347 *Prince had already been recruited*: Ibid.

347 *"I was looking at creating a small, focused capability"*: Ibid.

347 *"I grew up around the auto industry"*: Ibid.

348 *"unconventional means of penetrating 'hard target' countries"*: Ibid.

348 *"We have a rapidly growing, worldwide network"*: James Risen and Mark Mazzetti, "30 False Fronts Won Contracts for Blackwater," *New York Times*, September 3, 2010.

348 *"team of foreign nationals helped find and fix a target"*: Adam Ciralsky, "Tycoon, Contractor, Soldier, Spy," *Vanity Fair*, January 2010.

348 *Prince also embraced*: Ibid.

348 *"institutional osteoporosis"*: Ibid.

349 *"I put myself and my company at the CIA's disposal"*: Ibid.

349 *"what happened to me was worse"*: Ibid.

349 *"cartoonish show of force"*: Eli Lake, "Court Docs Reveal Blackwater's Secret CIA Past," *Daily Beast*, March 14, 2013.

350 *"defendants conspired to commit offenses against the United States":* United States of America v. Gary Jackson, William Wheeler Mathews, Jr., Andrew Howell, Ronald Slezak, Ana Bundy, U.S. District Court for the Eastern District of North Carolina, Northern Division, No. 2:10-CR-8-FL.

350 *One blackwater employee:* Ibid.

351 *the CIA had its own secure telephone line:* Eli Lake, "Court Docs Reveal Blackwater's Secret CIA Past," *Daily Beast,* March 14, 2013.

351 *"Blackwater was an extension of the CIA":* Ibid.

351 *providing guns to Jordans's:* Ibid.

351 *"The federal government's three-year prosecution":* James Risen and Mark Mazzetti, "Case Ends Against Blackwater Officials," *New York Times,* February 21, 2013.

352 *agreement with the State Department to pay $42 million:* James Risen, "Blackwater Reaches Deal on U.S. Export Violations," *New York Times,* August 20, 2010.

352 *pay $7.5 million more in civil penalty:* "Blackwater Successor to Pay Fine to Settle Arms Charges," Reuters, August 7, 2012.